Proletarians of the North

Proletarians of the North

A History of Mexican
Industrial Workers in Detroit and
the Midwest, 1917–1933

Zaragosa Vargas

UNIVERSITY OF CALIFORNIA PRESS
Berkeley   ·   Los Angeles   ·   Oxford

University of California Press
Berkeley and Los Angeles, California

University of California Press, Ltd.
Oxford, England

© 1993 by
The Regents of the University of California

Library of Congress Cataloging-in-Publication Data

Vargas, Zaragosa.
    Proletarians of the North: a history of Mexican industrial
workers in Detroit and the Midwest, 1917–1933 / Zaragosa Vargas.
        p.   cm. — (Latinos in American Society and Culture : 1)
    1. Mexican Americans—Employment—Middle West—History.
2. Mexican Americans—Employment—Michigan—Detroit—History.
I. Title.   II. Series.
HD8081.M6V37   1993
331.6'2172075—dc20   92-9122
                                                          CIP

Printed in the United States of America
9 8 7 6 5 4 3 2 1

The paper used in this publication meets the minimum requirements of
American National Standard for Information Sciences—Permanence of Paper
for Printed Library Materials, ANSI Z39.48-1984. ⊚

To Zaneta and Apolina

Contents

Illustrations follow page 130

Maps, Graphs, and Tables

Foreword

As we enter a new and no doubt challenging century, American society will be characterized by increased racial and ethnic diversity. Latinos, or people of Latin American descent, will represent a significant portion of this multiracial and multiethnic constellation. Composed of Mexican Americans, Puerto Ricans, Cuban Americans, Central Americans, other Spanish-speaking groups from the Caribbean and from South America, Latinos—so demographers predict—will constitute the largest racial minority in the United States in the twenty-first century.

A diverse, heterogeneous, and multidimensional ethnic group, Latinos are both an old and a new population. Some, such as the Hispanos in New Mexico, can trace their origins as far back as the initial Spanish colonial settlements in what later became the American Southwest, while others are only now arriving, as waves of immigrants and political refugees continue to cross the border, with or without permission.

Yet Latinos are important not only because of changing demographics but also because of their contributions to American history and culture. How American society changes in the next century will be significantly influenced by Latinos. At the same time Latinos will continue to be transformed by their experiences within the United States. This dialectical relationship constitutes the basis for a new and syncretic American culture.

With these developments in mind, the University of California Press is pleased to initiate a new monograph series, Latinos in American Society and Culture, for which it is my distinct pleasure to serve as series editor. This multidisciplinary series (history, literary criticism, cultural studies, and the social sciences) will explore the rich and diverse Latino experience and the role of Latinos in the reformulation of what it means to be American.

We are pleased to commence the series with the publication of Zaragosa Vargas's study of the Mexican immigrant community in Detroit, *Proletarians of the North*. Mexican Americans are the oldest and largest Latino group within the borders of the United States. A pluralistic population, Mexican Americans have roots in pre-Columbian and Spanish colonial culture; they include Mexicans from areas annexed by the United States in the nineteenth century, immigrants who came from Mexico in the twentieth century, and succeeding generations of Chicanos.

Professor Vargas's study concentrates on the important role that Mexican immigrant workers have played in the economic development of the United States despite the fact that they did not reap the full fruits of their labor because of race and class discrimination. Although centered largely in the Southwest, Mexican immigrants began also to work and settle in the Midwest by World War I. Professor Vargas calls attention to this geographic diversity and to the industrial character of the Mexican working class in the Midwest as it was recruited into auto, steel, meat-packing, and other forms of industrial labor. His study provides the most substantive description to date of Mexican immigrants in the Midwest. It broadens midwestern history to include the Latino experience—a significant encounter that needs to be included as we reconstruct American history as a multicultural and multiethnic saga. This book thus inaugurates a series that will focus on Latinos in the United States but will speak as well to the overall reconceptualization of American culture and society.

Mario T. García

Acknowledgments

Many people and institutions helped me during the eight years this book took shape. I wish to thank Guadalupe Aguirre, former Director of Casa Unidad, Detroit, Michigan, and Robert Muñoz for taking time out from their busy schedules to share with me their knowledge of Mexican Detroit and to help me arrange and obtain interviews with colony members. I am grateful to these former autoworkers and their families who so kindly shared their memories with me, enriching thereby my life as well as this book. The dearth of written materials and records of the early Detroit Mexican colony makes the testimony of these people invaluable.

I received valuable and able assistance in the early stages of my research. Yvette Addison, Rogelio Casanova, and Ernesto Quesada performed with patience the monumental task of gathering data from over 4,000 Ford Motor Company employment record cards. All were valuable research assistants. I owe special thanks to my friend Raúl H. Villa for his indispensable research assistance in the Archivo Nacional, Mexico City and his help with the oral interviews in Detroit. Thanks also to Jim Vieth for the word processing of the first version of this study and to Keith Farnsworth for designing the maps and charts.

For archival assistance I would like to thank the staffs at the following institutions: the Walter P. Ruether Library of Labor and Urban Affairs, Wayne State University; the Wayne County Clerk Office, Detroit; the Archdiocese of Detroit Archives; the Burton Historical Collection, Detroit Public Library; the Ford Motor Company Records Depository and the Ford Motor Company Industrial Archives; the Archives and Research Library, Edison Institute; the Minnesota Historical Society, St. Paul; the Bancroft Library of the University of California, Berkeley; the Chicano Studies Library of the University of California, Santa Barbara; and the Department of Labor Archives and the Judicial, Fiscal and Social Records Branch, National Archives, Washington, D.C. James R. Killeen, David Crippen, the Reverend Leonard P. Blair, Richard Ogar, and Raquel Quiroz González deserve special thanks.

I will always remain grateful to the late Charles Gibson and Marvin Felheim, eminent scholars in their respective fields of history and American studies. When I began my graduate studies at the University of Michigan they encouraged me to pursue Chicano history, at a time when many scholars questioned its validity and merits. My special thanks to my friends Dennis Nodín Valdés and Sara Deutsch. Dennis provided encouragement from the very beginning, and Sara read an early version of the manuscript and made helpful suggestions. The appearance of this book is due mainly to the efforts of Mario T. García. He recognized the value of this study to Chicano history when it was still a dissertation. I owe a special debt of gratitude to David Montgomery, friend to all workers. I have benefited enormously from David's wisdom and expertise. I thank both Mario and David for their generous support, helpful criticism, and warm friendship.

I am indebted to Laurie Sommers, Michigan State University Museum, Cynthia Read-Miller, Curator, Photographs Collection, Henry Ford Museum and Greenfield Village, and Marianne Letasi, of the Founders Society, Detroit Institute of Arts, for locating and reproducing some of the photographs that appear in this book. I particularly thank Señora María de Jesús Viuda de O'Higgins for granting me permission to use a detail of a mural painted by her late husband Pablo O'Higgins for the cover of my book. My special thanks as well to my friend Ramón Favela for his assistance in this regard.

Financial support for this project came in the form of a 1984–85 travel and research grant from the Whitney Humanities Center, Yale University, and a 1985–86 Postdoctoral Fellowship from the National Research Council and the Ford Foundation. I am obliged to friend and colleague Hal Drake, former chairman of the history department of the University of California, Santa Barbara, for providing me release time from teaching in 1991 in order to complete this study.

At the University of California Press, Scott Mahler expressed an early interest in this project. Mark Pentecost and Lynne Withey generously gave advice and assistance and helped prepare the manuscript. Mark deserves my special thanks for being patient and supportive. I especially want to thank Pamela Fischer, who copyedited the manuscript. Her competence made this a better book.

My personal debt is to my loving and caring working-class parents, Zaragosa and Herminia. My father instilled in me a passion for learning and to value patience and my mother taught me the meaning of hard work and to struggle. My greatest personal debt is to my two best friends, my wife Zaneta Kosiba-Vargas and my daughter Apolina. Poet, artist, scholar, patient and loving wife, Zaneta has been my pillar of strength. Apolina, you are a constant reminder of more important things in life. I dedicate this book to them.

Introduction: Coming to Work in Detroit

Chicanos, who constitute nearly two-thirds of the U.S. Latino population, are a significant part of the American experience. Great numbers of Chicanos have been Americans for generations—since before the Southwest became part of the United States. Although the Mexicans who settled in the Midwest played an important role in the history of Chicanos in the United States, they remain relatively unknown to scholars. They first made their way to the industrial heartland during World War I, establishing Mexican communities (colonies) in St. Paul, Chicago, Gary, Detroit, and other Midwest cities and towns. (See Map 1.) Although eclipsed by the great migration of blacks in size and scope, this early Mexican migration to the North represented a shift from previous patterns, in which Mexicans were confined to the Southwest. Over 58,000 Mexicans settled in the cities of the Midwest during the fifteen-year period from the end of World War I to the first years of the Great Depression.

During this time, Mexicans transformed the sugar-beet industry by supplanting European immigrants as the main source of labor. However, the greatest change in Mexican employment took place when these workers entered the foundries, steel mills, packing houses, and auto plants of the North and became industrial proletarians. The entrance of Mexicans into northern industrial employment is noteworthy in the history of Mexican workers as well as in the history of American labor, for it marks their move from the fringes of the American working class to full participation in its expansion and recomposition along racial and ethnic lines. The nature of the different kinds of factory work Mexicans

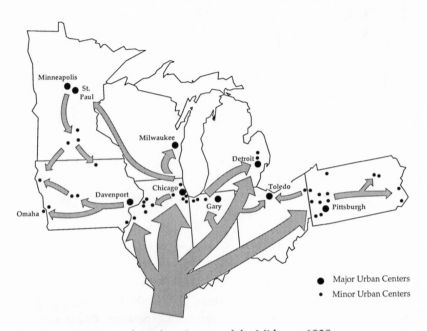

Map 1.   Mexicans in the Urban Centers of the Midwest, 1928

SOURCE: George T. Edson, "Mexicans in Our Northcentral States," 1927, Paul S. Taylor Collection, Bancroft Library, University of California, Berkeley.

NOTE: Arrows indicate migration flow from Texas and within the Midwest region.

performed, the rules governing the shop floors they worked on, their relations with co-workers, the meaning of work for them, the formation of Mexican colonies in which they lived, and the nature of institutions within these colonies—in short, the everyday lives of Mexicans—were all directly influenced by this move to the industrial setting of the Midwest.

Mexican immigrants came north shortly after World War I to work for sugar companies, railroads, and manufacturing industries. A continuing shortage of unskilled workers resulted from the restrictions imposed on immigration from eastern and southern Europe. Northern employers launched major labor-recruitment campaigns in the South, targeting both whites and blacks, and in this search for workers turned to the huge Mexican population residing in Texas. The Lone Star state received the greatest number of the more than half million Mexican immigrants arriving in the United States in the 1920s. As a result, for a period extending well into the post–World War II years, Texas would supply the rest of the nation with Mexican laborers.

At the turn of the century Anglo Texan ranchers and farmers had discovered the intrinsic value of low-wage and bountiful labor from across the border. The real value of the Mexicans was their penchant for hard work. Indeed, they made the huge fortunes of these Texans possible. Anglo political power sustained this system, and, by imparting certain negative qualities to the Mexicans, Anglos justified the repression of these workers in all facets of life. To these Texan landowners Mexican inferiority and the existing class structure were interwoven ideas. Accordingly, they treated the workers as a "God-given natural resource like land, water, and sunshine,"[1] and they often used violence to prevent Mexicans from leaving their jobs. The workers resisted nonetheless. They staged spontaneous strikes and work slowdowns or took advantage of their mobility to seek other kinds of work.

Because Texas agricultural employers considered Mexicans property, they covetously guarded them from the enterprising northern labor agents sent into the state by the Michigan sugar companies. These agents initiated Mexican migration to the North by recruiting Mexicans and their families in El Paso, Laredo, Fort Worth, and especially San Antonio, the city that all through the 1920s served as the gateway to the Midwest. The canny labor recruiters lured thousands of Mexicans north with the promise of higher wages. However, it was the self-reliant Mexicans who ultimately made the decision to sign the work contracts and head into this unknown region, where they were welcomed as suitable replacements for the now less-numerous European immigrants.

Mexicans traveled north on trains not only to labor on beet farms in the Midwest but also to work for eastern railroads, which hired them to maintain and repair tracks in the Midwest and in Pennsylvania and New York. For half a century Mexicans had built, then maintained, the train routes of the Southwest, and in the process these "watchmen of the rails"[2] created a work ethic and culture unique to the kind of labor they performed. Because Mexicans were familiar with railroad jobs and were willing to work for low wages, they became the main source of labor for many eastern lines. By continuously replenishing their supply of workers through recruitment, the railroads helped fix one more variation on Mexican migration routes to the Midwest.

Like the beet growers, the railroads served as intermediary employers of Mexicans before they entered factory work. Thousands secured jobs in the steel mills. Northern steel companies brought Mexicans to the Chicago-Gary area initially as strikebreakers during the 1919 steel strike. In some cases, this move caused resentment among immigrant European workers toward Mexicans, a resentment that occasionally surfaced as conflict in the working-class neighborhoods they shared. The insular world of these white ethnics was already being encroached on increasingly by blacks who had arrived in the cities of the North ahead of the Mexicans. Nonetheless, by the mid-twenties, with the adoption of the eight-hour day and adjustment to the three-shift sched-ule, thousands of Mexicans toiled in the steel mills of the region. Some employers sought Mexican labor to reduce their black workforce.

Through chain migration, relatives and friends of these Mexican pio-neers followed, so that expanding family and friendship networks sup-planted recruitment as the movement north became self-perpetuating. Mexicans utilized these networks to share information about job opportunities and to participate in the decision-making process before migration to the Midwest.

Mexicans made the decision to venture to the Midwest not out of economic necessity but to improve their living standards. The origins of this decision can be traced to the homeland of Mexico.[3] Capitalist de-velopment of this nation's rural countryside destroyed a way of life based on subsistence farming.[4] To survive, Mexicans had to depend on wage labor obtained through migration. Although they could earn a living in Texas, their second-class status propelled them to extend the search for a better life to the North.

By the end of the 1920s, Mexicans had been integrated into the in-dustrial workforce of the Midwest, and in some northern factories like those of Inland Steel they formed the largest racial group. Mexicans demonstrated a willingness to accept and stay with the hard and low-paying work, successfully adjusting to the factory regimen. "The men showed great endurance at work," observed George T. Edson, a field investigator for the Bureau of Labor Statistics, "sometimes working continuously without a day off in a year in metal foundries where others would not stay a month."[5]

Interrupted briefly by the 1920–1921 depression, a steady stream of Mexicans flowed into Michigan. At first the migrants used the routes established by the itinerant sugar-beet workers, half of whom now en-tered and left the Great Lakes states according to the planting and har-vesting seasons. A similar migration circuit was also established in the Chicago area by Mexican railroad workers, whose numbers on the pay-rolls of the local rail lines grew constantly because of track maintenance and repair work. Mexicans arrived in Chicago via the railroads that

linked the Windy City with major rail terminals like the twin cities of
Kansas City, Kansas, and Kansas City, Missouri, and like Fort Worth
and El Paso, Texas. A discernible pattern of migration from city to city
within the Midwest coincided with the cycles of employment in the various labor sectors. Shaping this migration as well were the individual
choices and priorities of Mexican workers.

"Dynamic Detroit" became a favorite destination of the Mexicans
venturing north. Detroit was the center of automobile manufacturing,
the nation's largest industry and one that was having a long-range impact on all aspects of American life. Henry Ford's mass production of
automobiles had contributed dramatically toward making Detroit the
worldwide symbol of modern technological progress. In their homeland, Mexicans knew that the Ford Model T cars and trucks on the city
streets and country roads were manufactured in Detroit. In addition,
work in the auto industry had gained wide publicity after Henry Ford's
announcement of the $5-a-day wage in 1914. Thousands left Mexico
and eventually arrived in Detroit. They joined other workers who came
to the Motor City in quest of the Ford wage bonanza. To work in the
Ford Highland Park plant was their primary objective. Crowds of Mexicans arrived in the Motor City and stood in long lines outside the gates
of the company's plants waiting for a chance at a job.

The migrants came predominantly from west-central Mexico and
were young, single men from all economic backgrounds. Farmers, miners, blacksmiths, garage mechanics, and grocery clerks all came to the
car factories of Detroit. Journalists, college students, and government
workers also came, for a small number of the migrants were educated,
middle-class professionals seeking opportunities in the Motor City that
the upheaval of the Mexican Revolution had prevented them from realizing in their home country. Both money and influence in the Mexican
government facilitated their migration.

A letter from the father of an eighteen-year-old engineering student,
Augustín Valdéz, from Mexico City expressed the fervent hopes of these
immigrants and their families.* Augustín's father wrote to Henry Ford
in advance of his son's arrival in Detroit. In the letter (penned in his
native tongue since he assumed that the great Henry Ford knew how to
read Spanish), the elder Valdéz praised the Ford Motor Company,
which had become synonymous with the city of Detroit. More important, the father revealed that many Mexicans were redefining the con-

---

* The names of interviewees and of all Ford Motor Company employees have been
changed to protect their privacy.

cept of manliness based on factory work when he expressed his firm belief that his son would be transformed into a man in the Ford factory. Augustín would become the embodiment of the modern industrial worker: "Within a few days my son, Augustín Valdéz, will arrive in Detroit to work in your highly esteemed factory. . . . I have accomplished one of my greatest aspirations—of sending my son to complete his education and build his character in the great city of Detroit. . . . I am placing my son under your care, for I know that you will turn him into a man." [6]

Lack of education prevented most Mexicans who moved to Detroit from expressing similar aspirations. Yet these men viewed Detroit as a city of promise and hope; it had influenced their decisions to leave Mexico and bypass Texas, heading expectantly for the North. In 1928, about 15,000 Mexicans lived in Detroit, and an undetermined number had arrived and left the Motor City as they continued their sojourns to other parts of the Midwest.

Constant innovations in machine production and organizational control increasingly made autoworkers efficient producers, as the giant automakers battled for dominance of the market, all the while concerned with keeping labor costs down. As efficiency became a hallmark of auto work, Mexicans were subjected to the inhuman pace of machine production. Perhaps Mexican anthropologist Manuel Gamio was referring to these autoworkers when he noted that in the United States Mexican workers had become "laborers of the modern type, much more efficient than before." [7]

The Mexicans who settled in Detroit and accepted the rigors of work in the car factories were progressively bound to a way of life dominated by the auto industry. Through hard work many became habituated to one type of industrial employment and enjoyed a sense of satisfaction and accomplishment in the labor they performed regardless of its hardships. Moreover, Mexican autoworkers attached meaning to the tasks they performed and thought of themselves as an elite group of industrial workers. Like their countrymen working in other kinds of factories, Mexican Detroiters were cognizant of the hierarchy of labor they were creating in the North and the social status that accompanied the different kinds of work. By the middle of the 1920s sharp divisions in employment had developed among Mexicans. Their social standing in their hometowns, but more and more in the northern colonies as well, was based on such factors as the wage level they had attained, the work they performed, and the reputations of the companies that employed them.

The identity of these autoworkers was shaped by their experiences in the departments and shops of the auto plants. The men tolerated conditions on the job in exchange for better living standards. Yet they opposed actions that challenged their dignity as workers. Mexicans worked in the large, noisy car factories alongside workers of different nationalities and alongside blacks who only recently had preceded them to the Motor City. The autoworkers performed demanding and monotonous work that, though mechanized and rationalized through managerial schemes, did not require any knowledge of machinery or any skill. They were supervised by foremen who had the authority to discipline the work crews under their charge and who did not hesitate to wield their power. Mexicans and blacks resisted cruelty and coercion in the workplace through insubordination, retaliation, sabotage, or quitting, thereby dispelling their long-standing reputations as passive and docile workers who deferred to the supposedly superior Anglos.[8]

Urban life was part of the process of industrialization that Mexicans encountered in the North. It had as much impact on the Mexican immigrants as their work in the rail yards, packing houses, steel mills, and car plants. Their settlement in predominantly ethnic, working-class communities meant that their life-style was determined by the work rhythms of the nearby factories. Bad conditions such as inferior, expensive, and scarce housing, and pollution, widespread racism, and periodic unemployment failed to dampen the expectations of Mexicans for a better life. The northern cities offered more opportunities than did the Southwest, and, as time passed, Mexicans also found they had little reason to return to Texas or Mexico. The colonies they established in the Midwest served many as havens from the regimen of the factories. These colonies differed according to the economic, social, political, and cultural life of the cities in which they were located, and they shaped the urban experiences of Mexican immigrants accordingly. However, nearly all the colonies were characterized by high transiency because of the teeming numbers of single men and intercity migration. Nevertheless, the early colonies prevailed and formed the foundation of the present-day Latino communities of the Midwest.

The history of Mexicans in the Midwest remains incomplete. It is based mainly on the pioneering studies that researchers from the University of Chicago conducted in the 1920s. *The Mexicans in Chicago,* by Robert C. Jones and Louise R. Wilson, and *The Tenements of Chicago 1908–1935,* by social-service worker Edith Abbott, are among the insightful works produced. The field studies of the economist Paul S. Taylor also serve as a basis for the early history of midwestern Mexicans. In the late 1920s Taylor documented the experiences of Mexicans in Chicago and the Calumet region for part of his series *Mexican Labor in the United States.*[9]

Taylor visited Detroit in the summer of 1928 as part of his field investigations of Mexican labor in the United States for the Social Science Research Council. He interviewed dozens of Mexican workers in Detroit as well as city and business officials who had contact with these factory workers.[10] Taylor's findings were never published. One year prior to Taylor's visit to Detroit, Edson investigated the Mexicans living in the Motor City and in Pontiac, Flint, and Saginaw. Edson was assigned by the Bureau of Labor Statistics to ascertain the status of the Mexicans living in the northcentral United States, an area defined for official purposes as extending from Pittsburgh to Nebraska, "from the Allegheny Mountains to the Missouri River."[11] Edson's extensive field reports likewise were not published. Both Taylor's and Edson's research notes furnish invaluable information for the study of Mexicans in Detroit and the Midwest. The early Mexicans described for these two researchers what it was like to work in the factories of the region and recounted as well their impressions of the urban industrial Midwest.

The extant scholarship explores the theme of immigration to the Midwest but focuses primarily on the Chicago-Gary region and then only on single communities or on selected elements of Mexican life. The dissertation by Louise Año Nuevo-Kerr, a history of the Mexicans of Chicago, centers on the post–World War II experience. Francisco Rosales has written on the Mexicans of Indiana Harbor, and the Mexicans of Gary, Indiana, are discussed in the work by Raymond Mohl and Neil Betten. Dennis Valdés has written a history of Mexican agricultural workers in the Midwest, capturing the distinct experiences of these workers as well as documenting the rise of agribusiness in the region. Much of the other research on the Mexicans of the Midwest originated in the early 1970s, when the first Chicano historians began the huge task of revising previous work or producing original work on aspects of the Chicano experience. Few of them captured the entire process of migration to the North, the forms of community building in the midwestern cities, and the ways the industrial nature of the region affected Mexican urban life by producing gradual and uneven changes. Regarding the workers, the studies fail to note the significance of an emerging and quite differentiated Mexican industrial working class. The various histories treat in a narrow and general fashion the work lives of Mexicans, depicting these experiences as one-dimensional and divorced of human agency. They tend to describe exploited workers who toiled for low wages and were burdened with the problem of workplace discrimination.[12]

Research has generally not kept pace with the innovations by labor historians who study American workers; they attempt in their work to capture all aspects of life in the factory as well as in the community, and they stress change. Thus left out of the history of Mexican workers are their daily work experiences (which varied by employment sector), the ways they responded to factory work, and the working-class life-styles they embraced in the colonies of the North. The profound changes that took place among these Mexican industrial workers remain undocumented, such as the internalization of a factory regimen, which infused new meaning into the jobs and tasks they performed. These men were not passive workers; indeed, they were active historical agents who found purpose in their labor tasks, continuously refashioning former conceptions of work.

The existing scholarship nonetheless has contributed to revealing the contours of Mexican experiences in the manufacturing cities of the American industrial heartland. Still, no study has successfully addressed the varied process of Mexican migration to the North or the lives of Mexican workers, the formation of their communities, and their adaptation to urban life in the Midwest as a whole. Little is known of the history of the Mexicans of Detroit. Before the 1970s, studies consisted of master's theses and dissertations. Outdated and with a social-science orientation, this research provides little historical interpretation of the living and working conditions of Mexicans in the once giant and legendary auto-manufacturing center of Detroit.[13]

This book reconstructs the experiences of Mexicans in Detroit and the Midwest from 1917 to 1933. During this time the first large-scale Mexican immigration to the United States took place, Mexicans became urbanized, and they expanded the boundaries of their world of work. Moreover, this era is important to the larger Mexican experience, for Chicano scholars concur that much change took place as a result of the growth of the Spanish-speaking population. Mexican culture was revitalized, concerns about identity were renewed, and American culture made an impact on all aspects of Mexican life, including gender relations. I argue that during the 1920s the migrants from Mexico became exposed to different kinds of factory labor, shared common conceptions about the value of work, and held expectations for a better life in the North that were shaped by the culture of consumption and new patterns of leisure activities. Thousands of these men entered work in the auto industry of Detroit and formed one of the major urban concentrations of Mexican workers in the United States in the 1920s. These autoworkers and the Mexicans working for the railroads, packing houses, steel mills, and foundries in other northern manufacturing centers formed the vanguard of Mexican industrial workers shortly after World War I.[14] Their history has been missing from the larger history of the recomposition of the American working class, which until recently also excluded the experiences of black Americans.

This book begins by concentrating first on the origins of the migration north in Texas, the source of the majority of Mexicans who settled in the Midwest. The purpose of this migration was to improve one's condition. The book then focuses on the first phase of Mexican settlement in Detroit between 1917 and 1921 and documents the Mexicans' varying perceptions of Detroit and their responses to the urban environment. Because of the overall importance of urbanization during this period, a discussion of the experiences of European immigrants and blacks in Detroit is incorporated, as are the conditions of Mexicans in southwestern cities and in other urban midwestern settlements. The demographic characteristics of the Motor City, its ethnic, racial, and class dimensions, form the context. Corporate and public officials shaped Detroit as the premier open-shop city in the United States; an overriding concern was producing a disciplined workforce from the largely immigrant and black working class. Americanization schemes, the Catholic Church, and colony leaders and organizations were used to encourage the adaptation of Mexicans to Detroit's urban industrial environment. The repatriations in the wake of the 1920–1921 depression undoubtedly demonstrated to the Motor City's Mexicans that their hopes for a better life could suddenly be dashed.

Mexicans engaged in different kinds of factory employment in the industrial Midwest. I examine the work lives of Mexican autoworkers in southeast Michigan, especially those employed by the Ford Motor Company. Data from Ford employment records, oral interviews, and secondary sources document the previous employment of these autoworkers, their job assignments inside the plants, and the status of Mexican and black autoworkers at the Ford River Rouge plant in 1928. Racial tensions, which mediated overall social conditions in working-class Detroit, existed between Mexicans and white co-workers and foremen, and race had an impact on their mutual perceptions. The working conditions in the Ford plants intensified existing racial animosities. Mexican autoworkers utilized a variety of strategies they had learned through previous factory work to resist speed-up, petty work rules, and the authority of shop foremen. These men also coped with illness and accidents and with pervasive unemployment in Detroit.

The second phase of Mexican settlement in Detroit took place between 1922 and 1933; this was the last migration of Mexicans to Detroit and to the Midwest until the late 1930s. Like the immigrants before them, these later Mexicans changed the make-up of the northern urban centers. The growth of the Detroit Mexican colony continued being determined by the fluctuations of the Motor City's business cycles, although the economy was beginning to show signs of slowing down. Against this backdrop, I examine the residential patterns of Mexicans, along with living conditions and discrimination; the founding of Mexican businesses; the situation of Mexican women in the colony, including their roles as service, clerical, and factory workers; the effects of proletarianization and urbanization on Mexican religious life; the establishment of mutual-aid and fraternal organizations; consumer habits; and leisure activities. Mexicans adapted to the consumer-oriented culture and its new value system, which defined their jobs as merely a means to achieve material well-being.

The book concludes with an assessment of the sharp decline of the auto industry and Detroit's financial crisis, which signaled the onset of the Great Depression and precipitated Mexican repatriation. The ways Mexicans responded to repatriation reveal the conflicting opinions and animosities in the Detroit colony regarding voluntary removal as a solution to mass unemployment. The crisis had devastating consequences for Mexican Ford autoworkers, testing their strategies in coping with unemployment and, for those still working, with the ruthless speed-up. Involvement in labor organizing was inevitable. At this time Mexican farmworkers in the Southwest engaged in fierce struggles to achieve worker rights and so did Mexican industrial workers in the North. These valiant efforts to gain dignity as workers and, more important, to recoup decent wages and material well-being were undertaken in a climate of fear of deportation. Mexicans in the North participated in the organizing efforts of the packing-house workers, steelworkers, and autoworkers in the early 1930s. These Mexican industrial workers later

joined the Congress of Industrial Organizations. Mexican factory workers in Detroit and elsewhere in the industrial Midwest helped achieve
union recognition.

The significant strides being made in U.S. labor history and in the
study of numerous immigrant groups require a reinterpretation of the
history of Mexican workers in the 1920s, including a critical examination of the overall impact of factory work and urban life on Mexican
industrial workers in the Midwest. As unskilled and semiskilled factory
workers, these early-arriving Mexicans demonstrated an eagerness and
a desire to work and proved to northern employers that they could indeed function in an industrial environment. Their actions also demonstrated the will to resist and to reject the exploitive factory workplace.
Mexicans in the Midwest created communities that withstood numerous challenges—namely, economic downturns and repatriation drives
detrimental to survival and growth. This study provides historical in-
sights into the work and life experiences of Mexicans in 1920s Detroit
at a critical juncture—when Mexicans were becoming mass-production
workers in the auto industry. Moreover, it supplies a historical base for
the study of the formation of the Mexican industrial working class in
the Midwest and offers a new interpretation of the history of Mexican
labor in the United States.

ONE

Mexican Migration to the Midwest

At the end of World War I one of the largest regional migrations of American workers was launched by the expansion of production in steel, automobile, rubber, and electrical manufacturing in the North. With the exception of a growing number of blacks from the South who remained in the North, the migration was circular, with men and women returning to their places of origin. An estimated 620,000 workers moved to Pittsburgh, Chicago, Detroit, and other manufacturing cities each year between 1920 and 1929 to fill unskilled factory jobs once held by eastern and southern European immigrants. These Europeans had constituted a large portion of the American workforce in both production and nonproduction jobs since the late nineteenth century, but the changes in immigration policy enacted when the United States entered the war substantially reduced their numbers.[1]

The continuing shortage of unskilled workers caused by production needs and restrictions placed on immigration from Europe prompted northern employers to send labor agents to recruit Mexicans in Texas. Labor-contracting agencies in San Antonio also recruited Mexicans for employment outside the state. Recruitment was thus the primary method by which Mexicans first entered the North, and, as with the black migration, labor agents played a necessary role in facilitating the initial stages of this migration.[2] Mexicans were thus offered an alternative to Texas, where most of these immigrants toiled primarily as low-wage, seasonal farm laborers, although the railroads also employed them in large numbers. Texan racism furnished an additional reason for

13

Mexicans to respond readily to the labor agents' call. Racial intolerance was shaping the emerging commercial agricultural order and spilled over into every facet of Mexican life.

Throughout the 1920s, and continuing well into the post-World War II years, Texas was the greatest contributor of Mexican labor to other states. Indeed, the sheer numbers of the Mexican labor reserve in the Lone Star State made it "the hub on which the wheel of the Mexican population in the United States . . . revolved."[3] Mexicans set out for work from the state's farms and railroad-section projects. The cities of El Paso, Laredo, San Antonio, and Fort Worth served as staging areas for this migration to the Midwest and as relay stations for returning immigrants.

The demand for workers added a new dimension to the migration patterns of Mexican labor within the United States that would prevail well into the post-World War II years. The demographic features of the migratory waves were shaped by employment demands in the North and also by the personal choices of the migrants in their search for work.

NORTH FROM TEXAS

Thousands of Mexican immigrants, many accompanied by their families, entered Texas at Eagle Pass, Laredo, and Brownsville, at the turn of the century and spread into the three distinct farm zones that emerged in the state's southwestern region. This great influx of Mexican labor contributed to the development of commercial farming in Texas. Abundant Mexican labor allowed farmers to make a profit. Mexicans undoubtedly "put Texas on the map agriculturally." In the Winter Garden area they planted and harvested onions and spinach; they picked citrus fruits in the lower Río Grande Valley and cotton in the Gulf Coast cotton belt. But before these workers performed the labor they became celebrated for, which created and ordered agricultural work in Texas, Mexicans laboriously cleared cactus, dense thickets of chaparral, and mesquite trees from hundreds of acres of land. The arduous task of clearing mesquite was called grubbing, a "Mexican job" according to a local Texas saying. The root system of mesquites sometimes went down fifty feet into the ground; the men either cut the roots or pulled them out by hand and then burned them with the cactus and chaparral. The workers wore down the wooden handles of pickaxes through prolonged use in removing undergrowth so thick that passage by foot or horse was nearly impossible. The tedious clearing of the land paid $8 an acre but this amount was divided among a Mexican work gang. Working in gangs often composed of relatives and friends made it hard for men to shirk their work and eliminated discord, which typically underlay agricultural labor systems. There was no reason to work against kin or close acquaintances. Mexicans also dug the ditches and dams that would irrigate the land, and they constructed the roads on which they and their countrymen would be brought to the fields and on which the bountiful harvest of fruits, vegetables, and cotton was taken to market.[4]

The rapid development of the cotton industry attracted Mexicans to Texas. But the repressive working conditions and low wages characteristic of this industry eventually motivated tens of thousands to seek alternative work in the Midwest. "Snow time in Texas," wrote a contemporary observer, "is not in the winter but in the fall, when cotton is everywhere and the fields are white with the open bolls." Mexican migratory labor made cotton king in Texas in these early years, and this achievement made Mexicans the agricultural laborers of choice. Farmers endlessly praised them as ideal laborers. Costing less and demanding less, efficient, and, more important, plentiful, Mexicans first replaced white sharecroppers and then blacks in Texas as the preferred workers. Few scholars have noted that the wide use of Mexicans in the Texas cotton industry helped fuel black northern migration. The spread westward of black cotton pickers from Louisiana and Arkansas was stopped in east Texas by the seemingly endless flow of Mexicans pushing into the area from the state's south and central sections during the cotton harvest season. And with the cotton industry in the Salt River Valley of Arizona and in California's Imperial Valley using Mexican workers, the labor of black migrants, like that of white sharecroppers earlier, became less important. In Texas, Mexicans in many instances were preferred over blacks because the expectations of blacks had been raised during World War I and caused a change in attitude on their part. Blacks were no longer satisfied with agricultural work; their inclination now was to leave the South entirely. The heretofore uncomplaining loyalty and trustworthiness of the black worker, who was referred to by Texans as the "befo' de wah darky," were now imputed to Mexicans. Mexican and Mexican American farm labor, based largely on the family unit, was establishing and shaping a "new labor frontier" in the Southwest; by 1920 it extended into the beet fields of Colorado, the Central Plains states, and the Midwest.[5]

Cotton picking in Texas took place in three areas and seasons: in south Texas from early June to the end of August, in central Texas from August to mid-September, and in north and west Texas from September to December. The cotton season thus afforded tens of thousands of Mexicans continuous, uninterrupted employment over a seven-month period. Moreover, the cotton-picking season followed the end of the fruit and vegetable harvest in the Winter Garden area and the lower Río Grande Valley. This pattern had a cumulative effect on the size of the labor force following the cotton crop; with the end of the harvest season in each farm zone additional Mexicans joined the pool of cotton pickers.[6]

The typical path of Mexican cotton pickers and the dangers many encountered and resisted as they followed this crop through Texas are illustrated by the example of Lauro Tienda. In 1916, Lauro and his mother entered south Texas at Laredo. They had been forced to flee their hometown of La Blanca in Zacatecas, Mexico, after Lauro's father, an army captain fighting against the Mexican government during the Mexican Revolution, was murdered and the family received death threats. The Tienda family had been the wealthiest residents of La Blanca, owning thousands of acres of land and hundreds of head of livestock. Their elevated economic and social status ended when they crossed into Texas and signed a contract to pick cotton on farms near Piersall. Later the Tiendas joined other Mexican families traveling south in a caravan of autos and trucks to the San Marcos, Harlingen, and Corpus Christi cotton areas in the Río Grande Valley and then going north to pick cotton near Hamilton on the Oklahoma border. The cotton harvest was finished just before Christmas and the farm workers returned south to winter in San Antonio. Many did not complete the cycle; they quit along the way, having satisfied family monetary needs, and additional families took their place. Hundreds of thousands of Mexicans like the Tienda family constituted the huge labor force that harvested ten million acres of Texas cotton, earning from $0.50 to $1.50 per 100 pounds. Wages varied according to location and yield per acre.[7]

The now-heralded big swing of the enormous reserve of Mexican workers who followed the cotton crop through each of these three areas suggested an army on the move to journalist Carey McWilliams:

> From the lower valley, where the season starts, comes the initial vanguard of about 25,000 Mexican migratory workers. As the army marches through the Robstown–Corpus Christi area, an additional 25,000 recruits join the procession. By the time the army has reached central Texas, it has probably grown to about 250,000 to 300,000 workers. Recruits join the army, follow it through a county or two, and then drop out, to be replaced with new families from the next county.[8]

Cotton picking in Texas had drawbacks. One was the result of utilizing the family as the center of production. The use of women and children as unpaid labor not only tended to lower wages but as a rule depressed labor standards. In addition, the demanding, backbreaking labor was performed in unrelenting heat, involuntary unemployment was caused by a rainy season, and many Mexicans suffered the blatant racial abuse of Anglo ranchers. Mexicans were isolated in rural areas and small towns and segregated by race from Anglos. Hatred of Mexicans was deeply ingrained in Texas culture, and in this climate of virulent contempt it was not uncommon for hostility to culminate in violence. Many Texas ranchers were members of the Ku Klux Klan and dictated a reign of terror. Violence, the threat of violence, and legal means regulated the movement of Mexicans; these became physical as well as ideological extensions of segregation necessary to control and maintain this labor force. The laborers were expected to accept their inferiority as part of the ostensibly rational separation of the Anglo and Mexican races in Texas.[9]

Lauro Tienda and his mother had a dangerous misadventure on a cotton farm outside Hamilton, Texas. Refusing to pick the cotton crop because it was overgrown with the troublesome Johnson grass, the Mexican laborers walked out of the fields. The Texan farmer attempted to use the labor contract to force the Mexicans to work, but this tactic did not persuade them to return to the fields. Infuriated by the workers' apparent arrogance, the ranch owner called nearby ranchers to his property and threatened the defiant Mexicans: "Why do you think you have been brought to the United States? To pick cotton! Now pick!" Though frightened, the men and women still stood their ground in defiance and refused to work. The ranchers charged their horses into the workers, began beating them indiscriminately with whips and rope, and prepared to lynch all the men. Public opinion regarding the treatment of "bad Mexicans" would have supported the ranchers' actions. Lauro bravely warned the enraged Texans that he had told a priest which ranch they would be working on and how long they would be gone. Fearing possible prosecution if they went ahead with the mass lynchings, the ranchers reluctantly released the men.[10]

Contrary to what has been written about the passive and docile nature of Mexican workers, to the surprise of Anglo farmers many frequently did not hesitate to walk out of the fields if working conditions were unsuitable—even at the risk of violence. De facto peonage, readily enforced through direct and indirect means, was a reality for Mexican farm laborers. Yet family and friends who had suffered indignities spread information about their mistreatment and the unfavorable working conditions at certain farms, implicating owners for the inequities. Indeed, the brash nature of Texas labor relations shaped the consciousness of Mexicans—men, women, and children alike—and was largely responsible for the ways in which they responded.[11]

Mexicans migrating from Texas to the Midwest therefore made conscious choices to leave behind working and living conditions made doubly oppressive by racism.[12] Distressing experiences in the Lone Star State underscored the inequitable social relations at work and prompted some Mexicans to "escape" from Texas by crossing back into Mexico. Others, however, headed North. In comparing working conditions in Texas with those in the Midwest, workers remarked that less supervision, interference, and subservience were required in industrial work. More important, the men gained dignity and respect, which they had not known in Texas. As a Mexican steelworker stated, in the North one was allowed to "talk with your hat on." [13]

San Antonio became a favorite city of the sojourners passing through Texas. This Southwest metropolis and cultural center antedated Los Angeles as the capital of Mexicans living within the United States. An estimated 20,000 laborers left each year from San Antonio to work in Texan cotton fields and in northern beet fields and factories, with the tip of this migration wave reaching into the north as far as Detroit and Pittsburgh. The Mexican diaspora scattered workers "like clouds . . . all over America." All railways and highways from El Paso to Brownsville converged at San Antonio, a virtual Ellis Island for the tens of thousands of newcomers from Mexico in search of work and new opportunities.[14]

Mexicans seeking work in San Antonio congregated at Milam Park, nicknamed La Plaza de Zacate, a popular gathering place for the city's Spanish-speaking population. A cross-section of the Mexican working classes assembled there: itinerant railroad workers from Mexico and east Texas, Oklahoma, Kansas, and Nebraska, previously on extragangs ballasting, laying ties, and doing ordinary pick-and-shovel work; experienced miners from the Mexican silver mines of San Luis Potosí and coal mines in Bridgeport, Texas, and southeastern Oklahoma; seasonal farm laborers finished with the Texas and Oklahoma cotton harvests, ready to join the migration to the sugar-beet, wheat, and corn fields in Colorado, Illinois, and Michigan; packing-house workers who had processed hogs and cattle in Kansas City, Omaha, and Chicago; and former foundry men from Indiana and Ohio who had returned to San Antonio until the next start-up of production.[15]

Milam Park was a lively place. Mexican and American anarchists, Wobblies, and Socialists came to Milam Park and drew small circles of attentive men. These committed labor agitators, survivors of the wartime hysteria and government suppression, were familiar with the plight of Mexicans. Many of the wayfaring Mexicans had been exposed to labor radicalism. In the vernacular Spanish of the workers or through translators these firebrands expressed their point of view to anyone willing to listen or read the leaflets handed out. At the risk of being jailed for advocating radical causes, the organizers appealed to the men to support their political agendas.[16] The contest for the hearts and minds of the Mexicans had a religious context throughout the twenties. Street preachers from various Protestant denominations, intent on spreading the Gospel, passed out pocket Bibles and religious tracts in Spanish. Leaflets announcing upcoming evening prayer meetings or tent revivals, where confessions and testimonies became public events, were also given to the men. The preachers hoped their fiery sermons would win over souls that had wandered away from the Catholic Church. Knowing that many Mexicans possessed anticlerical sentiments, the street evangelists probably sprinkled their exhortations with derisive remarks about the Pope and Rome. Food vendors, San Antonio's famous "chili queens," sold a variety of Mexican edibles popular with the workers who had come to San Antonio.[17]

Labor agents also circulated among the men, luring them with cash advances or train passes to work on area truck farms, to pick cotton in Texas, to plant and harvest sugar beets in the North, or to work in steel mills in Chicago, northwest Indiana, and Pennsylvania. Chalkboards advertised these jobs and provided instructions about where workers should meet to be processed.

Mexicans who were not recruited returned to Milam Park to repeat the routine the next day, and the next, until they were hired. They passed the time searching through the job listings in the Spanish-language newspaper *La Prensa* or perusing letters from home or reading translations into Spanish of favorite novels such as *The Count of Monte Cristo*. Those unable to read asked their friends to read for them or hired readers. *La Prensa* carried news about events in Mexico and the United States that, like the speeches and advice of the labor radicals and preachers, usually roused the groups of men to a lively discussion. Some Mexicans spent the afternoons in movie theaters, a popular form of working-class recreation at this time. Films were the basis of these workers' first impressions of the United States while they were in Mexico. On the American side of the border movies continued to change the cultural perceptions of the migrants and encouraged and shaped their materialistic desires. They joined the throngs of newspaper and shoe-shine boys who regularly flocked to the daytime matinees. The cost of admission was well within workers' limited budgets. For a nickel or a dime, they watched newsreels, laughed at Charlie Chaplin's antics, or were thrilled by one of the wild-West features. A piano player furnished the background music for the silent images flickering on the screen as well as for the foot stomping and whistling of the spirited and noisy audience.[18] Similar scenes were taking place in El Paso and Los Angeles, which were also major Mexican population centers serving as gateways to the United States.

The kinds of jobs Mexicans were recruited for in these cities often signaled a change in employment patterns. Although Mexicans in the United States were confined largely to the rural hinterland by the nature of their work, the decade of the 1920s was nonetheless an important transitional period in their history. At this time a growing number underwent a process of accelerated urbanization and through a range of work experiences were proletarianized, becoming incorporated into the American working class through habituation to industrial work and, for some, adaptation to an industrial life-style.

After the 1920–1921 depression, Midwest employers resumed pro-duction, and news spread that labor agents would again be recruiting workers in San Antonio. Acting through one of the forty-five labor agencies licensed by the state of Texas, northern companies contracted Mexicans, sometimes a thousand at a time, and shipped them out of state by the trainload. Labor agents worked on commission, so workers were never asked whether they had entered the country legally. Also, because of this monetary incentive, the agents signed the same men on multiple times under different names. Mexicans familiar with the loosely regulated hiring were not afraid to sign on and, once transported north, to break their contracts if the work was unacceptable; they then either looked for jobs elsewhere or returned to San Antonio to repeat the hiring process. Mexicans were thus making conscious choices; their self-serving decisions and actions demonstrated a degree of autonomy that contradicts assumptions about their passive behavior.[19]

Direct personal contact was the standard way for labor agencies to recruit new workers. This strategy was likely a response to the growing opposition of Texas farmers to the depletion of the local labor force (85 percent of which was migratory and Mexican) by northern agricultural and industrial concerns. By the mid-twenties labor agents understood the networks Mexicans had established and manipulated the information being passed on to their advantage. Mexicans were encouraged to send letters describing their contract jobs to relatives and friends in Mexico, and sometimes the agency's letterhead was supplied for this purpose. The immigrants were urged to give glowing accounts of the United States as well as of the liberal policies of their employers. This practice proved quite successful; upon entering Texas many new arrivals sought work with the companies named in the letters. Another recruiting method was assigning Spanish-speaking agents, usually Mexican Americans, to ride the trains heading out of San Antonio and Fort Worth to convince Mexicans on board to sign with their companies. To circumvent illiteracy and the language barrier, some labor agents wore special clothes, colored ribbons, or paper flowers on their coats to identify the employers they represented. At the turn of the century labor agents in New York had used similar means to recruit Old World immigrants pouring into the city.[20]

Recruitment by northern employers helped break the virtual quarter-century monopoly on Mexican labor held by Southwest farmers, railroads, and mining companies. Lured north by the promise of higher wages and their rising expectations for economic betterment, immigrants in increasing numbers bypassed work in Texas. Mexicans who went north returned home and told their relatives and friends about what they had seen in their distant travels in search of work. Through word of mouth the opportunities available in the Midwest became widely known. Brothers, uncles, and cousins drew their kin into railroad work, foundries, steel mills, and auto factories, showing them work routines and shortcuts, while cautioning them to avoid particular crew bosses and foremen unfriendly to Mexicans. Family and friendship networks thus not only influenced the paths of Mexican migration to the North and decisions about work but determined settlement patterns within the region and aided adjustment to the new urban, industrial environment.[21]

In 1927, the Mexican population in the Midwest totaled 63,700; it increased to 80,000 in the summer months, with the influx of migrants into the farming regions. This group was relatively young (half were between eighteen and thirty) and had a vast array of life experiences and backgrounds. (See Graph 1.) Most came from the states of Michoacán, Guanajuato, and Jalisco in Mexico's overpopulated west central region. Nearly two-thirds of the immigrants admitted into the United States had been laborers in Mexico.[22]

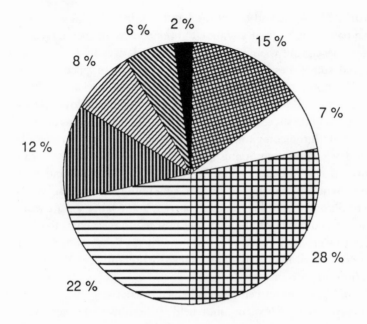

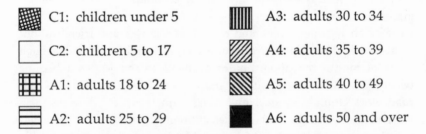

Graph 1.   Ages of Mexicans in the Midwest, 1926

SOURCE: George T. Edson, "Mexicans in Our Northcentral States," 1927, Paul S. Taylor Collection, Bancroft Library, University of California, Berkeley.

Moreover, these men had been active labor migrants in their home-lands. The majority had already traveled from their hometowns to nearby cities within Mexico to find temporary work. The expanding commercialization of agriculture in Mexico had rendered many of the migrants landless and triggered this movement to cities. The migrants who settled in the urban centers returned less and less to the countryside for the planting and harvest seasons, and continued to expand their search for wage labor. This quest took them to other parts of Mexico and then into the southwest border region for short-term employment before they permanently broke the cycle of seasonal migrations.[23]

Through this process the meaning of wage labor was reinforced or re-defined as the itinerants took on different kinds of work.

Pedro Escobar left his farm outside Guadalajara, Jalisco, and moved the short distance to the city, where he obtained work. He next traveled to Tampico, Tamaulipas, on Mexico's Gulf Coast, and was hired by the American-owned Eagle Oil Refinery. Pedro had learned that this company paid in U.S. currency, and understanding the favorable rate of exchange he made the long trek across the country to take advantage of this opportunity. When Pedro lost his job, he returned to Guadalajara and found work in a brick factory. Having grown used to receiving American dollars, he was now dissatisfied with the low wages in Mexico and migrated to El Paso, Texas, where he signed a labor contract to harvest sugar beets in Wyoming. From Wyoming, this mobile bachelor journeyed to Chicago and found employment in one of the packing houses. Like thousands of his countrymen who crossed the border in search of work, Pedro's extended migratory patterns began in Mexico and were based on demands for labor in the United States. As a bachelor, he could allow personal preference and opportunity to dictate his route and job selections.[24]

Some Mexicans recrossed the border two, three, and even four times to seek work. Unlike the immigrants from the Mexican states of Coahuila and Tamaulipas, who settled temporarily or permanently in adjoining Texas, workers from west central Mexico like Pedro Escobar chose the distant labor markets in the northern and eastern sections of the United States.[25] The peregrinations of Mexicans took them further away from the familiar border region and into the agricultural and industrial regions of the Midwest, to *el norte*.

Mexicans shared anecdotes about their adventures in the North. Like the Chinese sojourners who recounted tales of their "Golden Mountain" and the stories young southern Italians sent back to the old country about the land of *dolci dollari,* Mexicans too exaggerated their experiences to increase their stature among relatives and friends. Often left out of these glowing accounts were descriptions of the seasonal layoffs, the horrible work accidents, the bitter cold weather, and the poor living conditions in the cities. Yet when men came home in Model Ts and wearing American apparel, badges of success in the North, and were able to buy acres of land, their success further fueled growing dissatisfaction with local conditions and made the long trek north increasingly appealing.

Mexican migration to the Midwest was not haphazard; each sequence of the journey was well planned by the migrants and involved consultation with family members or friends and especially with those who had already made the extended trip north. These pioneers were familiar with the job opportunities, and their advice was invaluable. The migration generally followed the sugar-beet planting and harvesting seasons or coincided with the fluctuations of railroad and industrial work. The steady movement north was interrupted only by economic recessions, when a shortage of jobs prompted a return migration to Texas and Mexico.[26] (See Graph 2.)

The stream of Mexicans into the American heartland was thus facilitated by the unending demand for laborers during and after World War I and by immigration laws that stopped the flow of European labor and now favored Mexico. Throughout the 1920s Mexico was the primary source of foreign immigration to the United States. Labor historian David Montgomery has described this unrestricted Mexican immigration as a "revolving door for migrant field workers from Mexico." Southwestern employers, and soon northern agricultural concerns, had found a bonanza in cheap labor and lobbied earnestly in support of their self-interest. The desire for economic advancement was the underlying motivator for thousands of immigrants from Mexico. Labor agents initially aided this migration, but Mexicans soon developed it through informal kinship and friendship networks. The flow of Mexican labor northward originated in Texas, chiefly from the cotton-picking and track-maintenance-and-repair sectors. These seasonal migratory work patterns were extended by Mexicans to the North and adjusted to the fluctuations of industrial employment.[27]

Mexicans in the Midwest alternated between factory labor and work in agriculture and on the railroads. This tendency demonstrated the influence of the sugar-beet sector, the pull still exerted by previous work patterns and employment cycles, as well as the preferences and priorities of family and friends. The expanding domestic production of beet sugar in the Great Lakes region led to the active recruitment of Mexicans. Indeed, many of the men who entered factory employment in the region first worked on sugar-beet farms, family members working alongside the men, planting and harvesting this crop on a seasonal basis. Mexicans made sugar the agricultural queen in the North.

SUGAR-BEET WORK

The demand for Mexican labor by the northern sugar-beet industry was stepped up by the wartime restrictions imposed on European immigra-

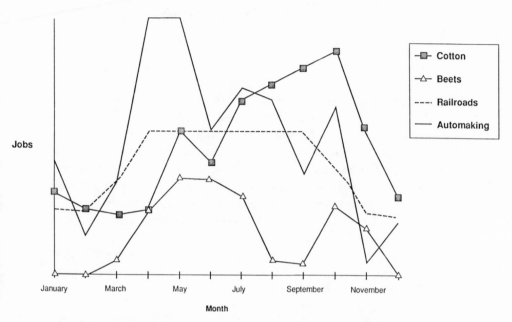

Graph 2.   Seasonal Occupations of Mexicans in the United States, by Industry and Crop, 1924.

SOURCE: Federal U.S. Mediation and Conciliation Service, Record Group 280, Subject Case Files 165/223, Box 13, National Archives, Washington, D.C.; and Rouge Area Hourly Workers' Employment Record Jackets, 1918–1933, Accession AR-84-58-1050, Ford Motor Company Industrial Archives and Record Center, Redford, Michigan.

tion. Throughout the sugar-beet areas of the Midwest, Mexicans replaced Russian, Slovak, and Bohemian immigrant families. Labor shortages were also created when white ethnics left sugar-beet work to become farmers or moved into higher-paying factory employment in the cities. *Braceros* (day laborers) were first used during World War I, but once the war ended Mexican families supplanted the previous willing workers as the mainstay of the northern sugar-beet industry. Supported by influential friends in Congress through a strong lobby, the sugar companies commissioned labor agents to recruit Mexicans in Laredo, San Antonio, and Fort Worth. South Texas also became a favorite recruiting ground because of the huge pool of Mexican workers who, once finished with the local planting and harvesting seasons, were available for northern sugar-beet work. The laborers who planted and harvested Michigan's sugar-beet crop were generally hired in San Antonio. Mexicans from all over Texas arrived in this city in early spring in anticipation of the beet season, and every day at dawn the long lines began forming in front of the labor-contracting offices.[28]

Contracting families was preferred because it was a profitable arrangement for farmers. To the Mexicans not only was family work familiar and customary, but declining wages demanded the effort of all who could work. Laboring together, a household could make sufficient money for the remainder of the year. (See Table 1.) The labor-intensive nature of sugar-beet work required ten to twelve hours of work, six days a week, from each worker to get the harvested beets to the refineries quickly in order to limit depletion of sugar content. Children had to take part, despite efforts to curb the exploitive excesses of child labor. The sugar companies thus did not want the urbanized Mexican worker but Mexican families from rural areas—that is, workers with seemingly boundless energy, according to Carey McWilliams.[29]

The newly hired beet workers rode north on trains of the Missouri Pacific Railroad; the railroad connected Texas to all points in the North, but the largest number of workers went to Michigan. Labor agents supplied the contract laborers with passes and prepaid tickets. Trainloads of Mexicans contracted by Michigan sugar companies left San Antonio this way. Others left from Fort Worth. The agents instructed the workers to carry only a few personal belongings, which they brought in cardboard suitcases or satchels. The workers had been told that the sugar companies would furnish all their necessities, including meals in transit. Warned about the harsh climate, the Mexicans packed warm clothing; some passengers brought along cherished items such as family photographs, and rosaries and small crucifixes made their way into the suitcases of the religious. One hundred fifty Mexicans were on board the Missouri Pacific train Lauro Tienda and his mother rode to Saginaw in 1926. Three years earlier, the Juan Martínez family joined 400 Mexicans who left San Antonio on the trip to Mt. Pleasant. Another Detroiter recalled that in 1918 her family was among the 1,000 Mexicans who departed from San Antonio to work on sugar-beet farms outside Saginaw. It took four to five days for the Mexican contract laborers to arrive in Michigan. During the trip food was provided as promised: coffee, canned meat, bologna, ham, and bread. The workers were let off the trains in St. Louis for the three to four hours required for an engine change. In Chicago they transferred to the Wabash line for the last leg of their journey. The Mexicans contracted for sugar-beet work were relatively well cared for during their trip, in contrast with the poorer conditions for men hurriedly sent north to perform repair and maintenance work for some eastern railroads.[30]

Table 1. Contract Earnings of Mexicans in the Sugar-beet Fields of the North Central States During the Season of 1926

	Number of Workers	Acres Tended	Price per Acre	Contract Earnings	Bonus Received	Total Received[b]	Average per Worker
Michigan	6,720[a]	42,000	$23	$966,000	—	$966,000	$143.75
Ohio and Indiana	3,264	20,400	23	469,200	—	469,200	143.75
Minnesota	1,506	9,375	23	215,625	$5,620	221,245	146.91
North Dakota	1,270	7,960	24	191,040	2,340	193,380	152.27
Iowa	2,018	12,460	23	286,580	11,550	298,130	147.74
Total	14,778[c]	92,195	$23.20 (avg.)	$2,128,445	$19,510	$2,147,955	$146.88 (avg.)

SOURCE: George T. Edson, "Mexicans in Our Northcentral States," 1927, PTC, 17.
[a]Of this number 3,048 were shipped from Texas by one company.
[b]Exclusive of any outside earnings.
[c]About 5,000 of these returned to Texas after the harvest was finished.

The contact on the trains with countrymen with diverse backgrounds and experiences continued to expand the social world of Mexicans beyond their home communities. It brought into focus the differing aspects of life in Mexico and the United States. One of these new experiences was contact with blacks. Mexicans were not always the only passengers on the trains; sometimes they traveled with blacks who were leaving the South in hope of better lives in the North. The blacks were from east Texas and Louisiana and were destined for St. Louis and Chicago packing houses and steel mills. Like the Mexicans, the blacks left as families. One can only speculate whether these black passengers knew that some of them had been pushed out of the Texas cotton fields by the quiet Mexicans sitting in their midst.[31]

In Michigan, the sugar-beet farmers met the incoming Mexicans at the train stations. Some farmers welcomed back families who had worked for them the season before. The distribution of the hundreds of contract laborers to their respective employers resembled a lively public auction and usually attracted a crowd of curious onlookers. Once on the farms the Mexicans were fed and given a chance to bathe in the nearby rivers or lakes since they had been unable to wash during the long and tedious train ride. The workers received straw mattresses, food allotments, and wood for stoves, and they were assigned living quarters. Next came the distribution of work implements—hoes, hooked topping knives, files to sharpen tools—and instructions for the tasks they would perform during the upcoming months. Veteran workers brought their own tools and had knowledge of the labor tasks. The travel-weary Mexicans started work the next day.[32]

The beet workers had a set assignment of between twenty and thirty acres. Three separate tasks were involved in the work. First came blocking and thinning, lasting about six weeks because farmers staggered their planting schedule. After a one- or two-week lull, hoeing generated about a month of work at the end of spring and in early summer. Workers were often idle until the harvest season began in late September; it lasted until late November or early December. With foot-and-a-half long topping knives the workers chopped the leafy tops off the swollen beets the farmer had lifted out of the ground with a tractor.[33]

The work performed in the northern beet fields cannot be casually dismissed, for Mexicans placed importance on their efforts beyond the wages earned. These industrious families could be relied on to care for the crops the following year because the Mexicans valued the reputations they acquired for their diligence and gladly returned to farms with acceptable working conditions. A distinct work ethic had evolved. Speed and endurance, in addition to withstanding grueling physical labor, were wellsprings of pride and respect from family, co-workers, and farmers. Reputations were built on how fast one could perform the work, resulting in contests between families and between individuals. In some instances the tenacious competition involved women, who by the end of the 1930s constituted over a third of the beet workers. The older women, often wearing dresses in the fields because of modesty and convention, set the work pace for the children. Younger women in bib overalls required less supervision than the children, for years of field work had accustomed them to the rhythms of a day's work. Some women picked more than their set acreage of sugar beets and had also established reputations as first-rate cotton pickers. Like the men, these hardworking women—mothers, daughters, sisters, cousins, and aunts—derived a sense of pride as workers even though their labor, like that of children, was unpaid. Moreover, domestic chores and childcare were part of their day's work.[34]

The use of Mexican labor in northern sugar-beet work was quite extensive and produced a silent invasion of the rural Midwest by a myriad of workers. With the promise of good wages and the enticements of free transportation and housing, the sugar companies contracted thousands of Mexicans to perform handwork on beet farms in Minnesota, Wisconsin, Ohio, Iowa, and Michigan. The Dominion and the Michigan sugar companies even sent Mexicans to work as far as Ontario.[35] Michigan sugar companies brought Mexicans to the state beginning in 1915, when it shipped them from Texas under contract with the Osborn Employment Agency. This recruiting agency of the Michigan Sugar Company became the biggest employer of Mexican contract labor. As a result of steady recruitment and the seasonal migration patterns, Mexicans constituted 33 percent of Michigan's sugar-beet workers in 1922, and that figure more than doubled to 75 percent by 1927. In 1927 the Michigan, Isabella, Columbia, Great Lakes, Continental, and St. Louis sugar companies employed nearly 20,000 Mexicans across the state.[36]

In addition, this extensive use of workers in the sugar-beet industry introduced crossing paths of Mexican migration within the region as workers searched for supplementary employment. The American Crystal Sugar Company first hired Mexicans to work in Minnesota in 1907 and steadily recruited them thereafter; by 1927, 5,000 Mexicans worked in this state and 7,000 by the following year. During the off-season some of the men obtained work in the meat-packing houses and on the railroads in St. Paul or picked corn and onions in North Dakota. Contracted in Texas and in Kansas by the Continental Sugar Company, Mexicans entered sugar-beet work in northwest Ohio in 1917. After the harvest season, Continental Sugar provided its employees with work at its sugar refinery in Toledo. Recruitment of Mexicans by this company reached a peak in 1926, when 2,697 were brought into Ohio. In the ensuing years the growing number of Mexicans present in the Toledo area, many men former sugar-beet workers who had found jobs with the railroads, furnished Continental Sugar with an ample labor supply, and it no longer needed to recruit outside the state.[37]

In 1927, some 58,000 Mexicans were employed on 800,000 acres of sugar-beet farmlands extending from eastern Colorado to northwestern Ohio; of these, half worked in the Midwest. Related through networks of family and kin, they formed an army of industrious field hands that was the northern equivalent of the multitude that harvested Texas cotton. And like their Texas counterparts, the Mexican sugar-beet workers gained the praise of farmers who endowed them with such characteristics as being "reasonable, obliging, . . . capable, less demanding," and showing "a willingness to take orders." Working as late as November and early December, when winter snowfalls blanketed the beet fields and the days grew colder and shorter, Mexicans harvested 7.5 million tons of sugar beets valued at between $60 and $65 million. One can appreciate why the sugar-beet industry lauded their boom years as the "Mexican Harvest."[38]

These workers were now part of a migratory labor force that left from San Antonio and the Río Grande Valley in Texas and entered the Midwest on a seasonal basis. Many came north to work for specific farmers. Accustomed to sugar-beet work—the intensive nature of planting, hoeing, cutting, and blocking performed in the chilly spring rains, the humidity of summer, and the first snows of late autumn— these itinerant laborers arrived each spring in a convoy of Model Ts and Reo trucks for the start of the planting season and left in late fall after the harvest. The use of these motor vehicles provided a new-found mobility, not only in Texas but outside the Lone Star State. The constant recruitment of Mexicans by the sugar companies produced a seasonal migration from Texas to the Midwest that became self-perpetuating. The migration routes, which passed through northern Texas, Arkansas, Missouri, and Illinois and which remained largely invisible to Americans, were followed by future generations of Mexicans coming to work on the fruit and vegetable farms of the midwestern region. Like their predecessors, they too left the migrant stream and settled in the cities in order to secure work in the local factories.[39]

Mexican sugar-beet workers were not immune to the many abuses that were associated with the work and that often went unreported. The independence they enjoyed working on the farms came with bad housing conditions, health problems, and destitution. Dishonest farmers cheated the Mexicans out of their wages or were cruel to the workers. However, none of the misdeeds proved as threatening as the encounters in Texas, where hostile Anglo farmers commonly said they "would rather kill a [Mexican] worker than pay him."[40] Beet workers did not passively accept bad treatment but applied lessons of resistance they had learned from agricultural labor in Texas. Complaints were filed with Mexican consuls about poor living and working conditions and wage discrimination, but sometimes the laborers simply walked out of the fields or staged work slowdowns to protest their objectionable treatment.[41] Farmers with bad reputations had trouble getting workers the next season because word spread quickly through the informal networks that were established in the northern agricultural region.

A vast number of Mexicans did not return to Texas at the end of the sugar-beet harvest season. Instead the workers repeated the patterns of their European predecessors and left sugar-beet work for jobs in the cities. Some Mexicans who stayed wintered in migrant camps and lived on their savings, which they supplemented with part-time farm work, until the start of the next beet season. (See Map 2.) Many more moved to small towns nearby or to industrial centers within the region like Milwaukee, Chicago, and Detroit.[42] With the help of family members and friends they were channeled into employment on railroads, on city maintenance and construction projects, and in foundries and factories.

Like the Texas farmers, sugar-beet companies experienced a flight of their Mexican labor from the beet farms. Aware that their diligent workers were leaving the farms and replacing them was costly, the sugar companies began using the newly created Mexican colonies in the cities as recruiting centers. The companies tapped the pool of idle factory workers during lax periods of employment. In Lorain, Ohio, Mexicans laid off by the National Tube Company enlisted for beet work in Kansas and Nebraska; in the Mexican colony of East Chicago, Indiana, workers secured beet work during the summer layoffs in the steel industry through the advertisements in the local Spanish-language newspaper *El Amigo del Hogar* (*The Friend of the Hearth*); in Chicago, men laid off

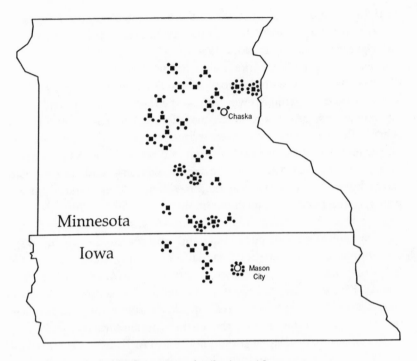

• = one family; average family size = 4.2 persons

■ = one farm

Map 2.   Mexican Sugar-Beet Workers Wintering Outside Chaska,
Minnesota, and Mason City, Iowa, 1927

SOURCE: George T. Edison, "Mexicans in Davenport, Iowa, and Moline, Illinois,"
1927, Paul S. Taylor Collection, Bancroft Library, University of California, Berkeley;
anα George T. Edson, "Mexicans in Galesburg, Illinois," 1927, Paul S. Taylor
Collection.

from the local steel mills and packing houses signed contracts with labor agents representing Great Lakes Sugar and left by train to Saginaw,
Michigan. And in Detroit workers answered notices that labor recruiters for the Michigan Sugar Company placed in pool halls frequented
by Mexicans. Advertisements for work at $23 an acre, free transporta-
tion to and from the farms, and discounted train tickets to San Antonio,
Fort Worth, and Dallas on completion of labor contracts enticed hundreds of jobless Mexicans to the beet fields.[43]

As time passed, Mexicans in the northern cities resorted to beet work
only during prolonged periods of factory unemployment and when alternative kinds of work were unavailable. This growing reluctance

stemmed from their habituation to city life and the routine of industrial work, which, despite periodic shutdowns, brought a semblance of permanence to their lives. No doubt the migrants from Mexico contrasted their hopes for a future with the uncertainty that had characterized their former lives in their homeland. Many considered a return to the farms as a regression. Conscious of the world of work, Mexicans thus made decisions in accordance with their desire to improve their overall situation. Family concerns were paramount in these choices. In addition, the immigrants were no longer interested in conveying the image of accomplishment to their countrymen. They had already gained respect through their successful adventures in the North, evidenced, for example, by the money they sent home. The priorities now were to achieve and enjoy the material rewards of good wages and steady work, to gain somewhat better living conditions in the cities, and to attain social status locally among their countrymen who likewise had made the decision to remain in the northern urban centers.[44]

The desire to disassociate themselves from farm labor became widespread because midwestern Mexicans recognized its lowly rank in the emerging hierarchy of obtainable labor that was an integral part of the social order they created in the North. In the Mexican colonies factory workers enjoyed the highest status and prestige; these relatively well-paid men were employed in unskilled and semiskilled operations in steel mills and car factories. Next in the ranking came the railroad workers, the men who repaired and maintained the local rail lines. Belittled by factory workers because track work entailed a transient life-style for the men and their families as well as living in deplorable boxcar camps, the proud track laborers nonetheless considered themselves better than the beet workers at the bottom echelon. Farm work was viewed as a last resort, casual labor performed only by greenhorns or by Mexicans who constituted the permanent labor migration force from Texas.[45]

By the middle of the 1920s Mexicans with relatives and friends working in the beet fields were encouraging them to leave the farms and seek factory employment. They argued that jobs in the foundries and factories, though beset by bad working conditions, were far superior to the hard handwork, low earnings, bad housing, and winter unemployment that characterized beet work. More important, their children were placed at a disadvantage by having to work when they should be enrolled in school, an indication that education figured prominently in their world. The constant prodding by relatives and friends already in the cities helped to reinforce cognizance of the contrasting experiences of beet work and factory work, between rural and urban life, and between poverty and material prosperity.

The shift to nonfarm wage work by Mexicans, however, was uneven or sometimes did not occur at all because of individual predilections and circumstances. The transition was abrupt for some, such as the men who used the train passes to get to the North but never intended to honor their beet contracts, taking packing-house, foundry, and factory work instead. For others the process was gradual, as in the case of Mexicans who tried out different kinds of jobs during the off-season, alternated between this employment and sugar-beet work, then left the migrant stream. Many Mexicans never severed their ties with migratory farm work but chose to return to the North each season, then depart for Texas when the cotton, fruit, and vegetable harvests began in this state. The majority of these migrant workers were *Tejanos,* Texas Mexicans with strong ties to family and community and deep pride in the Lone Star State. For thousands of sugar-beet workers, however, city life eventually became irresistible and a viable alternative. They gathered their families and meager belongings and loaded them on buses or into family jalopies and left the farms for the urban centers.[46]

Joining them in their trek to the city were Mexicans who came north to work for the railroads. Railroading, like agriculture, was an important frame of reference for Mexicans after their nearly fifty years of employment by this industry in the Southwest. Like the returning beet workers, track men relayed news about job possibilities in the region and established a parallel migration route that followed the network of eastern rail lines to and within the North.

WORKING FOR THE RAILROADS

Extensive employment of Mexicans by the railroads during World War I was synchronized with this industry's seasonal requirements for track laborers. It followed somewhat the hiring patterns of late nineteenth-century railroad companies in that procurement of Mexicans by labor recruiters in Texas coincided with the beginning of track-bed maintenance and construction in the spring.[47] Just as they had taken on Irish, Chinese, Japanese, and Greek workers a half century earlier, railroad companies aggressively recruited Mexicans for track work because native-born Americans, the "buckwheats," unless desperate, generally refused this physically demanding and low-paying labor. They enjoyed

better wage opportunities because the concentration of a black and ethnic labor force in certain jobs degraded this work. Nativism in combination with the needs of the southwestern rail lines for common labor,
which was plentiful along the border, made track maintenance and repair the work realm of Mexicans, the recent immigrant arrivals. It was
their turn to do the work considered fit for "lesser breeds." With picks,
shovels, crowbars, and sledgehammers put in motion through shouted
commands, whistles, or hand signs, and with a work pace set by the
gang leaders, countless Mexican track gangs helped in the construction
of the American railway system. Indeed, as one ex-railroad man in Detroit remarked, the sweat labor that Mexican track men performed
in the heat, dust, and storms "built the American railroads from
scratch." [48]

Among the Mexican recruits were seasoned railroad hands with
years of work experience in Mexico and the United States. Some had
been employed numerous times on six-month contracts in Arizona,
New Mexico, and Oklahoma unloading rails, laying switches and ties,
tramping, lining, and leveling roads. These road men, who had worked
for such lines as the Southern Pacific, the Santa Fe, and the "Katy" (Missouri, Kansas, and Pacific Railroad), had no problem securing railroad
work. [49] They were sought out by the railroads as foremen and gang
bosses for predominantly Mexican crews. Though veteran track workers were recruited, the railroad companies also contracted Mexicans by
the thousands chiefly for common labor and for work in the roundhouses.

The endless and backbreaking work done by Mexican track laborers,
at times in severe weather, became their hallmark. It was aptly described
by two contemporary observers:

> You see that poor devil out there lifting that heavy iron? He is as strong as
> an ox, but he can hardly lift it for the reason that it is so hot in the sun. Right
> now he has to have two pairs of gloves so as not to blister his calloused
> hands. Those are Mexicans. . . . They work when we are sleeping, mush
> around in the water in big rains. . . . When a wreck occurs, they are the first
> to get there though it be, as it usually is, at night. . . .
> The other rejoined: Yes, and what kind of a chance have they to enjoy
> their work? They are doing work that the average American would not and
> cannot think of doing. Last week . . . in the desert the heat killed three Mex-
> icans and prostrated a score more. The temperature was up to 120 degrees. [50]

Tens of thousands of Mexicans endured long periods of section work in
the countryside far removed from contact with anyone except co-

workers. At night the glowing fires from the men's campsites alongside
the rail lines seemed to extend to the skyline. The men enjoyed the sense
of independence their work gave them and the camaraderie of their co-
workers, who often were relatives. Mexican track workers took pride in
their work, from which they forged an identity based on tradition; they
thrived on the respect gained through such manly efforts. Common labor for Mexican railroad workers entailed experience and skill; daily
work patterns and rhythms learned on the job were taught to new recruits: knowing how to time lifting, hauling, and digging as the day
grew hotter, and being prepared to work all through the night by lan-
tern light after a derailment or washout. Many of these railroaders
passed on their knowledge of track work to their sons.[51]

Men drawn from these ranks in the Southwest headed for track work
in the North. Eastern railroad companies faced shortages of unskilled
labor and began contracting Mexicans in Texas, where the lines had
terminals. To justify their large-scale recruitment to the wary railroad
unions, which feared this flood of cheap labor, the rail companies argued that it aided the war effort because food and munitions were carried by rail. Furthermore, the companies contended that the Department of Labor sanctioned the use of Mexican contract labor by the
railroads for the duration of the war. At first most of the recruits got
their jobs through private labor agencies or through railroad employment offices set up in Texas cities. The companies soon tapped their
workers' networks of relatives and friends to reduce costly recruitment
expenses. Careful not to jeopardize the reputation of the family name,
the men would strive to be good workers.[52]

One of the railroad companies expanding its recruitment of Mexicans for maintenance-of-way service in Chicago was the Chicago, Rock
Island and Pacific Railway (referred to as Rock Island). This company
had a terminal in El Paso, and the Mexicans recruited shipped out on
its trains directly to the Chicago area. The Rock Island circulated an-
nouncements printed in Spanish among its Mexican employees so they
could send them to their relatives and friends in Mexico. In this way the
railroad circumvented the extra costs of direct recruitment. In turn,
Mexican kinship and friendship networks assured a steady flow of dependable and reliable men into the work crews of the rail line.[53]

In 1916, 206 Mexicans worked year-round in Chicago for sixteen
railroads with terminals there, but within ten years 5,255 were performing track labor in the area for twenty rail companies. This significant
rise in employment was noted by a field researcher who stated, "More

Mexicans worked for railroads than for any one single industry, over 25 percent of them being thus employed." Between 1923 and 1928, the percentage of Mexicans engaged in track maintenance in the Chicago area doubled from 21 to 42 percent. By the end of the 1920s stagnation of the rail industry set in, mainly as a consequence of competition with the automobile industry. The shrinking labor market eventually limited the choices of Mexican track laborers.[54]

The use of Mexicans by railroads in Chicago during the 1920s was not uniform; Mexican penetration of track work differed according to each company's needs for unskilled laborers and its hiring practices, as well as the personal choices and decisions of Mexicans. For example, Mexicans constituted only 4 percent of the Terre Haute Railroad's track laborers but accounted for 80 percent of the maintenance and repair crews on the Burlington Railroad.[55] Through their networks, the men learned of the reputations of the various eastern railroad companies. Even such things as a railroad logo could be the deciding factor in choosing which company to work for, as was the case with the Mexicans attracted to the Santa Fe line because of its bold white cross insignia, which was emblazoned on its locomotives and cars. Information about unfair treatment as well as bad working conditions was also passed on through Mexican information networks and influenced the distribution of Mexicans within the railroad industry. Disagreements about the terms of the contract, a strike, or a reduction in wages played an important role in the decisions of each worker regarding his railroad employment.[56]

After the 1920–1921 depression, as eastern railroads began employing large crews of Mexicans drawn from the labor pools emerging in Chicago, a familiar pattern began to emerge. Beet workers who migrated to Chicago during the winter from farms in Michigan, Indiana, and Ohio constituted a sizable number of the recruits during the track maintenance and construction season. These men supplemented a company's regular work crews of Mexican track men. In 1926, 650 Mexicans shipped out from Chicago to Detroit with the Palma Construction Company for work on the Michigan Central Railroad. Others hired on with the Detroit Railway Company as section hands. All these men were seasonal track laborers. Thus while some Mexicans were long-time employees, most hired on in the summer and later quit to seek jobs in the local factories.[57]

This became the pattern of employment for Mexicans in track work in the North. Several hundred Mexicans worked for the New York Central Railroad in the Toledo area. The close proximity of sugar-beet farms furnished additional numbers of workers if the company needed them during the maintenance and construction seasons or for emergency road work. In Chicago, Mexicans hired on as maintenance-of-way men with the Baltimore & Ohio Railroad and left for Maryland and West Virginia on six-month contracts. They seldom stayed on the job beyond the length of their agreements; if jobs were plentiful, they moved on to other employment. Winter found a large number of them back in the Windy City seeking menial labor until the call again went out by the railroads for track workers. Nonetheless this pattern confirms the significant influence of the American railroads in expanding the work horizons of Mexicans, as the eastern lines drew them into northern track work and distributed them in an ever-widening arc that now extended east of the Mississippi River.[58]

The experience of the Pennsylvania Railroad illustrates this pattern. By 1926, the Pennsylvania had shifted its recruiting drives from Texas to Chicago, which had become the main supplier of Mexican labor in the North. Five hundred Mexicans per month from the Chicago area worked for the company during the repair and maintenance season around East Liberty, Homestead, Pitcairn, and East Pittsburgh, Pennsylvania. Two years later, the Pennsylvania Railroad had 3,000 Mexicans on its payroll as maintenance-of-way men in Pennsylvania and New York. Turnover was quite high, with 80 percent of the track laborers breaking their contracts and leaving the region. The remainder moved into higher-paying work in the coal mines outside Wilkes-Barre and in steel mills around Pittsburgh.[59]

Notwithstanding the fact that a distinguishable labor sector within track work had been established with its own work ethic and culture, and based on family and friendship networks, Mexican track laborers in the North performed physically strenuous tasks, often in the ice and snow and in below-freezing weather where the frost line was a major obstacle. For example, men with the Burlington Northern in Minnesota worked in winter temperatures of twenty degrees below zero, which the wind chill reduced even more. Such amenities as housing, coal for heating (though often old and toxic creosote-treated railroad ties), water, and commissary food were accepted as adequate compensation by the hard-working men. Especially attractive was the offer of free transportation back to the border on completion of six-month contracts, an incentive that made brief visits home possible or brought family members north. Housing ranged from barrack-style shelters to makeshift homes built from discarded freight cars and railroad ties. Once they were steadily employed, many men began bringing their families north. The wives, although accustomed to the three- and six-month work assignments of their spouses, had grown tired of the long separations and of dependence on parents. They wanted to join their breadwinners, to experience what the men described in letters or in stories during brief visits home. As the pace of recruitment for northern railroad work accelerated, Mexican boxcar communities began to dot the landscape; they were the beginning of many of the Mexican colonies in the Midwest.[60]

The composition of the camps, which were established along the rail lines in Texas and ones extending north, varied and influenced social relations. Some consisted of families; some, just of single men. Some were entirely Mexican, while a few included Greek, Italian, Romanian, and Irish immigrants and blacks. The camp residents offered one another companionship as well as assistance with food, childcare, or during illness. They were bound together by the common experience of years and years of railroad work and hardship and coexisted relatively harmoniously.[61]

The camp tenants were resourceful in creating a livable environment and were well prepared for the off-season, when work was scarce, as demonstrated by the established site two miles west of Fort Madison, Iowa. It was home to several dozen Mexican employees of the Santa Fe and Burlington Railroads and the families of the men. Boxcars at this camp had porches, fences, and large vegetable gardens; meat and eggs were supplied by a flock of chickens housed in coops; the camp dogs had huts for shelter; the inhabitants had their own small sundry shop and eating establishments; and "blind pigs" (speakeasies), a dance hall, and even a makeshift motion-picture theater provided entertainment. The camp's movie house was evidence that the fascination with American movie culture extended even to these immigrants in the hinterland. Tom Mix, Rudolph Valentino, and Clara Bow movies likely were a consuming pastime in this rustic setting, providing another dimension to the colony's dynamism.[62]

Railroad camps were often located in isolated rural settings dozens of miles from towns and cities. When the men went out on maintenance and construction jobs, sometimes for six months, support systems broke down and caused hardship, especially when families were abandoned. While breadwinners were away families received little money or in some cases none at all because mail service was sporadic and dependent on the train runs. Women took on the added responsibility of running the camps in the men's absence. Mexicans living in camps near cities were more fortunate because local charities familiar with the dwellers' privations offered assistance, though in most instances they accepted aid only after the resources of family members had been exhausted. Sickness plagued the camps, exacerbated by improper nutrition among the children and adults and the dismal conditions in some camps.[63]

Racial prejudice figured in the location of some of the boxcar camps. The life-style of the camp residents, shaped by years of itinerant railroad work, was associated with transiency and poverty—a perception that language and cultural differences compounded. The era's prevailing image of Mexicans was one of impoverished undesirables accustomed to squalor and unfit to live among white Americans. This prejudice was fueled by the low status attributed to all foreign nationals. Mexican track workers were thus regarded as outsiders, much as the Chinese and Japanese track laborers on the Pacific Coast had been fifty years earlier. Competition for jobs was also a factor. Railroads were increasingly hiring Mexicans instead of local residents to perform seasonal repair and maintenance work. This practice caused resentment of the Mexicans, who did the track work for lower pay than did the townsmen.[64]

Given the low wages, hard work, and seasonal nature of track employment, labor turnover was a persistent problem for the railroads. Mexican laborers who felt little commitment to the lines, save for their paycheck, quit in droves and returned home or drifted out of track work and into cities. In addition to the pull of jobs in the urban centers, which promised material well-being through higher wages, family members influenced the decision of track laborers to head for the cities because of the transient nature of track work and the isolation and rusticity of boxcar camp life. Women found it hard to make the transition to a nomadic, often secluded existence and were disconcerted by the long absences of the men. The expectations of women for a better life—for having running water and electricity, owning a refrigerator, shopping in stores, putting their children in school—went unfulfilled as they faithfully followed their men up and down miles of rail line. These working-class expectations shaped and ordered the social world of the Mexican women, as they did the social world of their male counterparts. They too wanted good wages and the satisfaction of success along with the corollary high status among their countrymen in the northern colonies.

Eastern railroads continuously replenished their supply of workers. Mexicans with families were encouraged to sign contracts so as to maintain a stable labor pool and offset the desertions. Along with the sugar companies, the railroads thus fostered Mexican migration from Texas to the Midwest and helped to increase the Mexican population in the region. As the rail lines began recruiting laborers from midwestern cities, they aided the distribution of Mexicans throughout the heartland.[65] Once Mexicans established beachheads in the various railroad industries of the Midwest, networks of family and friends supported and sustained the influx into this sector. And incentives such as free transportation and housing made track work both accessible and attractive.

EMPLOYMENT IN STEEL MILLS AND MEAT-PACKING PLANTS

Likewise, the wages and bonus and benefit plans offered by some steel companies increased the number of Mexicans who decided to work in this labor sector. The industrial North became identified with steel work, and Mexicans' entry into this industry added to the differentiation of the Mexican working classes. Despite racism, which assured that Mexicans would perform only blue-collar work, their experiences in the mills altered their lives as workers as well as altering the general perceptions of Mexican proletarians in the United States in the 1920s.

Factory employment of Mexicans in the Midwest signaled their transformation into industrial workers and marked a major change in the work habits and life-styles of these migrants. As the newest members of the factory workforce, they helped reshape the composition of the American working class. More important, as factory operatives they internalized the values and culture of the industrial workplace and thereby refashioned their former conceptions of work. Diverse experiences in mills, foundries, and factories delineated this working-class culture.

Migration patterns that had been circumscribed by seasonal agricultural work were adjusted to industrial settings. A discernible pattern of internal Mexican migration within the northern region was timed to the cycles of each sector of manufacturing, with the constant circular movement of Mexican workers following the seasonal fluctuations of factory work.[66] This new migration pattern was prompted by the inexorable search for steady jobs, decent wages, and acceptable working conditions, underscored by personal choices and family preferences.

Relatives and friends were key sources of information. They alerted prospective factory workers to plants that were hiring or laying off men, to the kinds of jobs and pay available, and to whether the work was steady. They also helped the new factory workers understand what would be expected of them. For those on production jobs knowing how to make efficient use of time in the performance of their work routines was particularly valuable. Time took on a new meaning and significance. Work rhythms and patterns were refashioned to fit the performance of work based on hourly increments (or piece rates) rather than on daily wages or seasonal contracts. However, this clock-time ordering of work was fluid; it was continuously reshaped, redefined, as well as contested by both workers and employers within the different factory workplaces. Mexican industrial workers soon learned numerous ways to resist this imposition.[67]

The independence that mediated sugar-beet and track work no longer existed in the foundries and factories. The exceptions were in nonproduction jobs—warehouse work, maintenance and repair work. Employees in these areas enjoyed a modicum of freedom. In all other areas foremen cast long shadows and tyrannized Mexicans. The men followed instructions barked by the foreman and were alert to his whereabouts, a necessity if they intended to hold on to their jobs. Impersonal, anonymous contacts between Anglos and Mexicans, which had characterized migrant farm work, were supplanted by constant interaction with foremen who did not hesitate to bawl out a man for the slightest infraction. Foremen were the new intermediaries between Mexican laborers and their factory employers, replacing Mexican American interpreters, crew bosses, and timekeepers, who filled this role on the farms.[68]

As Mexicans internalized the regimen of the factory, they simultaneously infused new meaning into the jobs and work tasks that they performed and that they now described through an appropriated workplace vocabulary. Their employment became a source of pride and status, prompting respect from co-workers and families and gaining acknowledgment from factory bosses, who became familiar with their penchant for hard and steady work. Mexicans also placed importance on the firm they worked for, whether it was a top company or one considered at the technological forefront such as Ford Motors. No matter how hard or routine factory labor was, the men found purpose in their industrial work. Strength, courage, and endurance became sources of pride and respect and confirmed an individual's worth to himself, among his peers, and in the community. Mexican steelworkers thus fashioned an identity from their experiences in blast-furnace and open-hearth jobs, in the intense heat, smoke, and fumes of the mill environment.[69]

Continual labor shortages brought Mexicans north to the steel mills, as did the massive worker unrest that followed the end of World War I. Often unsuspecting at first that they were being hired as strikebreakers, these workers signed up in Texas and in Kansas City to take the jobs being abandoned by northern steelworkers striking for higher wages, better working conditions, and union recognition. The total number of Mexicans used as scabs is unknown, but it likely remained small because news of the strike soon reached the workers from compatriots returning from the North. (In 1923, Mexicans were again called on to abort organizing efforts in steel.)[70] Despite their small numbers, Mexicans were cast in the strikebreaking role eastern and southern European immigrant workers once filled, a recent experience that historical amnesia conveniently obliterated for most of them. The indissoluble image of Mexicans as strikebreakers generated animosity among white ethnics against them. It would subsequently affect co-worker relations in both the mills and the working-class neighborhoods, notably in the Chicago-Gary region and to a lesser extent in a few Pennsylvania mill towns like Johnstown.[71]

The strikes also made Mexicans victims of a northern brand of racism, one directly aimed at blacks. The steady flow of southern blacks into the North occurred as immigration from southern and eastern Europe to the United States ended. Blacks now became the chief targets of racial resentment, which was fed by competition for jobs and housing. Mexicans became part of this equation, victims of heightened racial and ethnic consciousness in the North. The situation in the mill towns of the Midwest became explosive in the summer of 1919 because of outbreaks of racial unrest, notably the race riots in Chicago. To exploit the tense racial situation, but, more important, to undermine the morale and resolution of the strikers, the besieged steel companies recruited 30,000 blacks from northern urban centers and the South to serve as strikebreakers. These exploited workers were conscious of their actions; strikebreaking did not seem like much of a betrayal to blacks. Employers, but more so unions and white workers, discriminated against them and denied them a livelihood.

The steady entrance of Mexicans into steelwork resumed after the 1920–1921 depression as employers expanded their recruiting efforts.

Edson reported that some steel companies distributed fliers printed in Spanish to Mexicans aboard trains of the Santa Fe Railroad, a tactic some rail lines had used to attract workers in Texas. The mill owners attempted to draw these contract laborers into steelwork as they headed to Iowa to work for the Santa Fe. The offer of higher wages and benefits persuaded dozens to desert.[72] Steel plants in the Chicago area relied on local employment offices or labor sources for recruiting Mexican workers. Like the sugar and railroad companies, the mills utilized the family and friendship networks of Mexicans already on the payroll to secure additional workers and thereby reduce recruitment costs. This practice benefited Mexican workers.

The U.S. Steel Corporation became the largest employer of Mexicans in steel, hiring thousands to work in its plants in Wisconsin, Illinois, Indiana, Ohio, Pennsylvania, and New York. The Carnegie Steel Corporation employed far fewer Mexicans, but the company helped disperse them into the steel-mill regions in Pennsylvania and Ohio. By the early twenties, nearly 900 Mexicans were working in the mills of Carnegie Steel in Homestead, Braddock, Duquesne, and Clairton, Pennsylvania, and in Mingo Junction, Ohio. Bethlehem Steel brought Mexicans into Pennsylvania, as did Jones and Laughlin and National Tube, both subsidiaries of U.S. Steel.[73]

Steel plants in Pennsylvania hired fewer Mexicans as steel production shifted to the Great Lakes region. The companies had stood firm against the organizing drive launched by labor organizer William Z. Foster in the summer of 1923, which the inauguration of the eight-hour day helped undermine. No attempt was made by Pennsylvania steel firms to replace Mexican workers who deserted by bringing in new shipments of these men.[74] In May 1925, the Pennsylvania Bureau of Employment reported that only 1,135 Mexicans worked in the state's steel plants. (See Table 2.) The use of Mexicans in the mills of western Pennsylvania was likely restricted by the presence in the region of second-generation European immigrants (37 percent of the workforce by 1930) who monopolized the unskilled jobs. Also, reliance on blacks (10 percent of the workforce by 1930) further limited job opportunities. Most Mexican steelworkers were found in the steel districts of the Chicago-Gary area and in Lorain, Ohio. If the Great Depression had not cut off migration from Texas, as did the short-lived 1920–1921 depression, Mexicans would have contributed far more than they did to the ethnic transformation of the region's steel labor force. In Ohio, the National Tube

Table 2. Number of Mexicans Employed by Pittsburgh-Area Steel Companies, 1925

National Tube Company, McKeesport, Pa.	300
National Tube Company, Pittsburgh	35
Jones and Laughlin Steel Company, Pittsburgh	50
Spang, Chalfant and Company, Etna, Pa.	150
Carnegie Steel Company, Clairton, Pa.	80
Carnegie Steel Company, Braddock, Duquesne, and Homestead, Pa.	520
Total	1135

SOURCE: George T. Edson, "Mexicans in the Pittsburgh, Pennsylvania, District," 1925, PTC, 11.

plant in Lorain had as many Mexican steelworkers on the payroll as did all the steel mills in the entire state of Pennsylvania.[75]

Mexicans responded to the call by National Tube for steady work at good wages when 1,000 arrived from Texas at its Lorain, Ohio, steel plant in 1923. Turnover of Mexicans at National Tube remained low, about 13 percent, because this mill carefully screened its applicants and required the possession of immigration papers. The local company paid the transportation costs back to the border for workers who entered the country illegally so they could obtain visas. National Tube also contacted former employers to verify applicants' work records. The slow but careful selection process proved worthwhile; as a result of its selective hiring policies and its willingness to employ these migrants, this steel plant gained the allegiance of its new employees. Three-fourths of the workers earned between $0.60 and $0.70 an hour on alternate eight-hour day and night shifts.[76]

The week's paycheck briefly rendered tolerable the resentment by white ethnic and black co-workers. White ethnics could not forget that the new Mexican workers had been hired as potential strike insurance, and blacks resented being displaced by "foreign" workers whose racial characteristics ought to have likewise penalized them. The pitting of one immigrant group against another created dissension and ethnic rivalry. National pride took on added meaning as the men competed to outperform one another on the shop floor. Meanwhile, black and Mexican workers silently acknowledged that despite their dislike of one another race relegated most of them to the meanest and roughest jobs.

Though subject to business cycles, the work patterns Mexican steelworkers established at National Tube in Lorain demonstrated that as a
group they were actively entering industrial employment and rising
above their newcomer status. More important, the desire to return to
Mexico was waning as immigrants resolved not to go back to their
homeland because of limited opportunities. Mexicans in the Midwest
were being integrated into the American blue-collar world. Their assimilation into an industrial work culture, an uneven process of adaptation,
was taking place through the creation of enclaves in ethnic, working-
class neighborhoods and the networks established there, all of which
were influenced by the pervasive factory environment.[77]

However, everyday life was far from idyllic for the Mexican proletarians. Alternating bouts of work and unemployment were ever present
and undeniably unsettling. The workers paid exorbitant rents for some
of the worst housing in factory districts. Overcrowding made living un-
healthful, and pollution was widespread in the neighborhoods located
in the vicinity of the steel mills, stockyards, and foundries. For many,
their situation probably triggered memories of the wretched living conditions of San Antonio's West Side, where they had temporarily settled
before traveling north. Notwithstanding, these ethnic working-class
settlements in the North were home to the Mexican immigrants, and
the hardships and sacrifices were considered worthwhile.[78]

As Mexicans in the industrial heartland adopted the work habits and
life-styles of factory laborers, national identity and cultural practices for
some took on new meaning and purpose. They insulated the immigrants
from the hardships and work regimen of the factory and the oftentimes
unfriendly urban environment. Evidence of the transformation taking
place in the mill towns of the North was recorded by Edson. In September 1926, he attended the celebration by Mexican steelworkers in
Lorain of Mexico's Independence Day. Three hundred of the men
and their families had gathered to observe this Mexican national holiday. The pride of the men in their new status as steelworkers was evident in their immaculate attire, though upon closer inspection many of
the men's faces likely showed burns from the tremendous heat emitted
by the blast furnaces, and scars covered their callused hands, some with
missing fingers.[79] That evening, the well-dressed Mexican workers from
National Tube surely made the most of their time off from the mill in
commemorating their national holiday with speeches, literary presentations, and the playing of both the Mexican and American national
anthems. For months, the women had eagerly anticipated the night out,

a well-deserved respite from the routine of childcare and domestic chores and of feeding and caring for their men. On such rare occasions the dresses they had scrimped to buy could finally be worn for a reunion with family members and friends. The pocket watches the men carried and fished out to quickly glance at indicated the importance of time as a regulating force in their lives. It was hard for those on the first shift to enjoy the ceremony. They knew that early the next day they would once again file back to their jobs in the mills to relieve their compatriots who had labored all night tending smelters and blast furnaces. As Edson observed: "[They] are laborers in the big factory a few blocks north, where at that moment one could see the fires that burn continually lighting up the smoke-clouded sky of the night and where their brothers were . . . toiling in the heat of furnaces, for one-third of the men are always at work." [80]

Steel production helped transform Chicago into a mecca for Mexicans migrating to the Midwest and into a staging area for those heading to other sections of the region. Chicago's steel mills offered thousands of Mexicans employment. In 1925, over half the 8,000 to 10,000 Mexican steelworkers in the Midwest held jobs in Chicago mills, and they constituted 14 percent of the total local workforce in steel. Wisconsin Steel and Illinois Steel employed nearly a third of these workers. The proportion of Mexicans working in Chicago's steel industry remained relatively constant until the end of the decade, at which time 82 percent of the 19,362 Mexicans in the Windy City were industrial workers. [81] They could be found at work in freight yards, steel mills and foundries, and packing houses. This was the case for all of the Chicago-Calumet region.

Northwest Indiana was another center of steel production. In the twenties, thousands of Mexicans traveled by electric tram and bus to Indiana Harbor and Gary, Indiana, located east of Chicago, to seek work in the local steel mills. Some left fruit farms in southwestern Michigan to take jobs there. The Department of Labor reported that in late fall 1924 approximately 4,000 Mexicans from Michigan orchards arrived at the local steel mills in Indiana Harbor and Gary and that applications for work averaged twenty to thirty per day. [82]

The number of Mexicans at the Inland Steel Company in Indiana Harbor increased in 1923, when the company expanded production and changed to the eight-hour day, adding an extra shift. Over the next six years Inland Steel hired 3,600 Mexicans, the majority from Gary, Chicago, and Pennsylvania, though some had come up from Texas. Despite the labor turnover, with men quitting to seek work elsewhere, the 2,526 Mexicans Inland employed in 1926 were nearly a fourth of the company's total employees. Their numbers declined thereafter, reflecting overall reductions of the company's workforce. However, the 2,000 Mexicans on Inland's payroll in 1928 still constituted almost a third of its workers and its main ethnic group. On the eve of the Great Depression, Inland Steel had the second largest number of Mexican workers of all U.S. manufacturing industries. Only the Ford Motor Company employed more at its massive River Rouge plant.[83]

Unquestionably, Inland Steel's Mexican workers played an essential part in Indiana Harbor's economy. This role was noted in an interview by Edson of steelworker F. M. Figueroa, who was also co-publisher of the local Spanish-language newspaper *El Amigo del Hogar*. The steelworker pointed out that the significant contributions of his industrious countrymen to local prosperity came with sacrifices. They were not appreciated, nor did their labor exempt them from discrimination, which was rampant in Indiana Harbor. This worker pointedly remarked:

> The Mexicans of Indiana Harbor earn pay amounting to $7,000,000 a year. Of this amount they [only] send to Mexico . . . $1,000,000. That means that they turn $6,000,000, which they earn by hard labor, back into the money drawers of the city. . . . For this wealth . . . they get little more than a miserable existence, snubbed by their neighbors, abused by the authorities, and exploited by everybody.[84]

As noted, the growing presence of blacks in the North had generated resentment, making race relations quite tense. Competition for jobs and housing increased with the arrival of Mexicans, who benefited somewhat from the discriminatory policies of some steel firms. Mexicans in the Chicago-Gary area had joined blacks as the main source of unskilled labor in steel manufacturing. In several plants Mexicans outnumbered blacks because steel companies began to set numerical quotas in an effort to contain the growth of the black workforce. No attempt was made to integrate blacks into the steel factories. Their subsequent assignment to the worst job sectors increased opportunities for Mexicans. This racial stratification, which was duplicated in segregated neighborhoods, resulted in black steelworkers in the Chicago-Gary region absorbing most of the shock of racism.[85] But dark-complected Mexicans were at a disadvantage and encountered some of the same discrimination as blacks. Mexicans were another visible racial group and were often assumed to be black by white workers who had no reference point other than blacks for comparison. Because Mexicans disliked having to contend with the stigma of color that blacks confronted, many distanced themselves from this racial group.

Like their co-workers in general, Mexicans were motivated by pay and benefits to remain loyal employees. Also, employment security was especially valued because already by the mid-1920s manufacturing jobs were becoming hard to find; an unstable job market remained a threat, and workers continually faced an unsafe working environment and related health problems. Mexican steelworkers enjoyed some upward mobility within the unskilled and semiskilled ranks despite limited opportunities. But although there was a tendency to move out of the low-paying, hazardous foundry jobs considered by many as the domain of greenhorns, some Mexicans chose to remain in the foundries. Less supervision by foremen was one reason for this decision. Foremen hardly made the rounds of the foundries because deadlines for job completion were not as stringent. Once Mexicans became familiar with the requirements of the job, they shrewdly manipulated the tasks so they worked less but earned the same amount of pay. The Mexicans reasoned that foundry labor, though physically demanding, offered steady employment and a regular income. Few white workers wanted the strenuous work even when jobs became scarce.[86]

In addition to finding railroad work and steelwork, Mexicans entered the northern meat-packing industry, and within a short time a sizable number were performing unskilled jobs in the packing plants of Wilson and Company, Swift and Company, Cudahy, and the Omaha Company in Nebraska, South Dakota, Kansas, Iowa, Minnesota, and Illinois. In 1928, Mexicans constituted 5.8 percent of the labor force in Chicago meat packing; they were concentrated primarily in entry-level positions, working alongside Polish and Lithuanian immigrants in the pickle, glue, lard, and fertilizer departments.[87]

The working environment in the meat-packing plants—the stench of putrefying meat, the noise of the machines, and the mix of languages— was captured in the following description by labor historian James R. Barrett: "Within the plants the atmosphere was dominated by the sight, sound, and smell of death on a monumental scale. . . . In the midst of all this squealing, gears ground; carcasses slammed into one another; cleavers and axes split flesh and bone; and foremen and straw bosses shouted orders in half a dozen languages."[88] Mexican packing-house workers attempted to keep up with the dangerously fast work pace, which added to the high number of work-related accidents and injuries that marked the industry. Former packing-house workers chillingly re-

called co-workers being killed because of the frenzied pace of the work
in the plants. Along with these hazards, erratic schedules and seasonal
layoffs were endemic to packing-house work. In Chicago, the meat companies usually hired men for only a day's work at the beginning of a
mass slaughter and sent them home once the job was finished. Every
morning men were chosen from the mass of laborers who congregated
around the stockyards. The relatively low number of Mexicans in meat
packing was a result of the huge ethnic and black workforce in this industry. However, a considerable number of Mexicans were employed in
meat-processing plants in Kansas City, and some were long-time
packing-house workers. Their presence in this industry contributed to
the diversity of the Mexican proletarian experience in the North.[89]

ENTRANCE INTO AUTOMOBILE EMPLOYMENT

Michigan's automakers played a central role in the development of the
emerging Mexican industrial working class. Large numbers of Mexicans migrated to southeast Michigan specifically to seek high-wage
work in the car and truck plants. However, the auto industry (except
for Buick Motors) neither recruited Mexicans, as had the sugar companies and the railroads, nor brought them north initially as strikebreakers, as had the steel mills. Rather, the car companies drew Mexicans
into their factories mainly from the ranks of sugar-beet workers on area
farms, though railroad workers, steelworkers, and a few coal miners
also yielded to the lucrative lure of auto work. As early as 1917 Mexicans began working in automobile factories in Detroit, Saginaw, Flint,
and Pontiac, Michigan. The majority had migrated to Detroit from
other parts of the Midwest; less than 10 percent were direct arrivals
from Mexico.

Once again, networks of family and friends helped spur the influx of
Mexicans into the Motor City, providing information about work and
how to obtain employment. In 1925, Guadalupe Morales came to Detroit from the coal mines near Toluca, Illinois, six years after crossing
the border at Eagle Pass, Texas. For three years Morales performed perilous work in the mines, digging coal on his knees in three- to four-foot-
high shafts. A friend employed by Ford Motors visiting the miner told
him about the work opportunities at the River Rouge plant. Morales
was warned that swarms of job seekers would be at the plant gates and
that the company hired men arbitrarily. The friend informed Morales
that few men applied for the unpopular and stigmatized foundry jobs,

instead claiming they were benchmen or assembly men. The Mexican mine worker was to follow his friend's instructions when he got to the Rouge plant: "He told me that when I get to the plant gates and am asked, 'What do you know?' I was to reply, 'Coremaker.'" Guadalupe did this and was immediately hired as a coreman in the foundry department.[90]

By 1920, about 3,000 Mexicans were in Detroit; the constant movement of workers to and from the city made an accurate count difficult. Detroit was the world's biggest manufacturer of cars, trucks, and tractors, and the nation's fastest growing metropolitan area because of its high-wage industry.[91] Ford Motors hired the greatest number of Mexicans, employing nearly 4,000 at its Highland Park, Fordson, and River Rouge plants in 1928. Over 200 young men carefully selected by their government from engineering and technical schools in Mexico enrolled as students in the Henry Ford Service School. They worked as apprentices on cars, trucks, and tractors in the Highland Park and Fordson plants as part of their training to become technicians for dealerships in Mexico and Latin America. Mexican colonies developed in the working-class districts near car plants in Saginaw, Flint, and Pontiac. By the end of the 1920s, General Motors and Dodge Motors employed approximately 800 Mexicans, Fisher Body had several hundred in its plants in Detroit and Pontiac, and nearly 1,000 worked at the Buick Motors plant in Flint and at Chevrolet's Detroit and Saginaw plants. Untold numbers of Mexicans also found jobs with auto-parts and accessory firms that did subcontract work for the major carmakers.[92] Because of the high labor turnover that characterized the auto industry, it is quite likely that thousands of Mexicans passed through the gates of the car plants of southeast Michigan.

Mexicans found employment with all the car companies and worked in most plant departments, though their distribution within the industry was uneven. Where they worked depended on the hiring policies of each auto and auto-parts maker and of plant managers and foremen who, with their own racial and ethnic preferences, determined job assignments. At some car plants Mexicans formed a considerable percentage of the men in the shops and even won promotions to foreman and supervisor. "There were lots of Mexicans at Chrysler Motors," retired autoworker Ramón Huerta remembered. "In my department were Mexicans, Spaniards, and Polackos [Poles], but no blacks. Our superintendent was a Mexican from Jalisco."[93] Fisher Body used few Mexicans because of hiring restrictions on foreign and black workers. In certain plants Mexicans and blacks were concentrated in the most hazardous areas, like the spray-paint department, because rigid job patterning designated some work as being exclusively for these racial groups. However, Mexican and black autoworkers quit or did not accept the shop-floor racism passively. On the contrary, straight razors, wrenches, and fists served as equalizers, contradicting the stereotype of Mexicans and blacks as compliant and docile workers who were grateful that they had employment.[94]

Exposed to dangerous working environments, untold numbers of Mexican autoworkers were blinded by flying metal, lost their fingers and sometimes their hands in the whirling machinery, inhaled poisonous gases, and suffered burns from molten metal. Work-related stress was an additional problem. Many could not withstand the fast pace of production and the regimented working environment, where discipline was strictly enforced by shop foremen. Foremen baited the Mexicans, racially harassed them, and did not hesitate to beat or kick them for minor violations. Outweighing the hazards of mass-production work, the sporadic prejudice of white autoworkers, the unsafe factory conditions, and the repressive forms of control, the promise of employment continued to attract Mexicans to Detroit throughout the twenties. The hope of achieving a better life prompted Mexicans to migrate to the Motor City. Good-paying jobs with the Ford Motor Company were greatly prized. To wear the silver Ford badge and short ("whitewalled") haircuts, which were the distinctive trademarks of the Ford autoworker, became the ambition of Mexicans in the climb for status.[95]

The immigrants' eagerness to obtain positions with the famous automaker is evident in the numerous letters the Ford Motor Company received from Mexicans inquiring about work. In 1923 a Mexican from Monterrey, Mexico, wrote to the Ford Employment Department: "[I] want to work for the Ford Motor Company because it is the best business on Earth and there must be a permanent position and a good future for a man who wants to work."[96] This letter clearly reveals adherence to the work ethic by Mexican immigrants. If a man was willing to work hard—and all of Ford's autoworkers were driven beyond capacity—a job with the popular auto company was a means to a better life and a way to attain pride and gain respect as a worker. This social status was sought more and more in the Mexican colony of Detroit, for thousands of Mexicans endeavored to become part of the elite corps of Ford mass-production workers. These new Ford men were the embodiment of the Mexican industrial proletariat.

The opportunity for work on the railroads, in the steel mills and foundries, in the packing houses, and in the auto factories brought thousands of Mexicans into the industrial heartland of the Midwest during the 1920s. (See Table 3.) Admittedly, sizable numbers were recruited by northern sugar companies, which with several eastern railroads helped augment Mexican migration to the North. Earlier legislation restricting immigration from Europe also proved favorable. Mexicans toiled in factories alongside immigrant and black co-workers and were prone to the same work slowdowns owing to swings in production cycles. During boom years Mexicans enjoyed full-time employment, enabling them to participate in the prosperity of the period. When industrial production shut down, as during the 1927 recession, Mexican factory workers faced layoffs and bouts of unemployment. Without work, thousands left the Midwest, though itinerant employment was commonplace. The Mexican proletarians of the North adjusted to their new environs and embraced the style of work of the different labor sectors though always attempting to modify or resist the social relations of the workplace as well as the demands for increased production. The following chapters will note that the search for steady work demanded frequent movement. As a result, high levels of mobility within the region as well as inter- and intracity migration characterized the nascent Mexican industrial working class. (See Table 4.)

Table 3. Nonagricultural Employment Occupations and Wages of Mexicans in the North Central States, 1927

Place of Employment	Number Engaged	Hourly Wage Rate					Average Hourly Wage
		$.30–.35	$.36–.40	$.41–.45	$.46–.50	over $.50	
Steel mills, foundries, auto plants	17,295	0	144	8,632	4,164	4,355	$.4973
Railroads[a]	7,572	77	7,070	339	60	26	.3914
Highway and building construction	3,727[b]	0	3,540	66	35	2	.4026
Packing houses	1,011	57[c]	68	692	180	14	.4269
Cement and brick plants	663	39	142	288	190	2	.4465
Tanneries	559	0	6	425	115	13	.4627
Total	30,827	173	10,970	10,442	4,744	4,412	$.4561

SOURCE: George T. Edson, "Mexicans in Our Northcentral States," 1927, PTC, 5.
[a]Extra railroad gangs employed in summer not included.
[b]This number decreased about 90 percent between October 15 and December 1.
[c]Of these, thirteen earned less than $.30 (ten women earning $.20, a girl and two men earning $.27).

Table 4.   Average Job Duration for Mexican Workers in Midwestern Cities, February 1927

	Kind of Work	Number of Workers	Years	Months	Days
Galesburg, Ill.	Foundry	36	2	3	3
Fort Madison, Ia.	Roundhouse, Shop	61	6	3	22
Moline, Ill.	Steel Mill	26	1	8	10
Silvis, Ill.	Roundhouse, Shop	40	2	5	2
Silvis, Ill.	Railroad Stores	31	4	11	22
Mason City, Ia.	Cement Plant	39	3	4	27
Mason City, Ia.	Packing House	66	0	8	4
South St. Paul	Packing House	105	4	11	7
Omaha	Packing House	91	9	10	1

SOURCE: George T. Edson, "Mexicans in Our Northcentral States," 1927, PTC, 11.

Mexicans in Working-Class Detroit, 1918–1921

The extensive urbanization of a rural, migrant people was the result of the movement of Mexicans into American cities. This transformation was well under way by 1920, reflecting the shift of half the nation's population to urban centers. Three southwestern cities were primary destinations for Mexican immigrants entering the United States: San Antonio, El Paso, and Los Angeles. As noted, San Antonio functioned as a principal distribution center for the workforce heading to the Plains States and the Midwest, and scholars have documented the overall importance of El Paso for Mexican labor recruitment and for distribution within the Southwest region and to other geographical regions. Los Angeles played a similar role for south-central and southern California, funneling thousands of workers to rail lines like the Southern Pacific and to farms in the Oxnard and Ventura areas and as far away as the San Joaquín and Imperial valleys. Circular and return migration accounted for the expansion and contraction of these large urban Mexican populations, whose growth was abruptly interrupted by the 1920–1921 depression. In 1920, 70 percent of midwestern Mexicans resided in cities; these migrants formed colonies in the North for the first time. The twin cities of Kansas City, Kansas, and Kansas City, Missouri, along with Chicago became main settlement centers, as did Milwaukee, Gary, Indiana Harbor, Detroit, and Toledo, as the immigrants fanned out seeking work.[1]

The comparatively small Mexican colonies of the urban Midwest did not have high population densities like those in the Southwest, where

Mexicans formed the main racial group. Other important features distinguishing the Mexican midwestern experience from the southwestern were the diverse ethnic composition of the northern cities, labor strife, and the presence of large black populations. Mexicans in the North occupied working-class districts established by eastern and southern European immigrants at the turn of the century. These European immigrants sometimes formed a third of a city's population. During World War I, intense nationalism permeated some of these immigrant neighborhoods, such as those in the Chicago area, and limited interethnic contacts. However, community identification was solidified by the 1919 steel strike, and it precipitated antipathy toward Mexicans, who as recent arrivals were perceived as outsiders imperiling white workers' livelihoods. Such discrimination made it hard for the Mexican newcomers to find housing, which was already in short supply. These circumstances did not confine Mexicans to the worst urban districts in just one city; on the contrary, they moved frequently between pockets of poverty in several cities through a process of circular migration. Discrimination was also a response to the increasing size of the black population, which began arriving during World War I. Blacks were the chief victims of housing segregation in the urban North.[2]

For the Mexicans who were migrating to the North, the short period from 1917 through the 1920–1921 depression was historically complex and varied. There is little information about these early experiences, which were compressed within several years but which encompassed substantial change. Most of the Mexicans moving into the Midwest were urbanized and to a certain extent Americanized. Thousands entered factory work, and many who migrated to the Chicago area became involved in the 1919 steel strike. As racial antagonism mounted with the economic downturn, opposition by white workers and local officials to the Mexican presence in the North culminated in calls for removal. This chapter examines what these early years were like for the Mexicans who migrated to Detroit and suddenly encountered a major manufacturing city, one that was shaped and ordered by the corporate heads of the automobile industry.

MEXICANS ENTER INDUSTRIAL DETROIT

Mexicans first arrived in Detroit at the end of World War I from area beet farms and cities within the Midwest. A small number came directly to the city from Mexico, including some who left because of the Mexican Revolution. Among these men were college graduates, those with technical educations, and those with sufficient government connections to facilitate their migration to Detroit and to procure employment in white-collar and skilled factory positions.[3] Mexican settlement generally corresponded to the seasonal nature of auto manufacturing. Making their way north from Texas, Mexican immigrants came to Detroit in the spring and left in the winter. The men returned to Detroit the following year to begin the cycle again, often accompanied by two or three companions seeking opportunities in the Motor City. This circular migration, shaped by the industrial nature of the northern environment, ended when the decision was made to stay in Detroit, at which time wives, children, and other family members were brought north.[4]

It is uncertain how many Mexicans settled in the northern cities because of the high number of transients. About 4,000 Mexicans lived in Detroit at the end of 1920, far more than were reported by enumerators from the Detroit Board of Education because scores of transients and single men living in boarding houses were undercounted. Having entered the United States surreptitiously, these men did not answer their doors to strangers for fear that they might be immigration officials.[5]

Mexicans came to "dynamic Detroit" motivated by the hope and desire for a better life, which rested with procuring work in the car plants. The letters the newcomers sent home vouched for Detroit and the abundance of well-paying jobs in the auto plants, where cars rolled off the assembly lines day and night. The job opportunities available with Ford Motors were repeatedly emphasized in the correspondence. During visits home in the off-season, Ford autoworkers told relatives and friends about the company's lucrative wages (averaging $0.75 an hour in 1919), their challenging experiences in auto work, and Detroit's vibrant city life. The conversations focused on the Ford assembly lines, which symbolized technological mastery and modernity; the embodiment of Ford technology was the Model T.[6] Machines captured the imagination of hundreds of Mexicans and drew them to Detroit. The remarks of one of these early arrivals typified the contagious excitement: "Almost everybody . . . where I lived talked of coming [to Detroit], . . . and the desire to go was in the atmosphere. Young fellows who had been up here told about how much they were earning [and] all became enthusiastic. I wanted to see that part of the world about which I had heard so much."[7]

However, on arriving in Detroit Mexicans had varied experiences. Obtaining jobs through kinship and friendship networks was not always feasible; relatives and friends preceding the immigrants to the city sometimes failed to find work themselves and did not have the resources to assist incoming workers. Countless arrivals did not get past the plant gates because they could not speak English. A few reached the city during production shutdowns and found themselves waiting months to get jobs, milling around the dozens of private employment agencies in the city or at the gates of the car plants. Others reached Detroit broke or in debt, having exhausted their savings during the passage north or else owing money to creditors who financed their trips. Desperation forced these ill-prepared men into menial jobs, into the beet fields, or back to Mexico. Newly hired workers did not avoid misfortune. Detroit's cost of living made housing and food expensive, and many men became discouraged, quit their jobs, and left the city with their dreams unfulfilled. Others fell sick or were injured in factory accidents or simply succumbed to homesickness.[8]

Yet work was plentiful in the Midwest at the end of the war, and the majority of Mexicans who came to Detroit found jobs. They entered an increasingly stratified factory environment (which was due mainly to Detroit's sizable black workforce). Spilling into the city's working-class communities, their influx would underline ethnic and racial divisions.[9]

Detroit's population had grown rapidly as a result of the tremendous expansion of automobile manufacturing; indeed, Detroit had become one of the country's great industrial cities. Between 1900 and 1910, its population increased by 63 percent. In 1920, the U.S. Census reported that 993,678 people resided in Detroit, making the Motor City the country's fastest-growing metropolitan area.[10] Migration was the chief source of this population increase. A seemingly endless demand for labor by the auto industry, coupled with high earnings, turned Detroit into a boom town as tens of thousands of workers poured into the city to seek their fortune. Of the 528,000 residents added to Detroit's population between 1910 and 1920, 412,000 were new arrivals and countless others continuously moved to and from the city in search of work.[11]

Detroit was a city of blue-collar workers. On the eve of World War I, nearly half of Detroit's workers labored in auto and auto-parts factories. In 1919, they produced $880,000,000 worth of automobile products, which constituted an estimated 60 percent of the city's total manufacturing revenue. In 1920, Detroit's automobile industry employed 135,000 workers. Twelve percent worked for General Motors (the result of the merger of Buick, Cadillac, Oldsmobile, and Chevrolet). Studebaker, Hudson, Packard, Maxwell, and Dodge Motors were major employers. The Ford Motor Company hired the greatest number, with 40,000 men on its payroll.[12]

Although the Motor City's car factories attracted native-born workers from the surrounding region, European immigrants constituted a large part of the auto workforce until restrictions ended the flow of these immigrants at the start of World War I. About 160,000 foreign-born immigrants came to Detroit between 1910 and 1920, more than came to any other American city except for New York and Chicago. In 1920, immigrants accounted for 29 percent of Detroit's population. The size and diversity of the auto industry's immigrant worker population was particularly evident at the Ford Motor Company. In 1914, they formed nearly three-fourths (70.7 percent) of the Ford workforce of 12,880, with Poles, Russians, Hungarians, and Romanians among the twenty-two nationalities working for the company.[13]

Restrictions on European immigration and the deplorable economic and social climate of the South soon triggered the migration of thousands of southern blacks to Detroit. (White southerners also began moving to the Motor City.)[14] The major black exodus to Detroit occurred between 1914 and 1917 and then picked up again after 1920. The migration repeated a trend established by blacks, who had previously traveled to the northern urban industrial centers in search of work. After leaving the rural areas many black migrants first stopped in southern cities, where they held temporary jobs before heading north. Others left for the North directly from the farms. Forty-two-year-old Ford autoworker Sargent Brown left farming in southern Louisiana to work on the docks in New Orleans before coming to Detroit, while twenty-seven-year-old Henry Carter and his wife and four children moved from their farm outside Georgiana, Alabama, directly to Detroit, where he was hired at Ford Motors. Though many blacks ventured north alone, most made the trek accompanied by their families and were determined to stay in Detroit. The men came from diverse backgrounds and altered the composition of Detroit's original black community, which had been established in the previous century.[15] Work and a better life than what they had left behind in the South motivated the black migrants pouring into the Motor City.

From World War I and through the 1920s Detroit received 34 percent of all blacks migrating north. Most were brought north by relatives and friends already living and working in the city. This migration was aug-

mented through recruitment by the Detroit Urban League in cooperation with the Detroit Employers' Association. In 1917, an average of
1,000 blacks entered Detroit each month, the highest influx coinciding
with the auto industry's peak hiring periods in May, June, and July. By
1920, this migration accelerated; 1,000 migrants arrived each week, increasing the city's black population to 40,838 (a ten-year growth well
over 600 percent). Five years later the number of blacks in Detroit
doubled to 81,831. Because of the industrial nature of the city's economy, 79 percent of the men worked in manufacturing, with most holding unskilled factory jobs.[16] Some Mexicans worked side by side with
blacks in the foundries and factories of Detroit and southeast Michigan,
establishing the stereotypes that distinguished each racial group and at
the same time helping to define irrevocably the social environment of
the workplace.

The bulk of the Mexican northern migration was made up of young,
single men. In Detroit the age distribution of Mexican factory workers
resembled the city's overall male-worker population. Despite the loss of
men to military service during World War I and the outmigration
of workers, the continuous entrance of single males maintained this
demographic trend. Information from Ford employment record cards
and local Catholic Church records indicates that at this time over three-
fourths of the Mexican workers in Detroit were in the twenty- to
twenty-nine-year age range, while those forty years or older constituted
just over 2 percent of the total. The youthfulness of Detroit's Mexican
population remained constant throughout the twenties.[17] This age characteristic illuminates an essential feature of the mass-production auto
industry. A young workforce was indispensable in a manufacturing system where speed, agility, and fortitude were necessary. Work on the line
quickly used up a man's youth; it exacted a considerable toll on the
laborer's physical as well as mental stamina. The work crippled many,
and the stress aged the men prematurely; autoworkers in their twenties
often were mistaken for older men.[18]

The highly seasonal nature of auto production made transients out
of thousands of workers. In 1920, more than 10,000 men were available for work in Detroit, and throughout the decade approximately
60,000 to 75,000 transient workers passed through the city.[19] Their
numbers declined somewhat as the city's job market stabilized. Detroit's
workforce reflected a national labor pool made up of mobile, unskilled
urban workers. The transiency of Mexican workers in Detroit must be
seen in this larger context. The high mobility of Mexicans in the north-

ern urban centers was more often the result of the changing labor markets of the industrial cities in which they resided rather than being a
particular flaw of this minority group.[20]

The Mexicans coming to work in Detroit encountered a city comparatively free of labor dissension. As workers in the least unionized city in
the country, Mexicans in Detroit were spared roles as labor scabs and
the consequent hostility their compatriots were greeted with in Chicago,
Gary, Indiana Harbor, and Milwaukee. Local labor struggles in these
cities had amplified solidarity in the ethnic working-class neighborhoods, which in turn fostered intolerance toward outsiders.[21] Detroit's
labor unrest occurred earlier, before the Great War. Attempts were
made in Detroit to organize autoworkers and stage strikes in 1913,
when the Industrial Workers of the World organized a strike over pay
grievances by 6,000 autoworkers employed by Studebaker. The strike
failed, although scholars contend that it was responsible for implemen-
tation of the $5 day at the Ford Highland Park plant. After World War
I, the Carriage, Wagon and Automobile Workers Union (CWAWU) organized skilled autoworkers demanding wage increases to compensate
for the rampant inflation. Despite growth in its membership, the
CWAWU drive collapsed because the union limited its efforts to only
one or two shops within a factory. Moreover, the members opposed
strike action in favor of arbitration and conciliation. The CWAWU was
re-formed as the more militant Auto Workers Union, whose membership declined rapidly with the start of the 1920–1921 depression.[22]

Because of the peculiar nature of mass production, "a minutely divided, closely timed, mechanized process," the auto industry was anal-
ogous to a huge synchronized machine—a disruption of any sort would
shut it down completely. Aware of this possibility, the Motor City's largest employers implemented a wide range of strategies to keep their factories free from union organizing. Their steadfast opposition to collective bargaining was aided by the Detroit Employers' Association; its
anti-union tactics contributed to making Detroit the nation's preemi-
nent open-shop city prior to the Great Depression. The Detroit Employers' Association maintained a list of safe, nonunion workers ("independent working men with clean records") and blacklisted suspected labor
agitators. It hired labor spies and Detroit policemen for surveillance to
keep the local labor supply free of "Bolshevik" organizers, and it had a
roster of 44,000 strikebreakers at the ready. The antilabor political
agenda of the Detroit Employers' Association involved lobbying efforts

at the local and state levels to challenge child-labor restrictions, factory-inspection regulations, and any other unfavorable legislation.[23]

Auto companies acting through the Detroit Employers' Association intentionally encouraged and maintained a worker surplus as a deterrent against union organizing, wage hikes, and labor unrest. Through its Labor Bureau the Detroit Employers' Association advertised for workers in about 200 American newspapers and eliminated the practice of employers' hiring away each other's workers. The Employers' Association published weekly reports of the number of workers on its members' payrolls in its bulletin *Labor Barometer*. When the massive black migration began, the association sent labor agents into the South and border states to recruit its share of this bountiful labor supply. It channeled many of the job-hungry black migrants into Detroit factories by financing an employment bureau within the Detroit Urban League. In January 1920, the Associated Industries of Detroit was organized along the same principles as the Detroit Employers' Association. Comprised of nonmanufacturing employers, the Associated Industries added to the Motor City's notoriety as an open-shop town.[24]

This was the backdrop for Mexican migration to Detroit shortly after World War I. The ongoing labor needs of this city's factories were augmented by the war effort and brought mainly young and single Mexicans to Detroit. As we will see, the highly transient Mexican residential patterns were distinctly defined by Detroit's rapid urban growth and by the proliferation of factory zones throughout the city.

THE EARLY PHASE OF MEXICAN SETTLEMENT

Housing for midwestern Mexicans in these early years was influenced by such factors as the size and diversity of the economy of each city, its growth rate, the need to locate as close as possible to work sites, and, in some cities, employer housing policies. There was no uniformity to Mexican settlement in the urban North. Severe housing shortages and the inflation that followed the end of World War I greeted the first arrivals. For Mexicans in Chicago, the dearth of housing resulted in exorbitant rents in the worst tenement districts. The noise from the rail yards, the stench of slaughtered animals, and the noxious fumes from the steel mills were constant nuisances. A Mexican woman living in Back-of-the-Yards whose husband worked in a local meat-packing house resignedly told Paul S. Taylor, "The smell and stench here are bad; . . . it makes me sick and makes me vomit at times. . . . Some of the other Mexican women around here feel the same way. It is very bad but what can we do? Our husbands work near here, the rent is cheaper, and we have to live." [25]

Housing conditions elsewhere were not better. The Mexicans brought to Gary as strikebreakers first boarded in company barracks adjacent to the noisy mills and thereafter inhabited cheap frame houses in the neighborhoods assigned to workers by the steel companies. In East Chicago, Mexicans employed by Inland Steel were charged $1.50 per day to live in company-operated barracks inside the plant. Their rent was nearly ten times the cost of housing in San Antonio, but their wages were considerably higher than those they could earn in San Antonio. Some men occupied tents because of East Chicago's housing shortages. After the 1919 steel strike, Mexicans moved from Inland's company housing to the adjoining mixed-ethnic working-class neighborhoods, where they resided in boardinghouses and hotels though continuing to pay inflated rents. [26] This housing typified that of most American workers at this time. Overcrowded tenements, tarpaper shacks, and tents were common shelters for working men and women in the world's greatest industrial power.

At the end of World War I, rapid population growth and the increase of factories in Detroit resulted in Mexicans settling in crammed working-class neighborhoods that formed in close proximity to the car plants. Detroit's port of entry was the near east side. At one time occupied by Germans, it was now heavily populated by newcomers who used it as a staging area before moving to different sections of the city. Concentrations of workers could be found living in Detroit's central district, in the recently formed factory zone west of the city, and in the Milwaukee Junction and Delray areas. [27] Mexicans followed the settlement trends of workers who preceded them to Detroit, and their movement westward within the city paralleled the shifting of Detroit's working population toward the new Ford plant in River Rouge. Mexicans entered these ethnic neighborhoods, and in certain instances lived with blacks, but never formed a majority on Detroit's city blocks. The propensity of single men to come and go kept these working-class neighborhoods in a state of flux.

The settlement of Mexicans in Detroit had changed little from this pattern as the 1920s began. In 1920, Mexicans dwelled in rooming houses, apartments, and flats on the city's near east side. Because of the shortage of housing, Mexicans on the east side shared quarters with

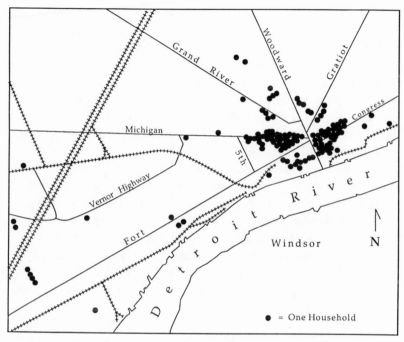

Map 3.   Mexican Settlements in Detroit, 1920
  SOURCE: *R. L. Polk's Detroit City Directory* (Detroit: R. L. Polk Company, 1920).

blacks who were probably paying the same exorbitant rents for lodg-
ings in these congested neighborhoods. Mexicans also occupied housing
east and west of Detroit's central district (see Map 3). The practice of
locating shelter as close as possible to car factories, auto-parts plants,
and foundries remained constant. Some Mexicans employed at the Ford
Highland Park plant and the men attending the Henry Ford Service
School found housing north of Detroit in Highland Park, most residing
in rooming houses and apartments.[28] Many of the city's Mexicans had
located in the Michigan Avenue area, in Corktown, the former Irish colony centered around Most Holy Trinity Catholic Church. Bordered by
Grand River Avenue on the north, the Detroit River on the south, and
Fifth Street on the west, Corktown was a mixed-ethnic working-class
neighborhood with only a small second-generation Irish population.[29]
Mexicans also began moving into southwest Detroit. Railroad workers
originally occupied this area, which was crisscrossed by track yards.

The high wages bringing Mexicans to Detroit were quickly eroded by the inflation following the end of World War I, the principal cause of the escalating cost of living in the Motor City. The immigrants clearly underestimated living expenses in Detroit. As one seasoned Mexican autoworker stated: "Many [Mexicans] are fooled, . . . not realizing that while they get higher wages expenses are also great." Single males did not escape the rising living costs, as revealed by a Mexican laid off from Hudson Motors: "I am a bachelor but I think that it costs me as much to live as if I had a family." According to the Department of Labor, Detroit had the greatest postwar increase in living expenses of the biggest American cities. As 1919 came to a close, food cost twice what it cost in 1914, clothing three times as much, and housing, fuel, and electricity were likewise very costly. What $1 could buy in 1914 cost $2.36 in 1920 (but $1.82 in December 1921).[30]

The wartime inflation and the depression that followed in 1920–1921 impeded the ability of Detroiters to maintain a reasonable standard of living. In 1921, an annual income of $1,698 was needed to support a family of two adults and three children, but the average income of an autoworker was $200 less than this. Workers bore additional burdens because they sent part of their earnings to family members in their home countries, saved money to help relatives come to Detroit, or set funds aside to buy land. Detroit's excessive cost of living required that Mexicans readjust their strategies if they were to attain their goal of economic betterment and improve their living standards.[31]

The reality of the inflationary living costs of the post–World War I period conflicted with the expectations built up in the glowing letters and stories that brought Mexicans to the Motor City. Detroit's reputation as a wage paradise was an illusion that quickly vanished once Mexicans came to know the challenges posed by city life. They braved a scarcity of housing, overcrowding, high rents, and a polluted factory environment accentuated by the ceaseless clamor of plant machinery, which operated day and night except during slowdowns or model changeovers.

The wartime housing decline meant that Detroit could not accommodate a population that had tripled in size in twenty years and was continuously augmented by new workers. This situation produced extensive tenement and rooming-house areas with neighborhood densities of 40,000 persons per square mile. Despite the high percentage of home ownership among Detroit's autoworkers (37.8 percent), a 1919 survey of metropolitan housing noted a shortage of over 33,000 units and revealed that 165,000 persons resided in substandard dwellings. (Much of Detroit's housing had been constructed during World War I and was poorly built.) Detroit's hotels were filled to capacity. This hotel population of mainly single men was easy prey for prostitutes, numbers runners, and bootleggers in the era of prohibition. To shelter the tens of thousands of persons unable to find housing, Detroit relaxed its health codes and sanitary regulations and in 1921 set up tent camps on the city's outskirts as temporary shelters.[32]

The scarcity of housing made workers adept at finding alternatives. It was not uncommon for several families to share living quarters and for breadwinners to pool their money to cover rent payments. Some families had resorted to these arrangements during their stays in other cities. Men sought out garages and vacant office buildings and stored their possessions in rail cars at the city's train yards. A few rented sleeping space in autos, while others slept in the local parks. Detroit's laboring men toiled in the world's most modern factory buildings equipped with technologically advanced machinery that was making this metropolis "the wonderful city of the magic motor," but ironically after their shifts they returned exhausted to dismal substandard housing.

Approximately two-thirds (62.2 percent) of Detroit's families were renters, half paying upward of $40 per month for run-down houses and overcrowded and unhealthy flats and rooms. Nearly a fifth of these dwellings did not have gas, electricity, or indoor bathrooms. Tenants in cottages and flats heated their units with wood stoves. Because of the cold climate scavenging for wood scraps became commonplace and was especially widespread during layoffs, when workers had no place to go and there was not enough money to purchase fuel. Stealing coal became a necessary pastime for youth. Single men paid about $5 per week for a room; two men sharing a room paid between $3.50 and $5 each. Board was $6 a week for two meals a day and $8.50 per week if lunch was included. In 1921, the combined cost of room and board for a single man in Detroit averaged $12 a week.[33]

The crowded living conditions of Detroit's largely single Mexican male population reflected the restricted housing situation in the city in general. In 1919, eleven Mexicans employed at the Ford Highland Park plant shared a house on West Adams Avenue, while three Mexicans from the plant lived in a room on West Davison with two other autoworkers. Rentals were sought on these two streets because of the proximity to the Highland Park plant. In downtown Detroit, five Mexican Ford autoworkers lodged together at the Brunswick Hotel on Grand River Avenue, and in Dearborn four Mexicans from the Fordson Tractor Plant rented one room at the Cahill Hotel.[34] The overcrowded conditions were indeed severe. Mexicans on different shifts shared cots and beds; some individuals slept while others worked. The men prepared food in their rooms in makeshift kitchens or frequented the hash houses, cafes, and lunchwagons parked outside the plant gates. Sometimes they ate their meals with families (both Mexican and non-Mexican) who supplemented their income by providing this vital service to the autoworkers.

Mexican track laborers discovered a housing alternative in the dozens of boxcar camps that were established in or near midwestern urban centers. Perhaps the biggest Mexican boxcar camps were in the twin cities of Kansas City, the nation's second largest rail center and a main hub for the Santa Fe, Rock Island, and Burlington & Quincy Railroads. The sprawling rail camps served as temporary housing for upward of 10,000 Mexicans heading to jobs as far away as Los Angeles. Seven camps were located in Chicago, the nation's major rail terminal, which was a locus for Mexicans. There were fifteen camps west of this city, and Mexicans formed several east of Chicago toward Gary.[35]

In Detroit, Mexicans employed by the Michigan Central Railroad established camps on the city's west side close to the train depot on Michigan Avenue and in the rail yards near Sixth Avenue and Plum Street. Some residents had resided in boxcars in Detroit and in rail camps in other parts of the country for two or more years. Men who left track work for factory jobs continued living in the boxcar camps, thus circumventing Detroit's severe housing shortage. For the men who stayed employed with the railroads, this housing was free during idle work periods and available as well for relatives and friends new to the city.[36]

Although offering some advantages, boxcars were not optimal living environments, and the Mexicans endured hardships unique to this living situation. For instance, metal cars became dreadfully hot when they were in the open without protection from the sun. Poor lighting and ventilation, lack of running water, bad sanitation, and overcrowding plagued certain camps and created a breeding ground for diseases like tuberculosis.[37] The intrinsically nomadic life-style of track work considerably influenced the social interactions of camp inhabitants. Ex-railroad worker Juan Martínez remarked that the boxcar camps in Detroit exemplified the ingenuity of the occupants, who made the best of a difficult situation, but lawlessness was pervasive. This situation was the basis for the disdain of Mexican track laborers expressed by their compatriots, local relief workers, and townspeople.[38]

Another tragic repercussion of itinerant camp life was the breakup of families. In Detroit, several Mexican women living in the rail camps had been abandoned by husbands who never returned from track construction and repair jobs. Placed in charge of the camps while the men were away, the women were usually able to subsist without resources except during prolonged periods, although those lacking family or friends to offer assistance were hard pressed. In the fall of 1920, a relief worker found Mrs. Elisia Estrada with her three-year-old and ten-month-old daughters and another woman living in a dilapidated freight car in the rail yard at Michigan and Central Avenues. The destitute and distressed women and children needed food and clothing and had run out of coal. Without help, a few women made their way to towns from boxcar camps after bravely wandering for miles along the railroad tracks. These women no doubt realized the rail camps were not the idyllic homes in the photographs sly labor agents circulated to induce Mexicans to sign work contracts.[39]

The hardships and frustrations of finding housing in Detroit forced some Mexicans to leave the city. They became discouraged by their inability to adjust to living arrangements that required extra compromise and cleverness. Ford autoworker Edward Soto decided that the good money he was earning in the Highland Park factory did not compensate for the costly sacrifice of living in crowded Detroit. In late July 1920, this disgruntled autoworker quit his job and left the city with his wife and two children because the only housing he could find was an empty office in a building on West Columbia Avenue in Detroit's busy central district. The autoworker had searched repeatedly for housing during his time off from a forty-hour-a-week job. Edward's wife did not assist him; she was providing care for their two children, did not know her way around the huge and bewildering city, and probably could not speak English.[40]

The Mexican colonies emerging in the urban Midwest were exceedingly transient. Immigrants traveled from city to city searching for work; and movement within the cities added to this impermanence. Proximity to work, better housing, or the desire to live closer to relatives and friends were the primary incentives. Mexicans also left urban centers to reunite their families. It was relatively common to temporarily leave family members at different points along migration routes as Mexicans continued their peregrinations in search of employment. Once a final destination had been decided on and jobs and housing obtained, the workers arranged for their kin to join them.[41] This practice was followed by many Mexican autoworkers in Detroit. Dozens of men hired by the Ford Motor Company had previously worked in car factories in Pontiac, Flint, and Saginaw. Granted short leaves of absence by Ford Motors, they returned to these cities to visit relatives left behind until arrangements could be made to move them to Detroit. For example, in June 1920, Ford machine hand Salvador Durán obtained a temporary leave of absence to travel to Pontiac to bring his wife and child to Detroit. This courtesy was not extended to all Ford autoworkers, but in certain instances during the early years of ample employment family obligations overrode employment considerations. Denied permission to leave work, Ford worker Jesús Ramos quit and went to Saginaw to relocate his family to Detroit. He then journeyed to Cleveland (where he had worked before migrating to Saginaw) to bring his mother to join the family. Fortunately for this worker, he was rehired by Ford Motors and got a job at the Highland Park plant.[42]

THE CATHOLIC CHURCH AND AMERICANIZATION

In these early years, and without any fraternal organizations yet formed, many Mexicans in Detroit in need of assistance received support from the Catholic Church. Given the ethnic mixture of northern cities, with their sizable immigrant populations, the Catholic Church viewed its community work as an investment that would support future growth. If the Church did not minister to the spiritual and physical needs of the growing Mexican population in the United States, the immigrants might become indifferent to the faith and susceptible to aggressive proselytizing by Protestant sects. Thirty-nine percent of Detroit's population was Catholic, over twice the percentage for the Midwest and the country as a whole. The Church took special interest in promoting the well-being of Mexican immigrants arriving in the city beyond meeting their immediate needs. It provided the bereft newcomers to Detroit with food, clothing, temporary housing, and financial assistance, just as it did for other immigrant parishioners in need of aid. But because assimilation of these immigrants was a primary concern, the Church also promoted adaptation to Detroit's unique industrial environment. To prepare Mexicans for Detroit's demanding structured society, the Catholic Church in the years following the end of the war adopted techniques for ushering in a new social order similar to those adopted by the corporations. Americanization was the key to this plan.[43]

Americanization programs advocated belief in Christian principles as a cornerstone in converting immigrants into good Americans and steering them away from negative external influences, particularly pro-union causes. Detroit, known as the "graveyard of organizers," was a bastion of Americanization. Fear of radicalism was endemic in the Motor City in the wake of the nationwide labor strife of 1919. It prompted Detroit businessmen and city officials, who equated unionism with un-Americanism, to join in the antiradical and antilabor activities of the red-scare movement.[44] Detroit's corporate leaders considered Christian principles a defense against rampant socialist ideas, which could imperil worker docility. Outside the workplace, the Catholic Church reinforced these ideas as it watched over its flock of immigrant parishioners.

Mexicans in the North had not yet established parishes with Spanish-language services. Consequently, the spiritual needs of the scattered migrants from Mexico were served by lower-east-side parishes catering to other immigrant groups. Holy Family Catholic Church on Hastings and East Fort Streets was a popular parish, and Mexican worshippers also went to St. Mary's on St. Antoine and Monroe Streets. Holy Family parish served the city's southern Italians, while St. Mary's was predominantly German but was attended reluctantly by members of different immigrant groups. A factor that motivated Mexicans to form their own parish was ostracism by white ethnic Catholics, who viewed their churches as cornerstones of their communities. The newcomer status of Mexicans and particularly their identifiable racial traits caused them, like the blacks, to be spurned. For instance, the southern Italian parishioners of Holy Family began to move further east in the city because of the near east side's encroaching black population.[45]

Father Juan P. Alanis took charge of investigating conditions among recently arrived Mexicans in Detroit. This exiled priest from Monterrey, Mexico, approached Bishop Michael J. Gallagher about taking responsibility for the welfare of the new arrivals, many of whom were having problems finding housing, feeding their families, and obtaining proper clothing. Within a short time Father Alanis helped a group of his less-burdened countrymen organize into the Mexican Catholic Society, which held its meetings and social events at St. Mary's Parochial School. The society's members included the middle-class and professional segment of the Mexican population as well as Mexican American autoworkers whose sense of social obligation impelled them to provide leadership and aid. This assistance was likely not well received by Detroit's Mexican immigrant factory workers, as the conflict and animosities along class lines that originated in Mexico prevailed in the North and would eventually split the colonies into warring factions. Nevertheless, in 1921, the Mexican Catholic Society, led by Detroit's elite Mexicans and with the help of a handful of native-born Americans, held a series of bazaars, concerts, and other activities to raise money to construct a building for their religious services. Although the fund raising was impeded by the depression, the 150 Mexican and American families involved raised $6,400 and $1,000 (respectively).[46]

Father Alanis was assisted in his work by Father Juan Mijares, who came to Detroit from Saginaw, where he had ministered to sugar-beet workers. The Mexican priest had followed these farm laborers to Saginaw from Kansas City. The two priests were overwhelmed by the requests for aid from their less-fortunate Mexican brethren, who had not anticipated that the cost of living in Detroit would be so prohibitive or that procuring employment would be so difficult. At the urging of the two priests, men from the Mexican Catholic Society joined the Society of St. Vincent de Paul. They received training from the American members of this Catholic organization in providing help to the impoverished Mexicans.[47]

Sunday services for St. Mary's small Mexican congregation consisted of morning mass conducted in Spanish and in the afternoon planned social activities supervised by Father Alanis. Sundays had special meaning for the women. Living in an unfamiliar city of nearly one million people and after a week spent cooking, washing, and cleaning for their families and often boarders as well, Mexican women looked forward to this respite. The women particularly appreciated one another's company, given the limitations Mexican tradition imposed on their activities outside the home and Detroit's male-dominated factory environment. At these Sunday gatherings women probably shared news about the past week or about relatives and mutual friends in Mexico, as most were related or were from the same hometowns and villages. For the men, the Sunday activities offered momentary escape from the regimen of the car plants. The workers played cards, those with a penchant for music sang *corridos* (folk songs), while others with political leanings discussed (likely out of earshot of the good priest Alanis so as not to dismay him) the affairs of their home country, which was wracked by revolution. Mexico was still an important reference point for these immigrants not long departed from their homeland. The assassination of Emiliano Zapata, arranged by President Venustiano Carranza in April 1919, and Carranza's own murder the following year likely prompted heated debates.[48]

Meanwhile, the children participated in a different kind of activity on these planned Sunday afternoons, which assisted their assimilation to their new home. They attended Spanish, English, and American history classes as part of the Americanization program Father Alanis directed. What better person to teach American values to these youth than a priest, a figure most Mexicans were taught to revere, respect, and fully obey. His classes stressed proficiency in two languages, much like the parochial-school curriculum for young Mexican immigrants at this time.[49] Yet, the Catholic Church also believed that the economic well-being of Mexican immigrants was enhanced by learning the language, customs, and values of their new land in an expedient manner. The Church thus advocated allegiance to both the Catholic faith and to the United States. The immigrants would be judged by their success as defined by the Motor City's business leaders.[50]

During these early years, the experiences of urban midwestern Mexicans with Americanization differed little from those of Mexicans in El Paso, in the villages of northern New Mexico, in the company towns of southern Colorado, and in the emerging barrios of Los Angeles. However, Mexicans in the North were taught the principles of Americanization mainly to prepare them for the ordered and efficient world of factory work. In Milwaukee, Mexican tannery workers studied English to become productive workers and U.S. citizens. At this city's YMCA evening English classes, the immigrant laborers from Mexico in unison repeated on their instructor's cue the short, sing-song elementary sentences and rhymes from the blackboard: "I have a nose." "He has a nose." "You have a nose." To improve worker efficiency and prevent accidents at work, the men were taught the basic commands of the foremen and the names of machine parts. Each pupil was given copies of the English lesson for home study. In Gary, Mexicans were targeted in a deliberate effort to eradicate immigrant cultural practices in support of the battle of the U.S. Steel Corporation against its large ethnic workforce. Some hapless Mexicans in Gary caught without naturalization papers were given the choice of either going to jail or joining the U.S. military. The Mexicans arriving in Detroit between 1918 and 1920 likewise experienced a range of Americanization practices, which included the required purchase of war bonds, and outside the workplace the

Catholic Church provided the men spiritual guidance with a patriotic undertone. All were designed to homogenize the workforce in order to consolidate an industrial economy based on mass production.[51]

The Catholic Church promoted the principles of Americanism following the policies established by the Detroit Americanization Committee. This committee spread the principles of American government and citizenship and, because it involved the city's biggest employers such as Ford Motors, supported the open-shop program. The goal of the Americanization drive was to make immigrants equate factory discipline with good citizenship—to educate and drill them in industrial work habits that would result in eager but complacent workers. As the first official spokesman for Mexicans in the Motor City, the Catholic Church laid the groundwork and provided the outreach programs necessary for their accommodation to city life. Through the Church's efforts middle-class Detroit saw the new arrivals in a more positive light than they otherwise might have. This perception was important because Mexicans in the Midwest were still relatively unknown compared with Mexicans in the Southwest, where most immigrants from Mexico resided.[52] Acting as the Church's spokesperson on behalf of Detroit's Mexican colony, Father Alanis expressed his belief that his compatriots would become good citizens and that Americanization served their best interests: "My countrymen will prove among the most useful aliens drawn to Detroit in recent years. They came . . . with the expectations of becoming useful citizens. . . . I am confident that we can . . . teach them a sympathetic understanding of the laws and liberties of this Republic." [53]

Mexican American autoworkers who were faithful Catholics also played a role in aiding their immigrant counterparts assimilate the culture of the factory, which was being shaped by the doctrines of the corporate world. Helping Mexicans understand what was expected of them in their adopted home of Detroit was thirty-two-year-old autoworker José V. Espriu, one of the founders of the Mexican Catholic Society. Born in Nogales, Arizona, but raised in Mexico until a young man, Espriu came to Detroit in 1916 to work in the auto industry. He enlisted in the army the following year, when the United States entered the war, and served overseas with the American Expeditionary Force. Upon his return to Detroit, filled with enthusiasm for having fought to preserve democracy in Europe, he recognized the extent of the problems faced by the Mexican population and began to work for the betterment of the community. Espriu's military service and the pervasive atmosphere of Americanism influenced his ideas about the proper conduct of

Mexicans in Detroit. His commitment to public duty reflected that of other World War I Mexican American veterans. Concerned with their status as Americans of Mexican descent, the men were dedicated to improving their communities and to achieving their rights as citizens. In the late 1920s war veterans in Texas would help in the formation of the League of United Latin American Citizens (LULAC), a Mexican American civil-rights organization with a rather conservative, bicultural notion of Americanism.[54]

Espriu's outlook was further colored by his own values as a Detroit autoworker. For him, to have Mexicans identify as Detroiters was even more meaningful than their becoming Americanized, though ultimately this was the goal. The civic-minded Mexican American autoworker told the Detroit News, "We are all Americans, though some of us were born north of the Río Grande and others south. . . . The Mexican is in Detroit to become a Detroiter. He needs little of what is called locally 'Americanization.' America to him signifies the same ideals as it does to the man born in Michigan." Espriu believed the Mexicans migrating to Detroit were motivated by the same forces that four years earlier had brought him and tens of thousands of men to the Motor City—the desire and willingness to work hard and to achieve success in the city's auto factories. Mexicans were to adopt and cultivate American work habits, they were to express loyalty to and identify with the auto companies, and they were to aspire to the American standard of living.[55]

Espriu and the Mexican Catholic Society were assisted by Ford autoworkers Reyes Padilla and Simón Muñoz, two devoted Catholics and members of the newly created Mexican Auxiliary of the Society of St. Vincent de Paul. Both these men were prominent figures in church-related affairs throughout the twenties. During the 1920–1921 depression, they helped distribute food and clothing to jobless Mexicans, found shelter for those evicted from their housing, and helped the Detroit Diocese with the repatriation of destitute countrymen who volunteered to return to Mexico. In addition to their work with the fundraising efforts of the Mexican Catholic Society, Reyes and Simón and their wives were asked to be sponsors at weddings and baptisms. Through this compadrazgo (coparenthood) they strengthened numerous bonds with Detroit's Mexicans, a working-class camaraderie that was also fostered through work in the factories.[56]

The Latin American Club had a similar influence on the middle-class and professional Mexicans enrolled in the Henry Ford Service School. The experiences of these aspiring Ford Motors company men, who were taught the basic principles of business management and adopted the spirit of boosterism, show another aspect of Mexican life in Detroit, which was not homogeneous but multifaceted. The Latin American Club was formed in 1919 by the Spanish-speaking students of the Henry Ford Service School. By 1920, three-fourths (100) of the Ford Service School's Spanish-speaking students belonged to the club; it disbanded at the end of 1923, when Ford Motors stopped its recruitment of foreign students. The club was encouraged and assisted by Ford Motors as part of the company's boosterism and steady drive to Americanize its foreign students; they were brought to Detroit from all countries where Ford had established its factories and dealerships. The Latin American Club supplemented the training the students received at the school, where American history, civics, and government were a mandatory part of the curriculum. The club's Mexican members were inculcated with the ethics, standards, and values of the Ford Motor Company, which were deemed essential to good business-management practices. It provided cultural and social activities for the students while they lived in Detroit and tried to maintain contact with members after they completed their technical training and returned home.[57]

Members of the Latin American Club continued their friendships through correspondence after leaving Detroit. These letters attest to the thorough indoctrination of the Henry Ford Service School graduates, apostles of the Ford credo, who became select members of Mexico's business and professional world. A letter ex-student Dennis Ayala sent from Mexico to his school chum Armando Díaz in Detroit contained numerous references to the Ford ethic of hard work, efficiency, and discipline—an ethic on which these new professionals based their interpretations of manhood. In reminiscing about his Detroit days, Ayala described the valuable lessons he learned at the Ford Service School and their lasting impression on him: "When I think of the time I spent in old Detroit I feel happy because . . . I was given a chance to train myself to be a man. I am proud to have worked at the Ford plant where I learned to value time, . . . to get out of it all the benefit possible."[58] Upon his return to Toluca, Mexico, Ayala joined his father's meat-packing company and assiduously used his training at Ford Motors to supervise the plant workforce. Ayala imparted the value of time management to the workers under his supervision. The Henry Ford Service School graduate concluded his letter by encouraging his friend in Detroit to learn as much about Ford methods as possible, specifically the auto company's emphasis on efficiency and the importance of work. As he did with his men, Ayala instructed Díaz to "get all the knowledge you possibly can out of the Ford system; learn by all means to save your time and value your work." [59]

These Mexicans believed that they were in the vanguard of "Fordization" of the world, that this was their role in life. Detroit was the champion of Americanization—the attempt by industrialists to impose their belief in "a new society in which everybody would share the same values, . . . an American system which struck a balance of moral qualities, orderly work, and prosperity." [60] The Ford Motor Company spearheaded this drive to remake American society and no doubt the rest of the world. Henry Ford had recently opened branch plants in Mexico and was annoyed by that country's continuing revolutionary turmoil. He publicly stated that if his philosophy for success were followed, it could end the Mexican Revolution. As the famous carmaker phrased it: "Villa would become a foreman; . . . Carranza might be trained to become a good time keeper." [61]

The ultimate goal of Americanization efforts was to assimilate Mexicans into American society. Yet beginning with Manuel Gamio in the 1920s, scholars have noted that assimilation of the early Mexican immigrants was never fully achieved because their own culture was constantly reinforced through immigration and return migration. Besides, most Mexicans were ambivalent about adopting the United States as their homeland. [62] Expressions of loyalty to the United States during the Great War proved futile for immigrant and American-born Mexicans. They met with discrimination, exploitation, and rejection. Native white workers, some joining the Ku Klux Klan, turned against Mexicans as they did against Catholics, Jews, and blacks. Racism thus played a decisive role in the lives of the Mexican working class. [63] Nevertheless, high wages, which promised economic betterment, and the romantic lure of modern technology continued to entice Mexicans back to the Motor City and to the cities of the industrial North.

For some Mexicans who stayed in Detroit, maintaining a cultural identity was crucial given Americanization and the total regulation of their lives in the workplace. Realizing the limitations placed on them by the larger society, Mexicans began participating in the life of the colony. National holidays and celebrations became restructured in Detroit as private commemorations of a Mexican identity and culture. [64] Detroit's Mexican immigrants began celebrating their country's *fiestas patrias* (national holidays), in part because of the nationalist sentiments aroused by the ongoing Mexican Revolution. The two most momentous occasions became Mexico's Independence Day on September 15 and the Feast of Our Lady of Guadalupe on December 11. Mexicans from throughout southeastern Michigan came to Detroit to join in the observance of the Feast of Our Lady of Guadalupe, first held in 1920. The *Detroit News* reported that 8,000 gathered in the city in early December of that year. In deference to Detroit city officials, a painting of the Virgin was blessed and presented to the city as a token of the first public celebration of this Mexican religious holiday in Michigan.[65] The weekend commemoration also marked the peace and friendly relations between the United States and Mexico.

Mexicans in Detroit had previously observed the holiday by taking the day off from work to attend mass but risked being fired because employers did not deem this or any other immigrant commemoration an American holiday. Company officials frowned on immigrant traditions; national or religious holidays, baptisms, or weddings impinged on industrial efficiency, and their observance was banned. Immigrant workers were therefore cautious about taking any time off for fear of reprisals.[66]

In preparation for celebration of the two holidays, the Mexican participants practiced dances, plays, and poetry, and an orchestra rehearsed traditional music. The extent of these activities suggested that some trained Mexican dancers, singers, musicians, actors, and actresses were in Detroit. For example, three sisters who were schoolteachers with dance training decided to perform. Fleeing the violence of revolution in Mexico, they had first settled in El Paso and then followed their husbands when they came to find work in the car factories of Detroit.[67] Scheduling the practice sessions and rehearsals may have been difficult because Mexican Independence Day took place during the auto industry's semiannual peak production period. Assigned to all three shifts, which included Saturdays, the autoworkers participating in the festivities risked losing their jobs. However, Church-sanctioned activities, coordinated with the Detroit Americanization Committee, were likely exempt from such penalties.

THE 1920–1921 DEPRESSION

These expressions of pride in national identity and culture by Detroit's Mexicans, heightened in response to the new experiences in the Motor City, were halted by the 1920–1921 depression, when a somber mood set in. The economic crisis ended further migration of Mexicans to De-

troit and prematurely curtailed formation of their colony and the creation of fraternal organizations. Many men lost their jobs. Their subsequent ordeals with mass unemployment and poverty foreshadowed the
problems the Motor City's Mexicans would confront a decade later during the Great Depression.

The economic depression began in the spring of 1920 and brought
extreme hardship to the Mexicans of the Midwest who had been in the
region for only a few years. Sugar-beet farmers could not afford a spring
planting and dismissed their Mexican workers. Realizing that farmers
would not continue to supply them with housing, the beet workers left
the farms and moved to nearby cities. There they joined countrymen
who had been discharged from their factory jobs. Thousands of Mexicans returned to Texas and Mexico, and immigrants waiting to enter
the United States wisely changed their plans. There was work only for
Americans. The extent of the crisis in the midwestern industrial cities,
where Mexicans were passed over for work in favor of Americans, was
tersely summed up by an unemployed Mexican worker:

> The good work lasted about a year and a half. Then came "la crisis" and I
> was laid off. So were many, many Mexicans. Some of them had worked there
> a long time but they kept the Americans. It made some of us mad but what
> could we do? Nothing.
>
> I went to Detroit in hopes things would be better. Then to Pittsburgh. But
> they were worse.[68]

Some American workers, unable to find jobs and never fully recovered from the defeats of the recent employer offensive, blamed Mexicans
for their loss of work. Violence escalated. Officials in cities gripped by
the fiscal crisis demanded that the federal government not feed the immigrants but promptly deport them to Mexico. Recently targeted for
Americanization, Mexicans were now "foreigners," a blanket label in-
dicting the mass of immigrants.[69] The tendency to blame Mexicans for
the country's economic ills, when these workers already were wrong-
fully charged with undercutting wages and cheapening labor, created a
precedent that would recur each time the United States confronted a
crisis and needed a scapegoat. Actually, Mexican workers performed
the hard, low-wage labor the majority of American workers shunned.
Only immigrants, blacks, and hoboes "on the bum" were considered fit
for these lowly jobs.

The depression caused Mexicans in northern manufacturing centers
to suffer great hardship. They were the first workers dismissed because
of employer-implemented discriminatory policies. Blacks too received

their discharge slips, in keeping with the historic racism that affected their work experiences.[70] In Indiana Harbor, one-third of the Mexican workers at Inland Steel lost their jobs once production shut down and management ordered all remaining jobs to go to Americans. Two-thirds of the Mexicans employed by Chicago-area railroads and industrial firms were idled between 1920 and 1921. At Chicago's South Works only 15 of the 203 Mexicans hired in 1920 stayed on the job. Once again, an undetermined number of these immigrants were drawn into the middle of labor unrest. During the following winter Mexicans entered Chicago's Packingtown at the height of the meat-packing strike. Some had been brought in two years earlier as strikebreakers, but most were local recruits, including laid-off steelworkers from South Chicago. Blacks constituted the main group of scab labor, however. The spectacle of 15,000 men, women, and children congregating in the Polish and Lithuanian neighborhoods west of the stockyards undoubtedly surprised the unsuspecting Mexicans. They were likely astonished when police unexpectedly fired their weapons at the courageous strikers and officers mounted on horses and motorcycles charged into the crowds and up to individuals gathered on tenement steps. From rooftops and windows snipers exchanged gunfire with the police down below.[71] (Fifteen years later in South Chicago, during the "Little Steel" strike, Mexican steelworkers and their families would similarly face police clubs and guns. This time it would be the Mexicans, some with proudly raised American flags and chanting "CIO, CIO," who braved the violence to help bring unions to the area mills.)

The beleaguered Mexicans in the Midwest received little assistance from the Department of Labor, local employers, or city officials. They were subjected to a policy of willful neglect that had distinct consequences. For example, Mexicans brought to work in the sugar-beet fields under Department of Labor exemptions were summarily returned to the border. However, railroad and steel companies refused even to transport their laborers back to Mexico. The firms claimed they had no obligation to these workers. Kinship networks and the few nascent fraternal organizations were tested to their maximum and soon broke down because of the swiftness and severity of the crisis.[72]

Even the recently established Mexican consulate offices proved unable to help their countrymen. City officials in Chicago refused Mexican Consul Francisco Pereda's repeated appeals to provide help for several hundred Mexican families who had abandoned hope for an economic recovery and were now seeking repatriation. In a letter to Mayor William Hale Thompson, the overwrought Mexican consul explained that his countrymen had underestimated the length of the crisis. They had believed it was just another production shutdown that would last only a few weeks. But after nearly five months without work, savings had been exhausted, and the immigrants were poverty-stricken and desperate. Chicago city officials referred Pereda's requests for assistance to the Department of Labor, which also did nothing.[73]

The depression dealt the hardest blow to the Mexicans of Detroit. The bad times in the Motor City were a consequence of overproduction and the resistance of the automakers (with the exception of Ford Motors) to reduce prices despite falling sales. The reconversion to peacetime production in Detroit at the end of World War I resulted in the cancellation of government contracts, which had formed the basis of the wartime prosperity. Costly capital investments, expansion, and speculation by the auto industry contributed as well to the crisis. The 1920–1921 depression seriously threatened the Motor City's economy and the welfare of its workers.[74]

Auto manufacturers began reducing their workforce in the spring of 1920. By year's end over 80 percent of Detroit's autoworkers were jobless. The one-industry nature of Detroit's economy made its unemployment the worst of all American cities. More than four-fifths of the industrial labor force was out of work by January 1921, and an estimated 75,000 individuals left the Motor City. The Michigan Manufacturers Association reported that this figure might have been higher, that 100,000 to 200,000 workers had left the state and probably half were from Detroit.[75] Property owners were further burdened by rising property taxes and many lost their homes. Children were taken out of school, as there was no money to purchase adequate clothing and shoes for them, or they were forced to leave the city with their families.[76]

The severity of Detroit's unemployment was evident from the huge deficits in the city's public-assistance program and from the futile attempts to create jobs for out-of-work heads of households. Relief costs jumped from $305,300 in 1920 to $1,958,300 in 1921, a 700 percent increase in a stopgap measure that failed. Detroit's Department of Public Welfare (DPW) established an Employment Bureau, which placed unemployed breadwinners in city jobs; however, work was found for only 17,175 of 40,270 applicants. (A similar blueprint for relief implemented by Detroit during the Great Depression eleven years later also ended in disaster.)[77]

Detroit's desperate workers vied for the few available jobs, and as this competition intensified so did prejudice toward the foreign-born, especially by World War I veterans. They alleged that immigrants had monopolized the work while they were away. American veterans apparently forgot or chose to ignore the fact that thousands of immigrants and blacks had served in the U.S. Army and fought in the trenches of Europe. Even native-born Mexicans, many of them war veterans, encountered antagonism. Because of this widespread nativism, foreign aliens applying for assistance to the City of Detroit and Wayne County were reported to the Immigration Bureau, which immediately issued warrants for their arrest.[78]

Almost all the Mexican Ford autoworkers lost their jobs, but before being discharged they suffered the most relentless speed-up in the history of Ford Motors. Henry Ford continued production to pay for the huge $75,000,000 loan he procured to buy out investors in his company. To repay this loan and simultaneously increase the profit margin, the auto company speeded up production and at the same time reduced its total workforce.[79] A few men continuing with the company voluntarily quit, sensing that the layoffs would eventually affect them. They left the city, but most planned to return in the spring, when hiring by the auto companies began again. These Mexicans had become habituated to the cycles of the auto industry, conditioned to expect that production would resume and they would soon be rehired. In the meantime, they would wait in more affordable environs and among family until they were recalled.[80]

Devastated by the economic crisis, some Mexicans left Detroit in search of work but never returned for their families, causing them much hardship. Without food, proper clothing for the winter weather, or shelter, and unable to obtain aid from a bankrupt DPW, Detroit's remaining Mexicans sought aid from the Society of St. Vincent de Paul. Members of the society's Mexican Auxiliary dispensed almost $1,000 in food and clothing to the Mexicans staying in the city and continued to solicit donations, but they were able to help only a small fraction of their countrymen. The circumstances of Detroit's Spanish and Maltese immigrants were likewise dismal; every day small parties of these impoverished individuals came to the offices seeking food and relief.[81]

The dismal state of Detroit's battered and bewildered Mexicans was made worse by the influx of hundreds of distressed, job-seeking beet workers who, according to the *Detroit News*, "had been induced to locate in Detroit by the promise of lucrative employment in the area auto plants."[82] Many more beet workers, part of a workforce of between 4,200 to 4,700 Mexicans brought to Michigan during the 1920 sugar-beet season, were stranded on rural farms. The hard-pressed sugar companies refused to cover the costs of their return to Texas. The needy workers migrated to nearby Michigan cities and also traveled to Chicago to seek aid. Their growing numbers in Saginaw prompted the city and county to seek ways to remove this pauperized population. Local officials refused to extend relief to the Mexicans on the grounds that they had entered the United States on their own initiative or had been brought to the area by the sugar companies. At the mercy of calloused Saginaw city officials, two hundred beet workers were repatriated to Mexico in February 1921.[83]

Government removal of destitute Mexicans was for the most part minimal despite repeated demands by city officials. The government claimed that it was not legally bound to deport Mexicans en masse or financially capable of doing so. This federal inaction resulted in locally initiated removal plans in lieu of relief. The removals were coordinated by Mexico's consulates (three of which were newly established for this purpose), the officially sponsored Comisiónes Honoríficas Mexicanas (Mexican Honorific Commissions), and charitable organizations like the American Red Cross.[84]

The immigrants braved daily harassment by agents of the Immigration Bureau of the Department of Labor. The bureau began the task of apprehending Mexicans suspected of breaking their 1917 labor contracts and now considered by the bureau to be undocumented residents. Workers unable to prove legal entry prior to 1921 were arrested and deported. These actions were an indirect consequence of the legislation restricting immigration from eastern and southern Europe and Asia. Immigration from Mexico was not affected by the restrictions, but the Department of Labor nonetheless ordered its agents to locate and remove all undocumented Mexicans. This search resulted in a dragnet through the working-class neighborhoods and, with the permission of cooperating employers, into the workplace.[85] In 1921, in a massive sweep that began in New York City and Chicago, deportation units from the Immigration Bureau arrested Mexicans without proof of permanent residence. The detainees were sent to New Orleans and then transported to the Mexican border for deportation. Agents continued their search in cities along the border, proceeding up to San Francisco, and then swinging back to the border.[86] For Mexicans, the repatriations of 1921 were a preview of the methods the United States would later use to rid itself of these surplus workers.

Fathers Alanis and Mijares assisted with the repatriations in Detroit. Father Alanis might have recognized the irony in his present work. He had previously stressed the positive rewards of Americanization to the Mexicans and extolled the merits of a free-enterprise system that rewarded hard work and built moral character. Now he could offer the immigrants little help other than to accept repatriation, the only viable option for workers whose foreign origins separated them from an insular American society. The Catholic bishops of Mexico and Mexican Consul Francisco Vera in Detroit assisted the Society of St. Vincent de Paul with the voluntary repatriations. The society paid for the transportation of Mexicans to the border, and the Mexican government then took charge of the return of its weary repatriates to the interior. A fund of $11,000 was raised by the society for this purpose, and the bishops of Mexico sent an additional $12,000. In groups of ten to twenty persons, 514 Mexicans were repatriated from Detroit by train to the Mexican border.[87]

The mass unemployment in Detroit ushered in by the production shutdown caused a rapid decline in the city's Mexican population. Between late November 1920 and February 1921, the number of Mexicans in the city dropped from 4,000 to 2,500. After a year passed, with the start of automobile production, Mexican migration to Detroit resumed. And as economic conditions improved, the call went out again for workers by Michigan beet companies. Elsewhere in the Midwest, the demand for laborers by the railroads and the steel industry also spurred migration.[88]

Nevertheless, in 1921, the initial, albeit brief, phase of Mexican migration to Detroit following World War I ended. A booming American economy and intervention by the U.S. government in the form of favorable legislation and regulation by the Department of Labor were responsible for triggering and sustaining this first wave of immigration from Mexico to the Midwest. However, just as important was the dream of increased opportunity shared by thousands of Mexicans who headed north. As they made their way into the manufacturing cities of the Midwest, Mexicans altered the makeup of northern urban populations. This midwestern Mexican experience diverged markedly from the southwestern. Mexicans in the Midwest settled in highly industrialized cities, moving into largely mixed-ethnic working-class neighborhoods with no previous Mexican settlements. Many lived with blacks. Adverse living conditions and inflation met the immigrants on their arrival in the cities. The Catholic Church helped in the adjustment to the new industrial environment. Guided by the belief that Americanization would bolster the economic well-being of Mexicans, the Church encouraged their full participation in the American dream. From the standpoint of business, Americanization was essential for educating and disciplining Mexicans in industrial work habits in order to make them efficient factory laborers. The proximity of the border, which always made return migration possible, dissuaded most working-class Mexican immigrants from embracing the principles of Americanism. Racial discrimination remained the main impediment to assimilation and prevented the acceptance of Mexicans by the dominant society. But factory work in the North continued to mold Mexicans into industrial proletarians; and their entrance into the ranks of the American working class fostered the recomposition of that class along ethnic and racial lines.

THREE

Mexicans and Factory Work in the 1920s

Mexican migration to the Midwest resumed at the end of the 1920–1921 depression. The northern sugar-beet industry became wholly dependent on Mexicans, and thousands of these workers in turn used beet work as intermediary employment, a staging area for entry into the packing-house, steel, and auto industries. The huge labor force of Mexican men, women, and children that followed the harvest seasons in the Great Lakes area contributed a steady flow of migrants to the cities.[1] The opportunity for factory employment contributed to the geographical dispersion and urbanization of Mexicans. In 1927, George Edson reported to the Department of Labor that 30,827 Mexicans held industrial jobs in northern urban centers from St. Paul to Pennsylvania's Monongahela Valley. By 1930, 53.6 percent of Mexican male workers in the Midwest held manufacturing jobs, and 36.6 percent worked for the railroads. These percentages were twice those for Mexicans nationwide (26 percent in manufacturing and 16.3 percent in transportation).[2]

The proletarianization of Mexican workers in different industrial employment sectors was thus well under way almost two decades before World War II, the period scholars demarcate as the time of large-scale entrance into factory work by this group. This trend toward factory employment reflected national labor patterns in the 1920s in that over half of all blue-collar employees did manual work in production. It was a restricted labor sector; only horizontal mobility was possible within the unskilled and semiskilled ranks. Mexicans entered industrial work just as manufacturing was reaching its peak of importance to the American economy. Their status as the latest newcomers to industrial work would have far-reaching consequences in later years.[3]

Racism played a role in the hiring of Mexicans for industrial work. Mexicans made up a workforce distinguishable by race in the farming regions of the Midwest. This distinct labor market was perpetuated by Mexicans through their practice of contracting as families—a practice that sugar companies supported and encouraged because of their total dependence on this labor. In contrast, Mexicans in the industrial cities entered factories already structured along racial and ethnic lines, with blacks constituting the largest minority. Black workers acted as a buffer against racism for Mexicans because distinctions between black and Mexican workers continued to be made by some employers. The recent period of Americanization notwithstanding, those employers that did not hire blacks and were unfamiliar with Mexicans but had immigrant employees tended to group the Mexicans with the immigrants and imbued them with the same qualities as their European counterparts: dull-minded brutes with a penchant for back-breaking labor at the lowest wages. As one employer in Gary plainly stated in 1923: "What we need is 'Hunkies', and lots of 'em. . . . The Mex doesn't come under the quota law and he's willing to work long and cheap, so we'll keep on importing him." [4]

In other instances, Mexicans were grouped with blacks. Discrimination, preconceived notions about Mexicans, and employment policies, which varied from company to company, then determined whether and where they worked. Company offices controlled overall hiring practices, but superintendents controlled hiring at the plants. At factories where the employment manager did not believe "in taking up the white man's burden," one of three situations resulted: the number of Mexicans was limited; they were confined to undesirable departments; or they were excluded entirely. Thus a few plants had a large number of Mexicans on the payroll but confined them to low-level jobs, while others had a negligible Mexican workforce. Companies like U.S. Steel expanded their recruitment and hiring of blacks and Mexicans and used them in the least desirable jobs and to depress wages as well. (Even in the face of ongoing labor shortages, employers were reducing manpower and wages as part of their campaign to undermine the job gains made by workers during World War I.) Mexicans may have benefited to some extent from the black presence in the North, but they did not escape the profound changes race had introduced into the workplace and the cities.[5]

Skin color hindered Mexican job mobility and prevented full acceptance by the general factory population. Often mistaken as black, dark-
complected Mexicans fared the worst. This situation did not change
with the fulfillment of citizenship requirements, which by the end of the
1920s was mandatory for employment. In general, however, the racial
atmosphere affecting working conditions in the North was an improvement over that in the Southwest, as many midwestern Mexican workers
repeatedly acknowledged. One Mexican in Chicago stated: "We like it
here better than in Texas. Wages are better . . . and there is no distinction." Another midwestern Mexican worker compared his bad experiences in Texas with those in Michigan and Pennsylvania. His remark
moreover reveals that Mexicans in the North were being affected by
racism against blacks, and they succumbed to this evil: "Distinction?
Yes, in Texas; the Mexicans look too much like niggers. In Flint, Michigan, no. . . . In Pittsburgh . . . I go every place; . . . that's why I was
living good and liked it in Pittsburgh." [6]

Scholars have overemphasized the structural limitations of labor
markets that inhibited the range of choices for Mexican workers.
Among the many factors omitted from these narrow and static assessments is the whole range of behavior and attitudes of these workers and
the element of human agency. Though encumbered by the special relations that underlined the different kinds of factory work, the Mexican
workers of the Midwest shaped their conditions through conscious action, using a variety of methods to create meaning and bring about
change in their lives. These workers had not one experience but a vast
array of experiences and belonged to a dynamic and diverse working
class. Through individual and shared encounters, Mexicans recognized
northern employers' strategies to exploit them, acknowledged the pervasive racism, and devised ways to counter the unjust practices.

This chapter assesses Mexican employment in the Midwest after the
1920–1921 depression. It traces in broad outline some of the characteristics of the working lives of these Mexican workers, particularly those
employed in the auto industry in Detroit and southeast Michigan during
the 1920s.

THE ROLE OF MEXICANS IN NORTHERN INDUSTRIES

In the winter of 1925, approximately 350 Mexicans lived in St. Paul,
one of the smallest and northernmost points of Mexican settlement in
the Midwest. St. Paul's Mexicans were mainly itinerant sugar-beet

workers who wintered in the city until they left again in the spring for work on beet farms elsewhere in the state and in Iowa and Wisconsin. Over a third were hired by the railroads and packing plants. However, this was only a small number of those seeking factory work. Mexicans in St. Paul wanted industrial jobs because their earnings from sugar-beet labor were quickly spent for food and housing, but local employers were reluctant to hire them. Present in St. Paul only during the winter and with only a limited number of them working, these new immigrants were invisible to all but the white ethnics who worked and lived among them and to the relief agencies that served the city's immigrant communities. As a result Mexicans remained strangers to St. Paul's American-born residents, who falsely perceived them "as a hot-tempered, lazy people with little energy." [7]

By 1928, the size of St. Paul's Mexican population was relatively unchanged; however, only one-third departed for the beet fields, with the remainder staying to work for the Milwaukee, Northern Burlington, and Rock Island railroads, and in the meat-packing houses of the Swift, Armour, and Cudahy packing companies. The few Mexicans employed in the packing houses as meat packers, janitors, cleaners of lard-waste containers, and butchers were long-time employees who enjoyed steady work and earned $0.42 an hour for a forty-hour week. This was better pay than they could earn doing sugar-beet and track work. The migratory nature of sugar-beet work and the absence of manufacturing industries persisted in stifling the growth of St. Paul's Mexican colony. It unexpectedly grew during the Great Depression with the influx of sugar-beet workers into the city. They had been denied employment by area farmers because of discriminatory policies favoring unemployed white workers, who competed with Mexicans for the scarce field work. [8]

Mexicans entered Milwaukee in 1917 under contract to local railroads and the Illinois Steel Company. Additional numbers drifted into the city from the state's beet fields. After World War I, work in Milwaukee's tanneries and steel mills lured additional Mexicans to the city such as Alberto Castro, who left Kansas City, Missouri, after losing his job with the Missouri Pacific Railroad. The ex-track laborer got off the train in Milwaukee when he saw the forest of factory chimneys on the city's skyline. "Oh boy!" Alberto exclaimed, "it's an industrial town." To this Mexican eager for work, industry meant a whole spectrum of blue-collar job opportunities. There was good money to be made in Milwaukee. Alberto found work with the Pfister & Vogel Leather Company, which was just beginning to increase its Mexican workforce, but not out of any benevolence toward these earnest workers—the local labor situation had become critical.[9]

In 1923, 750 Mexicans recruited in San Antonio arrived in Milwaukee anticipating working for Pfister & Vogel. However, two-thirds of the men were channeled to the Chicago, Milwaukee & St. Paul Railroad because the pay cuts precipitating the 1922 railroad strike had caused an urgent labor shortage. Like their countrymen who took the railroad jobs not knowing that they were hired as scabs, the Mexicans who went to work for Pfister & Vogel were unaware that a strike by the company's mostly Polish tannery workers had brought them to Milwaukee. This fact had been intentionally withheld by the local Mexican consul, who prepared their special six-month contracts. Among the contract laborers were former army officers, post-office employees, bank clerks, customs officials, and other government workers who had lost their jobs as a result of the ongoing Mexican Revolution. They now had the unenviable distinction of being scabs, doing work most would have refused in their home country. These ex-civil servants labored side by side with compatriots from working-class backgrounds; such daily contact between classes did not occur in Mexico.[10]

Predictably, the Mexicans were not well received by the striking tannery workers; to avoid further tension Pfister & Vogel lodged the strikebreakers in segregated housing and then in company-owned boardinghouses and fed them in its cafeteria. The cloistered Mexicans consequently knew nothing about Milwaukee because they saw little of the city. The ostracism and intolerable working conditions at the tannery led 20 percent to quit their jobs after one month and return to Texas. The Mexicans had the most unpleasant jobs; they had to wear rubber boots, aprons, and gloves to protect them from the caustic lime used to remove the hair from hides in the poorly ventilated, foul-smelling workplace. Despite the negative aspects, the tanneries offered the Mexicans who stayed relatively steady wages for tasks that were easily mastered.[11]

Throughout the 1920s, hundreds of Mexicans traveled to Milwaukee after hearing about the plentiful work from relatives and friends already in the city. The newcomers obtained employment in the tanneries, shoe factories, steel mills, meat-packing plants, and with the railroads. Mexicans unable to find work in the Chicago area went to Milwaukee, where work in the leather factories paid $27 a week and jobs with Illinois Steel paid $24 a week. In late 1926, 1,500 Mexicans lived in Milwaukee; however, 500 had left before this because of the slowdown in the leather industry, and the sugar-beet harvest drew others to area farms. Because of the phasedown at the Illinois Steel plant in 1928, workers faced two- and three-day workweeks and finally dismissal when this plant closed and moved to Gary, Indiana.[12] Milwaukee's potential as a point of destination for Mexicans and blacks migrating to the Midwest was limited by the proximity of Chicago, Indiana Harbor, Gary, and Detroit.[13] Sugar-beet workers were the most likely recruits because they used Milwaukee as a wintering site.

For Mexicans, Chicago served as the major point of entrance into the industrial North. The Windy City had the biggest Mexican population outside the Southwest, and it was on the main migration route from Texas to the Midwest.[14]

Chicago's diversified economy offered Mexicans choices for unskilled industrial work, and the availability of factory jobs brought thousands to the thriving city. The proletarianization of Mexicans in the 1920s was unquestionably taking place in Chicago. The Mexican population grew rapidly in the winter of 1922–1923, when jobs opened up in the steel mills, which had recently switched to the eight-hour, three-shift schedule. Despite the substantial wage reductions for common labor (50.2 percent by U.S. Steel), long waiting lists at plants and foundries were evidence that men eagerly sought any available employment. In 1924, Chicago's fiery steel mills employed 1,042 Mexicans and an additional 606 worked in foundries. The major industrial employer in this year was the railroads, the men often working on the lines that had brought Mexicans to Chicago for over a decade. Two thousand Mexicans worked for twenty principal railroad companies in Chicago and represented over one-fourth of the city's Mexican workforce. As in the Southwest, railroad maintenance and repair work in the Windy City became closely identified with Mexican labor.[15]

In early 1927, over 17,000 Mexicans lived in Chicago and were concentrated in six locales adjacent to their place of employment. Mexican women (1,650) and children (3,350) formed almost a third of the population. Of these Mexicans 761 worked for the meat-packing plants and stockyards, and an additional 300 were employed by the Chicago River & Indiana Railroad, which served the slaughterhouses. The Mexicans working at the Swift, Armour, Hammond, Omaha, and Wilson packing houses constituted 4 percent of the total workforce in meat packing, which would increase to 5.6 percent in two years. In South Chicago, 1,030 Mexicans worked for Illinois Steel, 665 worked for Wisconsin Steel, 500 for the Crane Company, and 1,500 for various small foundries. Those at Illinois Steel and Wisconsin Steel constituted 12.2 percent and 21.8 percent, respectively, of all the hourly employees at these two plants. The employment of Mexicans at Wisconsin Steel had increased in 1923 because the policy was to hire no blacks at all. With the only requirements being a minimal knowledge of English and a willingness to work, Mexicans filled the low-wage, unskilled positions abandoned by European immigrant workers who were by then making modest progress in moving up the job hierarchy.[16]

The railroads in Chicago remained the principal employers of Mexicans because many had terminals in the Plains States and the Southwest, and thus the companies and the Mexicans had a strong past association with one another. The railroads hired Mexicans because they were hard-working and efficient in carrying out assigned tasks, not simply because they were a cheap and abundant source of labor. Mexicans in turn could rely on steady work with advantages to compensate for the low wages: They performed familiar tasks on the track gangs and in the roundhouses, and they could bring their families north to live in the city. Certain rail companies preferred hiring Mexicans or hoboes before blacks; such selective employment policies benefited the migrants from Mexico, assuring steady work. In 1926, approximately 5,255 Mexicans worked for the Rock Island, the Santa Fe, the Illinois Central, the Chicago & Northwestern, the Chicago Great Western, the Wabash, the Erie, and additional lines. Mexicans made up 40.5 percent of track laborers on the twenty Chicago rail lines during this year. (By decade's end, almost half of the maintenance-of-way men in the Chicago area were Mexican.) In addition, Chicago public and private construction and street-paving companies employed 1,500 Mexicans, an indication of the size of the itinerant Mexican population in the Windy City available for short-term job stints. Five hundred found work in hotels, wholesale houses, and so on. About 95 percent of Mexican workers in Chicago held unskilled jobs, the huge number employed as track maintenance and repair men no doubt accounting for this high percentage. These men earned from $0.38 to $0.44 an hour, and the small number holding semiskilled and skilled jobs earned between $0.55 and $0.75 an hour. Earnings such as these far exceeded wages in Mexico and Texas and made the long trip north worthwhile.[17]

While Chicago furnished abundant opportunities in track, steel, and meat packing, the Inland Steel Company in nearby Indiana Harbor, Indiana, offered Mexicans jobs in steel manufacturing, as it had before the 1920–1921 depression. By now this company was the second largest employer of Mexicans in the Midwest. Just as the fast-paced machine work in the highly modern Ford plants fostered pride in the car company by the veteran Mexican autoworkers, the smoke-shrouded and fierce Inland mill created an aura of prestige for this steel company's hardened Mexicans because of the physically grueling and dangerous work. Being able to work in a rough-and-tumble company town became a rite of passage into the industrial working class and added to the attraction of Inland Steel.

From the beginning, Mexicans were a significant percentage of the workforce at Inland Steel. Although the company had cut back its labor force by 60 percent and had imposed hiring restrictions as a result of the 1920–1921 depression, 389 Mexicans worked for Inland as the year 1921 ended; they made up 12.9 percent of its workforce. The Mexican steelworkers included those who had been strikebreakers two years earlier. Unwilling to become embroiled in a labor dispute, a considerable number had left Indiana Harbor during the strike but returned in 1922 accompanied by relatives and friends, nearly tripling Inland Steel's Mexican workforce to 1,224, or 26.8 percent of the total. In 1923, Inland's Mexican steelworkers earned approximately $0.50 an hour for the newly implemented eight-hour day. About 10 percent held skilled jobs, 20 percent were semiskilled, with the remainder in unskilled positions. The 2,526 Mexicans who worked at Inland Steel in 1926 accounted for almost a fourth of the plant's hourly employees. The men's participation in bonus plans and insurance programs added to their identification with the company and to their job security. The Mexican steelworkers at Inland Steel, along with 450 employed by the Universal Portland Cement Company, 150 employed by Youngstown Sheet & Tube, and 500 women and 1,000 children, made up the more than 4,500-member colony living in Indiana Harbor, which was almost twice the size of the Mexican population of Gary, eight miles to the southeast.[18]

Steelwork brought Mexicans to Gary following the 1921 depression, and numerical quotas and job ceilings for blacks augmented the local Mexican worker population in steel production. In 1923, 474 Mexicans were employed at the Illinois Steel plant; they made up 4.1 percent of the total labor force. In 1925 the number of Mexicans at the plant nearly tripled to 1,117, or 7.8 percent of the workers.[19] In addition, 360 Mexicans worked for the American Sheet & Tinplate Company; 300 were employed at the Gary Tube Company; and the railroads employed over 260. Gary's Mexican steelworkers earned an average of $4.40 a day, most doing rough jobs with limited opportunities for advancement within the unskilled ranks because of prejudice. About 2,500 Mexicans lived in Gary in 1926: 1,950 men, 200 women, and 350 children. As in Indiana Harbor, the small number of Mexican women and children in Gary was due to racial discrimination and to the shortage of adequate housing compounded by high rents. Because of these unsatisfactory conditions, over half the married men had left their dependents in Mexico.[20]

Hundreds of steelworkers from Gary and the Chicago area eventually decided to seek jobs and economic betterment in auto manufacturing. As they had during and after World War I, Detroit and southeast Michigan remained a favorite destination for thousands of Mexicans. In 1922, the Detroit Mexican consul estimated that several thousand Mexicans worked in the city's auto factories. Nearly three-fourths of these men originally came to Michigan as beet workers but stayed because of the abundant opportunities in Detroit's auto factories. Auto work overall was remunerative employment. During this era of little job security car manufacturing led all industries combined in wages paid despite the seasonal nature of the work. It ranked fifth in average annual wages in 1919, first in 1925, and maintained these competitive wages into the depression years of the 1930s.[21]

The Mexicans of Detroit and southeast Michigan became part of an ethnically and racially diverse labor force, though large numbers of white southerners and rural midwesterners also worked in the car plants. Between 1919 and 1929, as members of this workforce Mexicans helped produce over twenty million motor vehicles, including trucks and tractors.[22] The participation of Mexicans in tractor and truck production had an indirect though distinct effect on the migration of their countrymen from Texas to the Midwest: as the mechanization of large-scale cotton farming in Texas increased, as well as the expansion of fruit and vegetable truck farming, the numbers of seasonal Mexican laborers rose proportionately. In turn, the continued growth of these low-wage agricultural employment sectors replenished and extended the flow of Mexican migration to the Midwest, a stream of which was directed to Detroit.[23]

A universal desire among Mexicans to work for Henry Ford, the man "who had given birth to the worker," according to one Mexican Detroiter, remained constant because this famous carmaker offered good wages and steady work. In 1923, 438 Mexicans worked for Ford; three years later this number tripled to 1,200; and by 1928 the Ford Motor Company employed the greatest number of Mexicans in Detroit, almost

4,000, or a 330 percent increase in two years. Ford surpassed the Inland Steel Company as the number one industrial employer of Mexicans in the Midwest.[24]

There was no double wage scale in the Ford plants—a higher wage for Anglos and a lower wage for Mexicans and blacks. Ford paid its Mexican employees the same as white autoworkers, hourly earnings varying from year to year. For instance, men hired in 1918 were paid the standard $0.50 an hour, those hired in 1919 received $0.75 an hour, while workers in 1928 earned hourly wages of $0.625. There was also equity in pay increments. Mexican Ford autoworkers received the same wage readjustments as their white and black counterparts. Neutralizing these wages were increased production quotas, manpower cutbacks, and the introduction of new, more efficient machinery. Moreover, as with all Ford autoworkers, the ability of Mexicans to make a satisfactory income was undermined by the seasonal nature of auto work. Idled Ford workers had to seek alternative employment if they wished to maintain the standard of living they were growing accustomed to and now expected for their efforts on the line.

Mexicans in Detroit knew of the work possibilities available locally in lieu of auto work and sought these jobs. Sugar-beet work was one alternative, and Detroit construction and utility companies were further sources of jobs. The increase in building construction in Detroit furnished plenty of opportunities for part-time pick-and-shovel work, and Mexicans joined mixed-ethnic work gangs on construction sites throughout the city. Track work was available with the Detroit Street Car Company and the Detroit Union Railway, and Mexicans willingly signed onto the graveyard shift, night work that whites usually avoided. To pay for food and housing, some Mexicans found jobs as janitors, baggage handlers, dishwashers, and waiters at downtown hotels and as cooks and bus boys in area restaurants. The boom in street construction in Detroit created hundreds of temporary jobs for common laborers with the Detroit Gas Company, Detroit Edison, the Detroit Department of Public Works (DDPW), the Wayne County Road Commission, and the Michigan Highway Department. Mexicans employed by the DDPW worked with blacks. (The DDPW was the city's second largest employer of blacks, with 2,200 workers.) Mexicans drove cabs for the General Cab and the Yellow Cab Companies, sold lunches, barbered, or worked at Mexican grocery stores and restaurants. Mexicans also secured jobs in the city's packing houses, fertilizer plants, and as roustabouts unload-

ing boats on the Detroit River.[25] The goal was to acquire steady employment, regardless of the kind of jobs, for Mexicans had come North to
work.

WORK EXPERIENCES OF MEXICAN AUTOWORKERS

Numerous studies exist on the work experiences of Mexicans in agriculture, but there is a paucity of research on Mexican industrial workers,
in part because of the routine destruction of records by many companies. However, data from Ford Motor Company record cards offer a
rare chance to profile one important group of Mexican factory workers
in the 1920s. The Ford employment data are used here to examine and
discuss the previous employment of Mexican Ford autoworkers in Mexico and the United States; the places where they held industrial jobs
previously; the integration of Mexicans into factory work, especially
auto work; the kinds of jobs held by Mexicans in the Ford plants; the
impact of racial discrimination in this company's plants; the responses
to working conditions such as speed-ups; the interaction of Mexicans
with co-workers and shop foremen; their strategies for coping with fluctuations in the availability of work; and the hazards they confronted on
the job. Specifically, this chapter focuses on the experiences of Mexican
autoworkers in the Ford River Rouge plant. Because they were mass-
production workers, their experiences were unique and not representative of those of the majority of Mexican industrial workers. Because of
their previous work experiences, these men often already embodied the
work culture of the industrial North. Nevertheless, an analysis of their
experiences allows us to reassess the image of the Mexican worker,
which is typically associated with agriculture.

PREVIOUS EMPLOYMENT

The small number of Mexicans who had come to Detroit directly from
Mexico had worked in their homeland as blacksmiths, garage mechanics, miners, cigar makers, and oil-field workers, indicating a wide range
of exposure to wage work. However, most of the Mexicans hired by
Ford migrated to Detroit from other parts of the Midwest, and most
had been employed in four major industries: railroads, foundries, steel
mills, and auto plants. (See Table 5.) These men had journeyed to Detroit from industrial urban centers within Michigan and from Illinois,
Indiana, Ohio, and Pennsylvania. The remainder came to Detroit from

Table 5.   Previous Employment of Mexican
Autoworkers at the Ford River Rouge Plant,
1918–1933

	Railroad	Steel Mill	Foundry	Auto Industry	Auto-Related Industry	Total
Number	123	223	221	747	461	1,775
Percent	6.9	12.6	12.5	42	26	100

SOURCE: Rouge Area Hourly Workers Employment Record Jackets, 1918–1933, Accession AR-84-58-1050, Ford Motor Company Industrial Archives and Record Center, Redford, Michigan.

New York, West Virginia, Kentucky, Missouri, Kansas, Oklahoma, and California. The employment paths of the men were not the same; business cycles, personal preference, and differing circumstances caused the paths to vary substantially.

Only a small number of Mexicans hired by Ford had worked for railroads because job opportunities in the city outside of auto work were limited. Those who had worked for southwestern and Mexican rail lines came to Detroit between 1917 and 1920, when Mexicans were just beginning to gain access to Midwest labor markets. After 1920, the ex-railroad workers were employed mainly by rail lines operating in Michigan and Illinois. That the majority of these Mexicans worked for northern rail lines confirms the argument that after 1920 Mexicans applying for work with Ford were already in the Midwest. (See Table 6.)

The Mexicans who came to Ford from steel and foundry work again came principally from the Midwest and from within Michigan and had previously been part of the region's industrial economy. Foundry and steel work in the Chicago-Gary region had been the previous employment of hundreds of these Mexicans. The ex-foundry men had worked for companies in Detroit and southeast Michigan that did the preparatory rough work for the automakers.[26] The foundries gave hundreds of Mexican sugar-beet workers their first exposure to factories. Though grueling, the work performed in the oppressive heat was steady and offered relatively regular wages. With little supervision by shop bosses, the men soon became familiar with the foundry routines and refashioned them to their advantage whenever possible. They attached meaning to the types of work they performed, and they valued the friendship

Table 6.   Location of Previous Employment of
Mexican Autoworkers at the Ford River Rouge
Plant, 1918–1933

	Mich.	Ill.	Ind.	Ohio	Pa.	Tex.	Mexico	Other	Total
Number	1,512	142	123	49	83	76	161	85	2,231
Percent	67.8	6.4	5.5	2.2	3.7	3.4	7.2	3.8	100

SOURCE: Rouge Area Hourly Workers Employment Record Jackets, 1918–1933, Accession AR-84-58-1050, Ford Motor Company Industrial Archives and Record Center, Redford, Michigan.
NOTE: Totals vary for Tables 6, 7, and 9 because of incomplete records.

of their co-workers and the sense of shared identity derived from doing the hard, dangerous work.[27]

Some foundry workers returned to the beet fields but most moved about the cities of southeast Michigan in search of work, following the job circuit Mexican workers had previously established. Family and friends supplied the job contacts and so did the veteran workers accustomed to the cycles of factory production. Transportation was easy because a tram route connected Saginaw, Flint, Pontiac, and Detroit. Mexicans used this interurban line much as their compatriots in the Chicago-Gary region moved back and forth between the local steel mills on an interurban line. These foundry workers also made their way to the other Michigan cities in buses or their own cars and trucks.

Sometimes women influenced decisions about the search for employment. Like the men, women were concerned with achieving economic betterment through work. Many were aware of the differences in status at the workplace and understood that advancement through the ranks of factory work was attainable for their spouses. In March 1920, the fifteen-member Montano family crossed the border into Laredo, Texas, after paying the head tax.[28] But legal passage into the United States quickly exhausted their funds. The Montanos headed for San Antonio, where the four male members of the family procured work on a dairy farm outside the city, each earning $10 a week. The high cost of living in San Antonio and the low-wage work in the area prompted the Montano family to start north. After talking among themselves and consulting with friends who had made the trek to Michigan, the family chose Michigan as their destination. "One day as we walked along West Commerce Street we saw a big [billboard] advertising a trip to Michigan with the Michigan Sugar Company with headquarters in Saginaw. . . . Our money was going very fast, . . . the income too small for 15 people. So after thinking it over . . . [we] decided that Michigan would be the best place for our family."

At dawn on May 10, 1920, the Montano family boarded a train and left Texas for the North. Five days later, they reached southeast Michigan and were transported by truck to their jobs planting and hoeing sugar beets on a farm outside Saginaw. All the members of this big Mexican family worked on the assigned acreage and contributed to the family income. However, the drudgery of hand labor caused the Montanos to reconsider whether they were willing to stick with this work for three months until the harvest season ended. As the hoeing season waned, the Montanos decided to move to Saginaw in time to answer the call for workers by the General Motors Central Foundry. There they joined dozens of Mexican beet workers who like themselves were lured by the exceptional wages. The four Montano men obtained work together at the foundry, earning $0.70 an hour each for a nine-hour day. These wages were more than sufficient to support the fifteen-member family as well as to accumulate savings. But work at the foundry became unsteady as the 1920–1921 depression set in, and three of the four Montanos lost their jobs.

Three years later, in April 1924, Venturo Montano left Saginaw for Detroit to search for work; he was accompanied by his wife, María, and their young daughter. María had persuaded her husband to seek work with the Ford Motor Company in Detroit, a city her parents in Mexico had repeatedly spoken highly of. María and Venturo were determined that they would never undergo again the hardships they had endured during the 1920–1921 depression. More important, the husband and wife had recognized that factory work, not farm labor, was the key to raising their living standards. A job with Ford could make this raise in living standards possible as well as prove that Venturo could obtain the status associated with working for an industrial giant. María remembered the details of their short trip from Saginaw to Detroit, which left a lasting impression:

> The weather was bitter cold, we just shivered in the interurban. But I was so anxious to know the city which my father was very fond of. At last about ten o'clock that night the conductor said "Detroit." Then my heart pretty near busted. . . . I got so excited that I almost dropped Carmen, my only child.

Our excitement grew when we got near the [Ford] Highland Park plant, for the sight of it with its hundreds of lights [recalled] the tales of our mamma when we were little. My husband, right away the next Monday, applied for work at the Rouge plant. . . . He got a job the same day.

INTEGRATION INTO FACTORY WORK

The lure of Detroit and its job prospects brought hundreds of Mexican steelworkers to the Motor City. The prestige associated with Ford motivated many of these men, as well as the opportunity to obtain experience in the car factories. The ex-steelworkers migrated to Detroit from Chicago, Indiana, Ohio, Pennsylvania, and New York. Most came from the steel mills of South Chicago, Indiana Harbor, or Gary. A few had worked at the Colorado Fuel and Iron Company in Pueblo, Colorado, and in steel plants in Monterrey, Mexico. Monterrey was known as the Chicago of Mexico because of its heavy-manufacturing plants.

Auto-parts factories were additional entry points into the car plants. The work was hot, hazardous, low-paying, and involved long hours, but it offered steady employment for men with the necessary grit to perform the metal-casting jobs. Ramón Huerta's first job in Detroit was at Michigan Steel Casting. For six months he worked on the night shift in the molding and shakeout department, earning $0.30 to $0.40 an hour for eleven hours of brutalizing piecework. The stifling heat and the noxious fumes made it difficult for Huerta to breathe as he feverishly cast motor blocks for cars and trucks. The gutsy Mexican, realizing that he was being overworked and underpaid, was determined to get out at the first opportunity and find work in an auto plant. On-the-job training for auto work—training that he lacked when he first applied for auto work in 1919 on his arrival to Detroit—would help Huerta get into one of the main car plants.[29]

Briggs Manufacturing was a major employer of Mexicans in 1920s Detroit; it recognized their reliability and industriousness in doing heavy work. Of the 5,000 to 6,000 men at the Briggs Mack Avenue plant in 1928, over 7 percent were Mexicans. Briggs exploited men to the maximum and because of turnover helped maintain a perpetual flow of Mexicans in and out of unskilled jobs in the car factories. Employment at Briggs served as an initiation into auto work; it tested a man's capacity for intense work in an intolerable environment. Detroit's workers derisively called the Briggs plants the "butcher shops" (Mexicans referred to the Briggs shop on Mack Avenue as *el carnicería*) because of the wretched working conditions, excessive accident rates, and low pay. "Briggs killed a worker for the least pay of all the auto plants," remembered Huerta. "It ran the fastest line." This sentiment, based on grudging admiration and an underlying contempt of the work, was echoed by many Mexicans in the Briggs plants and by those men who had heard rumors from friends about the miserable circumstances.[30]

In the eyes of Briggs management, the resolve of the Mexican workers to withstand the intense fatigue of fast-paced machine production was their most valuable attribute. It contributed as well to the self-esteem of the men and to their social standing among their compatriots. An average of six months of the inhuman pace was all that most men could bear before quitting, contributing to the 30 percent turnover rate for all Briggs blue-collar employees. However, the more hardy men adjusted to the intense pace and stayed with the auto-parts maker. A small number even attained status as die setters. Perhaps those who stayed reasoned that they gained stability, which was preferable to the erratic labor schedules at the major auto plants, even if the major companies paid better wages. These workers likely understood the cyclical employment trends that characterized the industry and resolved to obtain and keep the steadiest work.[31]

Still, securing jobs in the plants of the main car companies remained the goal of most Mexicans arriving in Detroit. Within the auto sector, Mexicans had created a hierarchy based not only on wages but on the kinds of jobs they held and the companies they worked for. Status in the Detroit Mexican working-class colony was thus determined.[32]

Almost three-fourths of the Mexicans who obtained jobs with Ford during this period previously worked in the auto industry. This number included the aforementioned auto-parts workers and former students at the Henry Ford Service School who chose to remain in Detroit with the company. The prevalence of ex-autoworkers indicates that Mexicans employed in the car plants throughout Detroit and southeast Michigan were being integrated into the region's auto labor force. About 500 of these men had worked for General Motors, the second leading employer of Mexican autoworkers. More than one-third of the Ford workers who had previously been employed in auto manufacturing had worked for General Motors at its Dodge, Buick, Chevrolet, and Fisher Body plants in Detroit, Pontiac, Flint, and Saginaw.

The number of Mexicans employed by Fisher Body was limited by the company's reluctance to hire unnaturalized citizens. In light of Fisher Body's stringent restrictions on hiring blacks, in effect at all of its plants, the employment of even limited numbers of Mexicans by this car company is notable. Only forty blacks were on Fisher Body's payroll in 1926; twenty years later the company still had fewer than forty black employees. Mexicans apparently had replaced blacks in Fisher Body's dirtiest and hottest jobs, but this was questionable progress because the Mexicans were stereotyped as having an innate ability to withstand terribly hot temperatures and physically arduous work. A contemporary scholar reported a Fisher Body official as stating that at his plant the "dirty hot jobs are filled by Mexicans. [They] seem to stand the heat better than either Negroes or whites." In evaluating this biased remark the researcher concluded: "This is an interesting and enlightening comment on the status of the newest entrant into the battle for the job. He has to take the poorest job and like it. It used to be reported of the Negro: 'He can stand the heat better than white men. Negroes like hot jobs.' Now the report comes of the newest competitor: 'The Mexican can stand heat better than Negroes.' "[33]

The bad working conditions and racism in the Fisher Body plants did not deter Mexicans from seeking jobs with the company. The men realized that a barrier of discrimination separated them and blacks from the rest of the workers. Based on their previous work experiences in the Midwest, they anticipated getting less desirable jobs because of market conditions, language and citizenship requirements, and prejudice.

Hundreds of Mexicans worked for Chevrolet Motors in Flint, Michigan. A small number of the men had been with the company since 1916, when Chevrolet first hired Mexicans at its Flint plant. The autoworkers were on nine- and ten-hour shifts and earned bonus pay, which increased their loyalty. Management did not favor hiring foreign-born laborers (aliens made up only 3 percent of the workforce). However, preference was given to Mexicans because they accepted the rough jobs as sanders and polishers and, unlike white autoworkers, were inclined to stay in these positions. Although Mexicans were assigned the hardest jobs, they still had more opportunities than blacks did. Nearly all the blacks held janitorial positions.[34]

Considerable numbers of Mexicans worked for Dodge Motors. In 1926, 300 Mexicans worked at the Dodge plant on Joseph Campau Street in Hamtramck and averaged $0.55 an hour on piecework for a fifty-hour week. Twenty Mexicans were gang bosses or assistant managers earning from $0.60 to $0.80 an hour. The Dodge plant's Mexican autoworkers "got along well," according to the employment manager, probably because of the unusually high number of their countrymen in supervisory positions. Management knew the Mexicans on the shop floor preferred working under Spanish-speaking foremen, who likely used national pride to drive the men, pushing them on and challenging them to show up their white co-workers. Evidently, however, having compatriots as work supervisors was not sufficient compensation for the unfair bonus plan, which complicated the piecework system. Discouraged, many Mexicans left Dodge. Some of these men applied for jobs with Ford Motors, where an absence of piecework production and a five-day workweek were appealing.[35]

Buick Motors began hiring Mexicans in 1922 and by 1926 employed 500 in Flint. Buick was the only car company that recruited Mexicans in Texas, although most of its Mexican autoworkers came from the area beet fields and the railroads. Buick respected its Mexican employees as dependable and productive because they endured long hours of factory work with little complaint and regularly outperformed their black co-workers. Mexicans on machine operations had attained proficiency in their work, and those on group piecework surpassed the output of their fellow black and Italian workers. According to the plant manager, Mexicans synchronized the work tasks and accelerated the pace of work to run blacks and Italians "off the job by crowding them with the work when they took a notion to it." [36] Yet the Mexicans were aware that the piecework system was unfair; it pushed them to a point where they became careless, resulting in terrible injuries, and they were not paid for "dead time"—when work stopped because machines broke down or the men ran out of parts. Therefore, Buick's Mexican workers may have been cautious not to set their work speed too high because production rates were continuously adjusted upward to compensate for their competence.

In the 1920s Mexicans at the Buick Motors plants in Flint on construction and maintenance jobs earned $0.28 to $0.40 an hour with time and a half for Saturday-afternoon and Sunday shifts. This overtime work was denied black autoworkers. Mexicans in semiskilled jobs earned $0.40 a hour, though the majority were on the piece-rate system and averaged $0.50 to $0.55 an hour, sometimes working the eleven- and twelve-hour night shift. Despite the occasional dead time, to the men these extra hours meant subsistence beyond the minimum, the purchase of material goods, and regular savings deposits. For the single men, the added income could buy a return train trip to Texas and Mexico in luxury aboard a Pullman car instead of the usual passenger cars. The Mexican Buick employees expressed overall satisfaction with their jobs and appreciated the car company's willingness to hire them.[37]

In all, approximately 1,500 Mexicans were employed by General Motors and its subsidiaries in Saginaw, Flint, and Pontiac in the 1920s. The preference for Mexicans over blacks for the least desirable work, piecework, and for overtime characterized Mexican employment with General Motors. Personal choice, family considerations, bonds of friendship established with co-workers, and the status derived from affiliation with General Motors, which by now was the nation's biggest manufacturer of cars, influenced the decisions of these men to remain with this automaker.

Mexicans had similarly made inroads in auto work with non-General Motors companies. Five hundred Mexicans resided in Pontiac in the fall of 1926. They came to the factories in this city from the beet farms beginning in 1922. About 25 Mexicans worked at Pontiac's small Oakland Motors plant, while the Wilson Foundry & Machine Company used 200 in the production of engine blocks for Willys-Knight Motors. Dozens of Mexicans had been drawn to this foundry from building- and road-construction projects or from the local rail lines, which employed about 200 of them. Mexicans at the thundering Wilson foundry averaged $0.50 to $0.60 an hour on piece production, mainly in unskilled jobs. Only 10 percent were semiskilled. They labored in gangs with different nationalities and blacks for piece rates with no complaints of prejudice. In this rare instance prejudices and differences were set aside by workers. These men maintained control over their work pace and production quotas to avoid rising beyond the limits set by management and thus having their piece rates cut. The Mexican turnover rate at Wilson Foundry was the lowest of all employee groups, averaging just 4 percent.[38]

The health and lives of Mexicans were put in jeopardy when they were lured to work in the car industry. This was the case with the men who obtained jobs with Hudson Motors, where fewer than 100 Mexicans were employed. They worked in the paint departments on jobs that paid a relatively high rate of $0.80 an hour but that exacted a much higher toll on their physical well-being. The expanding use of spray-painting machinery in auto work dramatically increased health hazards for workers. Aware but uninformed of the health risks, men consented for the most part to the high-paying work in dreadfully toxic environments permeated with acetone, lead, benzol, and wood alcohol fumes.

A great deal of the spray painting was done without protective masks, and the paint completely saturated clothing, resulting in the progressive poisoning of workers. The presence of sizable quantities of volatile chemicals increased the potential for accidents. For instance, an explosion and fire in the spray-painting department of the Harper Avenue Briggs plant in Detroit burned to death twenty-one workers and permanently injured innumerable men.[39]

Lauro Tienda worked at the Hudson Motors paint shop during this early period. He knew that this job entailed inhaling noxious vapors and being drenched in paint from his previous work in the Packard Motors paint shop, where he had earned $0.50 an hour spraying black enamel on car chassis. At the Hudson Motors plant, the extra $0.30 an hour kept Lauro on the job, though he wisely transferred out of the paint department during his seven years with the company.[40] The high wages paid for the perilous paint work at Hudson Motors did not induce many Mexicans to seek jobs with this automaker. Those on the paint jobs likely questioned sacrificing their health for high wages.

Relatively few Mexicans worked for Studebaker, Packard, Maxwell, Cadillac, or Willys-Overland in Toledo, Ohio. Like Fisher Body, these automakers required naturalization papers from all applicants except Canadians, and this policy denied the majority of Mexicans work. In addition to restricting hiring, Cadillac Motors and Willys-Overland preferred skilled men, which likewise eliminated most Mexicans even though they had auto-work experience. Area sugar-beet and railroad workers had little chance of procuring jobs at Willys-Overland. Mexicans employed by Willys-Overland and Cadillac had been hand-picked and were long-term employees, averaging seven to eight years with the companies. One Mexican autoworker at Cadillac was the brother-in-law of the secretary to Mexican President Plutarco Calles. Another Mexican at Willys-Overland in Toledo was the brother-in-law of the manager of Ford's branch plant in Mexico City, as well as being a recent graduate of the Henry Ford Service School. Rather than writing the standard letter of recommendation, the Mexican consul of Detroit personally accompanied the applicant to Toledo for his interview with Willys-Overland.[41]

Thus Mexicans who were hired in the Ford plants already had broad exposure to industrial work; at one time many of them had jobs with railroads, foundries, and steel mills, mainly in the Midwest. The majority of the men had been employed in auto and auto-parts factories in

Detroit and southeast Michigan. Within the auto industry certain plant superintendents refused to hire Mexicans, while others accepted the popular belief that Mexicans could withstand harsh conditions. Some placed Mexicans in the least desirable jobs as an alternative to black workers. Saginaw's General Motors Central Foundry and Fisher Body followed these practices. The Mexicans at the Buick Motors plants in Flint were on semiskilled piecework jobs; most of the Mexican Dodge autoworkers likewise did semiskilled group piecework. Over 6 percent of those employed at Dodge's Joseph Campau plant held positions as gang bosses and assistant managers, contrary to the general impression that menial jobs were the only ones held by Mexican workers at this time and that upward mobility within the blue-collar ranks was relatively restricted. In the Briggs plants Mexicans did machine production and dealt with fast-paced work schedules that exacted a heavy physical toll. Yet the contemporary testimonies of auto-company employers and Mexican autoworkers and particularly the statements of ex-autoworkers reveal that the men drew meaning from and found purpose in their labor and garnered respect from the other workers, their kin, and management.

KINDS OF JOBS IN FORD PLANTS

There was no uniformity in the job assignments of Mexican autoworkers because of the various factors affecting job placement and because of individual decisions. They filled positions relegated to the newest entrants to an industrial sector that was beginning to decline. One thing was certain, all Mexican autoworkers on assembly operations had to cope with the monotony and routine of machine production.

Developments in standardized machine production and the subdivision of work within the auto industry had by the 1920s eliminated dozens of jobs once held by skilled workers and common laborers. Expertise and brawn were now embodied in the multipurpose machine, the "iron man." The machine operator performed from 25 to 49 percent of auto work. Machine-production techniques blurred the distinctions between the categories of skilled, semiskilled, and unskilled auto work. The job classifications of machine operator, drill-press operator, punch-press operator, and so on, were conceptual categories rather than definitions of actual labor processes. Management used the labels to create artificial job hierarchies to control and manipulate workers. By the end of the 1920s, approximately thirty-four different jobs with their varying levels of status had been derived from the work previously executed by one autoworker.[42]

The proliferation of machine production in auto work created jobs that required little or no training and that were easily learned within a week.[43] A contemporary auto-industry analyst observed that reaching ("hitting") and maintaining a constant machine pace while eliminating unnecessary motions were the basic job requirements for a machine tender. An autoworker's efficiency was measured by the extent to which his production equaled or exceeded the rate set by time-series men. Machine production demanded the ability to withstand "fatigue, boredom, and pressure." It did not require thought or judgment. The Mexican ex-autoworkers interviewed by the author agreed that their work in the car factories of 1920s Detroit consisted of performing the same tasks over and over again, which became unbearable during times of speed-up. The work was made worse by the actions and attitudes of foremen. Mexicans easily mastered their jobs and, more important, devised strategies to circumvent the dreadful features of mass-production work as well as to confront the authority of foremen.[44]

In 1924, nearly half of the Ford workforce consisted of machine tenders and machine hands, and during the period under study the jobs of Mexican Ford autoworkers reflected this homogenization of the countless work processes entailed in the making of automobiles.[45] (See Table 7.) These men worked on drill presses, screw machines, lathes, metal polishers, and stamping machines, among others; the terrific whirring, grinding, and pounding filled the air. The helpers in this syncopated rhythm of man and machine assisted machine tenders, assemblers, inspectors, testers, furnace operators, and molders. Laborers were oilers, salvage men, sweepers, and shippers. The jobs, however, varied by shop and department and were governed by a specific set of rules fashioned to fit the immediate work environment as well as by the particular milieu created by the workers.

The mammoth size of the Ford Rouge complex, its buildings honeycombed by dozens of departments, along with the legions of workers and the hundreds of jobs, resulted in the wide distribution of Mexicans throughout the plant. There was no bunching up of Mexicans on jobs in the Ford shops. The great size of the Ford factories, the tens of thousands of workers of all races toiling together, and the diversity of work classifications made it difficult for Mexicans to be concentrated in any one particular locale. In the late 1920s, the Ford River Rouge plant was the world's premier self-sufficient and self-contained industrial com-

Table 7.   First Jobs of Mexican Autoworkers at the Ford River
Rouge Plant, 1918–1933

	Skilled	Machine Tender and Hand	Helper	Assembler	Laborer	Foundry Worker	Inspector	Total
Number	24	716	520	52	306	128	3	1,749
Percent	1.4	40.9	29.7	3	17.5	7.3	.2	100

SOURCE: Rouge Area Hourly Workers Employment Record Jackets, 1918–1933, Accession AR-84-58-1050, Ford Motor Company Industrial Archives and Record Center, Redford, Michigan.
NOTE: Totals vary for Tables 6, 7, and 9 because of incomplete records.

plex—"a microcosm of the industrial age." The Rouge consisted of ninety-three buildings, ninety-three miles of railroad track, and twenty-seven miles of conveyers constructed on over 2,000 acres of land. The foundry, where both casting and machining took place, was 590 feet wide and 1,188 feet long and employed 10,000 men in 1922 and 12,000 by 1924.[46] "There are a lot of us at Ford but we are scattered all through the plant," remarked a Mexican working at the Rouge. Ex-Ford employee Guadalupe Morales recollected that he knew that many Mexicans worked at the Rouge plant in the twenties, but he never saw more than a handful each day, and these were men in his department.[47] This anonymity and the inability of Mexicans to work together contrasted with the treatment of Ford's black autoworkers. The company's largest racial group, blacks were clustered in particular shops and departments because of segregation.

RACIAL DISCRIMINATION

The number of Mexicans at Ford never reached the level of black employment, which was 10 percent of the workforce at the Ford Rouge plant in 1926. Mexicans did not experience the degree of racial discrimination that blacks did, yet Mexicans did not escape assignment to departments considered the domain of black workers.[48] (See Table 8.) As in most manufacturing industries in the North, blacks were a buffer group for Mexican autoworkers against the inequities of racism. Of some benefit to Mexicans was Henry Ford's formula for maintaining a certain level of black workers in his plants, calculated according to the total population of blacks in Detroit.

Employers admitted complicity in discriminating against Mexicans, and their biased attitudes reflected the preexisting prejudice against blacks and the attitudes of the era. One plant manager explained: "When I hire Mexicans at the gate I pick out the lightest among them. No, it isn't that the lighter colored ones are any better workers, but the darker ones are like the niggers." Another manager rationalized his company's policy of hiring only light-complected Mexicans by equating skin color with intelligence. "The educated, higher type Mexicans are like us. . . . They're not damned foreigners; they're wise foreigners." His comments reveal pervasive discriminatory attitudes regarding immigrant workers. As previously noted, in certain instances employers unfamiliar with Mexicans and with limited numbers of blacks on their payrolls or no blacks at all tended to group Mexicans with white eth-

Table 8.   Locations of Blacks and Mexicans
within the Ford River Rouge Plant, 1928

Division	Black, %[a]	Mexican, %[b]
Foundry/Foundry machine shop	53.1	30.1
Rolling mills and blast furnaces	27.0	10.3
Steel stamping	11.7	21.0
Spring and upset machining	3.9	2.5
Chassis and parts manufacturing and assembly	0.7	4.6
Motor manufacturing and assembly	1.8	24.7
Tool rooms	1.8	n/a
Construction	0.0	6.8

SOURCE: Rouge Area Hourly Workers Employment Record Jackets, 1918–1933, Accession AR84-58-1050, Ford Motor Company Industrial Archives and Record Center, Redford, Michigan.
[a]Statistics based on a 5 percent sample of 8,400 blacks employed in July 1928.
[b]Statistics based on a 5 percent sample of 4,000 Mexicans employed in July 1928.

nics. During factory shutdowns this underlying nativist hostility surfaced and limited work to "deserving" Americans. Employers stopped making distinctions among Mexicans along color lines—all became foreigners and expendable. "When employment slackens," remarked a steel-mill employment manager, "the Mexicans are the first ones off. They are not Americans."[49]

The foremen expressed this racial prejudice and hostility in the decisions they made about hiring and firing and work assignments. Foremen set the tone for relations on the shop floor. The negative impressions that Mexicans had of the United States no doubt were often shaped by the high-handedness of the foremen, who assigned Mexicans to the heaviest work and did not hesitate to fire the men if they disobeyed orders. Plant superintendents had the final say on discharges, but shop foremen circumvented their authority through daily harassment, which provoked the workers to action. Moved from rough job to rough job, some Mexicans eventually quit or else were fired if they protested. Mexicans were cognizant of this racial animosity, and it shaped their new consciousness as industrial workers. Remnants of Mexican deference to the Anglo surfaced, as the men were careful to avert their eyes when looking toward and talking to foremen. They looked away not because they feared the foremen personally but because they were apprehensive about losing their jobs.[50] For simply petty reasons foremen could fire men or harass workers by transferring them to bad jobs. The despotic foreman personified the repressive nature of the system and became a focus of hostility. As in other industries, discrimination against Mexican autoworkers by foremen did not go unanswered, but the responses of Mexicans to maltreatment by these authority figures varied.[51]

In Detroit, the prejudice against Mexican autoworkers emphasized the job hierarchy, which with its proscribed divisions generated enormous resentment. Despite the nearly indistinguishable differences between jobs, variations in work categories and accompanying wage differentials exacerbated the racial and ethnic divisions among autoworkers. All the men expressed dissatisfaction with standardized machine production. But most whites were exempt from the harder tasks in the worst departments. Native-born white machinists, metal finishers, and toolmakers likely felt superior to the white ethnic immigrants and blacks who held lower positions. The immigrants and blacks in turn resented the native-born whites because they dominated the better-paying and less labor-intensive positions and enjoyed relatively good working conditions. The privilege of white skin in time allowed the immigrant workers some job mobility, whereas most blacks and Mexicans faced continued discrimination and limited opportunities.[52]

For some Mexicans, the loss of their dignity and the humiliation that accompanied poor work assignments or being passed over for promotion were too great a price to pay, and they left the factories. A Mexican who had recently left his job at an auto plant because he had been treated unfairly remarked bitterly to Paul Taylor: "I quit my job. I saw that they were giving me all the hardest and dirtiest jobs. I asked the boss about it and he said it was because I was the strongest. I know though that the real reason was because I am a Mexican."[53]

Animosity among white, black, and Mexican factory workers, which mounted over time in some shops and departments, flared into physical and, once in a while, fatal confrontations. In the late 1920s, racism in the Ford plants, fueled by the tense environment of the drive system, speed-up, and workforce reductions, took its toll on everyone. In March 1929, Ford machine hand Fernando Albaniz was fired from the Rouge plant for pulling a knife on a white co-worker, and two weeks later a Mexican was discharged for knifing a white autoworker in his department. Black autoworker James Harris was dismissed from the Rouge

Steel Stamping Division in April 1929 for stabbing and seriously injuring a white, as was black worker Charles Green in October of the same year after hitting a white co-worker on the head with a pipe.[54]

RESPONSES TO DISCIPLINE AND FOREMEN

Dealing with racial discrimination was easier for Mexican Ford autoworkers than contending with the fast production pace and intense regimen of work. Whereas an altercation with a co-worker could be taken care of at the plant (once the foreman made his rounds), in the factory parking lot, or at a neighborhood bar, Mexicans had little control over work conditions. These were the domain of the plant supervisors. The speed-ups tested both physical and mental endurance; nonetheless, Mexican Ford autoworkers resisted being transformed into "machine men." The men had learned ways to counter industrial slavery while passing through the foundries, steel mills, and other car plants of the Midwest.[55]

Between 1922 and 1929, speed-up in the auto industry increased output per man-hour by 63 percent, over twice the increased output in manufacturing as a whole (27 percent). The auto companies bolstered worker productivity as they continued their fierce competition for market dominance. To achieve maximum profits, carmakers combined speed-up with a shift from piecework to day-rate production. At the worker's expense, production was doubled and tripled to record levels. Ramón Huerta welded seventy cars per minute during speed-ups at Chrysler and was overwhelmed by the frenzied pace of the car shells coming down the line. The accelerated work pace was made doubly unbearable by the line foreman, who drove the men unmercifully in the crusade to attain production quotas and forced many to quit in frustration, including Huerta. "I had to jump into each car and then down again as they passed by me. Finally I jumped out of a car, turned off the gas on my welding torch, disconnected it, and told the foreman, 'Pay me off. I quit. . . . It's impossible.'" Several days later Huerta resignedly returned to the plant seeking his old job. Family obligations, loss of status, and the prospect of unemployment induced the Mexican autoworker to silently bear the quick tempo of the line and the haranguing of his line foreman as a trade-off for the $0.90-an-hour wage.[56]

As noted, the most intense period of speed-up at the Ford plants took place just before and after the 1920–1921 shutdown. Autoworkers unable to withstand the relentless speed-ups were immediately discharged, and new hires drawn from the enormous labor pool in Detroit quickly took their place. In 1925, as a direct result of speed-up the company produced 31,200 cars per week using the same machinery that had manufactured 25,000 automobiles per week five years earlier. In 1929, Ford produced two million automobiles, the third highest production record in its history, by sharply reducing its workforce, implementing a three-day workweek, and increasing speed-up through the stretchout, the practice of assigning more than one machine to a worker.[57]

Meanwhile, opportunities for work began declining in Detroit and nationwide. The need for jobs tested the dignity of workers who had to accept nearly any conditions of employment in the shrinking job market. On January 2, 1929, out-of-town Mexican beet workers, along with unemployed white coal miners, southern blacks, and other hopeful men, congregated outside the Rouge plant gates in expectation of a chance at the $7-a-day wage offered by the Ford Motor Company. Thousands of men had waited all night outside the plant or had arrived before dawn. A total of 32,000 men milled around the plant's front gates on that freezing winter day, and for the next two weeks hordes of men desperate for work made a daily pilgrimage to the Ford Rouge. For $7 a day they agreed to a reduced workweek, imminent layoff, and speed-up achieved through stretchout. At the Rouge, stretchout helped increase an autoworker's production by an astounding 47 percent. During this time of fierce speed-up Isidro Rivas operated two machines at the Rouge's Motor Assembly Division. Soaked in sweat, he hurriedly moved back and forth between the machines, so consumed by the relentless pace that there was no time to wipe the burning sweat flowing into his red-rimmed eyes.[58]

Hundreds of Rivas's countrymen were not as resolute. They quit. Good pay could not compensate for the rampant abuse at the Ford Rouge plant. Company records indicate the unwillingness or failure of a great number of Mexicans hired by Ford to strive, achieve, and be celebrated as members of the elite ranks of autoworkers. Of the Mexican autoworkers for whom information on their final status is available, over half quit their Ford jobs within six months. (The remainder were terminated as a result of layoffs or lost their jobs because of poor productivity or disciplinary problems; see Table 9.) Like numerous Ford autoworkers, Mexicans expressed their displeasure through chronic absenteeism, five-day and ten-day quits, or merely walking off the job. This resistance occasionally resulted in their not reporting to work yet remaining on the company's payroll. Moisés Cárdenas was discharged

Table 9.   Final Status of Mexican Autoworkers
at the Ford River Rouge Plant, 1918–1933

	Quit	Laid-Off	Discharged	Transferred	Granted Leave of Absence	Died	Total
Number	1,533	894	157	4	62	8	2,658
Percent	57.7	33.6	5.9	.2	2.3	.3	100

SOURCE: Rouge Area Hourly Workers Employment Record Jackets, 1918–1933, Accession AR-84-58-1050, Ford Motor Company Industrial Archives and Record Center, Redford, Michigan.
NOTE: Totals vary for Tables 6, 7, and 9 because of incomplete records.

in April 1923, when Ford Employment Office investigators discovered that for two months he had been punching in but never reported to work. Instead, Cárdenas had a friend punch him in while he stayed home working on his house. The dozens of departments (129 at the Rouge plant in 1929), the staggered work shifts, and the huge turnover of men each month made it impossible for Ford personnel managers to maintain proper records on the thousands of workers.[59] Apparently, the wizardry of Ford management was not as successful in organizing the company's record-keeping procedures as it was in organizing the workplace. Workers found weaknesses in the system and took advantage of them.

For the men who remained in the Ford shops, foremen were the immediate objects of retaliation against prejudice, an intense work pace, and the tyranny of managerial control. The idea that Mexican Ford autoworkers were passive and docile and that they cowered in the face of supervisory authority was contradicted by numerous discharges stemming from disciplinary problems. These incidents occurred when Mexicans could no longer bear the deliberate harassment by foremen, generally during peak production periods when the stress and tension of the workplace became unbearable. The incidents show that Mexicans were concerned with and expected respect and that they had a conception of proper treatment on the job.

Of the 157 Mexicans discharged by the Ford Motor Company for this reason, nearly half had confrontations with foremen, ranging from refusing work assignments that undermined their dignity or risked their safety to talking back and physical violence. In July 1920, Ford machine

hand Henry Ruiz was discharged by his foreman after refusing an order
to sweep the floors. Feeling humiliated by his assignment, Henry quit
rather than accept a discharge, telling the foreman that he was "too
good to sweep" and "would find a job elsewhere." In March 1925, machine operator Diego Linares quit rather than report to the dreaded
paint line as ordered by his foreman. Charged with poor productivity,
machine tender Juan Orozco was fired in July 1928. The indignant
autoworker responded by intentionally breaking the drill piece on his
machine and then angrily telling his foreman he quit. The patience of
some men wore thin. In November 1929 Ford worker Alfonso Guerra
was discharged because he got into a fist fight with his shop foreman.[60]

Insubordination was not limited to Ford's Mexican workers, men
whom prevailing social attitudes deemed complacent and submissive.
Blacks too refused to submit to the dictatorial power of the Ford shop
foremen at the expense of losing their jobs. Despite the rampant racism
of the 1920s, during this period black pride and militancy surfaced and
were heightened by a new sense of nationalist identity. The reawakening
greatly influenced black workers. Marcus Garvey appealed to thousands of the black rank and file. Ford employment records show that
the company had problems disciplining numerous black employees,
some of whom were followers of Garvey or members of local gangs.[61]

Blacks in Detroit were keenly aware of their identity and standing in
the racially hostile and segregated urban environment, and a segment of
this population did not hesitate to defend their dignity. During Fred
Davis's three months at the Ford Rouge foundry in 1928, the black
autoworker refused to work for three different foremen. He quit rather
than yield to authority. And in a last expression of righteous indignation
at autocratic Ford rule, he shouted to the plant superintendent, "Stick
the job up your ass," as he passed by him for the last time. In October
1929, black Ford autoworker Clarence Hill was fired for threatening to
punch his foreman in the jaw. Hill had grown tired of his foreman's
harassment and repeated instructions about how to do his work.[62]

The preceding cases are just a few of the documented instances of
resistance by Mexican and black Ford workers to the power wielded by
shop foremen. Given the racist atmosphere in the Ford plants, in addition to the tense work environment, one can only speculate on the number of cases that went unreported or that Mexicans and blacks resolved
outside the plant gates.

Ford also implemented repressive and petty methods to maintain
worker discipline. The most infamous of these was "Fordization of

the face," which meant complete obedience and silence. Humming, whistling, singing, talking, smiling, and sitting down at any time were viewed as forms of strictly forbidden insubordination. Even the brief lunchtime of the workers was governed by strict rules. Some men caught running to the lunchwagons or preparing for lunch before the whistle immediately received a dismissal slip.[63] In addition, spotters posted throughout the departments reported malingering, which was defined as "stealing time."

Company rules also prohibited smoking, chewing tobacco, and the consumption of alcoholic beverages in the plants. Several Mexican workers paid for their vices by being fired. In March 1923, Joe Galarza was caught smoking on the job and was immediately terminated. Woe to the men who arrived at work with liquor on their breath or tipsy after a night on the town! For many workers drinking became a way of dealing with the domination of machine work and the constraints placed on their freedom by the moral and social order of the factory. Alphonso Sáenz's four years at the Rouge plant did not prevent him from being let go in December 1927 after allegedly coming to work drunk. The Mexican was first viciously beaten by the gate watchman and then, dazed and bloodied, was dragged to the Employment Office for discharge.[64]

The quit rates of Mexican workers did not indicate incompetence; their ability to perform factory work had already been tested. Rather, they reflected an unwillingness to put up with the monotony and routine of machine production and with speed-up. Like many men, Mexican and black autoworkers resisted the fast-paced work by disrupting operations and causing slowdowns, leaving certain tasks undone, or damaging parts, while others simply soldiered—that is, loafed while pretending to work.[65] They defied shop foremen and often broke work rules. Unwilling to accept the insults to their manhood and pride for Ford's wages, these workers quit even though they faced the prospect of being out of work as jobs became harder to find at the end of the 1920s.

COPING WITH FLUCTUATIONS IN WORK AVAILABILITY

The specter of unemployment loomed constantly for American workers throughout the 1920s. Unemployment hovered at about 5 percent, but by the end of the decade it varied from 8 to as high as 13 to 15 percent. Low pay was also a problem; most of the real wage gains had taken place before 1923. The increase in wages of just 2 percent by decade's end did not allow workers to match the income they had enjoyed in 1919. Moreover, what factory workers earned lagged far behind the increases in output per man hour.[66] Periods of joblessness, a rising cost of living, and negligible pay increases created unsettling economic conditions for Mexicans in the Midwest. Yet even with unstable employment and low earnings, industrial work was better than agricultural work on Michigan beet farms and in the Texas cotton fields. A family of Mexican cotton pickers in the Lone Star State averaged below $300 for a season's work well into the 1930s. Continual migration from Texas to the Midwest throughout the 1920s was the response of many Mexicans to their dismal plight.[67]

In the Midwest Mexican workers responded to the unstable job market and inflation in a similar way: They moved about in search of steady work. A Mexican who worked in Gary and Illinois spoke for his compatriots: "As long as there is work in the steel mills, we stay; when work closes down we are away to any place we can hear of steady work. . . . Here, if one does not have work, one is lost." And a Mexican employed at a steel plant in the Chicago region expressed his sentiment about the cost of living: "You must think of your work and the money you earn every minute. . . . Here the little you have is soon spent if you do not work every day." [68]

Much has been made of the transiency of Mexican workers during this time. An erratic job market in the 1920s, however, has been largely overlooked as an explanation. In Milwaukee, Mexican factory workers reduced to a two- to three-day workweek left the city. Mexicans continued to come to Chicago despite waiting lists at local steel mills, assuming they could secure other kinds of work in the Windy City. Eighteen percent of the Mexicans in East Chicago at this time were without work because of a production slowdown at Inland Steel, the main local employer. Many of these men were seeking factory work for the first time, and their numbers were augmented by the continuous arrival of their countrymen, who apparently disregarded or were misinformed about the contracting job market.[69] The situation was similar for Mexicans in Detroit and southeast Michigan, where expansion and contraction of the auto industry was caused by seasonal model changes. Moreover, an upswing or downturn in car manufacturing had an impact on overall employment in the region.

By the mid-1920s the annual model changeovers in auto manufacturing caused periodic layoffs in Detroit. At this time machinery was retooled, new dies were put in place, the assembly line was reordered, and production rates and line speeds were revised. This model-changeover period brought partial workdays and three- or four-day work schedules, and culminated in layoffs lasting from three weeks to four months. Once production resumed, laid-off autoworkers were rehired along with men arbitrarily chosen from workers who congregated outside the plants. Autoworkers then put in ten- to twelve-hour days and sixty- to seventy-hour workweeks, and worked Sundays and holidays as well as on the graveyard shift. Many men welcomed this extra work as a chance to make up lost income and to cover the unemployment that inevitably lay ahead.[70]

Mexicans arriving in Detroit in the summer, during the model changes, had little luck getting work. The apprehension of these men and the accompanying hardships of joblessness were revealed by one Mexican who came to the Motor City in the summer of 1928: "[I have] to move from place to place, . . . never certain what is going to happen. This insecurity is hard on a person. I haven't found a job yet; . . . I am sleeping in a flop house with a fifteen cent bed."[71]

Partial workdays also caused uncertainties, leading men to quit their jobs, some after only a few days: "I worked several days, . . . eleven hours the first day, ten and a half the next, nine the next, and five the next. . . . When they began cutting my time down I quit. If they hadn't cut down the hours so much on us . . . I would have stuck it out for a month."[72]

As previously noted, laid-off Mexican autoworkers in Detroit who had problems securing factory work were resourceful in finding alternative types of employment. Searching for work was nerve-racking but the high cost of living demanded a constant income, as did the necessity of sending money home to support families that had grown dependent on such remittances for subsistence. Any type of employment became acceptable in the quest for a steady income and to avoid idleness.[73]

One means of gaining entrance into the factories was buying and selling jobs, an illicit practice widespread at this time though showing the range of survival strategies Mexican workers developed. In South Chicago, Mexican steelworkers sold jobs or else lent their work numbers and badges to fellow countrymen when they made short trips to Mexico or went looking for work. Mexicans in Gary left their jobs at the mills but kept their badges and returned to work just long enough to remain on the payroll. In the interim, badges were used to gain credit at local stores. This tactic was advantageous; despite a bout of joblessness workers could feed and clothe themselves. And when creditors came after workers for nonpayment of bills, they could only garnishee from the small amount of pay earned. In Port Huron, Michigan, Mexicans had to "buy" their work in the local foundries from enterprising Mexican job brokers and continue paying a fee to keep the positions. Mexican railroad workers outside Fort Madison, Iowa, used several aliases and collected pay under all the names.[74]

In Detroit, buying and selling work badges became a way for some Mexicans to offset factory layoffs or supplement incomes. The prices varied; according to the peaks and lulls of the hiring periods, a Ford job on the black market averaged from $10 to $35. Men acquired Ford badges by applying for work several times, using a different name when they filed each application. They knew the risks involved. Ford Motor Company officials were alert to this practice, and when its investigators discovered the men involved, they were immediately fired. In 1928, Ford machine hand Frank López was dismissed for selling jobs to Mexicans, and in the same year machine hand Miguel Luna was let go after the Ford Employment Office discovered that he had paid $25 for his job.[75]

Perhaps because they were new to the Motor City and unfamiliar with the methods by which jobs were obtained, men went to the notorious private employment agencies. Dozens of Mexicans milled around the employment offices in downtown Detroit waiting for job orders from car plants and metal foundries. The men were unaware that the shady job agencies provided work for short periods and that a good portion of their paychecks would eventually go for unreasonable commissions. The greenhorns from the beet fields were easily taken in by the Spanish-speaking Syrians and Jews who ran many of the employment agencies.[76] However, most Mexicans knew better, for in their sojourns they had encountered these agencies and were aware that they worked together with local employers to cheat the men. A Mexican in Detroit remarked that this problem was especially widespread in the city: "Most of the employment agencies are nothing but 'frame-ups.' They are in *combinación* [collusion] with the employers who agree to take so many men on in order to collect a fee for securing employment and then lay them off in a day or two. . . . Nowhere else that I have been or heard of have there been so many men taken on for just a day or two and then laid off."[77]

As the men became more desperate for work, so did their means of obtaining jobs. Contacting family members and friends about job prospects, which had earlier proved fruitful, progressively became less useful with the growth of company employment departments and a shrinking job market. Mutual-aid and fraternal organizations were without the resources to assist the hundreds of Mexicans without work during lay-offs. Formal letters of recommendation from the Mexican consul no longer helped to gain entrance into the car plants.[78] In their attempts to get into the car plants Mexicans also did not hesitate to misrepresent their qualifications when filling out job applications. As previously mentioned, they asked friends which jobs needed to be filled and then at the plant gates stated that they had experience in that type of work. At some factories citizenship requirements and the necessity of having naturalization papers became barriers to employment. However, the more determined Mexicans continued to apply for work. Men misstated their citizenship, claiming to be Puerto Rican, Filipino, or Mexican American. The Ford Motor Company did not require proof of U.S. citizenship; plant officials realized that the men would lie to gain auto work.[79]

Mexicans who reached Detroit in 1927 faced serious hardships because of the recession that year. The automobile industry began slowing down in November 1926 and halted the next year, when Ford Motors shut down production for retooling of the Model A. The nine-month auto recession caused Detroit's relief expenditures to climb to $2.5 million. About 6,600 families received relief, and dozens received referrals to the Motor City's community fund.[80]

The recession of 1927 coincided with the influx into Detroit of out-of-work Mexicans in search of jobs, and they were joined by Mexicans who had fled west-central Mexico because of the Cristero Revolution. Families whose breadwinners still had jobs took in unemployed men and their families for two to three months. Women who had lost their husbands to illness or accidents were provided for by kin, were befriended by caring Mexicans in the colony, or supported themselves as best they could, ironing and washing clothes, for example, before seeking help from relief agencies. Their children supplemented the family income by selling newspapers and finding other kinds of jobs. The dire economic conditions forced untold numbers of Mexican families back to the beet fields or to leave Detroit to try their luck elsewhere. The hard times unified the city's Mexicans, who two years later met once more with economic calamity—the Great Depression.[81]

THE HAZARDS OF AUTO WORK

The Mexicans seeking industrial jobs in the Midwest had work-related hazards and accidents awaiting them for which, with the exception of

Mexican workers in Illinois, they would receive no compensation. Injuries incurred on the job severely compromised a worker's ability to obtain future employment. And in the event of a worker's death, his survivors usually were deprived of death benefits. Track laborers mashed their hands and feet or were hit by flying spikes as a result of misdirected blows of hammers. Continually picking up and laying rails or railroad ties caused wrenched backs and hernias. Heatstroke and frostbite were additional dangers. Tannery workers breathed air polluted with dust and processing chemicals, and the treatment process required men to be "constantly bathed in water, . . . resulting in serious injury to their kidneys." [82] Steelworkers encountered poisonous fumes, and the heat from molten iron caused dizziness and hampered their vision. A slip-up while pouring the hot liquid metal into a mold or splattering molten metal could result in severe burns. The feet and legs of autoworkers on the foundry shakeout line were injured by the hot sand falling through the screens. Mexicans in core-dipping jobs complained that their feet stayed damp from the pools of water that collected, and men whose jobs required standing for long periods of time on cement plant floors developed varicose veins. [83]

A major obstacle to compensation was language, but unscrupulous employers, unfair worker-compensation laws, and the cost of legal aid added to the difficulties. In one year Detroit lawyer Charles Benjamin (a Panamanian) helped the Mexican consul with over 400 cases involving work-related accidents. More accidents than these occurred. Injuries on the job went unreported because men feared losing their employment, or else minuscule settlements were received because the workers could not speak English. Benjamin observed that local employers cheated Mexicans out of reparations on every possible occasion. Track laborers injured on interstate rail lines had substantial trouble receiving settlements because there was no coverage under Michigan's Compensation Act. Moreover, such cases were expensive and protracted when taken to federal court for adjudication. Problems also arose when a Mexican worker died and had no known heirs. Often the worker's records were inaccurate; names and places in Mexico listed in Spanish were often misspelled, and Mexicans frequently did not know precisely where they lived in Mexico. [84]

The drive system intensified the pace of machine production and increased on-the-job casualties among autoworkers. Sometimes injured autoworkers received compensation but faced dismissal by their employers, whose sole concern was increasing output. Missing eyes, fingers, or limbs, these men maimed at work had limited job prospects. For instance, Mexican Ford autoworker Abel Morales lost his right eye in an accident in the Rouge foundry in June 1926. He was rehired on light work in October of the same year but was laid off three weeks later because his impaired vision prevented him from adequately accomplishing his job.[85] Men who lost an arm or a leg through plant accidents pleaded out of desperation for the opportunity to work. The right leg of black Ford autoworker Sterling C. Jones had been amputated below the knee because of a work accident. He tried to convince Employment Office personnel that he could remain standing for eight hours in a futile attempt to regain his job as a drill-press operator. Men stoically ignored their work-related injuries and illnesses during difficult economic times. Indeed, Ford workers went to the plants with arms and feet badly bruised and sore from injuries, infected wounds, arthritis, rheumatism, bronchitis, and pneumonia.[86]

Injuries sustained in work-related accidents now and then led jobless workers to commit crimes. In 1928, a Detroit probation officer reported that a Mexican was arrested for allegedly stealing clothes. The suspect claimed he was destitute because of work injuries and needed to steal because he could not obtain employment. The toes on one foot had been crushed by a falling rail, and the man's other foot had been injured in a foundry accident when molten iron was poured onto his shoe. Unable to support his sick wife or pay the overdue rent on his apartment, the impoverished Mexican had turned to petty thievery.[87]

SUMMARY

The Mexicans hired by the auto industry came from throughout the Midwest, where they worked for railroads, foundries, steel plants, and in auto and auto-parts factories. The majority were already in southeastern Michigan when they applied for auto jobs, having initially entered the Midwest as beet workers. The car companies each determined the number of Mexicans it would hire. Following unwritten guidelines in place throughout the Midwest, various plant managers used citizenship requirements to exclude Mexicans, while certain companies hired Mexicans in place of blacks for undesirable work. The individual preferences of Mexicans also figured in their distribution within the auto industry.

In the Ford plants of Detroit, the standardization of machine production meant that Mexicans worked in nearly every unskilled and semiskilled job category. Previous experience was generally not considered a requisite. A job applicant recently arrived from the beet fields could end up as a machine tender, assembly-line worker, or core maker as easily as a laid-off machine operator from a local car plant. Few held skilled jobs however.

Working conditions for Mexican Ford workers varied according to their department assignment. The nearly half who held semiskilled machine-production jobs were closely supervised in their routinized tasks by foremen. Conditions in these departments at times became quite volatile, especially during speed-ups, leading to confrontations between Mexicans and the shop foremen and co-workers. The pressure to maintain production under strict supervision, the accompanying speed-up, and an undercurrent of racism led autoworkers to resist, and hundreds quit. In addition, men were discharged for failing to keep up with production, not completing work properly, or disobeying foremen.

Despite repressive working conditions, irregular employment, and numerous work hazards in the Ford plants, Mexicans achieved a modicum of success as autoworkers. They symbolized the adjustment of Mexicans to an important northern industrial work sector during the 1920s. Their efficiency on the job was noted in 1928 by a Ford employment manager at the Rouge plant. He expressed overall satisfaction with the swarthy men from Mexico, adding that 8 were assistant foremen, 300 had been with the company since 1918, and about 75 percent of those hired in that year still worked for the company.[88] The seasonal layoffs and erratic work schedules plagued Mexicans at Ford, as they did all of Detroit's autoworkers, and eroded the heralded Ford wages. Yet Mexicans accepted these conditions, for many had defined success in their own terms and reasoned that whatever hardships they endured were worth it in order to be elite industrial workers.

FOUR

Life in the Mexican Colonies of the Midwest

By 1929, on the eve of the Great Depression, 15,000 Mexicans lived in Detroit. The colony residents were mainly autoworkers and their families, though the sprinkling of Mexicans with professional and technical backgrounds had middle-class standing. The Mexicans were not a significant portion of the Motor City's ethnic population. Yet they constituted the second biggest urban settlement of Mexicans in the Midwest. Detroit's auto-manufacturing industry persisted in directly shaping their patterns of residence, and the immigrants were burdened by costly rents, overcrowding, and oftentimes unhealthy living conditions in working-class neighborhoods. A few Mexicans met with housing discrimination, which was a by-product of the widespread racism of the 1920s.

Mexican women began arriving in the Motor City during this decade. Some had accompanied husbands, brothers, and fathers in their peregrinations to Michigan's sugar-beet farms. The more adventurous women journeyed north together, drawn by the employment opportunities and the excitement of big-city life. More and more women came north as men sent for wives, fiancées, and families or returned to Texas or Mexico to bring their kin to Detroit. A number of these women obtained employment to offset living costs.[1]

Mexicans quickly established a colony in Detroit. To meet the spiritual needs of Detroit's mostly Catholic Mexicans, Our Lady of Guadalupe Church opened in 1923, though it had been organized three years earlier. It was the first Mexican Catholic parish in the northern region, the culmination of a fund-raising campaign launched by colony members with the help of Catholic societies. Community-minded Mexicans formed mutual-aid societies and fraternal organizations, which offered assistance and promoted social and cultural activities; their leaders attempted to retain interest in the affairs of the home country. Mexicans with an entrepreneurial inclination opened businesses. Most of the barbershops, billiard parlors, restaurants, and other establishments were small, short-term ventures because of the fluctuating, automobile-based economy of Detroit.

Having come north for economic betterment, Motor City Mexicans retained the goal of improving their living standards and that of their relatives still in the homeland. Also important now was fulfilling the desires fashioned by a consumer society and its corollary mass culture. This culture was the bedrock of the new social order Henry Ford had ushered in with mass production. Mexicans began internalizing the values of Detroit's automobile-centered culture, which had revolutionized American economy, society, and customs. They sought social standing, which was determined not only by the jobs they held, the wages they earned, and the company they worked for, but by accumulating consumer goods readily available through credit and installment buying. Although these purchases were primarily small, owning an automobile was also an objective within reach of many Mexicans through cash purchases or monthly payments. These autoworkers derived meaning and purpose from their work in the car factories, but their wages also allowed them to attain material desires and to have a life apart from the auto plants.[2]

SETTLEMENT PATTERNS AND LIVING CONDITIONS

The continued expansion of Detroit's borders was driven by the tremendous growth of its industrial base. This expansion influenced the fluidity of the Motor City's growing population and consequent housing needs. Like other blue-collar Detroiters, Mexicans sought affordable shelter in rooming houses, apartments, and multifamily dwellings close to the factories. In 1925, Mexicans still settled on the east side of Detroit, and small numbers lived in Highland Park and in Hamtramck to be near the area auto plants and metal-parts factories. However, many Mexicans had established households along streets west of Woodward Avenue. (See Map 4.) Several miles further to the west was the Ford River Rouge plant.[3]

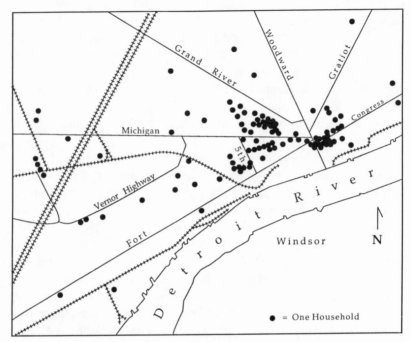

Map 4.   Mexican Settlements in Detroit, 1925
Source: *R. L. Polk's Detroit City Directory* (Detroit: R. L. Polk Company, 1925).

Mexicans moved frequently in an attempt to improve their lodging arrangements. This intracity movement, as many as twelve times in a one- to two-year period, was characteristic of Motor City workers generally, and, moreover, it was the norm for American cities. Adding to the Mexican transiency rate were the sugar-beet workers who flocked to Detroit each fall in search of jobs or when a bad season cut short their time in the fields. The peripatetic sugar-beet workers, noted Department of Labor field researcher Edson, "tended to inflate and deflate the population of Mexicans in Detroit."[4]

By 1929, most of Detroit's Mexicans lived on the southwest side. (See Map 5.) There they shared streets with Hungarians, Poles, Romanians, and Armenians, and contributed to the distinct ethnic character and high density of the city's working-class districts. Because of its diverse population, West Michigan Avenue was popularly known as "International Avenue." A number of Mexican workers from the Ford Rouge plant and Great Lakes Steel also began settling beyond Detroit's city limits, in the neighboring blue-collar communities of Springwells, Oak-

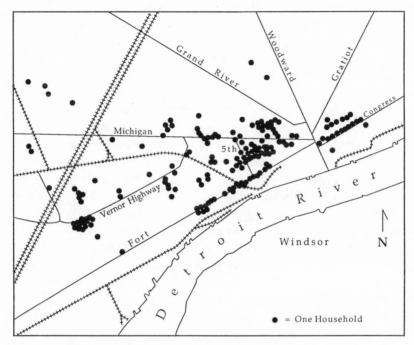

Map 5.   Mexican Settlements in Detroit, 1929
SOURCE: *R. L. Polk's Detroit City Directory* (Detroit: R. L. Polk Company, 1929).

wood, River Rouge, Dearborn, Lincoln Park, Ecorse, and Wyandotte. In addition, groups of Mexicans could be found living in crowded rooming houses and hotels as well as flophouses near downtown Detroit in the area between Michigan and East Grand River Avenues. These individuals may have been recent arrivals who worked downtown, men just hired by the factories, or those unlucky men thrown out of work.[5]

Most Mexicans in the Motor City did not purchase homes. The main reasons were their short time in the city; an unstable job market, which made a steady income impossible; and the prohibitive cost of real estate. Similar factors limited homeownership by Mexicans elsewhere in the urban Midwest throughout the 1920s.[6] By local standards homeownership by Mexican Detroiters was minimal, but it exceeded that for Mexicans in the North. In 1928, about 100 to 200 Mexican families in the Motor City owned homes. However, the shaky economy made their homeowner status quite precarious, and many forfeited their property because canny real estate agents routinely misled the immigrants about

the actual costs involved. Two- or three-month layoffs drastically reduced incomes and depleted savings, making it difficult for breadwinners to make mortgage payments, and inevitably they lost their homes.
Those able to buy houses often resorted to renting out rooms because
maintaining a family and meeting additional financial obligations did
not allow them to keep up with the mortgage debt they had incurred.[7]

The new Mexican arrivals in the northern cities crowded into the
working-class neighborhoods and were victimized by greedy landlords,
who profited from these crammed living conditions. Because of the
shortage of housing as well as the workers' need to save money, some
dwellings were packed with as many as three dozen people. Also, Mexican boarders often took in relatives recently arrived in the cities. These
conditions bred disease and crime. The 1925 city survey of housing for
Chicago Mexicans described the extraordinarily high density of occupants per household. Twenty-eight percent of the homes averaged four
or more individuals per bedroom, and 40 percent had lodgers. Mexicans in Gary's crowded South Side inhabited run-down tenements and
multistory dwellings, damp and poorly lit basement apartments, and
alley houses. The absence of building codes resulted in poorly constructed houses and apartments in this working-class zone populated by
Mexicans, eastern Europeans, and blacks. It also had many health problems and elevated crime rates.[8]

Nowhere in the Midwest or the Southwest was crowding more severe
for Mexicans than in Indiana Harbor. In 1930, the 4,500 to 5,000 Mexicans living in this tough mill town were concentrated in less than a
square mile close to the Inland Steel plant—the densest population of
Mexicans in the United States. They paid excessive rents for inferior
dwellings that they shared with Hungarians, Italians, and blacks under
less than friendly circumstances. Overcrowded, run-down row housing
was similarly the norm for Detroit's Mexicans at this time of Mexican
colony formation in the Midwest.[9]

Many Mexican families took in boarders and converted their homes
into *casas de asistencia* (boardinghouses), a popular form of lodging for
Mexican males. Partly because of the desire to be with their own countrymen, Mexicans made up the largest proportion of lodgers of all nationalities in the Midwest. Proprietors occasionally named the *casas de
asistencia* after their place of origin in Mexico, thus expressing regional
loyalty as well as offering cultural havens for sojourners from these
areas. The *casas de asistencia* served as centers for social life in many of
the Mexican colonies, and their significance was not missed by employ-

ers interested in keeping turnover among these workers to a minimum.[10] In Detroit, mortgage payments took up 25 percent of an autoworker's income by 1930. Therefore it was necessary for the city's working-class homeowners to take in boarders, sometimes up to six men. As a Mexican Ford autoworker knowingly observed: "If a family is to live decently it is . . . necessary to keep boarders. . . . Otherwise the working man cannot make ends meet."[11]

In addition to having to live where the weather was cloudy and gloomy most of the year, with snow and ice in the winter, exposure to disease was a sacrifice Mexicans made for the good money they were able to earn in the North. Unhealthy living conditions and improper nutrition coupled with cold weather produced a high incidence of tuberculosis, measles, and rickets. "The health of the Mexicans seems to be worse up here," stated a Gary social worker who had worked with these immigrants in both the Southwest and the North. "They have more money but less air and fresh vegetables and are more crowded."[12] In windy Chicago, Mexicans had a morbidity rate from tuberculosis eight times greater than that of the general population (but not as high as the occurrence for blacks). Mexican children suffered from rickets because of a lack of fresh fruits and vegetables, which were particularly rare during the winter. The disease was aggravated by the inclement weather and the scarcity of open areas in the city. Also, urban children spent their time primarily indoors, and when they were outdoors it was usually in dark courtyards and alleys. Mexicans in Gary were likewise afflicted with tuberculosis and other respiratory diseases as a result of crowding and workplaces polluted with dust, smoke, and coal gases. Rickets was a serious health problem in this city.[13] Tuberculosis, influenza, and pneumonia plagued the Mexicans of Detroit. Prolonged illness or injuries led to loss of employment, impoverishment, and dependence on family and friends or as a last-resort reliance on private charities and public assistance.[14]

DISCRIMINATION

Residential discrimination in the northern urban centers varied in kind and degree from that which Mexicans experienced in the Southwest. Mexicans moving into midwestern working-class settlements were assaulted and had their property destroyed but not as frequently as in Texas, where law and custom confined most urban Mexicans to segregated sections called Mexican Towns or Sonora Towns. As recent arrivals in the northern cities, Mexicans raised the same suspicions in these blue-collar neighborhoods as the southern and eastern European immigrants had when they first arrived. Residents invested in working-class mobility feared that their property, gained through years of hard work, would decrease in value when Mexican families moved in. These residents already saw their neighborhoods as being under siege by the growing number of blacks. In the Chicago area, resentment still lingered against Mexicans for their role as scabs during the 1919 steel strike. This anger generated fights between European ethnic groups and Mexicans because past strikes had involved entire neighborhoods and had forged feelings of solidarity. Overcrowding and housing shortages pitted these groups of workers against one another and added to the interethnic and racial conflict.[15]

Another source of hostility was the controversy surrounding Mexican immigration to the United States, much of which was illegal. The population of Mexicans in the United States was growing at a time when immigration from Europe had been halted. Less integrated than Europeans into American society, Mexicans rarely became naturalized citizens; most were reluctant to relinquish their ties to Mexico for rights and privileges American citizenship did not guarantee and this reluctance compounded their predicament. Edson noted that the white ethnics "loudly condemned the Mexicans." Often only a generation removed from Europe and having been subjected to the propaganda of Americanization yet insecure as to their own status as Americans, the white ethnics believed they were superior to Mexicans. In turn white ethnics' arrogance and presumptuousness annoyed and angered the proud Mexicans, who declared themselves the true Americans and pointed to their birth on the North American continent as proof.[16]

However, some Mexicans who were aware of the way in which factory work was divided along racial and ethnic lines claimed that the European ethnics were their equals because together they occupied the lowest rung on the industrial job ladder. A Detroit Mexican autoworker's exchange with a contentious white ethnic co-worker revealed this sentiment:

> The other day, one of these tramps approached me and asked me what nationality I was. I told him that I was a Mexican. He then remarked: 'So you are one of those who are in this country reaping benefits without paying for them are you?" This sort of got my goat and I answered—"You think you own this country don't you? Well, you are mistaken. You came over from Europe thinking that you would get rich and now look at yourself."[17]

1. Detroit riverfront, 1927. Courtesy of the Burton Historical Collection of the Detroit Public Library. The world's largest manufacturer of automobiles and the nation's fastest-growing metropolitan area, "dynamic Detroit" became a favorite destination for Mexicans venturing north.

2. Ford River Rouge Plant, 1939. Courtesy of Henry Ford Museum and Greenfield Village, Dearborn, Michigan. Containing some ninety-three buildings and twenty-seven miles of conveyors, "the Rouge" was the world's premier self-contained industrial complex—"a microcosm of the industrial age."

3. Henry Ford and Mexican Ford employees, 1919. Courtesy of Henry Ford Museum and Greenfield Village. Henry Ford was the most sought-after employer among Mexicans coming north because he offered steady work and good wages (although not as good as they were reputed to be.)

4.   Open Hearth Building, River Rouge Plant, 1934. Courtesy of Henry Ford
Museum and Greenfield Village. "The [Mexicans] showed great endurance at
work . . . sometimes working continuously without a day off in a year in
metal foundaries where others would not stay a month."—George T. Edson

5. V-8 cylinder block casting shakeout assembly line, 1935. Courtesy of
Henry Ford Museum and Greenfield Village. Workers on the foundry
shakeout line were frequently injured by hot sands falling through the screens.

6. Ford Model A Tudor sedans on the assembly line, 1928. Courtesy of
Henry Ford Museum and Greenfield Village. Mexican autoworkers easily
mastered their jobs and devised strategies to alleviate or circumvent the more
stressful or stultifying features of mass-production work.

7. *Mutualistas* with women of the Cruz Azul, Detroit, 1925. Courtesy of
Michigan State University. Mexican autoworkers and their wives formed
several mutual-aid societies, fraternal organizations, and women's auxiliaries
in Detroit.

8. Our Lady of Guadalupe Church, Detroit, c. 1928. Courtesy of the Burton Historical Collection of the Detroit Public Libary. This was the first Mexican Catholic parish in the region.

9. Orquesta Juvenil of La Liga Filarmonica Mexicana, Detroit, early 1930s. Courtesy of Michigan State University. Factory workers or their children often entertained at Mexican national celebrations, where their talents were sources of pride and identity.

10.   José Alfaro and "Chiquita," 1920. Courtesy of Michigan State University. Ford autoworkers and their partners won many tango contests staged by the Mexican community in Detroit.

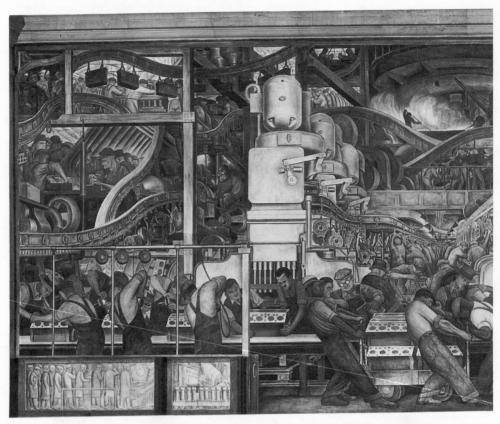

11. Diego Rivera, "Production and Manufacture of the 1932 Ford V-8 Motor at the Rouge," North Wall/Automotive Panel of "Detroit Industry" mural, Detroit Institute of Arts, 1931–32. Courtesy of the Detroit Institute of Arts. Many unemployed Mexican autoworkers went to the Detroit Institute of Arts to watch Rivera paint his murals.

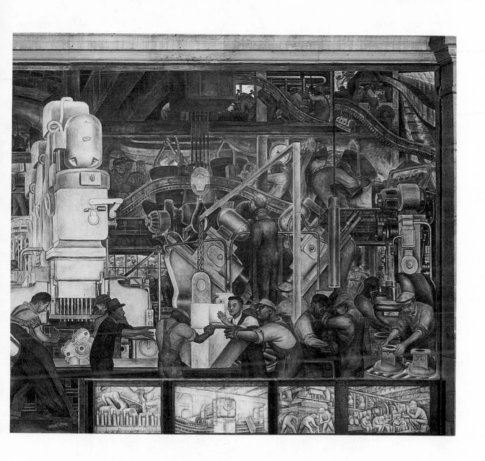

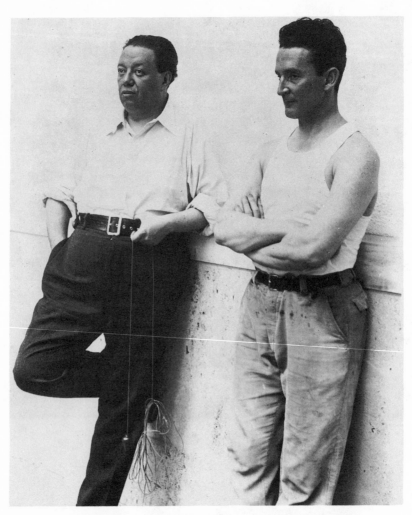

12. Diego Rivera and his chief assistant, Clifford Wight, Detroit, 1932. Courtesy of the Detroit Institute of Arts. Rivera's participation in the repatriation program was motivated by progressive, idealistic hopes for the Mexican working class.

Racial discrimination was a greater and more formidable obstacle for midwestern Mexicans than was occasional interethnic friction. The large black population had set the pattern for this northern brand of racism. Dark skins and Indian features made some Mexicans visible in the race-conscious North. In some northern cities Mexicans were reputed to be a bad element. They allegedly were prone to fighting among themselves and to stealing, and were accused of being sly, treacherous, and wily. Because they were thus equated with blacks, they became subject to residential segregation. As a result, just as Mexicans lied about their racial and ethnic background to secure work, some out of necessity denied their nationality to obtain housing.[18]

Discrimination against Mexicans was evident wherever they lived in the Midwest. In the cities of Waukegan and Aurora, Illinois, prejudiced landlords refused to rent to the large number of Mexican families, and a few local barbershops and theaters denied the newcomers service. Because Mexicans were East Chicago's largest ethnic group and there was a sizable black population, fear of an invasion by these dark races surfaced in the white community. The growing numbers of Mexicans in East Chicago prompted a quarter (24 percent) of the white workers to move outside the city, a 1920s version of "white flight," which would accelerate in the post-World War II years. Not considered white, Mexicans attending East Chicago's two movie theaters were seated with blacks, as were their compatriots in South Chicago at the Commercial Theater. Relations between Mexicans and East Chicago's police were also strained because of racial discord. In Gary, Indiana, whites held the same contemptuous attitudes toward Mexicans as they did toward blacks. Many Mexicans in the Steel City had problems renting apartments, and those purchasing homes outside working-class neighborhoods were sold overpriced and substandard property, a deliberate attempt to shut Mexicans out of white housing areas. Nor could Mexicans attend Gary's movie theaters. Until 1925, Mexican steelworkers traveled to Chicago for entertainment. This discrimination extended to the cemeteries, where a special section had been designated as the final resting place for Mexicans.[19]

Mexicans in Detroit might have encountered less racial discrimination than did their countrymen in East Chicago and Gary because they were a small fraction of this giant city's population. Nevertheless, Detroit's rampant racism reflected the low ebb of race relations nationwide. Racism, directed largely at blacks, undercut Mexican expectations, which had been raised by job opportunities in Detroit car factories. A color line had gone up restricting blacks to an east-side ghetto, and white neighborhood "improvement associations" hampered the efforts of blacks brave enough to purchase homes outside their enclave. In 1925, a small race riot erupted in Detroit when the black physician Ossian Sweet and his family tried to move into a white neighborhood. The Motor City had its share of "whites-only" movie houses, and most theaters restricted blacks to balcony seating. Blacks were barred as well from dance halls; however, certain establishments like the Greystone Ballroom set aside special days exclusively for this minority group. Detroit's police maltreated blacks; the rate of black convictions for such crimes as burglary, disturbing the peace, and prohibition infractions significantly exceeded that of whites, and they were given stiffer penalties.[20]

Within this context incidences of racial discrimination against many Mexicans did occur. In order to rent rooms and apartments they usually had to claim Spanish, Italian, or American Indian origins. Language differences compounded the problem. Poor command of the English language resulted in high rents for housing of inferior quality and led to continuing antagonism. Certain barbershops, restaurants, and bars denied Mexicans service. Dark-complected Mexicans had more problems than light-skinned Mexicans in Detroit; for example, those who tried to attend dances at the Greystone Ballroom were mistaken for blacks and were turned away.[21]

Discrimination against Mexicans in the northern urban centers was the result of the larger society's racist conceptions and the nativism that fed the drive to restrict Mexican immigration. Mexicans, always sensitive to the slightest criticism of their national origin, remained cognizant of ostracism along racial lines. Some were made aware of this racism by blacks whom they worked and lived with. In Iowa's railroad camps, for example, blacks urged their Mexican co-workers to fraternize with them and not with the white workers, "insinuating that they [were] two races of color separate from the 'white folks.'" Though friendly with blacks, Mexicans tended to keep their distance for fear of being further stigmatized. Many Mexicans, however, developed racist attitudes toward blacks. And black workers resented Mexicans, who were crowding into unskilled jobs and reducing already limited opportunities.[22] Northern racism thus was a central obstacle to full acceptance of Mexicans. Nevertheless, the midwestern working-class Mexicans advanced more than their countrymen in the Southwest, where color distinctions relegated them to a racially segmented labor market and to segregated housing.

Interactions between Mexicans and European immigrant groups, despite their differences, were relatively friendly. Occasionally Mexicans received sympathy and support from white ethnics who had not forgotten that they had suffered similar prejudice only recently. Like the Mexicans, these people had sold all their possessions to come to the United States and had endured countless hardships in their newly adopted homeland. As time passed, some white ethnic groups admitted the Mexicans into their neighborhoods, and even intermarriages gradually became acceptable. The intermingling that was taking place in the factories thus had its corollary in some of the working-class neighborhoods, where new relationships, though limited, expanded the social world of residents from different backgrounds. Cordial relations were enjoyed among Mexicans, Spaniards, Portuguese, and Latin Americans because all shared certain cultural interests.[23] Because of the need to assimilate the large ethnic populations in the urban Midwest, employers, city officials, and society placed pressure on Mexicans to cast themselves into the melting pot, as they had during the Americanization drives of the World War I years.[24]

MEXICAN WOMEN IN THE LABOR FORCE

Mexican women's work experiences show the inevitable changes they were undergoing as a result of socialization into an American urban context. Though their entrance into the northern urban workforce was limited, Mexican women helped attain acceptable living standards by supplementing family income and taking some of the burden off primary breadwinners. The high cost of living in the cities of the North required that they work. Hundreds of Mexican women as a result became wage earners but in a manner that took into account patriarchal concerns. Mexican women earned money by cooking and taking in laundry, working as domestics, and obtaining factory jobs. Work may have been viewed by married women as a stopgap measure, a familial obligation. However, young single women often ventured outside the home to seek employment. Like their male counterparts, the Mexican immigrant women of the North came from all classes and backgrounds; some had formal educations, while others had previous experience in wage work. These women had cooked for dozens of men in the railroad camps and worked long hours in garment factories, and a few had been teachers. However, low wages, few skill requirements, and the absence of job mobility and security typified the world of work for Mexican women. Women who were heads of households as a result of the death of their spouses, separation, or abandonment probably suffered most from the limitations of this unstable and low-wage work.[25]

Sometimes the wives of Detroit's Mexican autoworkers supplemented the family income by running *casas de asistencia*. Usually their daughters helped with this endeavor. Some girls dropped out of school so they could work full-time washing, cooking, and making lunches for the boarders. Widows and women abandoned by their husbands also supported themselves and their families this way, though relatives, friends, and countrymen probably took in these impoverished women, who became extended members of the family. In 1928, Mrs. Joseph Pino augmented her husband's autoworker income by renting furnished rooms and cooking meals for her tenants at their house on East Columbia Avenue. From 1926 to 1929, Detroiter Jennie Godina rented furnished rooms and offered board to workers at a house on East Congress Street, where she lived with her two brothers, who worked in the car plants. The widow Mrs. Gonzáles supported herself and three children by operating a boardinghouse after her husband died from tuberculosis in 1927.[26]

Operating a *casa de asistencia* was hard work for Detroit's Mexican women, often as exhausting as the labor the men performed in the factories. In addition to family duties like child rearing, the women likely kept up a hectic pace all day as they fed the men coming and going on the different shifts. They had to reorder cooking schedules, as some men wanted breakfast at dinnertime while others wanted their dinner in the morning. Long hours were spent not only cooking and shopping for food but doing laundry and performing additional housekeeping tasks. More important, the women probably had to sacrifice privacy, put up with overcrowding, and endure occasional drinking and quarreling by their male boarders.[27]

A number of Detroit's Mexican women met the financial needs of their families by working outside the home in a variety of jobs ranging from domestic work to factory labor. This situation reflected national patterns of employment of Mexican women entering the workforce at this time and work trends of women wageworkers in Michigan. Investigators in the 1920s reported finding Mexican women throughout the Southwest employed in cigar factories, cotton mills, and the garment industry. Deskilling in cigar making opened up job opportunities for women, while manufacturers such as those in the garment industry were shifting their operations to the South and Southwest to take advantage of the cheap and nonunionized labor markets.[28] Based on a 1926 statewide survey, women in Michigan of all nationalities and races worked in three fields of employment: domestic and personal services, manufacturing and mechanical industries, and clerical and sales occupations. Class background, marital status, and family composition also determined the kinds of jobs Mexican women obtained in Detroit.[29]

Over a third of the Mexican women working in Detroit during the 1920s held jobs in domestic and personal services. They worked as boarding and lodging housekeepers, janitors, and laundry workers, and as cleaning ladies in hotels, office buildings, and private homes. (See Table 10.) Laundry work was a low-status job and involved heavy work such as shaking out freshly washed items from the wringers. Others got jobs as dishwashers, waitresses, and cooks in area restaurants and lunchrooms. (The women in food service usually were responsible for buying and maintaining their uniforms.) Mexican women also worked as elevator operators, store cashiers, and office messengers. The dressmakers and seamstresses often worked out of their homes, but others found jobs in small neighborhood shops or were hired in the alteration units of major department stores like J. L. Hudson's. The majority probably worked seasonally. The homeworkers may have performed low-skill tasks such as assembling and finishing, but they had flexibility in finding time for childcare and domestic responsibilities.[30] A few women were skilled needle workers like Manuela Alvarez, the wife of Ford autoworker Mariano Alvarez. Fluent in French and Spanish, Manuela, like hundreds of Mexican women, had learned lace making in Mexico while enrolled in a Catholic academy. Before moving to Detroit, Manuela first supported herself and her ailing father in Saginaw by washing floors but soon obtained a job sewing theater curtains at a local factory. In addition, a few Mexican women worked as cigar makers, as hairdressers in beauty salons, and in health care as nurses or doctor's assistants. (The health-care workers made up the corps of nursing volunteers of the Mexican Blue Cross, which provided health care to Mexicans in the colony.)[31]

Given the propensity for factory employment in Detroit, it is not surprising that almost a third of the Mexican women who worked prior to 1930 were employed by manufacturing industries. These factory workers held light jobs as inspectors, packers, markers, sorters, box washers,

Table 10.   Occupations of Mexican Women in
Detroit, 1918–1929

	Domestic and Personal Service[a]	Factory jobs[b]	Clerical and Sales Jobs[c]	Students	Total
Number	254	211	176	18	659
Percent	38.5	32	26.7	2.8	100

SOURCES: City of Detroit and Wayne County marriage affidavits for 1918 through 1929, and *R. L. Polk's Detroit City Directory* (Detroit: R. L. Polk Company, 1918–1929).

[a]Women in domestic and personal services worked in boarding and lodging houses and as janitors, laundry workers, cleaning ladies, elevator operators, store cashiers, office messengers, dressmakers, seamstresses, cigar makers, hairdressers, nurses, and in food service.

[b]Women who held factory jobs worked as inspectors, packers, markers, sorters, box washers, candy dippers, glass cutters, solderers, and on punch presses, drills, lathes, sewing machines, and in auto work.

[c]Women in clerical and sales jobs worked as clerks, typists, secretaries, stenographers, bookkeepers, translators, milliners, and saleswomen.

fur finishers, candy dippers ("the aristocrats of the candy trade"), glass cutters, and solderers. A few women operated punch presses, drills, lathes, and sewing machines. The jobs required less physical exertion than male assignments did but demanded dexterity and speed. The women may have been on piece rates. Achieving and maintaining high levels of speed on the job—"getting the work out"—did not guarantee promotion by supervisors, who as a rule were mostly male. The Michigan Malleable Iron Company, the Michigan Paper Box Company, and the American Can Company all employed Mexican women in light machine operations. By 1928 a small number of women worked in auto and auto-parts plants.[32]

Factory employment was attractive to the young, single women, some of whom took English-language courses at the Gershom Center, principally to get jobs in the auto plants. As motivation, the instructors promised the teenage students that if they completed the courses, the staff would help them obtain work in the car shops. This strategy ensured regular attendance by the young women. In contrast, the training Mexican women in the Southwest received through similar programs prepared them primarily for work as domestics, seamstresses, and laundresses.[33]

Slightly more than one-quarter of the Mexican women employed in Detroit during this time worked in clerical and sales jobs. Such firms as the Kelsey-Hayes Wheel Company, the Michigan Central Railroad Company, and the Prudential Insurance Company employed a few Mexican women as clericals. A small number were employed by Hudson, Dodge, Studebaker, and Packard Motors. Some Mexican women worked as translators in firms that employed Mexicans or had Mexicans as clients, like Prudential Insurance. Those in sales worked for small shops or large department stores like J. L. Hudson's. The clerical workers might have received vocational training in typing, shorthand, and language courses, which were popular among Mexican women at this time despite resistance from males. A Detroit International Institute staff member reported that this training was opposed by Mexican fathers and husbands who strongly objected to the women attending school. Paradoxically, if it was night school, some men declared that "women should not go out at night," and if it was day school, women were told that "they should stay home" to do housekeeping.[34]

In the Midwest as a whole in the 1920s a small though growing number of Mexican women were employed outside the home in service and light manufacturing jobs, finding work as domestics, waitresses, laundresses, and in meat-packing houses, railroad shops, tanneries, and cotton mills. These were low-skill and highly seasonal jobs. Only clerical work offered some stability, but it was characterized by low pay.[35]

The start of the Great Depression disrupted the formation of the Mexican colonies and momentarily halted the progress women were making in the world of work. The manpower shortages produced by World War II, however, saw the entrance of Mexican women into male-dominated job sectors. More and more Mexican women in Detroit entered the local workforce by the late 1930s and during World War II, according to Ford Motor Company records. Many were *Tejanas*, Mexican American women from Texas, though most were Detroiters and high school graduates, the daughters of Mexican Ford autoworkers. These men had lost their jobs as a result of the depression, had failed to qualify for New Deal work programs because of citizenship restrictions, or had joined the military at the beginning of World War II. Work in war-related industries presented new experiences and opportunities for the first generation of Detroit-born Mexican women. However, after the war most lost their jobs to the returning servicemen, and with this loss of employment their sense of economic independence likely decreased as well.[36]

The entrance of Mexican women into the labor force met with considerable opposition from the men. Fathers and husbands did not object when their daughters and wives worked in agriculture because they could watch over them, but resistance flared once women began leaving the confines of the family. This was surely the case for married women, whose upbringing emphasized, and household needs necessitated, that they be the epitome of motherhood and domesticity. Greater forces were at work over which the men had little control however. Mexican males in the Midwest resignedly accepted women becoming wage workers, recognizing that because of the expense of city living additional incomes were more important than loss of pride.[37] This dilemma was shown in the attitude of a Mexican in Chicago whose wife took a job in a local meat-packing plant:

> We were getting quite desperate as my funds were getting low. My wife resolved to go to work even though in Mexico she had never, never worked. I felt at first very ashamed . . . because I was not able to support her. I never would have approved of it but . . . economic circumstances in this country are different from Mexico. . . . My wife is now working cleaning casings. Sometimes she works six hours a day, sometimes eight and sometimes ten hours.[38]

A few Mexican Detroiters expressed the prejudice of the time regarding Mexican women. Some jealously feared their spouses would be lured away by other Mexican workers because of the scarcity of Mexican women in the city, while others claimed that women worked only to buy frivolous items for social outings: "In this country they go to work in order to buy silk stockings and silk dresses . . . so that they can go to a lot of dances."[39] This complaint indirectly revealed heightened consumption by young Mexican women wage earners—a trend created by work-group norms. Women purchased consumer items to symbolize the achievement of independence and as a reward for hard work. Dressing in the latest fashions also enabled them to fit in and to disguise their status as newcomers. In Mexico these women had been exposed to the wealth of new American consumer goods through conversations with women who had immigrated to the United States and through the catalogs, magazines, and picture cards that circulated among local residents.[40] The movies also played a role in conveying the image of the United States as a land of material prosperity. Consumer items were available in Mexico but beyond the reach of most women because they lacked purchasing power. Once in the United States, these women found their desires shaped by the consumer culture.

Mexican men in Detroit predictably feared also that women might replace them in certain jobs and at lower wages. One autoworker voiced this apprehension: "There are lots of men walking the streets who have no jobs and families to support while young girls are working at $.25 to $.30 an hour." [41] This worker himself was similarly perceived as a competitor for jobs by white workers. Now Mexican men felt their female counterparts could potentially undermine their economic advances.

Not all the Mexican women fit this profile; many were occupied with household duties and child rearing and hardly ever left their homes without permission from their husbands. But for Mexican wage-earning women, their expanding role in maintaining or raising family living standards gave them increased economic responsibility and a degree of autonomy. For young Mexican women, work freed them from the restricted home environment. However, the acculturation and assertion of independence by Mexican working women, which differed for those who were married and those who were single, did not dissolve traditional obligations. Instead the interplay of employment with historic cultural patterns, the need for a second income, and family preferences produced new relationships on an individual rather than group level. [42]

MEXICAN BUSINESSES

Hundreds of Mexican businesses could be found in the northern urban centers in the 1920s. Most were small ventures that lasted for short periods of time because of population fluctuations, the financial risks involved, and reliance on customers who often needed credit to make purchases. Edson noted that many of these Mexican-oriented enterprises were not run by Mexicans but by Spaniards or Spanish Jews. [43] Nonetheless, the establishments contributed to the emerging internal social structure of the Midwest's Mexican colonies. They ranged from sundry shops in boxcar camps, bookstores, tailor shops, and bakeries to a half dozen grocery stores in several cities owned by one Detroit Mexican family. Some Chicago Mexican businesses even sent trucks to the outlying colonies, where they sold their specialized foodstuffs door to door. Three types of businesses predominated: pool halls, restaurants, and barbershops, which serviced a clientele of primarily single male workers. For example, poolrooms catered to bachelors and were located in downtown neighborhoods or along heavily traveled streets, where they attracted a walk-in clientele. The proprietors had operated businesses in Mexico or else had saved money to finance these enterprises from their work in the United States. [44]

Mexicans in Detroit began setting up businesses in the early years of their settlement. Mexican barbershops, billiard parlors, restaurants, grocery stores, and rooming houses appeared in the working-class sections of the city. (See Table 11.) As the number of Detroit Mexican businesses increased, demand grew for the formation of a Mexican Chamber of Commerce, but this ambitious project was terminated by the Great Depression. The more successful establishments, small enterprises with few exceptions, stayed in operation until the Great Depression also forced them out of business.[45] The number and types of Detroit Mexican businesses were determined by the same factors Paul S. Taylor outlined for Chicago: the size and concentration of the Mexican colony, the proportion of single male workers to families, changes in place of employment in the city by workers, total number of workers in an area, and whether similar businesses were present. For example, a high number of single men meant an increase in the number of Mexican pool halls. Mexican grocery stores would not be likely to open where Mexicans were already served by food stores, and there would be a low proportion of Mexican restaurants in areas with *casas de asistencia*.[46]

Detroit's Mexican businesses in the 1920s were scattered throughout the city and not centrally located as they were in East Chicago's "Little Mexico" section. There seventy Mexican restaurants, billiard rooms, barbershops, and grocery stores were crowded onto one city block but some were operated by Jewish and other ethnic proprietors. Their Mexican clerks had talked them into putting up signs and advertisements to take advantage of the Mexican clientele, who were "good customers" and liked "to buy on credit, too." The closest approximation to this concentration in Detroit was on East Congress Street. Six Mexican restaurants, four barbershops, five pool halls, a tailor shop, a bakery, a candy shop, and numerous boardinghouses opened and closed along this street. Several enterprises operated from the apartments and boardinghouses where the proprietors lived. Hours of operation varied because owners worked at other jobs.[47]

Businesses opened, closed, or relocated in accordance with the shifts in the Mexican working population, indicating both the permeation of the North's factory environment into the everyday life of Mexicans and this group's transiency. South Chicago's Mexican businesses suffered when steelworkers from South Works moved to the Illinois Steel plant in Gary.[48] In the Motor City, the sizable number of Mexicans transferred from the Ford plant in Highland Park to the company's River Rouge plant in southwest Detroit had an impact on Mexican businesses. High concentrations of workers usually ensured a steady patronage. For example, Detroiter Samuel Rodríguez's tailor shop on Baker Street had patrons of various nationalities who lived in the area. The Mexican tai-

Table 11. Number of Mexican Business Establishments in Detroit, 1918–1929

	1918	1919–20	1920–21	1921–22	1922–23	1923–24	1924–25	1925–26	1926–27	1927–28	1928–29
Barbershop	2	—	1	5	2	3	8	7	4	3	8
Restaurant	—	1	7	1	1	6	7	9	11	6	2
Grocery	—	2	3	1	1	1	6	6	7	5	11
Billiards	—	—	3	1	3	4	1	2	—	5	5
Furnished rooms	—	—	—	—	1	1	1	2	5	5	5
Tailor/Dressmaker	—	—	1	1	1	3	1	1	1	4	6
Dry goods	—	—	—	—	1	—	1	1	1	—	—
Bakery	—	—	—	—	1	1	1	1	—	2	1
Shoe repair	—	—	—	—	1	1	1	1	—	2	3
Trucking	—	—	—	—	1	1	1	1	2	2	2
Auto repair	—	—	—	—	—	1	1	1	—	1	1
Jeweler	—	—	—	—	—	—	—	1	—	1	—
Physician	—	—	—	1	1	1	—	1	2	—	1
Lawyer	—	—	—	—	—	—	—	1	—	1	—
Notary public	—	—	—	—	—	—	—	—	—	1	—
Printing	—	—	—	—	—	—	—	—	—	1	1
Bookstore	—	—	—	—	—	—	—	—	—	1	1
Music teacher	—	—	—	—	—	—	—	—	1	1	1
Beauty operator	—	—	—	—	—	—	—	1	—	—	1
Cigar maker	—	—	—	—	1	—	—	3	—	—	1
Laundry	—	—	—	—	—	—	—	—	1	—	1

SOURCE: *R. L. Polk's Detroit City Directory* (Detroit: R. L. Polk Company, 1918–1929).

lor's knowledge of English no doubt accounted for his mixed clientele.[49] Mexicans set up businesses near factory sites because of the potential for walk-in customers. In Detroit the El Buen Gusto Restaurant and the adjacent Everybody's Pool Room were located in the 6400 block of Russell Avenue in the Milwaukee Junction area near the Studebaker Motors plant and American Car and Foundry. The name of the poolroom was a message to workers that all were welcome to test their skill, to watch the players (and gamble on the outcome), and to meet friends. From 1918 to 1924, Raúl Perez worked as a barber out of his home on Gratiot Avenue southeast of the Packard Motors plant. And from 1926 to 1929 Arthur Rocha and his wife managed a dry-goods store on Charlevoix east of Conners near the Continental Motors, Hudson Motors, and Chalmers Motors plants.[50]

Although most of Detroit's Mexican businesses were small enterprises, several Mexican grocery stores had a sizable clientele and a wide assortment of goods available. The Spanish-language newspaper *La Prensa Libre* reported in 1929 that the Romana Market had sold enough meat in one week from four cows, six oxen, eighteen sheep, and twenty pigs to feed 20 percent of the Detroit Mexican community. In the same year, the Surtidora Grocery advertised in *La Prensa Libre* that it carried nearly 200 medicinal herbs, an assortment of dried chilies, *metates* (stone mortars and pestles), sugar cane, and additional Mexican and Latin American foodstuffs. Spanish-language music records and paperback novels and magazines could be purchased as well.[51]

Detroit's Mexican poolrooms, barbershops, cafes and restaurants offered settings where the immigrants could socialize with their countrymen and discuss politics, neighborhood news, and work. Information about factory hires and layoffs first reached workers at these businesses, and because of the prevalence of kin and friendship networks so did news of births, marriages, and the arrival and departure of families. Poolroom owners, whose daily contact with the factory workers made them colony caretakers, occasionally furnished money to pay the fines for Mexicans arrested by the police because they lacked a passport or had committed minor offenses. Though food and specialty items in the Mexican grocery stores were more expensive than in non-Mexican stores, the patrons usually knew credit was readily available and that their transactions could be conducted in Spanish. As time passed, however, shopping at a chain food store like A&P and at Detroit's Eastern Market, where food items could be purchased at wholesale prices, became the choice of the city's Mexicans.[52]

THE CHURCHES

Like the buying habits of Mexicans, the immigrants' religious practices were also changing, although Catholicism remained an influential force in their lives. The Catholic Church accommodated the members of the growing Mexican working classes in the Midwest, but its efforts at providing assistance were plagued by a lack of funds and of Spanish-speaking priests. The northern Mexican colonies remained without their own parishes and priests, at times because of the prejudice of the local Catholic priests, who detected an attitude of indifference to the Church among the predominantly male Mexican population of the North. As one scholar noted of Gary's Mexican steelworkers, "Unlike east European immigrants . . . Mexicans had an anti-clerical tradition which intensified under the pressures of migration and industrial life." Years of acquiescence to the Church in Mexico had probably made the men disenchanted with Catholicism. Valuing their independence, they disliked the intrusion of the Church into their lives and resented the power wielded by parish priests. Because Mexicans did not tithe or regularly attend services, the priests declared that the immigrants were Catholic in name only.[53]

After 1926, however, thousands of strictly devout Catholic immigrants flowed into the Midwest from west central Mexico, the site of the Cristero Revolution. They made Catholicism a powerful force that less ardent followers had to reckon with. These devout and politically conservative men provided much of the leadership of the Mexican Catholic societies. Dissension flared in the Mexican communities of the North because the pro-Cristeros and the less earnest Catholics—some of them suspected of being spies employed by the Mexican government—had not resolved ideological differences that had originated in Mexico. Sometimes this factionalism was stirred up by the priests, who accused Mexican President Calles of deliberately persecuting Catholics. Aside from partisan disputes, the religious leaders, who formed part of the elite of the northern Mexican colonies, also had to balance both Mexican and white community demands with their allegiance to the homeland.[54]

Accustomed to religious ceremonies that were in their native tongue and that venerated the Virgin of Guadalupe, Mexicans encountered a less ritual-oriented, English-speaking Catholic Church in the North. These differences may have further contributed to weakening the formal ties of Mexicans to the Church. Protestant proselytizers took advantage

of the fact that Mexicans were more disillusioned with the Catholic
Church than were most other ethnic groups. Numerous Mexicans had
converted to Protestantism in Texas or had been exposed to these reli-
gions in Mexico. However, ethnic and class differences proved immune
to Protestant conversion, which was also impeded by prejudice.[55]

Catholicism remained an important aspect of the migrants' cultural
identity. For Mexican women tradition weighed heavily. Church services were often the only acceptable social outing and a welcome re-
prieve from the demanding daily household chores. Religion for some
women became a means for community building, and their presence at
and participation in Church functions were notable. Religious services
such as baptisms, first communions, marriages, and cultural events
brought Mexican family and friends together, creating and strengthen-
ing bonds.[56]

Mexicans in the Midwest satisfied their need for their own parishes
and church buildings. In 1926, Mexicans in Lorain organized into the
first Mexican parish in the diocese. Their church building was a converted auto paint shop purchased through individual contributions and
monthly pledges. Half of the 500 parishioners were National Tube
Company steelworkers and their families. The three-shift work schedules of the mill probably interfered with regular attendance by the
men.[57] A Mexican congregation did not develop in Gary until 1924,
when the immigrants established Our Lady of Guadalupe Church with
the help of the Gary-Alerding settlement. As in Lorain, the parish priest
was non-Mexican, and the chief pastor was hostile toward the Steel
City Mexicans and called them "uncivilized." Mexicans in Indiana Harbor who practiced their faith were without a church building so they
attended the Catholic parishes of eastern and southern European immigrants, who no doubt disapproved of these intruders at their services. In
the meantime, the newly formed Mexican Catholic societies undertook
fund-raising drives to build a church. At the Eola boxcar camp outside
Aurora, Illinois, Mexican track laborers in 1928 built their own church,
using lumber and nails furnished by the railroad. This project demon-
strates once more the ingenuity and resourcefulness of track workers,
whose nomadic work required that they improvise as the need arose.
And in the same year in South Chicago a group of local Mexican steelworkers raised the money for their parish, Our Lady of Guadalupe.
Four exiled Mexican nuns assisted the two Spanish priests with the parish work there.[58]

The Catholic Church in Detroit began assisting Mexicans as soon as substantial numbers first began arriving in the city in 1918, and its work with and spiritual guidance of this group continued throughout the twenties. As they established residences west of Detroit's central district, Mexicans stopped worshipping at St. Mary's Catholic Church downtown. They began attending St. Leo's Catholic Church on Fourteenth and Grand River Avenue and Holy Trinity Church on Porter Street, drawn to the parishes for marriages, baptisms, and funerals.[59] Discrimination had also played a part in the departure of the Mexican worshippers from St. Mary's parish as it would at St. Leo's. In August 1923, St. Mary's priests asked the Mexicans to leave the parish school, which the immigrants had used as a meeting place since first coming to Detroit, because the white parishioners no longer wanted to share their facilities with the migrants. And the number of Mexicans at St. Leo's dwindled because the white members shunned them. Evidently, participation in Church-sponsored programs had not Americanized Mexicans to a level acceptable by the white parishioners. The ostracized Mexican parishioners left to attend Holy Trinity Catholic Church on Detroit's west side.[60]

In 1922, the newly formed Our Lady of Guadalupe Church of Detroit was sponsored by four Mexican Catholic societies. As noted, through functions such as bazaars they raised funds for a lot and building on Kirby and Roosevelt streets north of Grand River Avenue. A few of the male parishioners volunteered their labor for the restoration of the building. These endeavors received official support from Detroit Mexican Consul Joaquín Terrazas.[61] Our Lady of Guadalupe Church was officially dedicated on October 12, 1923. The day chosen for the dedication had significance because Latinos celebrated it as Dia de la Raza (Day of the Race). About 500 Mexicans made up the parish; they were delighted to hear services in Spanish and sermons relevant to their lives. Father Alanis observed that the overall impact "of the new church on the . . . Mexican people is incalculable" and that the immigrants expressed their gratitude when "each Sunday the church is filled to overflowing."[62]

By 1926 Our Lady of Guadalupe Church had become a focal point for the 10,000 Mexicans in the Motor City through its sponsorship of social and community activities for the colony. In December of that year, Bishop Michael J. Gallagher confirmed 500 Spanish-speaking children as part of the annual celebration of the Feast of Our Lady of

Guadalupe. For the twelve feast days a mass was performed by Bishop Gallagher in honor of each of the Hispanic groups in Detroit. This religious observance revealed the diversity of Detroit's small Hispanic population of Spaniards, Puerto Ricans, Cubans, and Central and South Americans, who were bound together by a common language and culture.[63]

The growth of Our Lady of Guadalupe Church was halted by the 1927 recession, when hundreds of Mexicans left the Motor City, and its limited resources were strained by the needs of the influx of sugar-beet workers. In addition to the hard times brought on by the recession, the eventual decline of Our Lady of Guadalupe Church was due to its location several miles from southwest Detroit. The location had been chosen by Bishop Gallagher, who had anticipated that Detroit's fast population growth would go on for some time. Accordingly, he wanted parishes created in advance of population settlements. The bishop's misjudgment became an inconvenience for the Mexican parishioners of Our Lady of Guadalupe Church. The constant movement of Mexicans to and from the city also made support of this parish by all but the small core of stalwarts unpredictable. Finally, low attendance was caused also by indifference to the Catholic Church, which was the result of discrimination within the Church and of displeasure over the arrival in Detroit of fervent Mexican Catholics fleeing the bloodshed of the Cristero Revolution. These Catholics made their presence and opinions known in church-related affairs and in the colony. Some Mexican factory laborers disliked the religious and nationalistic fervor of those in charge of the Church-sponsored organizations (who even forbade members from speaking English during meetings).[64]

The variety of diversions available in the North also contributed to low church attendance by the men. These amusements brought complaints from the Catholic priests, who were already displeased by what they interpreted as disrespect by Mexicans for the Church. In Lorain, one priest grumbled that National Tube's Mexican steelworkers chose to pass their leisure time playing cards, thronging to weekend dances, or haunting the pool halls. On weekends the movies also drew Mexican workers away from services and Church-sponsored events in the colony. The men, exhausted from a week's work, often preferred spending several hours at a Sunday matinee rather than being lulled to sleep at mass by the droning of a priest.[65]

Motivated by the lofty duties of conversion, the Protestant sects competed with the Catholic Church for the immigrants. The conversion drive in the North mirrored similar attempts being undertaken in the Southwest to incorporate the burgeoning Mexican population both spiritually and culturally into the dominant American Protestant culture. Denominations like the Presbyterian Church had opened missions along the Texas border as well as in New Mexico and California. This religious work entailed recruiting recently converted Mexicans as auxiliaries to preach among their countrymen. Protestant religious workers utilized the forms of popular culture through which Mexicans were exposed to the American way of life. Movies, dances, organized sports programs, literary presentations, and counseling became vehicles for instruction in the Bible and the English language by Protestant missionaries, whose purpose was to educate young Mexican men and women in Christian principles.[66] More important, the missionaries and settlement-house workers saw their role as protecting Mexicans against atheistic, radical tendencies: "The thousands of Mexican immigrants . . . are just now in a receptive mood. Mentally, socially, religiously, they are in a state of transition, and the forces of evil are at work among them. The question . . . is whether they are to be won over to . . . Bolshevism or to Democracy; to Trotsky or to Christ." [67]

A small number of Mexicans were attracted to the Baptist faith because the Baptists did not have Americanization as their goal. Instead the objective of the preachers was quite simply to win souls for Jesus Christ. As one Southern Baptist Convention spokesman remarked, the aim was "not to Americanize, not to culturize [sic], nor to educate, nor to emancipate, but to deal with [Mexicans] wherever they are, and in whatever circumstances . . . in order to impart to them the gospel of the Lord Jesus Christ." "Full gospel" churches carried the cause of Protestant fundamentalism directly to Mexicans. Broadsides declaring that "God is Love" and "Jesus Saves" were posted in the Mexican colonies to announce the evangelistic campaigns.[68] Pentecostal tent revivals attracted these migrants because of their informality, lack of ritual, and emphasis on repentance acknowledged publicly against a background of touching hymns. Mexicans, who had come in contact with Baptist preachers in Texas, were fascinated by literal translations from the Bible of stories of the creation and of Christ's birth, death, and resurrection, and by visions of apocalypse and the coming of a new millennium. The impassioned preaching and public professions of faith at the lively revivals was commented on by one Mexican immigrant in Moline, Illinois: "Few could resist the soulful, toe tapping melodies calling upon the sinners to repent and accept God. The period of individual prayer and public confession was irresistible. . . . Each evening there would be a parade of faithful coming forward to receive Jesus and to be healed." [69]

The Protestant churches profited from the indifference of the Catholic Church toward the migrants from Mexico, who were also often ignored by aloof white parishioners. In the Chicago-Gary region, twenty-seven denominations worked among the area's Mexicans. Every effort was made by the Protestant sects to recruit Mexicans: providing social, charitable, and recreational services; having Mexican preachers conduct street meetings in Spanish; setting aside rooms at churches for meetings with full-time Mexican pastors; as well as using adjacent settlement houses for recruitment. Moreover, some of the Protestant ministers attempted to find jobs in the local steel plants for unemployed Mexican members in their congregations. The Protestant missionaries were able to gain converts despite the Mexicans' transiency, the dissension when the congregations appointed Mexican preachers from outside the neighborhoods, and hostility from staunch Mexican Catholics. [70]

Several Protestant churches in Detroit began religious and charitable work among Mexicans when the Mexicans first arrived in 1918. St. Peter's Episcopal Church opened a mission on Michigan and Trumbull Avenues, though it later closed for lack of support. In 1926, La Misión Bautista Mexicana (Mexican Baptist Church) opened on Jones Street in the Michigan Avenue–Bagley Street area. It held Spanish-language services on Sunday afternoons and evenings, prayer meetings on Wednesday evenings, and English classes on Saturday. To attract as many Mexicans as possible, religious services were scheduled according to factory shifts and days off, and evening services accommodated the wives and families of men on night shifts. La Misión relocated to Baker Street in southwest Detroit, a pocket of Mexican factory workers and potential converts. Two more Mexican Baptist churches opened in 1929: La Luz Iglesia Bautista Mexicana (Holy Light Mexican Baptist Church) on Bagley Street with a Mexican preacher and the Primera Misión Bautista Mexicana (First Mexican Baptist Mission) on 25th Street with an Anglo preacher. Mexican Baptists joined these Spanish-speaking congregations because they felt uncomfortable attending the mainly middle-class, English-speaking Baptist churches in downtown Detroit. [71]

The social life of the Mexican colony of Detroit in times of prosperity and crisis was promoted by the Catholic Church as well as by Protestant churches. A few men and women attained prominence through their demonstrated leadership in the Church and their activities helped sustain the community. Often the success of Church-sponsored events was achieved largely through the devoted efforts of the women.

However, the dispersion of Mexicans in Detroit and their movement made maintenance of stable church congregations difficult. Some did not appreciate being directed to Our Lady of Guadalupe Church by the paternalistic white Catholic priests just because it was "better for Mexicans." By the late 1930s, Our Lady of Guadalupe Church of Detroit had a mixed congregation because of population shifts. Mexicans gained mobility again as their economic status improved through war-related factory production. With their earnings, and from the desire to better themselves, large numbers moved out of southwest Detroit to outlying communities like Dearborn, Ecorse, and Lincoln Park. The Mexicans remaining in the original colony began attending St. Anne and Most Holy Trinity Church, both parishes conveniently located in southwest Detroit and offering services in Spanish. Membership in Mexican Catholic societies filled the spiritual vacuum created by the demise of Our Lady of Guadalupe Church. Religion was but one meaningful aspect in the lives of Mexicans in the Midwest. Its institutional influence was considerable. However, the extent of this influence must be considered in light of the larger forces at play in shaping the experiences of Mexicans in the northern cities.[72]

MEXICAN MUTUAL-AID SOCIETIES AND FRATERNAL ORGANIZATIONS

Like religion, mutual-aid societies and fraternal organizations became for some immigrants an essential part of their lives outside the factories. The scores of Mexican mutual-aid societies and fraternal organizations that developed in the United States brought greater participation than cooperative associations in Mexico did. These formal efforts at self-help by Mexicans fulfilled the need for camaraderie and provided some insurance for work accidents, injuries, and illness, which plagued the colony residents. The orientation and goals of the mutual-aid societies and fraternal organizations ranged from mutual welfare and relief to Masonic, social, literary, artistic, and religious pursuits. All served as mediating forces, advocating ethnic consciousness to preserve a Mexican patriotic spirit while creating a sense of community. Far removed from the well-established Mexican colonies in the Southwest, Mexicans in the Midwest found this emphasis on Mexican identity and culture important.[73]

The Mexican government was directly involved in protecting its countrymen in the United States because it had a vested interest in its wayward compatriots. Cultivating an interest in things Mexican preserved allegiance to the mother country. Mexico did not want to lose workers across the border because they were potentially beneficial to the Mexican economy. Accordingly, Mexican Honorary Commissions and local branches of the Mexican Blue Cross were founded with the support and supervision of the Mexican consuls. The purpose of these organizations was to give aid and relief while at the same time promoting and sustaining interest in Mexican culture and in the affairs of Mexico.

These goals were articulated by leaders of the organizations, who often were nationalists in their sentiment and outlook. For these men, prestige in the Mexican colonies accompanied election to office in the mutual-aid societies and fraternal organizations; these positions also allowed them to act as representatives to the larger community.[74]

However, not all the compatriots in the colony approved of these opinionated leaders. Just as some Mexicans abhorred the interference of the Catholic Church and were resentful of the authority and admonishments of parish priests, many avoided the patriotic rhetoric of countrymen seeking to replicate the type of onerous society they had left behind in Mexico. Mexicans had no qualms about expressing pride in their national identity but resented meddlesome individuals who prescribed how they should express loyalty to the homeland. This attitude was shaped not only by the experience of years of revolution in Mexico but by the independence Mexicans were gaining from exposure to the urban industrial United States. The men were repelled by the authority asserted by some of the organizations, which dictated a member's family and community obligations. Though amenable to the mutualistic nature of these organizations, the men likely were annoyed by the accompanying mutual supervision. This was another aspect of the worker consciousness arising in Mexicans in the North, where an industrial work culture was actively molding a new point of view.[75]

Approximately thirty-five different Mexican societies existed in the Chicago-Gary region by 1928, with twenty-three in Chicago, eight in Indiana Harbor, and four in Gary. Because of the overwhelming working-class composition of the midwestern Mexican colonies, the most prevalent of these organizations was the mutual-aid society. It disbursed sick benefits to its members (as well as nonmembers) from the modest monthly dues and fund-raising events. The societies took up collections to assist the gravely ill and the survivors of deceased breadwinners, and credit was also extended when needed. Religious societies were sponsored by the local Catholic churches or by the YMCA's International Institute and had social and recreational functions. Others had a cultural focus: they maintained small libraries; offered enrichment programs; presented speeches, poetry recitals, and musical presentations; and organized celebrations of Mexican national holidays. Certain societies emerged after a crisis involving local Mexicans. For example, La Sociedad Protectora Mexicana (Mexican Protective Society) of Gary and its women's auxiliary, La Sociedad Mutualista Feminina (Women's Mutualist Society), were formed in 1924 after a series of altercations between Mexicans and city police. Most of the Mexican societies in the North were short-lived, lasting from one to six years.[76]

One of the more outstanding midwestern Mexican societies was Los Obreros de San José (Workers of St. Joseph) of Indiana Harbor, a working-class organization founded in 1925 by a group of Inland Steel's Mexican workers. It appealed for allegiance to Mexico and promoted its patriotic views in its newspaper, *El Amigo del Hogar*. Los Obreros sponsored numerous cultural activities for the benefit of enlightening the Mexican steelworkers of Indiana Harbor and nearby Gary. These events included plays, poetry readings, cello concerts, and even an exhibition of original works by the Mexican artist David Alfaro Siqueiros. National pride overshadowed the knowledge that this Mexican painter embraced contrary, radical beliefs. Members of Los Obreros undertook several fund-raising drives to build a Mexican Catholic Church, mindful of the need to offset both the successful conversions of countrymen by Baptist missionaries and Inland's raucous and vice-ridden environment.[77]

Mexican societies provided a wide range of cultural activities. Another society established by Mexican steelworkers in Indiana Harbor was Cuauhtémoc, which complemented the efforts at cultural enlightenment by Los Obreros de San José. Cuauhtémoc sponsored bazaars, dances, Mexican-style vaudeville shows, and baseball games, which promoted ethnic pride. The baseball games were played against other area teams such as the Mexican Athletic Club of Gary, a recreational association that also had boxing, bowling, and track teams. Upward of 3,000 spectators packed the baseball park for these games. Local support of the home team engendered pride in the community and indicated as well that the Mexican steelworkers of the Calumet region had adopted the national pastime as a premier recreational activity. The well-planned holiday celebrations of East Chicago's Mexican societies featured parades, carnivals, and dances, and the selection of a festival queen brought beauty to the urban grit and smoke of East Chicago.[78] All these diversions gave Mexican steelworkers momentary respite from the drudgery of the local mills.

Contributing to the diversity of cultural events available to Indiana Harbor's Mexican steelworkers were five theater groups supported by the local Mexican societies. The groups drew their casts, stage crews, musicians, and ushers from the surrounding communities, thus directly involving steelworkers and family members. Professional theater companies and vaudevillians from Mexico also toured the area. The societies of Indiana Harbor planned in 1926 to open a movie house to show Spanish-language films. This effort not only indicated the influence of movie culture but demonstrated the willingness of Indiana Harbor's Mexicans to unite for a common purpose—to defend themselves as a community and to make local officials responsive to them. The societies had earlier boycotted the local movie theaters because of segregation and had met with the city police chief in an attempt to improve the strained relations between Mexicans and the local police.[79]

In southeast Michigan and Ohio, Mexican mutual-aid societies and fraternal organizations formed, as did women's auxiliaries, and efforts were made to develop recreational youth groups. In Detroit, a Mexican Honorary Commission and a chapter of the Mexican Blue Cross were sponsored by the Mexican consul, and the Catholic Church supported the Sociedad de San José (St. Joseph Society). About ten societies were created in Detroit, which, after Chicago, had the largest number of such organizations in the Midwest. As they did elsewhere in the North, workers made up the membership of Detroit's Mexican societies.[80]

The societies assisted Detroit's Mexicans in observing national holidays as early as 1920, and the colony became involved in all aspects of the celebrations. For Mexico's Independence Day, the Mexico Universal grocery stores contributed to the festive atmosphere by stocking specialty items such as flags, garlands, streamers, tricolored sashes, confetti, and patriotic records. Many of the entertainers for the celebration were autoworkers such as Ford employee Fausto Lara, who composed several musical pieces for the 1926 Mexican Independence Day festivities. Lara's original compositions were heard by over 1,000 Mexicans at the Cass Technical High School, where the ceremonies took place. These men were obviously more than factory workers. Their artistry evinced talents that also were sources of pride and identity. Moreover, Lara's musical ability was probably acknowledged by his fellow countrymen as an indication of culture and learning and was thus given respect. The accomplishments of such workers went unnoticed except during festive occasions such as Mexican holidays or at community meetings. Such cultural events allowed Mexicans to be among their countrymen. For one afternoon or evening a little piece of plebeian Mexico was re-created in the streets, parks, halls, and gymnasiums of the industrial Midwest.[81]

In April 1925, the Motor City's celebration of Nationality Day attracted a gathering of 3,000 Mexicans, who heard a keynote address by Detroit's mayor, John W. Smith. The mayor's popularity with the Mexicans was due to his extensive travels in Mexico, in addition to being the guest of honor of the president of Mexico during one of these trips. (The colony's contingent of ex-Cristeros no doubt frowned on this distinction.) Mexicans wisely cultivated their cordial relations with Detroit city officials. For example, they sent a telegram of congratulations in 1927 to Charles Lindbergh after his successful goodwill flight to Mexico. Lindbergh was Mayor Smith's nephew and the son-in-law of Dwight Morrow, the American ambassador to Mexico. The heads of the Mexican colony used such functions and occasions to establish and maintain contacts with local officials. These connections probably enhanced their standing among their countrymen, and if any problems arose involving members of the colony, the leaders, acting as spokesmen, could use these contacts with city representatives to seek solutions.[82]

El Circulo Mutualista Mexicano (Mexican Mutualist Circle) had the longest continuous history of all the Mexican organizations founded in Detroit. It was established in 1924 with a membership of 150 Ford autoworkers, professionals, and businessmen. El Circulo funded and promoted social and cultural activities along with the Sociedad Anáhuac (Anáhuac Society), and it donated $5,000 to help establish the monthly newspaper El Eco de la Patria (The Echo of the Mother Country). The organization also extended financial assistance in founding Our Lady of Guadalupe Church.[83]

In keeping with its goals of creating a spirit of unity among Latin Americans and promoting Hispanic culture, El Circulo invited Puerto Ricans and other Spanish-speaking groups to attend its meetings. In October 1927, despite the hard economic times of the recession, El Circulo organized its first multi-Latin American celebration of Dia de la Raza to unite Detroit's Spanish-speaking groups. Over 1,000 people attended the pan-Hispanic picnic and dance at a park outside the city. Each year El Circulo held an official fiesta, Gran Conferencia Cultural Pro-México. During the Christmas season in 1927 the society held a fund-raising festival to buy toys for Mexican children, thus assuring that the children of autoworkers laid off by the recession would have a good Christmas. Evidently, celebration of a commercialized American version of the Christmas holiday was widespread among the Detroit colony residents. El Circulo also opened a library and obtained books from the city's secretary of public education.[84] El Circulo also maintained a close relationship with the International Institute of Detroit and represented the Mexican colony at institute-sponsored events. It also arranged conferences and lectures in Port Huron, Pontiac, Flint, Toledo, and Lorain.[85]

As they did elsewhere in the Midwest, transiency and conflicting work schedules restricted membership and inhibited participation in the Mexican mutual-aid societies and fraternal organizations of Detroit. And class and ideological differences caused internal divisions, which tended to weaken these associations.[86] Also, their effectiveness at self-help was reduced because their limited funds could not possibly offset widespread economic hardship during layoffs or economic downturns. Rather than pay dues to a society or organization, workers had to give priority to the purchase of necessities. The difficulty in maintaining the mutual-aid societies and fraternal organizations was summed up by a Mexican in Chicago: "It is very hard to organize societies and collect dues. [Mexicans] do not work regularly; they have to move with the work. If there is no work they fall behind in their dues. Now the question presents itself. Here is $10; shall I buy a pair of shoes and some stockings and shirts that I need, or shall I catch up on my dues? The answer is only natural." [87]

Membership and participation also depended on the priorities and goals of each Mexican worker. These men were progressively perceiving themselves as Detroiters, individuals who understood that their sweat and toil in the shops contributed to making the Motor City a great industrial center. They alone chose how they would spend their leisure time away from the factories. Baseball games, dances, movies, and park outings were forms of recreation popular with Detroit's working masses. And these leisure activities reduced membership in formal organizations. At the end of a long week of work in the auto plants and foundries, Mexicans happily opted for a weekend movie or an outing in the family automobile, or spent their free time catching up on sleep. In addition, the local pool halls and barbershops served as recreational and social centers for working-class Mexicans; here freewheeling political debates took place unencumbered by procedural rules, guidelines, and ascribed philosophies. Workers also took advantage of activities offered by the International Institute neighborhood house such as sports, English lessons, and similar self-improvement courses. Finally, some Mexican workers attended city-sponsored night classes like those offered at Highland Park High School.[88]

The Mexican mutual-aid societies and fraternal organizations did appeal nevertheless to some of the diverse Mexican population of Detroit, with its multitude of agendas. In addition to the limited help the societies and organizations furnished compatriots in times of sickness or need, social activities reinforced pride in Mexican culture and, more important, developed a sense of community. The events provided occasions for family reunions. And the eating, drinking, dancing, and marching in parades that took place during these festive holiday celebrations and pageants built and strengthened bonds among Mexicans.[89]

LABOR ORGANIZING

These mutual-aid societies and the events they sponsored caught the attention of factory bosses, who were aware of their influence and of the assembled large numbers of workers they attracted. Northern employers frowned on these societies for fear they would become vehicles for union organizing. This apprehension was not unwarranted; the immigrants from Mexico brought with them an awareness of the issues affecting them as workers who were especially susceptible to abuse. Mexican workers passing through Texas had gained a clear understanding of their vulnerability at the hands of sinister ranchers and farmers and of the need to guard against this exploitation. In the Midwest some had learned the lessons of class conflict the hard way—through participation in and exposure to the 1919 nationwide steel strike, the 1922 meatpacker's strike, and the local tannery strike in Milwaukee. And day-to-day experiences in the factories impressed on Mexican workers, conscious of the barriers race created, the inequities of the industrial system. A concern with and involvement in worker causes was also being generated among Mexican factory workers who came in contact with American and Mexican labor organizers during their peregrinations.

Mexicans' collective actions as workers were tied to their ethnic identity. Meetings, walkouts, protest demonstrations, and organizing were

often undertaken as an ethnic group. Awareness that the United States
was responsible for much of the political turmoil in Latin America was
another important aspect of the different perceptions of Mexican workers and their place in American society.[90]

In October 1926, Mexicans in Gary attended a labor meeting where
they were addressed by the Texas labor radical Charles Cline. Cline had
finished serving a thirteen-year prison sentence for allegedly killing a
south Texas deputy sheriff while leading a group of Mexican Americans
across the border to fight in the Mexican Revolution. The International
Labor Defense sponsored Cline's speech at Gary's Spanish Hall on October 17, the anniversary of the Bolshevik Revolution. The extent of the
involvement of Mexican steelworkers in labor activities was revealed by
the superintendent of the Alerding Settlement House in Gary. He publicly stated that "there are 560 organized communists in Gary and they
consist almost solely of Mexicans and Russians." [91]

The following year, Mexican steelworkers at the East Chicago
Youngstown Sheet and Tube plant walked off their jobs to protest dis-
crepancies in calculating hours worked. In 1928, labor agents in the
Chicago-Gary area were alert to union organizing among Mexicans
being recruited for sugar-beet work. Sugar-beet workers may have been
exposed to radical ideas because in 1928 Mexican sugar-beet workers
in Colorado had organized La Liga Obrera de Habla Española (Spanish-Speaking Workers' League) with the help of the militant Industrial
Workers of the World. The influence of La Liga was widespread; it extended into northern Colorado, the Denver area, and northern New
Mexico among a workforce that was largely migratory. The fear that
Mexicans in the Calumet region would similarly transform their
mutual-aid societies into unions thus had a basis. A labor agent expressed this apprehension: "I am absolutely opposed to the Mexicans
organizing, regardless of the object. These organizations . . . soon develop along bolshevistic lines of thought." [92]

Labor organizing and political activism surfaced among Mexicans in
Chicago and Indiana Harbor. In early 1929, a delegation of these workers traveled to Kenosha, Wisconsin, where they joined Mexicans from
Milwaukee and Racine in a demonstration supporting a strike by local
Mexican workers. The men were also protesting the assassination of the
anarchist Julio Antonio Mela in Mexico City. Before the Chicago delegation of Mexicans left for Kenosha, they distributed leaflets and staged
a spirited rally. The parade of marchers, automobiles, and trucks carried

banners and signs with words and phrases boldly condemning "Yankee Imperialism." The gathering aroused the local Mexicans, who "shouted their approval all along the line of the parade." Local police watched but did not intervene, as they had at a previous demonstration. That many Mexican workers harbored resentment of intervention by the United States in Mexico on behalf of American investors was revealed in the angry remarks of an Indiana Harbor Mexican steelworker: "The American government [invaded] our country and wrest from it a large part of its territory. . . . American money has fomented revolution in Mexico and . . . the United States has interfered with our sovereign right as a free country." [93]

Just as Marcus Garvey's Universal Negro Improvement Association attracted upward of 7,000 black Chicagoans, the visit to Chicago in 1928 by the Mexican intellectual José Vasconcelos drew hundreds of jubilant countrymen to his stirring speeches. The cultural nationalism he espoused of a *raza cosmica* (cosmic race) cultivated racial pride and identity in a great number of these northern Mexicans. [94]

Detroit's Mexican autoworkers likewise became involved in local organizing efforts and built worker societies as early as 1927. The workers, always careful of the company spies in their midst, secretly began making contacts with co-workers in other plant departments, attending worker meetings, and distributing union information. About forty to fifty Detroit Mexican steelworkers and autoworkers formed Los Obreros Unidos Mexicanos (United Mexican Workers), also known as Sociedad Obreros Libres (Society of Free Workers). This working-class collective established English- and Spanish-language classes for the colony, aided fellow Mexicans seeking employment, and purchased a cafe in southwest Detroit that members planned to run as a cooperative. When Mexican muralist Diego Rivera came to Detroit in 1932 to paint the Detroit Institute of Art murals, he considered Obreros Unidos important enough to donate money to their ventures. [95]

In the summer of 1927, Mexican workers in Detroit joined in heated discussions about the trial of Nicola Sacco and Bartolomeo Vanzetti. The two Italian anarchists had become symbols of discrimination against foreign-born workers, an issue repeatedly raised by Mexicans. Interestingly, some of the men who had recently arrived in the United States argued about whether the late Samuel Gompers of the American Federation of Labor (AFL) was aware of the prejudice encountered by Mexicans in the North. The crusty labor leader had accepted the temporary use of Mexican labor during World War I but staunchly opposed their expanding numbers in industry and referred to them derisively as a "great evil." In addition, the AFL was hostile toward Mexican laborers because many affiliated with the IWW. The more disgruntled workers, however, questioned why AFL unions denied Mexicans membership when unions in Mexico admitted American and Asian workers. Topics such as these were debated by Mexican workers in Detroit in informal settings. The men did not need conventional forums for open discussion of issues pertinent to workers.[96]

CONSUMERISM

As the 1920s ended, the jobs Mexican workers held had gained importance in determining their place in the social hierarchy of the Mexican colonies. A good-paying and steady job enhanced a worker's reputation among his countrymen. It assured a degree of independence, a relatively exceptional standard of living, and active participation in the American consumer life-style, with its emphasis on accumulating material goods. Mexicans in the Midwest were being integrated into an American culture of consumption. The migrants from Mexico were good spenders; they bought automobiles and home appliances, and life, health, and accident insurance appealed to the practical. Most, however, made small-item purchases reflecting general buying trends.[97] Mexican workers in Detroit justified their spending because they had jobs or would soon get one. For them, consumer items became rewards for hard work—one of the tenets of the new American society Ford had ushered in for the common man.

Mexican women in Detroit used home appliances bought on installment and tried new approaches to homemaking, which some women learned by attending home-management classes at the International Institute.[98] The new conveniences may not have reduced housework, but they did make tasks easier and faster to finish. Gas stoves cooked food more rapidly than charcoal; perishable food lasted longer refrigerated so that women did not have to shop every day; using a washing machine was easier than washing, rinsing, and wringing clothes by hand; and vacuum cleaners were more efficient than brooms against the constant soot and dust from the smoke-belching factories. Admittedly, the use of new products and the adoption of American homemaking habits by Mexican women were not uniform. Such factors as individual preference, how long the women had been in an urban environment, and their husbands' incomes determined their choices. Although some women preferred to grind corn for tortillas by hand, others became habituated to buying ready-made tortillas at the markets or American foodstuffs at chain grocery stores.[99]

Attractive advertisements in newspapers and magazines and merchandise carefully displayed in department and drugstore windows persuaded Mexicans to buy. Mexicans succumbed to the enticements of fast-talking salesmen who made the rounds of the plant gates or came door-to-door offering goods on the installment plan. When the salesman spread out the kaleidoscope of curtains, tablecloths, bedspreads, colored cloth, and other merchandise and made his pitch, it was hard for the wives to resist a purchase. Fifty cents or a dollar was often the down payment. Installment payments would be arranged later if the husband agreed to the purchase; if not, the item was returned and the down payment refunded. These salesmen conned many Mexicans into accumulating debts through installment purchases of furniture, washing machines, sewing machines, victrolas, and automobiles.[100]

Automobiles prevailed as a favorite and practical consumer item few Mexicans could refuse to own. After all, the technology involved in automobile manufacturing and the fascination with machines had lured them to Detroit's car factories in the first place. Autos constituted over one-third of the consumer goods brought back to Mexico by the returning immigrants. Half the Mexicans in the Motor City owned an automobile or had plans to acquire one, and both passenger cars and trucks were purchased. Mexicans bought cheap models new like the popular Model T and more costly vehicles used. Sometimes six to eight men pooled their money to buy the high-priced models and shared ownership of the vehicles. Because of the popularity and status associated with owning a car, Mexicans did not always make wise purchases in their hurry to possess this ultimate consumer product. They commonly paid for junk cars on questionable installment plans. This problem came to the attention of employers through notices of garnishments from used-car dealers. Frustrated with the mounting paperwork, plant officials, Edson reported, notified the dealers that "they would no longer honor orders against the wages of any Mexican . . . buying a used car." Employers also informed their Mexican employees that they would not extend credit or advance money to anyone purchasing a car. Edson also reported that sugar companies likewise opposed Mexicans' purchasing used cars on credit. Because of the beet workers' short employment season, it was feared that a laborer would "spend for an old car the money which he needs to keep him through the winter." [101]

Making and accumulating money persisted as the primary reason Mexicans came to the Midwest to work. At the same time Mexicans were becoming active consumers, their savings accounts showed not all forgot the value of thriftiness. About 10 percent of the workers in the North had savings accounts, and in some cities over a fourth saved money, as much as $100 to $250 per year.[102] The prudent men banked their earnings, and those continuously employed participated in life-insurance and company stock-purchasing plans. These wise practices prompted comments by employers such as the following by a Bethlehem steel executive: "You don't have to coax the Mexicans to buy stock in the company. The Mexicans as a rule take up the limit allowed, or if they don't, they give a good reason why they don't. You don't even have to sell it to them; they realize that preferred stock is a good purchase." Those who had been in the Motor City for long periods anticipated the hard times brought on by unemployment and frugally saved their money. As a veteran Mexican Ford autoworker observed: "I have been forced through necessity to be more practical—to save my money for one thing. . . . I have learned that through bitter experience." [103]

Sending money to Mexico became the foremost use of extra cash. Because Mexicans in the Midwest were paid industrial wages and few had families with them to support, they sent more money to Mexico than did their countrymen elsewhere. Twenty-five percent of their wages were mailed home as savings to support dependents or to repay loans extended for the passage north.[104] For example, Lorain's Mexican steelworkers made regular remittances to Mexico. Mexican steelworkers in Indiana Harbor sent over $1 million to Mexico. Immigrants in Gary sent home postal money orders averaging $20 to $25 a month and maintained savings accounts, as did Milwaukee's Mexican factory workers.[105] Detroit's International Institute reported that half the Mexican autoworkers in the city sent from $10 to $50 a month to relatives in Mexico in addition to maintaining bank accounts.[106]

Economic standing in the Mexican colonies of the North thus became a priority of the migrants from Mexico. It was defined by the possession of household goods, good-quality clothing, automobiles, ample groceries, and savings accounts, and by having extra money for family celebrations such as baptisms and weddings. Social standing in the Detroit colony was assured by having one's name appear in *La Prensa* of

San Antonio for contributing money to various benevolent causes in the homeland such as the construction of schools or aid to flood victims.[107]

LEISURE ACTIVITIES

Enough money still remained to engage in leisure pastimes, for Mexicans saw their stay in the cities of the Midwest as a magnificent adventure and not just a time of hard work. Even Mexican families from out of town dressed up in their "Sunday best" and spent an exciting day in the large cities taking in the sights while visiting friends and relatives. Few could let pass the allure of big cities and the wealth of choices the dazzling urban culture of the 1920s afforded.[108]

Recreational activities were always an integral aspect of the factory culture of Mexicans. Railroad workers in Moline went to the movies and the circus, and carnivals that came to town were popular amusements as well. In Lorain, Mexicans spent their off-hours from National Tube's steel mill playing pool, taking strolls around town in the company of countrymen, dancing, or going to the picture shows. Movie watching was an activity that East Chicago's Mexican steelworkers particularly enjoyed, even though seating at certain local theaters was segregated.[109]

The 1920s were the golden age of sports, and in addition to baseball games, wrestling matches were a popular spectator sport for Mexicans in Indiana Harbor and Chicago. Colorful posters printed in Spanish pasted onto building walls and displayed in barbershop windows and at pool halls announced the upcoming matches. The 1928 wrestling contest between the champion of Mexico, Francisco Aguayo, and the Yugoslavian George Mack, both steelworkers at Inland, drew a big crowd from the two ethnic groups. Competition between the steelworkers was symbolized in the ring by their respective country's wrestling champions. Aguayo wrestled another European in a widely touted match in Chicago. The heroic personality of Aguayo and his exploits in the ring endeared him to local Mexicans. The Mexican colonies of the Chicago-Gary region could proudly boast that their valiant compatriot Aguayo, a former mining engineer from Sonora, Mexico, had defeated "every opponent he had tackled" and had "only a few wrestlers standing between him and the world championship."[110]

Like wrestling, boxing engendered hero worship and social solidarity among Mexicans. The ability to fight was a sign of manliness and symbolically proved ethnic superiority. Promoters exploited these rivalries to draw large audiences. Mexicans in South St. Paul, Minnesota, had their own local sports hero—the courageous Mexican boxer George Galvin—and they filled the Stockyard Pavilion every time he was billed. He had a job at the local Swift meat-packing plant and had worked in packing plants since the age of nine. He began boxing at age twelve to earn extra money. This young, hard-working Mexican shined shoes in the evening after his shift at the packing house and did sugar-beet work in the summers. Galvin turned professional in 1924 and by the end of 1926 had fifteen victories by knockout and ten wins by decision. Billed as "Kid Galvin," "Kid Peewee," or "Little Dago," the teenager boxer fought throughout Minnesota, and in Sioux City, Iowa, Fargo, North Dakota, and Milwaukee, drawing crowds of Mexicans to his boxing matches in these cities. Galvin kept his job at Swift, which sponsored this champion Mexican boxer. He put away his boxing gloves and joined the labor movement during the first organizing drives of the Great Depression. In 1933, the charismatic ex-prize fighter with a strong sense of social justice had his first organizing experience supporting local Minnesota farmers in their protests, and in 1934 Kid Peewee became a full-time organizer for the packing-house workers of St. Paul.[111]

Recreation for Detroit's Mexicans included picnics, boat rides, and concerts at Belle Isle and other parks, and they also enjoyed movies and the spectator sports of boxing and baseball. A late-afternoon or weekend automobile ride with the family was a main diversion, as Mexicans owned cars and Michigan's countryside was perfect for camping trips. A streetcar ride to explore the city was also a cheap diversion.[112]

Detroit's city parks offered public recreation and became extensions of its working-class neighborhoods. Certain parks were visited by particular ethnic groups. Such was the case with Van Dyke Park, where a segment of the city's Poles congregated on afternoons and weekends. Polish autoworkers who befriended Mexicans at the plants invited them to their outings. On Saturdays and Sundays, a few Mexican workers attended the Polish dances at Van Dyke Park. "This Saturday I am going to a Viennese dance at the same place," a Mexican autoworker told Paul S. Taylor. "They dance a dance that they call the Polka and they dance it very strenuously. One has to rest up a week getting ready for such a dance!" It was not important for the Mexicans to understand their host's language; women outnumbered the men, and thus there was no shortage of obliging dancing partners. Because Poles were such a large ethnic group in Detroit, Polish, not English, was occasionally the first language Mexican workers learned in the factories. At the Van Dyke Park dances eager Mexicans even mastered a few Polish phrases from the women: "One of them told me how to say 'bottle of pop' in Polish so that I could buy refreshments." [113]

Mexican autoworkers escaped the fast pace of the city by going to Belle Isle Park on Sunday afternoons. They ate $1 chicken dinners at the park's casino and were entertained by the house piano player during their meal. A few spent their Sunday outing at Belle Isle on a quiet park bench reading the *Detroit News, Detroit Times, La Prensa,* or magazines and books purchased at La Librería Español, Detroit's Spanish-language bookstore.[114] The content of the Spanish-language papers was nationalistic, and religion was a prominent topic, obviously reflecting the contemporary issues debated in the homeland, which was mired in the issue of Church-state relations. However, the tabloids did address the concerns of each midwestern colony and printed news of interest to workers.[115] For many Mexicans, the cartoons and comic strips said as much about newsworthy events as the editorials and did so more poignantly. The cartoons of Salvador Pruneda in the widely distributed Los Angeles *La Opinión* targeted Mexican political leaders, unrest in Mexico, Catholicism, relations between the United States and Mexico, as well as American popular culture and everyday life. The comic-strip antics of the Katzenjammer Kids and the travails of Krazy Kat were also widely liked by the workers.[116]

Attending Detroit's neighborhood movie theaters was an inexpensive activity, costing $0.10. The workers, of course, avoided the "whites only" movie houses. Mexican autoworkers on shortened workweeks spent their off-time at the movies, now and then attending two or three times a day. Men rewarded themselves for a hard week of work by going to some of Detroit's better theaters even though they paid extra for the ambience. "When I go to a show," stated one Mexican autoworker, "I almost always go to The Michigan. The music is better and the show is high class." [117] The younger Mexican generation attended movies regularly. They were being integrated into mainstream American culture via the movies, which fostered new patterns of consumption, leisure, and recreation. The travails of Charlie Chaplin as the Little Tramp were popular among Mexicans, but many enjoyed films with Latin themes or Latin stars, showing their participation in and enjoyment of both American and Latin culture. Mexicans flocked to the theaters whenever the movie idol Rudolph Valentino, the Mexican screen stars Lupe Vélez (the

"Mexican Spitfire"), Ricardo Cortéz, Ramón Navarro, and Dolores "Lola" del Rio were featured. In the 1920s, *The Sheik* was the quintessential movie; it attracted Valentino fans in droves. The personal lives of these actors and actresses were frequently discussed by the loyal Mexican fans, who regularly read the Hollywood movie magazine *Cinelandia* or its Mexican equivalent *Ovaciones*.[118]

Listening to Spanish-language phonograph records was popular home entertainment for Mexicans in the North. The enthusiastic reception by Mexicans of these recordings inaugurated an era in which record companies such as Vocalion, Okeh (Columbia), Decca, and Bluebird (RCA) targeted a Spanish-language market. The whole range of traditional Mexican music was available, from patriotic selections to popular dance music to corridos, reflecting the divergent musical tastes of the Spanish-speaking listeners. Mexicans in Detroit could buy phonograph records at Guzmán's Mexico Universal grocery stores; these recordings came from a Chicago company that produced and distributed them throughout the United States. Tango music was much in demand. This Latin ballroom dance was quite the fad among Mexicans in the Midwest, who danced to music provided by Mexican orchestras like Irondale's jazz orchestra, the Azteca. When Mexican Detroiters staged tango contests, the best dancers often were Ford autoworkers. Their female partners were likewise accomplished dancers. The couples gained recognition for themselves through their tango dancing because it manifested Latin culture. Mexicans also enjoyed listening to the radio, a popular and inexpensive entertainment. Songs like "Tango Argentino" could be heard played live by the Spanish Serenaders Band on Detroit radio station WMBC, which presented ethnic programming.[119]

During their free time away from the car factories, Mexican autoworkers patronized the hundreds of poolrooms, taverns, dance halls, and various downtown burlesque shows. The burlesque shows, oftentimes "wicked" diversions, catered to Detroit's huge population of single men and were part of the city's rampant vice. The gambling, bookmaking, and prostitution that flourished in the "sporting houses" of the downtown district were all by-products of the Motor City's prosperity. A popular kind of night recreation in this time of prohibition was the Mexican dance halls, which often operated out of private homes. Groups of Mexican autoworkers purchased bootleg liquor at "blind pigs" (illegal bars), hired a taxicab, and made the rounds of the private dance halls. Autoworkers spent the evening drinking bootleg liquor and dancing with "nickel snappers," women whom they paid to dance with them. During the Great Depression Mexicans used the dances and parties in basements to raise money to help tenants make their rent payments.[120]

CULTURAL ADAPTATIONS

Through mass entertainment Mexicans in Detroit were exposed to the larger American experience and no longer remained insular in outlook. Time away from factory and home was enjoyed by the immigrants dressed in the attire of American urbanites. Adapting to the social scene of midwestern cities was as essential as adjusting to the routine of the industrial workplace.[121] Newly arrived countrymen in the northern urban cities received advice on how to fit in, which entailed dressing and behaving properly and getting a haircut. (Blacks similarly instructed recently arrived migrants from the South not to wear bib overalls or sit on stoops and porches barefoot.) Mexicans in Pennsylvania's mill towns alerted newcomers to conduct themselves according to the local standards, admonishing them "you are not in El Paso, you are in Pennsylvania." [122] The purpose of this counsel was to reduce the prejudice and discrimination encountered in the North. Mexican immigrants were sensitive to the derogatory stereotypes that circulated in these communities, such as their image as brutes, and helped their compatriots camouflage their newcomer status.

Young Mexican males emulated the "sheik" style of Rudolph Valentino, who had wide appeal because he popularized the Latin type in the United States. The men wore short, pomaded hair with pointed sideburns, dressed in expensive, fashionable clothing, and called themselves sheiks. The flamboyant sheiks of Chicago gained local popularity; the impeccably groomed and smartly dressed Mexican males were hired in dining rooms of big hotels, in department stores, and in other positions where contact with the public was required. Thus, while some Mexicans in the North denied their nationality because of racial prejudice, others chose to assert themselves as Latins and profited from this affirmation of race and culture.[123]

Young Mexican women were also adopting the new American dress modes. Silk dresses, "blond" stockings, and fashionable pumps were in vogue as were short skirts and bobbed hair. The fashionable women criticized their counterparts in Mexico who "all dress alike, in black" and claimed that the married women didn't "care about clothes any more." Along with their new dress styles and brilliantined hair, Mexican women's attitudes were changing through exposure to American mores and the evolving role of women.[124] Many Mexican men did not appreciate these changes, nor approve of women asserting their equality with men. The men believed the younger women tended to go to extremes as they copied the "disrespectful" Americans. Among the criticisms frequently raised by the men was that the new attitudes made Mexican women "'like American women,' independent, sassy, and no longer content to remain submissive"; they added that the women "go to pieces when [they] get freedom . . . in this country." Moreover, the men complained that Mexican women were aware of their small numbers in the North and used this shortage to their advantage.[125]

Mexicans in the Motor City dressed well, and their clothes generally made them indistinguishable as a class. Clothes became a means of personal expression and freedom. At the end of their shifts the men put on hats, suit coats, and dress shoes, for many believed that clothes made the man. Felt or Panama hats, suits, and polished shoes rather than the blue jeans and khaki overalls of the manual laborer were often the standard dress of the Detroit autoworker. Mexicans did work in overalls, but these were washed regularly. Once dressed in street clothes, Mexican workers boarded the trams and headed home or to the local pool halls and restaurants, or else roared off in their cars.[126]

SUMMARY

Detroit's Mexicans appreciated their experiences in this huge metropolitan center. These urban dwellers had established a colony and improvised to cope with the housing shortages and high rents. The residents tolerated the bad living conditions they shared with other ethnic groups, most of whom eventually accepted Mexicans into Detroit's working-class neighborhoods. Motivated by the desire to get ahead, Mexicans strove to achieve a relatively good living standard. Mexican women helped in this regard by obtaining employment throughout the city; the jobs also assisted the young women in gaining a degree of independence. Our Lady of Guadalupe Church, the Protestant missions, and the mutual-aid and fraternal organizations aided many colony inhabitants in their adjustment to an industrial urban environment and occasional encounters with prejudice and discrimination. Workers were reluctant to relinquish their new-found freedom and therefore did not heed the call to attend church regularly and selectively chose participation in the societies.

Exposed daily to city life, with its emphasis on consumerism and mass culture, Mexican Detroiters recounted their experiences to families and friends in their hometowns in Mexico. Stories that described the newly purchased stove or refrigerator, learning to dance the tango, listening to recordings on the victrola or radio, and adopting the latest fashions were as meaningful as descriptions of the work regimen in the car plants. The Ford Model Ts, in which hundreds returned to Mexico, were proof of success in the United States. Prestige in the neighborhoods now took precedence however. As autoworkers, Mexicans were earning decent wages, and the factory jobs instilled in them a sense of pride for working at the biggest manufacturers of mass-produced goods; the automobile work provided Mexicans with a means to enjoy a higher standard of living and enabled these urban trendsetters to take part in Detroit's array of activities.

Mexicans were too busy enjoying the glitter of urban life and improved living standards to notice the problems of the American economy. Imminent signs that the Coolidge Prosperity was coming to an abrupt end were evident in Detroit as early as the 1927 recession. Record production levels were reached by Ford in 1929 but were followed by layoffs of autoworkers in the fall of that year. Ford's workers believed that the layoffs would be of short duration, but they were not. Mexicans began leaving Detroit, despite ties to the Motor City—homes, children in school—content to live on the money earned and saved while in Detroit.

As did Mexicans elsewhere in the Midwest, the recently laid-off autoworkers began making preparations to depart for either Texas or Mexico. The trains took them out of Detroit, although scores departed in the cars and trucks they had purchased. The men left just as they had arrived, in groups of two or more, sharing the cost of transportation and food and enjoying one another's company as they reminisced about Detroit. A common scene in preparation for the exodus from the Midwest was the bustle of Mexicans buying suitcases and trunks at local stores or from the Jewish merchants who sold these goods out of their cars and trucks on the neighborhood streets of the Mexican colonies. These shrewd salesmen could depend on a brisk business from the departing Mexican factory workers. The migrants from Mexico had become accustomed to bargaining and anticipated the sales pitch.[127] The

men did not question the quality of the goods because they were principally concerned with getting belongings back to Mexico and easily gave
in to the persuasion. The Mexicans who stayed in Detroit could not
foresee the severity of the hardships they would undergo as the shutdown of the auto industry plunged the Motor City into its worst economic crisis.

FIVE

Detroit Mexicans in the Great Depression

Mexican workers in the Midwest lost their jobs as steel and automobile manufacturing shut down following the market crash of 1929. Those who survived the wave of job cuts worked two- and three-day schedules and acquiescently accepted pay reductions for the privilege of having a job. Working-class expectations, which rose in proportion to wages in the 1920s, plummeted for Mexicans in the 1930s. The Mexican worker's share in U.S. prosperity ended. Like other workers, they were no longer assured that "security and well-being" were within their reach.[1]

As the crisis deepened and factory jobs became scarce, many unemployed American workers in the Midwest began to blame Mexicans. They believed that Mexicans either were unfairly receiving relief or were being retained by employers so they could have a cheap and tractable source of labor. Once again, Mexicans were cast in their role as scapegoats for the economic hard times. Although hostility was directed at all foreign aliens and unnaturalized immigrants, much of it was aimed at Mexicans. Moreover, white Americans failed to distinguish between Mexicans who were citizens, those in the country legally, and the undocumented.[2]

The anti-Mexican feelings irate American factory workers in the North shared were communicated in the letters some wrote to government officials in Washington. For instance, in September 1930 a laid-off Gary steelworker bitterly complained about the large number of Mexicans in the area in a letter to the Bureau of Immigration: "Most of these Mexicans are not citizens . . . and don't care to be citizens. . . . They are about the lowest class of people that have entered this country. Because they will work cheaper than Americans will, that's the reason there is so many out of work. The American has to walk the streets and a Mexican has the work. That's not justice toward the American citizen."[3] And earlier in the same year an unemployed steelworker in Mansfield, Ohio, offered his suggestion as to how the government could become more involved than it was in alleviating the problem of unemployment—get rid of the Mexicans: "The place to start [is] by deporting thousands of these foreigners. [They] can live in shanty towns and eat from a garbage pail. Their money is either sent for more of their kind to come . . . or saved to take back when they go."[4]

Despite Mexicans' good work records, some companies singled them out for discharge when they began to restrict the few available jobs to American citizens.[5] For this reason, a dozen Mexicans at a steel plant in northwest Indiana, who over the years had proved they were reliable and earnest mill hands, were told by their superintendent that they had to be let go. The Detroit City Council, at the request of the mayor, ruled that no foreign-born workers would be hired even if they filed first papers or became naturalized citizens. Consequently, Mexican Detroiters employed on public track and sewer projects were discharged. Competition intensified for the shrinking pool of factory jobs, and it was difficult for Mexicans to find work. To discourage migration to Detroit, Mexico's Office of Migration Service circulated a notice explaining the bad economic conditions in the city. If Mexican workers wanted to come in spite of the warning, they were legally prevented from doing so by U.S. Bureau of Immigration restrictions placed on travel from Mexico.[6]

The terrible hardships experienced by Detroit's Mexicans can best be understood in relation to the dire economic situation, which was rapidly worsening. The sudden collapse of the auto industry triggered mass layoffs. Idle Mexican autoworkers who had grown accustomed to fluctuations in employment believed the slump would end sometime in the winter of 1929–1930 and that by spring they would be back to work. This, after all, was the pattern in previous years. However, as circumstances in Detroit grew progressively worse, Mexican autoworkers became resigned to the city's economy not improving. Many found it impossible to survive; rent payments and grocery accounts were past due, furniture was repossessed, and as the number of families applying for relief increased, so did the incidence of petty crime involving Mexicans.[7]

The few Mexicans fortunate enough to draw public assistance were struck from the welfare rolls when private and public relief efforts failed. For the first time Detroit faced a major relief crisis. Like other Midwest municipalities, the Motor City was no longer capable of financing its operations, especially its expanding welfare rolls. Detroit's severe fiscal crisis was not remedied until federal aid was received after 1933. More important, Mexicans found it difficult to qualify for relief because of discrimination and mandatory citizenship requirements.

In early 1931, with no end to the depression in sight, Mexicans in Detroit were faced with the choice of staying in the city or volunteering for repatriation. Detroit officials agreed to participate in a statewide program of Mexican repatriation in an attempt to eliminate the relief problem. The Mexican artist Diego Rivera and the newly formed La Liga de Obreros y Campesinos (The League of Mexican Workers and Peasants) of Detroit had appealed to the governor of Michigan to initiate this program. The most hard-pressed Mexican workers, those without money or hope of returning to work, conceded that perhaps the best solution to the problem was to return to their homeland. But city officials quickly grew dissatisfied with the slow pace of removing hundreds of impoverished Mexicans. Confronted with a rapid increase in the number of requests for aid, the DPW began to coerce those who applied for relief to accept repatriation. A degree of racism underlay the attempts of DPW case workers to eliminate Mexicans from the welfare rolls and to pressure them to leave.

An undetermined number of Mexicans left Detroit on their own at the first signs of economic downturn, just as they had during the 1927 recession and the 1920–1921 depression. They joined other Mexicans leaving the Midwest, including unemployed steelworkers and railroad workers from Illinois, Indiana, and Ohio, and sugar-beet workers from throughout the region who were released from their labor contracts. These jobless workers, many of them relatives and friends who had originally come north together, left by car and truck, pooling their cash to pay for gasoline. Others departed in railroad freight cars, and some hitchhiked.[8]

The most resolute of Detroit's Mexicans remained in the city and endured long bouts of unemployment and erratic work schedules. Their chief concern was acquiring food, shelter, coal, and clothing. During the crisis families and friends helped share these burdens. Because of Detroit's dependence on one industry, the decline of the auto industry signaled the beginning of Detroit's financial troubles, and this city's workers bore the brunt of this ruinous collapse.

THE COLLAPSE OF DETROIT'S AUTO INDUSTRY

Mass unemployment increased throughout 1930. At the beginning of 1931, nearly 250,000 workers were idle, and the unemployment rate in Detroit was 32.4 percent. Large crowds of jobless workers assembled expectantly at public and private employment bureaus, at the city's DPW relief stations, at factory gates, and on street corners. "Workers sometimes slept at the plant gates," recalled Lauro Tienda, who was one of the thousands of jobless workers trying to get a job at the Ford Rouge plant.[9]

The sudden drop in employment at the Ford Motor Company reflected the devastating effects of the depression on Detroit. In mid-December 1929, employment in the Ford plants stood at 100,500 workers. By spring 1931, Ford Motors had 84,000 workers on the payrolls at the Rouge and Highland Park plants. By late summer only 37,000 autoworkers were on the job; however, half of these were on a three-day workweek. This system of job sharing and rotating workers had been put into effect throughout U.S. industry. It would be supplemented by extending credit to workers, creating new jobs, prepaying pension plans, and providing garden plots. This version of welfare capitalism at the Ford plants resulted in significant wage reductions but without an easing of the punishing speed-ups.[10]

The workers paid a dear price for their jobs. The $6-a-day wage was instituted by Ford Motors in October 1931 as part of the automaker's cost-cutting measures. All workers experienced these wage cuts, including those with seniority, who previously earned $9.60 and more per day. Guadalupe Morales remembers that the $6-a-day wage was rarely attained because when workers reached the $5.80 rate the company conveniently discharged them and hired others to take their place. Men deemed "inefficient," which meant unable to withstand grueling speed-ups, were arbitrarily discharged. Some Ford jobs disappeared when additional machinery was installed and work was subcontracted to the notoriously low-paying auto-parts makers, like Briggs Manufacturing. Mexicans in the Briggs shops who had built reputations for tenacity were inhumanely subjected to the fierce speed-ups. The general feeling of discontent among Briggs workers would shortly manifest itself as strike action, the first of the preunion era.[11]

Stunned by the initial impact of the depression, Detroit officials predictably blamed the auto companies for bringing to the city a surplus of workers who were now without work. Because feeding and taking care of these men became the responsibility of Detroit's taxpayers, city officials tried to persuade the auto companies to take an active role in providing assistance. Most of the criticism was directed at Ford. Its plants were located outside the city limits in the townships of Dearborn and Highland Park. Thus the powerful and wealthy Ford Motor Company paid no taxes to Detroit, yet thousands of its unemployed workers resided in the city and received relief.[12] DPW officials estimated that 5,000 unemployed Ford blue-collar workers were on its welfare rolls, 15.6 percent of all heads of households receiving relief. These figures were resoundingly refuted by Harry Bennett. The despotic head of Ford's Service Department fired back that Ford's Welfare Office would take care of any worker in need of assistance.[13]

In 1928, 928 Mexicans had been hired at the Rouge plant when production of the Ford Model A started, but only 185 got work the following year. All were let go between 1929 and 1931. The prestige and status that Mexicans employed by Ford had enjoyed as industrious and highly paid workers came to an end. "Once the Mexican Ford autoworkers lost their jobs," Detroiter Pedro Escobar recalled, "they were no longer special. They were like everybody else—broke." [14]

RELIEF EFFORTS

Detroit's fiscal crisis compounded problems for those thrown out of work. The Motor City's mounting financial troubles severely impeded its ability to implement and maintain programs to feed and house the legions of unemployed. Several innovative programs were established early on by the city through the bold leadership of Mayor Frank Murphy, but all these programs failed, with serious and far-reaching consequences for Detroit's Mexicans.

The shutdown of auto plants and factories forced the challenge of dealing with unremitting joblessness on Detroit city officials and businessmen. The Motor City had always been plagued with the problem of a worker surplus; therefore, one immediate measure proposed was stopping the flow of workers into the city. Advertisements were placed in newspapers warning prospective workers not to come because of the rampant unemployment. The Detroit Chamber of Commerce suggested as a remedy that Michigan establish an immigration service to patrol

the state line. This was not an isolated proposal; other states implemented similar programs to alleviate the problem of jobless men who in
the hundreds of thousands now roamed the country seeking any kind of
work.[15] The deteriorating economic situation in Detroit and in Michigan's other manufacturing cities, already overcommitted to the needy,
prompted Governor Wilbur M. Brucker to issue a press release to dissuade further job seekers from entering the state:

> Those who come to Michigan under the mistaken impression that work is
> plentiful will but add to the thousands already without work or any prospect
> of securing it.
>   It is appalling to consider the misery into which such unfortunates may
> be plunged. . . . I see no way in which newcomers can be provided with food
> and shelter at this time, without adding to the suffering of those who are
> already dependent upon public and private charity.[16]

Having used up their shrinking resources to pay for the essentials of
food and shelter, thousands of the city's residents were forced by their
dire circumstances to seek assistance from the DPW. The widely praised
DPW attempted to provide care for the unemployed, but in one month
its relief caseload jumped sevenfold: In March 1930, it paid the most
public relief of all the nation's cities, $762,228.[17] The situation in De-
troit, where mass-production autoworkers reputedly could make a fortune overnight, had reached a critical point.

The Mayor's Unemployment Committee (MUC) was established in
an effort to keep pace with the increasing number of people needing
assistance. MUC was the brain child of Murphy, the new city mayor,
who had been elected on a welfare platform. Its first task was launching
a registration drive among the jobless. Through MUC's Employment
Bureau the most needy cases were given work specially created by the
city and the private sector. In its seven months of operation, the bureau
registered 112,282 families and found work for 23,926 persons, only
half of those who applied. Still, the MUC's Employment Bureau was the
last opportunity for Detroiters who had exhausted all options for procuring work.[18]

This courageous struggle to help the unemployed was stymied by an
outstanding debt of $378 million, which resulted from the rapid expan-
sion of Detroit's public services in the twenties. Because of the debt,
many relief work projects were postponed, and private businesses
stopped hiring referrals from the MUC's Employment Bureau. In the
spring of 1931, Detroit was forced to borrow $5 million to cover its
operational expenses; two months later, it had to borrow an additional

$5 million from the tight-fisted Ford Motor Company to meet its expenditures. Without the funds to feed and shelter the swelling numbers of unemployed, MUC resorted to enterprising measures that proved unsuccessful in the end. It sponsored a citywide garden project, and Mayor Murphy introduced a plan whereby unemployed men paid for their welfare allowances by working on city jobs.[19]

Laid-off autoworker Lauro Tienda was one of the participants in this program. He was hired by the city to collect garbage and wood scraps. Isidro Rivas was also hired. This unemployed Ford worker, steadfastly determined to maintain his pride, pleaded to be put on a job—any kind of job—because he could not stand being idle and did not want to go on welfare. Rivas busily maintained park gardens, cleaned concrete garbage dumpsters, and dug ditches on construction projects. Fortunate to still have an automobile, he earned extra money by charging men a quarter a week to ride with him to work.[20]

In July 1931 the DPW made further cuts in its operating expenditures when it decreased the weekly food allowance for dependent families. This action was followed by a 50 percent reduction of the city's 1931–1932 relief budget of $14 milion. These draconian measures, however, were not enough to make up for Detroit's huge tax delinquency, which in two years had risen to an alarming $18,993,519 and had plunged the city deeper into crisis.[21] Mayor Murphy continued his desperate crusade to resolve the city's financial problems. He cut city-employee salaries, laid off public-works personnel, and ordered the DPW to reduce its relief commitments even more. Eleven thousand families were removed from the relief rolls, a reduction of 25 percent.[22] Additional budget cuts in the summer of 1932 diminished DPW relief expenditures further. Welfare recipients were ordered to move in with other families when the rent-allotment program was terminated, which led to additional evictions of families on assistance. Some households were moved into tent camps set up in city parks such as Clark Park in southwest Detroit, the former center of the Mexican colony. As summer ended, the DPW had exhausted its resources, and family relief was reduced to its lowest figure; only 21,500 families were provided for.[23]

Relief from other sources also was not adequate. At the beginning of the depression Detroit Mexican Consul Ignacio Batiza established relief programs that supplied needy Mexicans in Detroit with food and housing, and he continued to provide letters of recommendation in a futile effort to help the men find work. In the past these official letters did help, but now they had little effect. As early as the recession year of 1927, manufacturing concerns (many pressed by workers trying to protect their own jobs) established stringent hiring policies that restricted employment to U.S. citizens. Inadequate financial resources and manpower shortages soon hindered Consul Batiza's ability to manage the expanding number of requests for aid. The ill-prepared Mexican Honorary Commissions could no longer be relied on for help, owing to constant and widespread demand for assistance and shrinking resources. The Catholic Church provided some aid, but because it was financially hard-pressed, most of its assistance was in the form of opening soup kitchens to feed the hungry. By 1933 the Diocese of Detroit was virtually broke.[24]

The New York banking trust that managed Detroit's debt feared its client would default on its loan payments and refused to refinance the city's short-term loans until it cut $6 million from its budget. Mayor Murphy had no choice but to agree to the terms of this recommended budget reduction, but it proved impossible to achieve. Rising tax delinquency and a payment due on past loans of $27 million left Detroit with only $20 million in operating funds. Only federal aid, the Mayor concluded, could save his city from bankruptcy.[25]

Mexican repatriation from Detroit took place in this bleak financial setting, in a city without adequate relief resources to deal with mass unemployment and threatened by impending bankruptcy. If the Motor City was unable to meet its fiscal obligations or to care for its native-born American residents, how was it to care for its population of foreign-born, many of whom had arrived only recently?

REPATRIATION

As the depression swelled the ranks of unemployed workers in Michigan, the state's Welfare Department came to believe that Mexican repatriation would help alleviate rising relief costs in the local communities. Organized removal campaigns in the state were begun during the first winter of the depression and continued throughout the early thirties.[26] The Mexican government cooperated fully with state and local officials in organizing the voluntary removal of its countrymen, and once they arrived at the border, it arranged and paid for transportation to their homes in the interior. The Mexican National Railways charged the destitute passengers from Michigan only one cent per mile beyond Nuevo Laredo, Tamaulipas, just as it had the poverty-stricken repatriates who left Chicago earlier. However, many newly arrived Mexicans who now resided in Michigan had entered the United States illegally and thus were subject to immediate deportation. In fact, 1,500 of these newcomers without proper documentation were removed from the state in 1931. Mexican Consul Batiza was aware of the growing apprehension regarding deportation and requested that it be played down in order to allay fear and suspicion that the repatriation program also was ordered by the U.S. Immigration Bureau. Mexicans repatriated from Michigan were to leave as organized groups rather than on an individual basis. Their home government believed that this course of action would less likely be interpreted as deportation; moreover, it would facilitate the removal.[27]

The DPW knew that the removal of Mexicans from the city would be more efficient than providing them with relief. Hence it willingly cooperated with Consul Batiza by referring Mexican relief cases and new applications for aid to his office for immediate processing. Hundreds of Mexicans had reached Detroit only recently and therefore were unable to meet the one-year residency requirement for assistance. Prejudice kept many others off the dole. The DPW agreed to pay the train fares of Mexicans returning to Mexico who had come to Detroit after 1929. In accordance with the current immigration statutes regarding admission into the United States, the federal government paid for the train fares of those who had been in the city prior to 1929.[28]

On October 10, 1931, sixty-nine Mexicans boarded trains at the Union Depot on Michigan Avenue and left for Mexico. Fifty-four left on November 6, followed by fifteen on November 20. On December 31, fifty-four more left from Pontiac, and on February 4, 1932, an additional seventy-six Mexicans left. Most were from the Pontiac area, but several Mexicans from Ohio had joined them. Half the repatriates were married couples with children; the remainder consisted of single men and women, almost all returning to towns in the states of Jalisco, Michoacán, and Guanajuato in west central Mexico.[29] Consul Batiza was obviously heartened that the repatriation program was helping alleviate the problems besetting his countrymen in Detroit, where the state's largest concentration of Mexicans resided. He made the following apologetic statement to the *Detroit News:* "The Mexican colony of Detroit is young. The majority of the 15,000 Mexicans have not been in the United States more than five years. They have not yet adapted themselves to the American ways and have been hit hard by the current depression." [30]

Detroit's Mexicans cooperated with the Mexican consul in his efforts to help those who decided to leave. Organized groups in the colony took steps to assure that the repatriation program was successful by helping everyone in the city and throughout Michigan who wanted to return to their country. La Liga de Obreros y Campesinos spearheaded the state-wide effort. This Mexican working-class organization was founded in August 1932, when 264 Mexicans, the majority from the Ford Motor Company, met in the Hispano Unidos Building on Vernor Avenue. Some of these men were laid off; some had managed to stay on the payroll. All were committed to the welfare of the colony and had responded to the handbills La Liga distributed throughout the city. The workers were brought together under the direction of the Mexican artist Diego Rivera, who helped model La Liga after the Communist organization he was affiliated with in Mexico while a member of the party.[31] Rivera was the most famous figure to become involved in the welfare of Mexican nationals in any American city. His participation in the repatriation program, already underway in Detroit before his arrival, was fueled by a progressive and idealistic vision regarding the Mexican working class. Rivera's wish was to see the proletarians of the North return to Mexico to live on worker cooperatives.

Rivera arrived in Detroit on April 22, 1932, accompanied by his wife, the artist Frida Kahlo. The director of the Detroit Institute of Arts, Dr. William Valentiner, invited Rivera to paint a series of panels in the courtyard of the institute. Edsel Ford, the president of the Detroit Arts Commission and the Ford Motor Company, was the patron of the monumental mural project. He provided the financial support for Rivera's series of powerful paintings of Ford autoworkers entitled "Detroit Industry." Rivera's other connection to Ford was through Kahlo. Her father, the photographer Guillermo Kahlo, helped design the Ford branch plant in Mexico City.[32]

Rivera resided in Detroit for almost a year as he painted the murals, and he became well aware of the plight of the city's jobless factory workers. What Rivera saw dampened his enthusiasm for Detroit, though his fascination with machines and with the vision of workers of different nationalities and races toiling side by side at the Ford Rouge plant endured.[33] The image of sullen unemployed autoworkers in Dearborn waiting in bread lines surely remained in the artist's mind. Rivera knew that in early March 1932 Dearborn police had fired on the 3,000 participants in the Ford Hunger March. He saw scenes of destitution in Detroit as he made his way to and from the Institute of Arts on Woodward Avenue. At this site 20,000 Detroiters began their funeral cortege to pay homage to the three workers killed during the Ford Hunger

March. Rivera soon became involved in the efforts to help out-of-work Mexicans. He spent as much time as possible aiding the local colony and taking an active part in many of the colony's functions, some of which he inaugurated. Given the charged environment in Detroit produced by mass demonstrations and actions by the unemployed, Mexican autoworkers had already begun debating the problem of joblessness; Rivera's intellectual intervention served to spur collective action.[34]

Rivera assisted Detroit Mexicans in establishing La Sociedad Cultural (The Cultural Society) and in reorganizing the community newspaper *La Prensa Libre*. The editorials in *La Prensa Libre* became more politically strident than they had been and served as a vehicle for the progressive ideas of Ford autoworker Luis Gasca and other writers tutored by Rivera. Despite its mission of political indoctrination through culture, during the early depression years La Sociedad Cultural provided a social outlet for Detroit's colony. For a dime Mexicans could attend one of the many dances the society sponsored.[35]

The weekly meetings of both La Sociedad Cultural and La Liga were attended regularly by 50 to 100 Mexicans. Small knots of men from the same plants, departments, and shops likely sat together, an expression of their affiliation, which was nurtured by shared work experiences. In his efforts to politicize them, Rivera gave lectures on the evils and inevitable demise of capitalism and on the promise and ideals of the communist world that would take its place. He carefully explained that under communism everything workers received would be obtained through their labor and that in the new classless society they would never go hungry. The Mexican artist told the attentive men why he went to the Soviet Union and extolled the communist way of life. Two former autoworkers recalled the cool reception to Rivera's leftist ideas; the audience remained silent as he lectured, awed by the tall, heavy-set artist with the frog-like eyes. None of the factory workers openly expressed their thoughts about what Rivera said but clearly understood his message. The men had gained their political knowledge about capitalist exploitation and its attendant racism in the heat and noise of car factories and in the smoke and noxious fumes of foundries and not through pilgrimages to the Soviet Union or through books. They learned their lessons about worker inequality through numerous experiences with fierce speed-ups, monotonous machine work, and accidents, all the while being threatened and cursed by gruff shop foremen. This singular work experience gained on the shop floor in combination with ties to friends, family, and community forged the solidarity that became evident in the upcoming labor struggles. Class and privilege thus no doubt separated the cosmopolitan Rivera (he had addressed the New York City John Reed Club in French) from the hardened autoworkers.[36]

Rivera's activities and inflammatory speeches may have won the admiration of certain groups in Detroit, but his actions were harshly criticized by the city's clergy. The controversy raised the ire of devout Catholic Mexicans and took their minds off the urgent problems of the depression long enough to attack Rivera for his atheistic, communist teachings. Certain members of Detroit's Catholic clergy, responding to the heightened communist activity in the Motor City, believed that La Sociedad Cultural did not just engage in parlor talk about Mexican culture and the arts but instead was "designed to instill Soviet principles into 'Mexican souls.'" Other clergy alleged that the vociferous newspaper *La Prensa Libre* "was another attempt to spread socialism among Mexicans."[37]

For their part, the city's devout Mexican Catholics wrote a letter of protest to Bishop Gallagher. In their letter, translated by Simón Muñoz, they fervently complained that members of La Liga had begun an attack on the Catholic Church and were inducing Mexicans to become communists. Muñoz named "the great Mexican painter" Rivera as one of the leaders of the assault on the Church. Muñoz with other Mexican Catholics had launched the newspaper *La Chispa* in an attempt to counter the socialistic and communistic writings of *La Prensa Libre*.[38] Evidently, not all Detroit's Mexicans appreciated Rivera's propaganda or his intervention in helping them return to Mexico. Perhaps this small group of zealous Mexican Catholics, many of whom had recently fled the religious persecution of the Cristero Revolution, preferred to risk unknown hardships in Detroit rather than live and work in godless worker cooperatives in Mexico. More important, this segment of the population was weighed down by Mexican tradition, which acknowledged the paternal authority of the Catholic Church. Detroit's Mexican autoworkers would have to circumvent this narrow-mindedness as they became involved in their collective effort to aid their less fortunate countrymen.

The state of Michigan helped direct the repatriation program, and Governor Brucker was approached by Rivera and La Liga for his assistance. The governor realized the magnitude of the task and contacted Detroit District Director of U.S. Immigration John L. Zubrick for additional help. Consul Batiza, Zubrick, and local city and welfare officials gave Brucker their full cooperation.[39]

For its part in the program, La Liga helped 850 Mexicans register at its local Detroit office within two weeks after its formation. La Liga established branch offices in other cities in Michigan and Ohio with large Mexican populations; the branches agreed to aid La Liga and the state of Michigan by providing funds. Altogether, between 4,000 and 5,000 Mexicans registered with this progressive organization or with the Detroit Mexican Consulate, which had jurisdiction over a large section of the Midwest. Almost 1,600 of these registrants were residents of Detroit.[40] Following the example of Governor Brucker, Consul Batiza attempted to get as many Mexicans as possible to participate voluntarily in the repatriations before the onset of winter, when it would be even more difficult to provide shelter and food for everyone in need. He made his appeal on October 17, 1932, in a circular written in Spanish, thousands of which were distributed to the Mexicans in Michigan and Ohio:

> As winter approaches, life in this region becomes more and more difficult for persons without work. All of the circumstances which produce the crisis still prevail without possible hope of amelioration in the near future; for which reason this Consulate reiterates its call to our Mexican residents that for their own interest they accept this opportunity . . . for their repatriation and return to our country.[41]

District Director Zubrick had special reasons for enthusiastically agreeing with the governor's proposal to remove indigent Mexicans from the state. If this first attempt at a statewide organized removal of Mexicans proved successful, Zubrick envisioned the launching of similar programs by other states in the Midwest, including one for destitute European aliens. Zubrick therefore recommended to U.S. Commissioner General of Immigration Harry Hull that both his bureau and the Department of Labor make an intensive study of the matter.[42] Zubrick went on to express the feelings of many state and local officials in Michigan regarding the repatriation of Mexican nationals who, in addition to being a burden to the welfare system, allegedly were taking jobs away from American citizens: "The elimination of such a large number of alien laborers and mechanics will work a tremendous benefit. . . . [It] will remove from the economic field a group that . . . is able to get first consideration in employment, . . . and by their removal the openings in industry will be left for residents and citizens of the United States." [43]

The special transportation arrangements were handled by the Central Passenger Association of Chicago with the cooperation of the railroads. Trains were chartered for the repatriates at $17 per person, rates considered acceptable by Consul Batiza, Director Zubrick, and the Detroit DPW. In light of its austerity measures, the DPW expressed particular satisfaction over this low cost. It represented a considerable savings, the equivalent of two to three months' welfare payments.[44]

Mexicans were sent by train to the processing center at Nuevo Laredo, across the border from Laredo, Texas. For many, the train ride reminded them of an earlier journey when they were first brought by railway car to Michigan by the beet companies eager for their labor. On the afternoon of November 15, 1932, approximately 432 Mexicans boarded a Wabash Railroad passenger train at the Union Depot and left Detroit on the forty-hour trip to Nuevo Laredo. The repatriates carried most of their personal belongings by hand, in suitcases, and in bags, just as they had when they first came to the city. Rivera and Kahlo walked through the railway cars to bid the Mexicans farewell. The portly artist no doubt was pleased that some of Mexico's finest sons (and daughters) were on their way to settle in worker cooperatives in northern Mexico. Mexicans leaned out of the train's windows to say good-bye to relatives and friends amidst the crowd gathered on the platform to witness the removal. A few men idly strummed guitars, while some of the women passengers modestly breast-fed their hungry babies, a portent of things to come.[45]

It was a cold and snowy Tuesday afternoon. There had been a fierce snowstorm the night before, a final reminder of the harsh climate the repatriates were leaving behind in the North. Four hundred of the departing Mexicans were from Detroit, the remainder came from nearby Dearborn, Highland Park, Melvindale, Hamtramck, and Muskegon. Because Detroit's DPW did not provide relief assistance to single males, almost a third of the repatriates were single men. Many of the Mexican children on board were American-born or of mixed parentage, the sons and daughters of marriages between Mexican men and Polish, German, Italian, and Hungarian women. The sullen children had cried as they were made to leave schools, friends, and a way of life different from the one they would find in Mexico. Some of the non-Mexican spouses accompanying their husbands and families had renounced their American citizenship. Only four deportees were with the two trainloads of Mexican repatriates.[46]

Because of the continuing snowstorm, the trains carrying the repatriates from Detroit arrived in St. Louis three and a half hours late. The need to wire for a doctor because some passengers on board were ill and the considerable wait for the doctor also contributed to this delay. No food was provided for the nonpaying passengers—that is, children under five years of age. Consequently, seventy-eight children received only milk three times a day and whatever portion of their parents' meager rations that could be shared. In St. Louis, the tired and hungry travelers were moved into cars of the Missouri Pacific Railroad for the trip to San Antonio. They arrived in the city the afternoon of the next day, November 17. In San Antonio, the travel-weary and hungry repatriates were transferred to a train of the International and Great Northern Railroad for the final leg of the trip to Laredo, arriving in this border town in the early evening.[47]

Twenty members of La Liga and an inspector from the U.S. Immigration Bureau had accompanied the repatriates from Detroit to the border, where Mexican health officials examined and inoculated them as they disembarked. Half were scheduled to return to their homes in the Mexican interior. The others were destined for various agricultural cooperatives that Rivera told them the Cárdenas government had established specifically for them.[48]

Another train carrying 430 Mexicans left Saginaw on the afternoon of November 22. Having learned of the misfortunes of their countrymen on the first trains, almost all the passengers brought food with them and purchased milk for the young children when the train stopped in Decatur, Illinois. When the train reached San Antonio about a dozen repatriates requested to leave but were refused permission. Two disgruntled passengers jumped through the windows of the train when it arrived in Laredo on November 24. These two Mexicans undoubtedly had changed their minds about returning to Mexico. Both were found wandering in the rail yards, probably waiting to catch an outbound train that would take them north. The next day they were returned to Mexico.[49]

In his report to the Mexican department of migration on November 28, Batiza noted that 864 Mexicans had been repatriated from the colonies in Detroit and Saginaw. He mentioned that a third party of 282 was scheduled to leave on December 6 and that plans were being made to send out a fourth party of 133 Mexicans on December 20 from Port Huron, Mt. Clemens, Flint, Pontiac, and Lansing. This would be the last organized repatriation handled by the Michigan Welfare Department.[50]

Determined to help as many poverty-stricken Mexicans in Michigan as possible, Rivera and the loyal members of La Liga began traveling throughout the state to contact their compatriots. Their efforts focused on their countrymen living in rural areas, mainly the hard-to-reach pockets of indigent sugar-beet workers stranded on farms throughout the state. Governor Brucker initiated a registration drive to estimate how many additional Mexicans desired state assistance to return to their homeland. State agents began this process in Saginaw, Shiawassee, Genesee, Lapeer, Bay, Tuscola, St. Clair, Macomb, and Oakland counties. The Mexicans had only recently made their way to the towns and cities from the outlying sugar-beet farms and were ineligible for relief assistance. However, because of apprehension about the actual purpose of the registration drives, the destitute men, women, and children did not cooperate fully with the state agents. Afraid that they were being processed for deportation, those in Saginaw not only refused to be listed with the state officials but impeded the agents' efforts. The state officials subsequently solicited the aid of Consul Batiza to explain the exact purpose of the procedure to Saginaw's Mexicans and to convince them how it would especially benefit the neediest.[51]

Batiza traveled to Saginaw and called a meeting of the Mexicans in the city. He soon discovered that their refusal to register was due in part to their intentionally ignoring the previous attempts of La Liga members to inform them about the repatriation program. Furthermore, a Catholic missionary, doubting the real purpose of these efforts, had told the Mexicans that they were being taken to Mexico to be drafted as soldiers in the war against the Cristeros. The men became frightened because most were from west central Mexico, where a large part of the fighting had taken place between Cristero and government forces. Mexicans in Pontiac, Flint, and Mt. Pleasant, who arrived recently from the outlying sugar-beet fields and had been shut off from reliable news sources, expressed a similar fear of military conscription.[52]

Voluntary removal from Detroit and the rest of the state proceeded as planned through November and into the first week in December, but shortly thereafter the Mexican government requested that it be terminated. On December 10, the Mexican department of migration wired Consul Batiza to inform him that additional returnees could no longer be assisted because of Mexico's own mass unemployment.[53] Repatriates were also not being hired by employers in Mexico for fear of fomenting labor dissension. Hardened factory laborers from the North were likely to know when they were being exploited. These were men who walked off their jobs because of dissatisfaction with poor working conditions and who thought nothing of disobeying, talking back to, or assaulting foremen. One employer (who happened to be American), when asked by an interviewer whether he hired many of the returning Mexicans, retorted: "I don't like to employ them [Mexicans] once they have been [to the United States]. They get too smart; . . . they talk to other workmen and spoil them."[54] The news of grim conditions and the lack of work in Mexico, which was relayed to Detroit in letters and by disheartened Mexicans returning to the city, began hampering the removals.

In addition, the accounts filtering back to Detroit of the first trip described a long delay in Nuevo Laredo for nine hours because of a rainstorm. This delay disrupted plans of the Mexican government to transport its returning citizens to the interior on trains of the Mexican National Railways. The passengers had to remain in the rail cars on the Mexican side of the border all night without light or heat, and the Mexican train company failed to make arrangements to furnish them with food. This time they had to rely on handouts from local people. The distraught, hungry, and unbathed repatriates were finally sent into Mexico in boxcars and not in the passenger trains as Rivera, La Liga, and Batiza had promised. When they arrived at the farm cooperatives, they discovered that the land was poor and lacked irrigation, and the financial assistance, tools, and seed they were promised by the Mexican government never arrived.[55]

The vision of workers' cooperatives created by Rivera in his eloquent speeches and lectures was shattered. In Michigan, officials feared that reports from Mexico about the cooperatives would jeopardize further repatriation efforts from the state. This fear soon proved justified.[56] Discouraged by the reports on the cooperatives and frustrated with delays in transportation, many Mexicans left stranded in Nuevo Laredo began selling their personal belongings to pay for the return trip to Detroit. Others headed back to the Motor City because their homesick American-born children and wives could not adjust to the new surroundings.[57]

Consul Batiza and Rivera no longer persuaded Mexicans to leave for Mexico but instead encouraged them to remain in Detroit. Rivera realized that the voluntary repatriation program failed to serve the best interests of his countrymen. Rivera had devoted much time and the money earned from painting the murals to organize the repatriation of Mexicans in Michigan. He now told Mexicans that like other unemployed factory workers their struggle was in Detroit. Consul Batiza had not had a change of mind; rather, he had been ordered by the Mexican government to cease the program. Aware that similar economic hard times awaited Detroit Mexicans in Mexico, he urged those referred to him by the DPW to stay. La Liga no doubt learned of this fiasco from members who had accompanied the repatriates on their journey. They probably reported on the appalling conditions of the trip and on how Mexico officially greeted its countrymen. In practice, repatriation was sorely wanting. To see fellow Detroiters begging for food like paupers and learning that the cooperatives were poorly administered was the final insult to Detroit Mexicans.[58] The hope for a better life in Mexico had been dashed in a little over a month's time.

The Detroit removal program received the strongest opposition from the Communist Party's International Labor Defense (ILD), and Rivera became a special target of this radical organization's protestations. In its push to organize protests and demonstrations against the city and the auto industry, the ILD was deeply involved in striving to gain the interest and support of Detroit's working classes, including the besieged Mexicans. Circulars written in Spanish, which attacked the repatriation program and criticized the work of Rivera and La Liga, were distributed by the ILD to those who remained in the Mexican colony. The Detroit chapter charged that Rivera was a "renegade from the Communist Party"—a renewal of the attack on the Mexican artist launched earlier at New York City's John Reed Club by party member William Dunne, editor of the *Daily Worker*. On that occasion, when Rivera responded to an invitation to speak at the club, he encouraged the audience to "join hands in the coming struggle against capitalism, against imperialism." At that point, he was interrupted by Dunne and the other party loyalists who branded him "an opportunist" who sold "his talent to the Rockefellers and other capitalists." The attack was premeditated and carefully planned by party headquarters in New York City. Detroit ILD members knew that Rivera was being ousted from the Communist Party. Their vituperative circular also condemned the Mexican government's unfulfilled promises to provide land, agricultural tools, and food for the repatriates, and it accused the United States of breaking up families in its forcible deportations of Mexicans.[59]

Coercion was the primary method used to convince Mexicans in Detroit and elsewhere in the Midwest that repatriation was a feasible option to relief. As the crisis deepened, the level of coercion increased in each location in proportion to its jobless rate and the fiscal status of the municipality. In St. Paul, the movement to repatriate Mexicans was underscored by efforts to remove these workers from heretofore undesirable field jobs, labor now coveted by unemployed white workers. In

East Chicago, Mexicans had already left at the first signs of the down-turn in the steel industry. Subtle pressure was placed on those staying to persuade them to accept repatriation. Mexican families were grudgingly given assistance but only after enduring considerable harassment by case workers. In Gary, Mexican families were automatically cut from welfare rolls if they refused to participate in the city's repatriation pro-gram. The Mexicans had been unable to understand the English-speaking case workers and were suspicious of their assistance. One Gary resident recalled that "many Mexicans were forced into repatria-tion while others, because of the language barrier and fear of the gov-ernment, were sort of fooled into it." [60]

Mexicans in Indiana Harbor were not asked by local welfare officials whether they wanted to return voluntarily to Mexico. Lists compiled by the relief department specified the number of hours Mexican steelwork-ers had worked for the week. When transportation to the border be-came available, those not making enough money were told by case workers that they had to be taken off the dole and removed from the city. An ex-steelworker bitterly remembered the conversation with and clever strategy of his case worker:

> "You are making $7.00 or $8.00 per payday for your family. You can't feed them . . . so we are going to take you off welfare."
>
> "Oh, God, what are you going to do, take us off welfare? We'll starve."
>
> "No, no, you have an alternative; . . . go to Mexico. We have a train that is available. . . ."
>
> So actually they weren't forcing you to leave, they gave you a choice, starve or go back to Mexico. [61]

Detroit DPW officials continued to battle the problem of dwindling funds and multiplying relief requests. The DPW scrutinized all new re-lief applications and ordered additional cuts in the number of families receiving assistance. Like most of Detroit's needy workers, Mexicans coping with joblessness and hard times applied for relief as the final recourse. Applying for welfare was a degrading experience and one tainted by racial prejudice, as black relief applicants knew. Case work-ers had various methods to vent their prejudice and dissuade those seek-ing aid. Often they meticulously reviewed the Mexican caseloads in an attempt to frustrate the applicants. Relief workers tried to humiliate families by accusing them of being lazy, for example, or of having too many children. Different files for Mexican and white applicants were maintained. "We had our own color," recalled ex-autoworker Ramón

Huerta. Mexican relief recipients were warned that if they did not cooperate, all assistance to them would be cut or else they would be repatriated.[62]

This was the experience of forty-two-year-old Pedro González, a
laid-off Ford autoworker from Dearborn. Accompanied by his wife and
four children, González had entered the United States in 1923; in 1925
the González family arrived in Detroit, where González obtained a job
with the Oldsman Foundry. A short time later, he was hired at the Ford
River Rouge plant and worked there for nearly six years before being
laid off in July 1931. Now, with a wife and nine children to support, he
applied for relief and inquired about repatriation at the Dearborn Welfare Board. One of his sons convinced the distraught Mexican autoworker to rescind his application for repatriation.[63]

In September 1931, González was rehired at the Ford Rouge plant
and worked sporadically for nearly five months until March 1932,
when he was laid off indefinitely. He again applied for assistance at the
Dearborn Welfare Board but was refused aid. Instead, pressure was
placed on him to return to Mexico. González protested vehemently that
he did not want to go back to Mexico but to no avail. He was subsequently ordered to appear before the immigration authorities to verify
his legal residence, which was easily proved. The Dearborn Welfare Department began threatening him by saying that he had to return to Mexico on the day scheduled. In a formal complaint, filed with Consul Batiza, González recounted how police officers dragged him and his family
out of their house and forced them into an ambulance, which took them
to the railroad station in Detroit. He further charged that he and his
family were treated like criminals and publicly humiliated in front of
their neighbors and the people at the Union Depot.[64]

González's experience was not an isolated incident of intimidation.
In Chicago, where acute joblessness and insufficient relief resources
forced some of the hungry to sift through garbage dumps for food,
Mexicans seeking relief were harassed by the U.S. Immigration Service.
On the morning of August 11, 1932, two field agents from the U.S.
Immigration Bureau entered the home of Ignacio Romero, Jr., detained
him without an arrest warrant, and harassed his family. The agents had
not bothered to determine whether Romero was in the country legally.
Mexicans in Gary were likewise bullied by relief officials determined to
rid the city of them. One agitated welfare applicant told the Gary International Institute that he had been ordered by a city relief worker to
surrender his "first papers" after refusing removal to Mexico.[65]

In their dealings with Mexican families seeking aid, Detroit DPW workers placed some on public cafeteria lists. After September 1932, the Reconstruction Finance Corporation paid for nearly all of Detroit's assistance programs. To save money, the city discontinued issuing its own food orders and began using federal funds to set up public cafeterias. Ten cafeterias were opened in Detroit where 6,000 unemployed workers and their families were fed each day. These proud and normally self-sufficient families had to walk to the cafeterias, and they suffered the embarrassment of this daily trek and the long wait in the municipal soup lines. To accept food from the city meant a further loss of their self-esteem.[66]

Not every Mexican felt this way—food for their families came before their pride. Given the bleak conditions in Detroit, with scores of the jobless resorting to stealing food to eat, workers welcomed the opportunity for a hot meal at the public cafeterias. Some Mexican Detroiters survived on a diet of carrots and potatoes from their backyard gardens. Those with children had to be constantly watchful of hungry workers, heretofore decent people, who stole milk off their porches. Ford autoworker Reyes Padilla made daily rounds of local bakeries to collect day-old bread, which he distributed from his garage to needy Mexicans.[67]

A total of 1,426 Mexicans repatriated from Detroit at a cost of $21,716 meant considerably lower relief expenditures for the DPW. By the middle of December 1932, only 3,000 Mexicans remained in Detroit. By 1936 the population dwindled to 1,200, a nearly 90 percent reduction of the population residing in the city in 1928. According to a report by Consul Batiza, just 15 percent of the city's Mexicans had work, 50 percent received assistance, and 35 percent "were having a hard time of it" and in a "precarious condition."[68]

Significant reductions in the number of Mexicans in other midwestern communities revealed the extent of the drive to remove this group from the region, which generated a climate of fear in the colonies that persisted for most of the 1930s. Six trainloads of Mexicans (1,032) left from East Chicago between June and October 1932. They represented one-third of the city's 1930 Mexican population; if the Mexicans who left on their own are included, about one-half of East Chicago's pre-depression Mexican population no longer lived in the city. Of those remaining, 50 percent were on relief and working at whatever jobs they could find. During 1932, about 1,500 Mexicans were repatriated from Gary, and another 1,800 left for the border from other parts of Lake County. In October 1933, only 1,500 of the estimated 3,500 to 4,000

Mexicans who had lived in Milwaukee up to 1929 remained, and half were on relief. St. Paul was one of the first midwestern communities to institute a repatriation program. In 1934, as Teamsters Local 574 was waging a violent trucker's strike in adjacent Minneapolis, 328 Mexicans (including American-born citizens) were repatriated from St. Paul, and those who failed to return to Mexico were denied relief. The Chicago Mexican newspaper *La Defensa* reported in 1936 that the percentage of unemployed Mexicans in the city was the highest of all foreign groups. More than 25 percent of the Windy City's Mexicans were jobless; some had not worked in industry for several years.[69]

THE PLIGHT OF LAID-OFF FORD WORKERS

Mexicans in the manufacturing centers of the Midwest underwent considerable hardship as northern employers discharged them en masse, relief assistance from local welfare agencies was denied, and thousands were forced to leave the region. An examination of the hardships Detroit's Mexican Ford autoworkers endured as the Great Depression unfolded reveals the severity of their suffering.

Little is known about how Mexican blue-collar workers in Detroit coped with the hardships in the first years of the depression. However, the case studies of the Ford Sociological Department and employment record card data illustrate the dismal conditions of the company's Mexican autoworkers. This information documents a wide range of experiences shared by workers who were laid off. Their ability to contend with the daily reality of the depression was determined by such factors as household situation, number and availability of dependents who could serve as wage earners, amount of savings, and preceding bouts of unemployment. The men depended on odd jobs to keep active and to generate cash. They shoveled snow, cut hair in exchange for coal, collected junk outside the city to bring back and sell, and hundreds left Detroit on two-week railroad cleanup and track-laying projects.[70]

As the depression wore on, the Mexicans from Ford developed alternative strategies for coping. For instance, family members hospitalized at the Henry Ford Hospital would delay paying their bills because they knew that breadwinners would be kept on the job until the debt they incurred could be paid off. The sons of unemployed men who could qualify enrolled in the Ford Trade School. In addition to obtaining a technical education, these young Mexicans received wages in the form of a stipend that helped support the family. Meanwhile, the wives and daughters of the unemployed workers could go to the Ford Sociological Department and request assistance, though it was not always forthcoming.[71]

Some Mexican Ford autoworkers drew on their modest savings accumulated during better times to help them through the jobless periods.[72] These men, however, were unusually fortunate. The majority of Ford's laid-off Mexican workers faced not only the challenges posed by unemployment but also overdue rent payments, payments on cash loans drawn from local credit unions, food bills, and medical expenses. There were also additional bills from consumer items purchased on credit such as radios, stoves, refrigerators, and cars. Ford records indicate that the small number of Mexicans in Detroit who owned homes lost their property during the depression.[73] Mexican Ford autoworkers with job seniority were not exempt from the ravages of the depression. There were no rewards for loyalty and years of hard work, nor just compensation for those grateful to Henry Ford for the chance to work in his factories.[74]

The experiences of Fidencio Mata were typical. Mata entered the United States in the spring of 1919 and worked at the railroad station in Laredo before he migrated to Detroit and obtained work at the Ford Highland Park plant. Despite the huge number of layoffs in September 1920, this autoworker managed to stay on the job. The following November, during the 1920–1921 depression, he married seventeen-year-old Fidela Suarez. One year later, not sure he could keep his job at the Highland Park plant, Mata quit and returned to Mexico with his wife. The Mexican couple waited until conditions improved before they returned to Detroit in 1923.[75]

That year, Mata was hired at the Ford Rouge foundry as a helper, and he remained steadily employed until his layoff in early October 1931. Investigators from the Ford Sociological Department were sent to visit Mata in southwest Detroit, where he lived with his wife and five children. The investigators reported that he had accumulated $675 in debts and nearly half were unpaid commercial loans. These bills included: $68 for two months' rent, an additional $135 in rent for a house previously lived in, $113 for milk, $40 in doctor bills, $22 in dental bills, $255 in loans from the Morris Plan and the Edwin Leonard Finance Company (both loans borrowed against Mata's car), and $42 to Crowley's Milliner Company for clothing. Mata's only income was the

$10 a week his brother paid him for room and board, but even this income stopped when his brother lost his job at the Ford Rouge plant.[76]

At the recommendation of the Ford Sociological Department, Mata was rehired at the Ford Rouge in November 1931 but worked sporadically for several weeks before he was laid off again. He spent December and January without work. In early February 1932, he was rehired at the Rouge plant but spent less than a month on the job before being placed on indefinite layoff. Mata had worked for the Ford Motor Company for a total of eleven years and three months. Three years would pass before the autoworker was called back.[77]

Detroit's unemployed Mexicans turned to relatives, "the inner ring of support networks," for help with housing, food, clothing, and small cash advances. Those who planned to leave depended on kin for help with final arrangements and to raise gas money for the long trip. Family networks became a key feature of the survival strategies of jobless Ford autoworkers who remained in the Motor City.[78] The following accounts from two Ford sociological case studies present contrasting examples.

Ford autoworker Fred Gutiérrez had been laid off four months when he was visited by investigators from the Ford Sociological Department on October 26, 1932. The fifty-five-year-old Mexican had been on the payroll of the Ford Motor Company for twelve years, since the summer of 1920, when he arrived in Detroit from the steel mills of Indiana Harbor with his wife, Rafila, their two teenage sons, Fred, Jr., and Marcos, and two daughters, Ida and Ruth. Both of Fred's sons eventually obtained jobs with Ford.[79] Now older, Fred could no longer keep up a fast work pace nor do the heavy lifting for eight to ten hours that he had done for a dozen years. Moreover, failing vision limited the old timer's opportunities to find a job. Although his wife obtained work and brought in some income, Fred's two sons were unable to help their parents. They had not worked full-time in nine months. Nor could Fred's two daughters, twelve-year-old Ida and eighteen-year-old Ruth (who was married to Ford autoworker Arthur García), assist their family. Without shoes or coats, they could not look for work. Ruth's husband did not assist his in-laws because he had recently lost his job at the Ford Rouge plant. Fred was provided some assistance by the Dearborn Welfare Department to pay his rent, food, and doctor bills so that he and his family were able to survive the winter. In April 1933, four months after his case came to the attention of the Ford Sociological Department, Fred was transferred to the Ford Dearborn commissary, where this old and nearly blind autoworker was given light work.[80]

In late October 1932, Ford Sociological Department investigators visited thirty-four-year-old Cecelia Peña, the widow of Ford auto-worker Gilberto Peña, who died in 1929. Peña's late husband had worked steadily for Ford Motors from 1919 until his death, except for one year of work with Carnegie Steel in Homestead, Pennsylvania. The widow and her seven-year-old daughter, Olivia, lived in a small, three-room apartment in southwest Detroit that they shared with Peña's two brothers, nineteen-year-old Henry and twenty-one-year-old Robert Saucedo. Both men had not worked in six months; Henry lost his job at the Ternstedt Foundry, and Robert was laid off from the Ford Rouge plant. Peña and her daughter received $11 in monthly payments from the Detroit DPW and along with her two brothers ate at one of the public cafeterias set up by the city. The two brothers were expected to pay the rent on the apartment, which was now $110 in arrears.[81]

The meager assistance payments were not enough to live on, so the Peña household depended on the support of their brother-in-law, Ford autoworker Alfredo Talamante, but he was also down on his luck.[82] Talamante was working three days a week at the Rouge plant, earning $18 weekly. In addition to providing for his wife and daughter, sister-in-law, and two brothers-in-law, Talamante helped his sister and her husband, Manuel Guerra, and their three children. A Ford autoworker since 1927, Guerra had lost his job at the Rouge plant. The Guerra family lived in a two-room apartment in southwest Detroit but quickly became destitute. Two years earlier, Guerra received a loan of $100 from Talamante to help pay his living expenses for the year. Guerra sent one son to live with his grandmother in Texas so he would have fewer family members to support.[83]

Some Mexican Ford autoworkers did not have family to depend on or else had households with ailing relatives or children too young to work. Bernabe Gutiérrez was earning $18 a week for three days' work at the Rouge plant and owed $127 for rent, utilities, food, and doctor bills. The Mexican autoworker's wife was unable to contribute to the family income, as she was nursing a three-month-old child and caring for four others, all under eight years of age. The Gutiérrez children had no winter clothing or shoes and consequently stopped attending school. Thirty-three-year-old Ford autoworker Henry Tafoya supported his wife, Elma, their three sons, and his sixty-three-year-old father-in-law on the $16 he earned for three days' work at the Rouge plant. All three of Henry's sons needed tonsillectomies and ate their meals at school because the father could not afford to feed them at home. Ford Sociological Department investigators rejected Tafoya's request for aid, deciding that the factory wages the Mexican autoworker made were "sufficient for proper food and fresh milk." [84]

The self-esteem of many Mexican Ford autoworkers was shattered by the experience of unemployment and the domestic strife that went with it, the lack of food and clothing, mounting bills, and no money to pay a doctor when loved ones were sick.[85] This was the experience of Jesús Huerta, a thirty-eight-year-old laid-off Ford autoworker. He was hired at the Rouge plant as a helper in late January 1930 and spent a year and a half employed intermittently before he lost his job. In January 1932, Huerta was called back to work but at a $0.12 reduction in hourly wages, thereby earning even less for the few hours on the job. This work lasted two weeks, until he was again laid off, this time indefinitely. He was confronted with the ordeal of day-by-day survival. The autoworker owed his landlord $35 for the house he rented in southwest Detroit, $35 was due a neighborhood grocer who had recently canceled Huerta's credit, and a one-time $50 emergency loan from the DPW remained unpaid. The struggle to support his family was not Huerta's only concern because he was also helping an unemployed friend and his family by letting them live at his house. The friend already owed Huerta three months' rent. Joblessness, the added stress brought on by steadily mounting bills, and the overcrowded living conditions all took their toll on Huerta's waning perseverance. When they visited Huerta and his family on May 31, 1932, Ford investigators reported that the Mexicans were "destitute and dirty" and that a distraught Huerta had just been arrested by city police for fighting with his wife.[86]

Most Mexican Ford autoworkers could not survive on the reduced work schedules and the assistance and mutual support of relatives and friends who shared similar circumstances. Their plight required intervention by the Mexican consul, the Ford Motor Company, and the DPW. They had the option of returning to Mexico, but the immigrants were determined to stay in Detroit and cope as best they could with the daily problems of the depression. Detroit had become home to these Mexican workers.

THE CONTINUING DEPRESSION AND LABOR ORGANIZING

Some Detroit factories started up production in April 1933 with an upturn of the economy and in the wake of an unsuccessful strike wave.

Mexicans expected a call back to work when factories began full production of new car models. Although the number of workers laid off in
Detroit continued to increase, by June some jobless Mexican autoworkers were finding employment.[87] In the meantime, Mexicans continued
to leave Detroit, having given up on fulfilling their dreams in the Motor
City. These workers survived periods of unemployment in the past but
never as long as during the depression. They had come to the United
States for a better life but now were returning poor and hungry, an embarrassing turn of events.[88]

In other parts of Michigan, the beet fields and foundries provided
work for Mexicans. Unemployed Americans generally refused to accept
this work, despite their impoverished condition. One hundred Mexicans chose to stay in Port Huron because they were employed part-time
at the Holmes Foundry. Their relief payments were cut, they were having problems paying their rent, and many were unable to buy clothing,
but the foundry supplemented their wages with modest food supplies.
Holmes was generous in supporting its hard-working Mexican employees; their labor was crucial to the company's survival because only
they would take on the difficult and dangerous foundry jobs. Grateful
for the help they received, the company's Mexicans hoped that local
economic conditions would improve so they could be reinstated to full-
time work. In Saginaw, 175 Mexican foundrymen likewise decided to
stay. All worked at the Gray Iron Foundry, one of the state's most dangerous workplaces, which had a large black and Mexican workforce.
One hundred Mexican families waited out the depression in the Mt.
Pleasant area. They had worked on sugar-beet farms but now received
some assistance from farmers and charitable organizations, all the while
hoping that the economy would recover so they could return to work
and save enough money to eventually leave the area.[89]

The economic picture brightened momentarily for Mexicans living in
other midwestern cities. In Chicago, where industrial jobs were scarce,
hundreds of Mexicans found pick-and-shovel work in February 1934
with the Chicago Northwestern Railroad Company. Two years earlier,
several hundred Mexicans obtained similar work with the Illinois Central Railroad when it needed 1,500 day laborers. And in East Chicago
conditions among the remaining Mexicans, on the dole or else making
due with menial work, improved as local industry recovered. However,
the monopoly on low wage labor by Mexicans in the Midwest was eventually eliminated. The depression increased competition from urban laborers and jobless farmers, just as it did in the Southwest, where the

flood of desperate Oakies and Arkies replaced Mexicans as the chief source of stoop labor. Sometimes farmers preferred to hire only white Americans. In Minnesota in 1933, Mexicans began to compete with laid-off American workers for sugar-beet work. "Only White Labor Employed" signs greeted Mexicans in the fields outside St. Paul.[90]

In Detroit discontented Mexican factory workers began to become involved in union organizing. Some workers had known about unions in Mexico, while others, like Ramón Huerta, gained first-hand experience with labor organizing in the United States. The ex-Chrysler worker stated, "I learned about unions in Colorado, in the coal mines where I shoveled coal for a dollar a ton. Frankly, I left the mines because I was a unionist. My compadre and I left when the strike at our mine was broken."[91]

Routinely exposed to the worst working conditions and placed in compromising positions during strikes, Detroit workers had also come in contact with union organizers, who urged them to join the labor movement. In the Motor City, many Mexicans actively participated in the marches, demonstrations, and strikes held by workers. Lauro Tienda recalled that a German American co-worker told him about the union after the co-worker went to the office of the United Auto Workers (UAW) on Woodward Avenue to volunteer for union work. At first Tienda was skeptical of his friend's advice and told him, "The union will not work. We will have two masters." But he had a change of heart:

> I wound up working for the UAW, passing out applications. We used to go to the Rouge plant in a union car to recruit members. "Come out and work for the union," we would yell to the workers on their breaks. My brother-in-law worked at Ford. I remember him telling me the union would never come to Ford's. He took one of my leaflets anyway. He later joined the union. Many Mexicans became involved in union work.[92]

Autoworker Pedro Escobar walked out of his shop and joined the union after being prodded by his black co-worker. For years these two men had worked across from one another, and together, in silence, they had endured the racial insults and abuse. Every day on the line they inspired one another with their willful perseverance; quitting was not the solution. Both believed that industrial unionism would remedy their discontent with the awful working conditions, low wages, and discrimination.[93]

Mexican autoworkers, at great personal risk, participated in the organizing efforts inside the plants. Ford worker Isidro Rivas became involved in the secret union activities at the Rouge because he could no longer bear the work regimen. Workers were being discharged for petty infractions. They had work badges ripped from their shirts and were literally kicked out of the Rouge plant. On the shop floor, Bennett's Service Department maintained strict surveillance of the men to prevent union activity.[94]

Former Ford worker Guadalupe Morales stated that he was involved in labor organizing at the Rouge plant as early as 1927, though he had become aware of worker inequities as a seventeen-year-old in Mexico. Morales and other Ford workers met during their lunch breaks to secretly talk about union organizing. Morales's commitment to the labor movement grew. He attended gatherings in downtown Detroit and at city parks and heard Walter Reuther, Homer Martin, and other UAW leaders speak. The former Ford worker also participated clandestinely in worker demonstrations. Morales remembered that during a Labor Day parade held on Woodward Avenue he and his co-workers wore masks so as not to be identified by the Ford Service Department men in the crowds, the "stooges" who spied on company employees engaged in pro-labor actions. Morales's tireless union organizing activities—a product of his lifelong yearning to "do something for humanity"—kept him away from home so much that one day his wife remarked: "I hope the union comes so I can have you home once and for all." [95]

In the first months of 1933, the outbreak of a strike against Briggs Manufacturing had a dramatic impact on the hundreds of Mexicans who worked for the company. The Briggs strike involved upward of 14,000 workers and continued into March, when it was crushed by the use of strikebreakers and widespread police interference. About 60,000 autoworkers were directly affected by the strike because Briggs was the major supplier of car bodies for Ford, which shut down certain plant operations when these essential parts were no longer produced. The Briggs strike, along with those taking place elsewhere in Detroit, reduced the already limited amount of work available, and the plant closures aggravated the dreadful conditions in the shrinking Mexican colony. Without work and witnessing their unionizing efforts blocked at every turn by overwhelming obstacles, some Mexicans who participated in the Briggs strike also left Detroit. Those who stayed had gained valuable organizing experience.[96]

SUMMARY

Detroit's industrial economy was hit especially hard by the Great Depression. The Motor City's Mexican population, which had grown to 15,000 by 1928, was reduced to a little over a thousand by the crisis.

Like other midwestern municipalities in the grip of economic hard times, Detroit could no longer manage its expanding welfare rolls. City officials agreed to take part in a statewide program of voluntary removal of indigent Mexicans as a means of eliminating the relief problem. However, repatriation was marred by civil-rights violations.[97]

The belief that repatriation could end the depression on a local level was illusory. If the repatriation program had ever really been a humanitarian effort as well as a method of cutting relief costs, the effects of the cruel removal of Mexicans by the trainload and the arbitrary withdrawal of their rights might have been somewhat mitigated.[98]

The depression took a heavy toll on the Detroit Mexican colony on both an individual and a collective level. The depression mocked the Mexicans' work ethic and destroyed their dream of a better life. The case studies of the Ford Sociological Department show the hardships of Mexican Ford autoworkers and their families. Unable to make their mortgage payments, homeowners lost their houses, and renters moved into cheaper dwellings or doubled up with relatives and friends because of the lack of money. Savings were exhausted and insurance policies lapsed. The inability to make regular payments on furniture, autos, and other personal possessions bought on credit and installment plans meant eventual loss of these goods. The deterioration in the standard of living continued even after Mexicans were called back to work because much of the money they made went toward repayment of the debts they accumulated during the layoffs. These debts included grocery and doctor bills, rent payments, DPW emergency loans, and the cash loans made by relatives and friends.[99]

The lowering of working-class standards and the blow to the pride and self-confidence of workers were not the only impact of the depression: The community Mexican workers had created in Detroit was destroyed, along with close friendships cultivated over the years.

The depression-era experiences of Mexican Detroiters were made worse by a current of discrimination that resulted from their alien status, reluctance to become naturalized citizens, language problems, and pronounced racial characteristics. These factors made it difficult for Mexicans to mix with others, and frequently led to the denial of work. On many occasions the rights of Mexicans were threatened by the anti-foreign campaign being waged against them. Even as economic conditions improved after 1933 through the intervention of New Deal programs, these anti-Mexican attitudes prevailed. The ill feeling toward Mexicans was evident in some of the letters Americans continued sending to government officials. A letter protesting the presence of Mexicans in Chicago, written by a Chicago worker to Secretary of Labor Frances Perkins, was typical: "The American people are now looking forward to better times thanks to the efforts of the present administration. But I see a dark cloud on the horizon which causes some anxiety and that is Mexican immigration. Will the government allow these peons to . . . displace American working men? . . . Surely some measures should be undertaken to stop this migration before it is too late." [100]

Unprecedented numbers of Mexicans in the industrial Midwest participated in the strikes of the early 1930s and several years later in the union drives and mass strike actions. These depression-era union efforts, which brought into the labor movement large numbers of Spanish-speaking workers who in many instances also supplied the rank-and-file leadership, have been omitted from U.S. labor history. Mexicans joined the struggles to gain higher wages, better working conditions, and union recognition. These men faced blacklisting by employers and intimidation by U.S. immigration officers who coordinated their actions with county and city welfare officials. In Chicago, Mexicans participated in the unemployment demonstrations held by the Chicago Workers' Committee and other local worker organizations. In May 1933, one month before President Franklin Roosevelt signed the National Industrial Recovery Act (NIRA) into law, Mexicans in the Windy City demonstrated to pressure the state legislature and the federal government to begin public-works programs and pass an unemployment compensation law. The NIRA brought Mexican steelworkers of the Great Lakes region into the labor-organizing drive. Many were members of mutual-aid associations, and others belonged to the Amalgamated Association of Iron, Steel, and Tin Workers Union. In 1936, Mexican steelworkers at South Works joined the Steel Workers Organizing Committee, as did those in East Chicago, Indiana Harbor, and Gary, Indiana, and in Youngstown and Mansfield, Ohio. In 1934 in South St. Paul, Mexicans like the ex-boxer George "Kid Peewee" Galvin helped organize packing-house workers at the Cudahy, Swift, and Armour packing plants. Mexican autoworkers assisted in bringing the union into Detroit's car shops and Great Lakes Steel, and those in Flint took part in the 1937 sit-down strike against General Motors and the great evil of speed-up. [101]

The optimism of the New Deal raised the hopes of Mexicans, who no longer felt as powerless as they had during the repatriation period. Though discrimination did not end, Mexicans, like blacks, pushed for racial equality and increased participation in the New Deal. The working-class expectations of Mexicans in the North entered a new stage. It was not until 1940, with the start of factory production on the eve of World War II, that Detroit's Mexican population reached levels akin to those of the 1920s. A collective struggle against discriminatory employment practices opened the way for Mexicans into Detroit's defense-related industries.

SIX

Conclusion:
Reinterpreting the History of
Mexican Industrial Workers

Chicano historians have included Mexican workers as part of their studies of the Southwest, where the majority of this population traditionally resides. This scholarship describes the Spanish-speaking working class in the different labor sectors of the region. Most of these studies were the outgrowth of the revisionist writing of the 1970s and early 1980s and were informed by the methods of the new social history, which emphasized the everyday lives of "ordinary people." Chicano historians have enriched our understanding of an important segment of the U.S. workforce whose experiences have been diverse and shaped largely by race. However, the story of Mexican workers in the Midwest has not received the same kind of close attention by Chicano scholars. Nor have U.S. historians devoted much scholarship to these working men and women; the historians' well-meaning and valuable efforts to incorporate racial minorities have been limited to blacks. No studies like those that have illuminated the dramatic saga of the great migration of blacks to the industrial cities of the North trace Mexican migration northward.

In this book I have attempted to document the varying features of the working-class life and community-building efforts of the thousands of Mexicans who underwent proletarianization and urbanization in the Midwest in the 1920s. Using an interdisciplinary approach, I have examined this history from different, wider perspectives: Chicano history, social and labor history, the divisions of race and gender. I have focused on a heretofore unknown dimension of Chicano history and of American labor history, that of the Mexican workers of the Ford Motor Company, to dispel perceptions of the monolithic, nonevolving nature of Mexican labor in the United States. Mexicans are not just transient agricultural workers, laborers who appear and disappear like phantoms with each harvest season. By building on the concept of the common laborer eloquently refined by David Montgomery, I have attempted to expand on his essential idea of the endless variations and contributions of the men and women who constitute the U.S. working classes. The experiences of Mexicans in the Ford plants and in urban Detroit expand our knowledge of the diversity and changing work relations of this group and revise our understanding of the Mexican working class during this critical period. Moreover, my study will, I hope, encourage other scholars to reconceptualize the larger history of Chicanos in the United States; if an accurate perspective on the making of the Chicano working class is to be attained, the midwestern record must be integrated into this examination and assessment.

Detroit in 1920 was the major industrial center of the Midwest. Its factories produced 2.2 million motor vehicles in this year. An army of unskilled and semiskilled blue-collar workers, most of whom were machine tenders and assemblers, engaged in the production of automobiles. The steadily increasing numbers of Mexicans in Detroit, beginning in 1917, entered a mass-production industrial environment that was ethnically and racially diverse. In their encounters with this industrial milieu, which mediated all aspects of their lives both inside the factory and away from work, the newest arrivals to Detroit shared the experiences of compatriots living and working in other midwestern cities.

The differences were vast between them and their counterparts in the Southwest, those much-disparaged wage earners whose sweat work established and sustained the large-scale agricultural and mining economy of the region. Tens of thousands of Mexicans settled in cities of the Southwest but only a small percentage entered industrial employment because of limited opportunities, the persistent barriers of race, and resistance on the part of organized labor to participation by Mexicans. The role of factory laborers in the Southwest was actually filled by Mexican women; they were a cheaper labor source than the men because gender compounded racial exploitation. In contrast, the prevalence of factory work in the Midwest, the high percentage of ethnic workers and of black workers (who deflected the prevailing racism for Mexicans) and the lack of unionism underlay the experiences of the proletarians of the North.

The movement of Mexicans north was but another chapter in a continuing search for wage work that began initially in their homeland and that was then in ever-widening circles extended across the border and finally to the Midwest. Exposure to wage labor prepared these workers for their entrance into northern employment, as they expanded their migration over 1,000 miles beyond Texas. Once in the North, the men established migration routes within the region, and mobility continued to be necessary in their search for work.

Largely through family and kinship networks, Mexicans were channeled into railroad work, meat-packing houses, steel mills, metal foundries, and auto plants. Most who entered these employment sectors had previously worked on northern sugar-beet farms. Like work in the other sectors, industrial employment was distinguished by its own distinct culture. As was the case for European immigrants, familiarity and custom figured in the preference of some Mexicans for certain kinds of work over others, though steadiness of employment was an important consideration and took precedence.[1] Mexicans came to Detroit specifically to earn the high wages promised by Henry Ford to all workers. Migration to the Motor City became synonymous with obtaining a job in the Ford plants because for many auto work represented both the apex of modern industry and the essence of mass production.

The high cost of living in Detroit, the erratic work schedules, the seasonal fluctuations of its factories, and recessions and depressions had an impact on Mexican workers. The situation in Detroit was typical of that in the Midwest. The search for work necessitated frequent movement, and families could not always depend on the earnings of one breadwinner. To offset living costs some women entered domestic, clerical, and factory employment. By the close of the 1920s Mexican women were working in Detroit's auto plants, adding yet another important dimension to the history of these midwestern proletarians.

Material well-being and consumerism were essential features of working-class culture in the 1920s. The desire for consumer goods fueled the pursuit of industrial jobs on the part of Mexican workers and their families. My study shows that, like most workers, Mexicans accepted the conditions of the job as a trade-off for an American standard of living with its emphasis on mass consumption.[2] Identification with the popular urban culture of the period, from stylish dress to downtown excursions, introduced changes as well in the immigrants' social structure. Some women, especially the younger ones, challenged values and norms stipulating conformity and "proper" behavior. Just as the work lives of Mexicans changed with their entrance into industry, their social realm was also undergoing marked change by exposure to the cities they encountered in the North. At the same time that American culture was altering Mexican life, ongoing immigration from Mexico and the proximity of the border reinforced Mexican culture. Traditional cultural institutions were transplanted to the Midwest. Next to work and the family, religion served as an important socializing force.

Although institutionalized religion was used to Americanize the immigrants, most Mexicans recognized that neither U.S. citizenship nor assimilation would help them achieve acceptance. Edson reported to the Department of Labor that the percentage of naturalized Mexicans in Detroit was higher than that in other cities in the North, but larger institutional forces impeded assimilation for most. The full incorporation of this minority group into the American working class was halted by the first nationwide repatriations, which were ushered in by the 1920–1921 depression. These repatriations mark the beginning of the recurring scapegoating of Mexicans when the country had economic problems; at each downturn, non-Mexican workers threw down the patriotic gauntlet of "American jobs for American workers." Although these ambitious immigrants continued to cross the border, recognizing the need to find jobs in the United States, many hoped to return one day to a better life in Mexico. Racism contradicted the American dream. Edson observed that to the majority of Mexicans the United States remained "the great hobgoblin, the fork-tongued dragon." Confidently, and mistakenly, he predicted that the pessimistic attitude of the immigrants toward the United States would change, that they would eventually become American citizens "when the effects of their bad dream . . . passed away." [3]

Throughout the twenties, various members of the dominant society frowned on Mexicans in the United States. American workers feared that the growing number of these "foreigners," whom they deemed cheap and illegal labor, would seriously undermine the little progress that had been achieved. White workers pleaded with their elected representatives "not [to] press the Mexican crown of thorns on the brow of American labor." [4] Organized labor claimed that further Mexican immigration jeopardized the standing of American workers. But in reality Americans rarely took the work assignments Mexicans accepted, even during hard times. The stigma of race had tainted these jobs.

Having gained first-hand experience in the racially stratified northern labor market, Mexicans understood how close they were to the bottom rung occupied by blacks. Government officials, some of whom were controlled by strong grower lobbies, succumbed to the eugenic theories then in vogue and loudly warned that continued immigration threatened the "white race." They wondered aloud whether the United States

could accept its eventual mongrelization. Mexicans now figured prominently in the historic dilemma of race in the United States. Resigned to
this enduring problem, a Mexican ex-autoworker concluded: "The
question of race between the Anglo and the Mexican will never end." [5]
Race, language, cultural differences, and questionable citizenship status
set this group of minority workers apart.

Seen in this larger context, the formation of self-help organizations
by these immigrants in the fledgling midwestern colonies was an ob-
vious way to ease adjustment, to furnish assistance, and to reinforce
cultural practices. Accompanying the strive for economic betterment as
the Mexicans became urbanized was the desire on the part of many to
improve their communities. However, the immigrant proletarians had
brought with them unresolved regional conflicts and animosities that
caused dissension. Because of differing philosophies and a high transiency rate, the Detroit Mexican societies and organizations were unable to retain members. Factory work schedules, family commitments,
and the city's various social activities, from park outings to movies, also
limited membership. More important, the immigrants were developing
a sense of independence influenced largely by their working-class encounters. Jobs in the auto plants and the shared experiences gained on
the shop floor shaped and reinforced the identity of these workers and
for many overrode all other considerations. They were beginning to
loosen their ties with the old country; despite the obstacles posed by
discrimination, they were defining themselves as Detroiters whose des-
tiny was inextricably linked to this great industrial center. The working-
class neighborhoods where they resided and where many were beginning to raise families had become home.

Although labor historians have stressed the demeaning nature of factory labor, the day-to-day shop-floor encounters of Mexican Ford
workers indicate clearly that their work lives were much more complex
than the existing generalizations suggest. These men demonstrated an
awareness of both limitations and possibilities and acted accordingly.
For this segment of the Mexican working classes, industrial employment in the Midwest represented an upgrading of economic status and
social well-being. Work provided the opportunity to improve their living standards. This possibility was repeatedly confirmed by ex-
autoworkers like Ramón Huerta: "Here in Detroit you had the opportunity to work and to live well." Indeed, auto work assured relatively
high wages, a cornucopia of consumer goods, and the promise of leisure
time to this urban Mexican population. [6]

Mexican industrial workers were active agents in their own history, which was demonstrated not only by their desire to better themselves but also by their behavior on the shop floor, by their ability to shape and contest their work, and by their desire for respect for their efforts in the factories. Like their counterparts working elsewhere in the Midwest, they produced a work ethic that not only valued manliness but also placed importance on the intrinsic value of work. The son of a Mexican railroader affirmed this value, recalling: "Work was one of the main topics of family conversation. We looked upon work as a provider of dignity and a sense of achievement. The nature of the work was not as important as the service it rendered. In rendering service we felt important and fulfilled." [7]

In the northern factories Mexicans performed mostly unskilled labor and were exposed to management schemes and innovative production methods regulated by shop foremen. Detroit's Mexican autoworkers earned their wages by following demanding production schedules and an armylike discipline. The Ford workers labored in all the company's plants and departments, taking on work assignments in the foundry as well as in assembly production. They neither had to have special skills nor exert much athletic effort in performing auto work. Speed and the stamina needed for their repetitive jobs were requisites to keep up with the pace of production, which at times accelerated to inhuman levels. [8] Notwithstanding, Mexican autoworkers demonstrated to the plant managers and their supervisors that they had the wherewithal to persevere on the line.

Labor historians have emphasized the monotony and routine of auto work, but another dimension has become apparent: workers found meaning in their work. Mexican autoworkers viewed machine tending as an improvement over previous forms of labor. They made good money, but more importantly, they considered their work modern and at the technological forefront. These men took pride in their labor as machine production workers and in their mastery of work routines. The deskilled work was not the source of their discontent; the fierce speed-up, the unfair piecework, and the onerous stretchout, inflicted on them by management and all complicated by discrimination, were the culprits that upset an honest day's work. [9] However, the high quit rate of Mexican Ford workers suggests that not all were willing to conform to or accept the shop-floor conditions. Through acts of cunning, by quitting or merely walking off the job, these free-thinking autoworkers expressed their resistance to exploitive labor processes and abusive foremen. Retaliations against foremen challenge the image of Mexicans as docile and servile workers.

Unemployment, another factor that characterized the 1920s, has not been explored by scholars in assessments of Mexican working-class reality. American manufacturing reached a peak during the years of Mexican migration to the Midwest, but factory work, which was abundant in the post-World War I period, became harder to find in the 1920s. Bouts of joblessness were particularly numerous in the auto industry. Ford's Mexican workers had to contend with two- and three-day work-weeks and irregular employment because of the periodic slowdowns in production. Life in Detroit for laid-off autoworkers was especially difficult during the 1920–1921 depression, the cutbacks in Model-T production during the 1927 recession, and the years leading up to the Great Depression. Mexican autoworkers coped with joblessness in a variety of ways at a time when there was no unemployment compensation.[10]

"There is no other city in the world for the worker like Detroit. But there is no other city that makes so many jobless."[11] So concluded one Mexican autoworker about the grave economic crisis that befell Detroit in 1929. By 1932 the Mexican colonies of the Midwest were in the grip of the Great Depression, and the majority of the immigrants lost their jobs, endured significant hardships, and were forced to leave the region. Thousands left because of coercion as repatriations removed them from the Midwest. My study shows that in Detroit individual circumstances and how each person coped with joblessness determined who left. Moreover, rather than acquiescing to the pressures to leave the United States, as scholars have assumed, members of the Detroit Mexican colony coalesced against repatriation once its shortcomings became known.

Those who remained in the Midwest understood that they shared common interests and concerns with other industrial workers, principally a desire for a humane working environment and a living wage. The working-class militancy that ensued was directed toward regaining pride and dignity and restoring conditions enjoyed in the 1920s, of which an acceptable standard of living and material well-being were the primary concerns. An end to discrimination on the job also became a rallying cause and led to widespread participation in the Congress of Industrial Organizations (CIO). Many white, Mexican, and black workers momentarily set aside their differences, which had contributed to working-class fragmentation and hindered unity across ethnic and racial lines. The CIO favored the organization of minority workers and furnished Mexicans with a vehicle to achieve worker rights, which the AFL had never provided. Mexicans who invested their energies in carrying the message of unionism into the auto shops of Detroit, Pontiac, and Flint brought meaning back into their work lives. As Joyce Shaw Peterson has argued, the sit-down strikes originated in working conditions that wrested pride away from the jobs the men performed. Pride was restored when the working men united and took a determined stand to demand workplace equality from the automakers.[12]

By the late 1930s only several thousand of the original Mexican settlers remained in Detroit. The population was soon replenished by the arrival of Mexican Americans from Texas coming to the Motor City to work in the revived auto industry. Detroit and the Midwest continued to serve as a safety net for these hard-working *Tejanos*—it provided the hope of escape from racial discrimination, which barred service in public places, restricted housing and employment opportunities, and often resulted in police brutality. In the Lone Star State, employment outside farm work was almost nonexistent for Mexicans and blacks.[13] Detroit and the Midwest offered the promise of a better future. This second phase of migration from Texas, this time by Mexican Americans, occurred during and after World War II. It paralleled another significant migration by blacks and white southerners coming north to find work in war-production centers like Detroit. These latter-day migrants encountered a wholly different industrial and urban environment even more fractured along racial lines than it had been in the 1920s.

Today, the American labor force is again undergoing extraordinary recomposition as Latinos, African Americans, Asians, and women are replacing white, native-born males as the mainstay of the American working class. A large percentage of the total increase in the nation's jobs has been the result of the entrance of Latinos into the labor sector, of which they now constitute a large segment. Historically among the most poorly paid and most exploited workers, they have long played a key role in worker struggles in the Southwest, and they occupy the front ranks of the current labor battles. Chicano workers have fought against plant closings, phasedowns, and deplorable working conditions in low-wage industries caused by the restructuring of the American economy. For Chicanos and other Latinos, the loss of manufacturing jobs has resulted in their economic ghettoization in low-wage, service-sector employment. And Chicanos and other Latinos will be among the first workers affected if the North American Free Trade Agreement is successfully carried through.[14]

These and other experiences of the Chicano population, of a people whose past has been omitted from the overall narrative of American labor history, are being researched and documented. Still, huge gaps exist. My study of the Mexican industrial workers of the Midwest is a contribution to constructing this larger history. It is a chronicle of the hard-working and proud individuals who trod back and forth to the factories and joined the endless tumult of the industrial workplace. Their history needs to be incorporated into the larger American mosaic.

Notes

ABBREVIATIONS

EIA   Edison Industrial Archives, Edison Institute, Ford
               Motor Company, Dearborn, Mich.

Minn. HS   Minnesota Historical Society, Archives and
               Manuscripts Division, Oral Histories Collection, St.
               Paul

PTC   Paul S. Taylor Collection, Bancroft Library, University
               of California, Berkeley

SMCC   St. Mary's Catholic Church, Detroit

SRE   Secretaría de Relaciones Exteriores, Archivo Nacional,
               Mexico City

USINS   U.S. Immigration and Naturalization Service, Record
               Group 85, National Archives, Washington, D.C.

USMCS   U.S. Mediation and Conciliation Service, Record
               Group 280, Washington National Records Center,
               Suitland, Md.

INTRODUCTION

1. Arthur F. Corwin and Walter F. Fogel, "Shadow Labor Force: Mexican
Workers in the American Economy," in Arthur F. Corwin, ed., *Immigrants—
and Immigrants: Perspectives on Mexican Labor Migration to the United States*
(Westport, Conn.: Greenwood Press, 1978), 266.

2. Carey McWilliams, *North from Mexico: The Spanish-Speaking People of the United States* (1949; reprint, Westport, Conn.: Greenwood Press, 1968), 167.

3. Ewa Morawska, *For Bread with Butter: The Life-Worlds of East Central Europeans in Johnstown, Pennsylvania, 1890–1940* (Cambridge: Cambridge University Press, 1985), 55. The transformations of the late nineteenth century resulted in the proletarianization of the Mexican rural population. This process is similar to the one East Central European immigrants underwent in their homeland, as noted by Morawska. My ideas on Mexican migration, working-class formation, and the values and behavior patterns of these workers have been inspired by Morawska's work.

4. By the late nineteenth century there was extensive migration from Mexico's central plateau to Mexico City and the city of Monterrey and to Sonora and other northern Mexican states. For example, many of the Santa Fe Railroad's Mexican workers in Kansas came from nonrural backgrounds, previously alternated between farm and railroad work, or else worked as casual laborers in Mexico. Judith Finchar Laird, "Argentine, Kansas: The Evolution of a Mexican American Community, 1905–1940" (Ph.D. diss., University of Kansas, 1975), 97.

5. George T. Edson, "Mexicans in Our Northcentral States," 1927, Paul S. Taylor Collection, Bancroft Library, University of California, Berkeley, 24. (Hereafter cited as PTC.)

6. Henry Ford Service School, Foreign Student Research, Box 1319, Accession ARG-15, June 10, 1920, Edison Industrial Archives, Edison Institute, Ford Motor Company, Dearborn, Mich. (Hereafter cited as EIA.)

7. Manuel Gamio, *Mexican Immigration to the United States: A Study of Human Migration and Adjustment* (Chicago: University of Chicago Press, 1930), 49.

8. "There were 495 man-hours needed to build an automobile in 1920, and the definition of a person's workday, family life, and hopes rested very much on what specific task of this complex process he or she could perform." Olivier Zunz, *The Changing Face of Inequality: Urbanization, Industrial Development, and Immigrants in Detroit, 1880–1920* (Chicago: University of Chicago Press, 1982), 309. See Stanley Aronowitz, *False Promises: The Shaping of American Working Class Consciousness* (New York: McGraw-Hill, 1973), 154–155; Richard C. Edwards, *Contested Terrain: The Transformation of the Workplace in the Twentieth Century* (New York: Basic Books, 1979), 111–129; David M. Gordon, Richard C. Edwards, and Michael Reich, *Segmented Work, Divided Workers: The Historical Transformation of Labor in the United States* (Cambridge: Cambridge University Press, 1982), 100–164.

9. Robert Redfield, "Mexicans in Chicago, 1924–1925," 1925, Robert Redfield Papers, Special Collections, University of Chicago; Robert C. Jones and Louise R. Wilson, *The Mexicans in Chicago* (Chicago: Comity Commission of the Chicago Federation, 1931); Edith Abbott, *The Tenements of Chicago 1908–1935* (Chicago: University of Chicago Press, 1936); Anita E. Jones, *Conditions surrounding Mexicans in Chicago* (1928; reprint, San Francisco: R&E

Research Associates, 1971); Paul S. Taylor, *Mexican Labor in the United States: Chicago and the Calumet Region* (Berkeley: University of California Press, 1932) (hereafter cited as Taylor, *Chicago and the Calumet Region*).

10. Paul S. Taylor, "Mexicans in Detroit, Michigan," 1928, PTC.

11. Edson, "Mexicans in Our Northcentral States," 1.

12. Louise Año Nuevo-Kerr, "The Chicano Experience in Chicago: 1920–1970" (Ph.D. diss., University of Illinois at Chicago Circle, 1976); Francisco A. Rosales, "Mexicanos in Indiana Harbor during the 1920s: From Prosperity to Depression," *Revista Chicano Riqueña* 4 (1976); Raymond A. Mohl and Neil Betten, *Steel City: Urban Patterns in Gary, Indiana, 1906–1950* (New York: Holmes & Meier, 1986); Dennis Nodín Valdés, *Al Norte: Agricultural Workers in the Great Lakes Region, 1917–1970* (Austin: University of Texas Press, 1991). See also Gilbert Cárdenas, "Los Desarraigados: Chicanos in the Midwestern Region of the United States," *Aztlán* 7 (Summer 1976); Louise Año Nuevo-Kerr, "Chicano Settlements in Chicago: A Brief History," *Journal of Ethnic Studies* 2 (Winter 1975); Ciro H. Sepulveda, "Research Note: Una Colonia de Obreros: East Chicago, Indiana," *Aztlán* 7 (Summer 1976); Ciro H. Sepulveda, "The Origins of the Urban Colonies in the Midwest, 1910–1930," *Revista Chicano Riqueña* 4 (1976); Francisco A. Rosales and Daniel T. Simon, "Chicano Steel Workers and Unionism in the Midwest, 1919–1945," *Aztlán* 6 (1975); Francisco A. Rosales and Daniel T. Simon, "Mexican Immigrant Experience in the Urban Midwest: East Chicago, Indiana, 1919–1945," *Indiana Magazine of History* 77 (December 1981). In his study of Mexican labor in the United States prior to World War II, Mark Reisler devotes one chapter to the Mexicans of the Midwest. *By the Sweat of Their Brow: Mexican Immigrant Labor in the United States, 1900–1940* (Westport, Conn.: Greenwood Press, 1976), 96–126.

13. Dennis Nodín Valdés, *El Pueblo Mexicano en Detroit y Michigan: A Social History* (Detroit: Wayne State University Press, 1982); Sharon Popp, "Exploratory Study of the Mexican-American Community in Detroit, Michigan" (Master's thesis, Wayne State University, 1970); Norman D. Humphrey, "The Mexican Peasant in Detroit" (Ph.D. diss., University of Michigan, 1943); Christopher Louis Murillo, "The Detroit Mexican 'Colonia' from 1920 to 1932: Implications for Social and Educational Policy" (Ph.D. diss., Michigan State University, 1981); Gumecindo Salas and Isabela Salas, "The Mexican Community in Detroit," in Margaret M. Mangold, ed., *La Causa Chicano: The Movement for Social Justice* (New York: Family Service Association of America, 1972); Marietta Lynn Baba and Malvina Houk Abonyi, *Mexicans of Detroit* (Detroit: Wayne State University Press, 1979); Edward Adam Skendzal, *Detroit's Pioneer Mexicans: A Historical Study of the Mexican Colony in Detroit* (Grand Rapids, Mich.: Little Shield Press, 1980). During the late 1930s Humphrey investigated the Mexican colony of Detroit through his work as a social case worker with the Detroit Department of Public Welfare. Humphrey obtained his research information from case records of Mexicans on relief in the fall of 1938, which he corroborated with data obtained from additional case records of Mexicans on relief in the summer of 1939. After he became a sociol-

ogist, he and his students conducted a series of interviews with Mexicans (1940 to 1943). The articles by Humphrey that appeared in academic journals in the 1940s are based on his dissertation. See, for example, "Migration and Settlement of Detroit Mexicans," *Economic Geography* 19 (October 1943); "The Integration of Detroit's Mexican Colony," *American Journal of Economics and Sociology* 3 (January 1944); and "Employment Patterns of Mexicans in Detroit," *Monthly Labor Review* 61 (November 1945).

14. David Montgomery, "Thinking about American Workers in the 1920s," *International Labor and Working-Class History* 32 (Fall 1987), 10–11.

CHAPTER ONE

1. David Montgomery, *The Fall of the House of Labor: The Workplace, the State, and American Labor Activism, 1865–1925* (Cambridge: Cambridge University Press, 1987), 460; Stanley Vittoz, "World War I and the Political Accommodation of Transitional Market Forces: The Case of Immigration Restriction," *Politics and Society* 8 (1978), 66–77.

2. Carole Marks, *Farewell—We're Good and Gone: The Great Black Migration* (Bloomington: Indiana University Press, 1989), 23; E. J. Henning, assistant secretary of labor, Washington, D.C., to Secretary of Labor, Washington, D.C., August 1, 1927, U.S. Mediation and Conciliation Service, Record Group 280, Subject Case Files 165/223, Box 13, NA (hereafter cited as USMCS); Paul S. Taylor, *A Spanish-Mexican Peasant Community: Arandas in Jalisco, Mexico* (Berkeley: University of California Press, 1933), 44–45; David Montejano, *Anglos and Mexicans in the Making of Texas, 1836–1986* (Austin: University of Texas Press, 1987), 162–163, 199.

3. Lowell L. Tubbs, "Texas Migrants," in Matt S. Meier and Feliciano Rivera, eds., *Readings on La Raza: The Twentieth Century* (New York: Hill and Wang, 1974), 174.

4. Carey McWilliams, *Ill Fares the Land: Migrants and Migratory Labor in the United States* (1941; reprint, New York: Barnes & Noble, 1967), 247–249; McWilliams, *North from Mexico*, 170; Charles H. Hufford, *The Social and Economic Effects of Mexican Migration into Texas* (San Francisco: R&E Research Associates, 1971), 32, 37; Montejano, *Anglos and Mexicans in the Making of Texas*, 169–170; author interview with Guadalupe Morales, November 24, 1986, Detroit; interview with Manuel Contreras, July 16, 1976, Minnesota Historical Society, Archives and Manuscripts Division, Oral Histories Collection, St. Paul (hereafter cited as Minn. HS). On job-pacing among African-American work gangs, see Gerald D. Jaynes, *Branches without Roots: Genesis of the Black Working Class in the American South, 1862–1882* (New York: Oxford University Press, 1986), 159.

5. McWilliams, *Ill Fares the Land*, 230; Corwin and Fogel, "Shadow Labor Force," 257; Charles T. Connell and R. W. Burton, "Survey of Labor Conditions on the Mexican Border and Contiguous Territory as Related to Unskilled Labor," 1922, report for the secretary of labor, USMCS, 165/223B, Box 13. The derogatory phrase describing supposedly servile blacks is that of the Texas folklorist J. Frank Dobie. See Robert J. Lipshultz, "Attitudes toward the Mexican,"

in Meier and Rivera, eds., *Readings on La Raza: The Twentieth Century,* 69.

6. Connell and Burton, "Survey of Labor Conditions."

7. Author interview with Lauro Tienda, November 20, 1986, Detroit.

8. McWilliams, *Ill Fares the Land,* 231–232.

9. Ibid., 246; Montejano, *Anglos and Mexicans in the Making of Texas,* 160–161; "Mexican Rights in the United States," *Nation* 115 (July 12, 1922), 52–53. Ex-Ford autoworker Guadalupe Morales recalled that a feudal-like order existed on the south Texas ranch where his family picked cotton. The owner, on horseback, carried a carbine and a revolver and habitually mistreated the Mexican workers. After they finished harvesting the cotton, the ranch owner prevented the Mexicans from leaving and forced them to cut cane and perform extra work without pay. In effect, the Mexican laborers were kept in bondage. "He had us like slaves," reminisced Morales. Author interview with Guadalupe Morales, November 24, 1986, Detroit.

10. Author interview with Lauro Tienda, November 20, 1986, Detroit.

11. Montejano, *Anglos and Mexicans in the Making of Texas,* 217–219; McWilliams, *Ill Fares the Land,* 254.

12. A Mexican in South Chicago told Paul S. Taylor a story similar to those recounted innumerable times by these migrants: "I worked in Texas for a while and there the Texans were bad. I have seen many people treat Mexicans bad but they are the worst of all. Whenever I was out on the range riding bareback, they stopped me, asked me who I was, where I lived, where I worked, and if I did not answer fast enough they hit me with a whip. I did not like that and hated them for it. I had no gun or would have killed some sometimes the way they treated me and the way I felt." Taylor, *Chicago and the Calumet Region,* 259.

13. McWilliams, *Ill Fares the Land,* 255; steelworker quoted in Taylor, *Chicago and the Calumet Region,* 259.

14. Hufford, *Social and Economic Effects of Mexican Migration,* 34; Richard A. García, "Class, Consciousness, and Ideology—The Mexican Community of San Antonio, Texas: 1930–1940," *Aztlán* 9 (Spring 1979), 29–32; Connell and Burton, "Survey of Labor Conditions"; William J. Knox, *The Economic Status of the Mexican Immigrant in San Antonio, Texas* (San Francisco: R&E Research Associates, 1971), 33, 37; McWilliams, *North from Mexico,* 178; McWilliams, *Ill Fares the Land,* 249.

15. Kathleen May Gonzáles, *The Mexican Family in San Antonio, Texas* (San Francisco: R&E Research Associates, 1971), 3, 6–7; García, "Class, Consciousness, and Ideology," 38.

16. One of these Mexican Socialist activists was F. A. Hernández. In 1915, Hernández was arrested and sentenced to prison on a charge of sedition, of "inciting rebellion against the United States," after addressing Mexican workers at the Market Place in San Antonio. Emilio Zamora, Jr., "Chicano Socialist Labor Activity in Texas, 1900–1920," *Aztlán* 6 (Summer 1975), 229; James R. Green, *Grass-Roots Socialism: Radical Movements in the Southwest 1895–1943* (Baton Rouge: Louisiana State University Press, 1978), 332.

17. "Beautiful Girls—the chili queens—; Smiled as the crowds passed by; They sold tortillas and chili beans; And a peculiar sort of pie." *AFL-CIO Weekly Dispatch* (San Antonio), February 11, 1938, p. 4. For a contemporary

description of the social life of Mexican San Antonio, see Green Peyton, *San Antonio: City in the Sun* (New York: McGraw-Hill, 1946). A frequent visitor to 1920s Milam Park was future labor organizer Emma Tenayuca. This San Antonian recalled that her father frequently took her to the park to hear radicals present their divergent points of view. Author interview with Emma Tenayuca, May 4, 1990, San Antonio, Tex.

18. Gonzáles, *The Mexican Family in San Antonio,* 6–7.

19. The year 1923 was an especially busy one for recruiting Mexican workers. Between March 1 and August 31 the Department of Labor reported that 42,780 Mexicans (nearly 1,700 workers per week) contracted to work outside Texas. It is unknown how many of the recruits were repeats. Connell and Burton, "Survey of Labor Conditions." This government survey listed the following businesses as recruiting Mexicans in 1923: U.S. Steel Corporation, Lorain, Ohio; Michigan Sugar Company, Saginaw; Bethlehem Steel, Bethlehem, Pa.; Pittsburgh Steel, Monessen, Pa.; Carnegie Steel Company, Pittsburgh; American Bridge Company, Ambridge, Pa.; and the Baltimore & Ohio Railroad, Baltimore.

20. Ibid; Montejano, *Anglos and Mexicans in the Making of Texas,* 210–212.

21. John Bodnar, *The Transplanted: A History of Immigrants in Urban America* (Bloomington: Indiana University Press, 1985), 61–62.

22. Taylor, *Spanish-Mexican Peasant Community,* 41; Edson, "Mexicans in Our Northcentral States," 6–7; J. E. Trout, inspector in charge of immigration, Laredo, Tex., to Captain W. M. Hanson, inspector in charge of immigration, Laredo, Tex., October 14, 1923, U.S. Immigration and Naturalization Service, RG 85, Subject Case Files 54224/358, Box 316, NA (hereafter cited as USINS); Captain W. M. Hanson, inspector in charge of immigration, Laredo, Tex., to E. J. Henning, assistant secretary of labor, Washington, D.C., November 5, 1923, USINS, 54224/358, Box 316. The nonagricultural background of the migrants was confirmed by the assistant secretary of labor: "The statistical records . . . clearly indicate that we are getting very few farmers or agricultural laborers from Mexico; . . . on the other hand, nearly two-thirds of those who come are . . . unskilled laborers who . . . have for the most part been employed in towns and cities." In the same year only 14.3 percent of the total immigrants from all sources were classed as laborers. Henning to Secretary of Labor.

23. Henning to Secretary of Labor; David Ward, *Poverty, Ethnicity, and the American City, 1840–1925: Changing Conceptions of the Slum and Ghetto* (Cambridge: Cambridge University Press, 1989), 190–191; Montgomery, *Fall of the House of Labor,* 73.

24. Author interview with Pedro Escobar, November 20, 1986, Detroit.

25. Lawrence A. Cardoso, *Mexican Emigration to the United States, 1897–1931: Socio-Economic Patterns* (Tucson: University of Arizona Press, 1980), 77–78.

26. For instance, after Detroiter Ramón Huerta was laid off from his job at Chrysler Motors during the 1920–21 depression, he and his wife, Olga, left Detroit for Dallas, waiting until conditions improved in the auto industry. Author interview with Ramón Huerta, November 19, 1986, Detroit. The distinct

pattern of northern migration and return migration by Mexicans was noted by U.S. immigration inspectors stationed along the Texas border: "The immigration that comes in February, March, and April is nearly all northbound, and goes to the railroads . . . and to the sugar beet fields of Illinois and Michigan. . . . Part of them go north to take positions with . . . automobile factories, steel mills, etc., in the industrial centers of the North and East. . . . The Mexican, unlike other nationals, goes home when times in the United States begin to get hard and work is scarce."

27. Montgomery, *Fall of the House of Labor*, 460; Ward, *Poverty, Ethnicity, and the American City*, 191; Mexican Embassy, Washington, D.C., to Department of Labor, Bureau of Immigration, Washington, D.C., May 7, 1919, USINS, 54261/202-G, Box 243. The various kinds of controls imposed on Mexican farm laborers in Texas are discussed in Montejano, *Anglos and Mexicans in the Making of Texas*, 197–219. For an example of the terror experienced by Mexican track laborers working on lines of the Southern Pacific around Echo, Tex., during this time, see William Z. Foster, *Pages from a Worker's Life* (New York: International Publishers, 1978), 28–29.

28. Harry Schwartz, *Seasonal Farm Labor in the United States: With Special Reference to Hired Farm Workers in Fruit and Vegetable and Sugar Beet Production* (New York: Columbia University Press, 1945), 112; Dennis Nodín Valdés, "Betabeleros: The Formation of an Agricultural Proletariat in the Midwest, 1877–1930," *Labor History* 30 (Fall 1989), 550; McWilliams, *Ill Fares the Land*, 260–261.

29. Valdés, "Betabeleros," 554; McWilliams, *North from Mexico*, 180–181; Schwartz, *Seasonal Farm Labor*, 110–111; Sepulveda, "Origins of the Urban Colonias in the Midwest," 101. Sugar companies instructed labor recruiters to avoid hiring "musicians" or "barber types" or any other Mexicans deemed ambitious. It was believed that these individuals were likely to take advantage of the free rail transportation and leave the trains as they passed through northern cities. D. J. Lister, general agent, Passenger Department, Missouri Pacific Railroad, to Leo B. Russell, inspector in charge of immigration, Department of Labor, Washington, D.C., September 16, 1924, USINS, 55/608/128; *Detroit News*, November 10, 1932; Paul S. Taylor interview with Mrs. Larsen, June 25, 1928, Detroit, PTC; Paul S. Taylor interview with Dr. Morris, August 2, 1928, Detroit, PTC.

30. Author interview with Lauro Tienda, November 20, 1986, Detroit; author interview with Juan Martínez, November 23, 1986, Detroit; author interview with Manuela Alvarez, July 14, 1986, Detroit; Charles A. Thomson, "The Future of Mexican Immigration," n.d., report for the director of conciliation, Department of Labor, Washington, D.C., USMCS, 165/223, Box 13.

31. Morawska, *For Bread with Butter*, 59. See, for example, Spencer Crew, *Field to Factory: Afro-American Migration, 1915–1940* (Washington, D.C.: Smithsonian Institution, 1987).

32. Author interview with Juan Martínez, November 23, 1986, Detroit.

33. George T. Edson, "Northern Sugar Beet Mexicans," 1927, PTC, 12; author interview with Juan Martínez, November 23, 1986, Detroit; Valdés, "Betabeleros," 543–544.

34. McWilliams, *Ill Fares the Land,* 276.

35. F. J. Klemp, manager, Labor Department, Michigan Sugar Company, Saginaw, to Commissioner General of Immigration, Washington, D.C., July 21, 1919, and Supervising Inspector, U.S. Department of Labor, Immigration Service, El Paso, Tex., to Commissioner General of Immigration, Washington, D.C., June 9, 1919, USINS, 54261/202-I, Box 243.

36. Klemp to Commissioner General of Immigration. Some companies later formed the Beet Growers' Employment Committee to coordinate the development of this prosperous industry; Baba and Abonyi, *Mexicans of Detroit,* 41, 44; Valdés, *El Pueblo Mexicano en Detroit,* 10.

37. Norman S. Goldner, "The Mexican in the Northern Urban Area: A Comparison of Two Generations" (Ph.D. diss., University of Minnesota, 1959), 29–31; interview with Alfonso de León, Sr., July 8, 1975, Minn. HS; interview with Manuel Contreras, July 16, 1976, Minn. HS; George T. Edson, "Mexicans in the Toledo, Ohio, Area," 1926, PTC, 2–3.

38. Schwartz, *Seasonal Farm Labor,* 112; McWilliams, *North from Mexico,* 180–181; McWilliams, *Ill Fares the Land,* 272; John R. Martínez, *Mexican Emigration to the United States, 1910–1930* (San Francisco: R&E Research Associates, 1972), 61–62.

39. Valdés, "Betabeleros," 551.

40. Interview with David Limón, August 5, 1975, Minn. HS; Edson, "Mexicans in Our Northcentral States," 14; McWilliams, *North from Mexico,* 181; author interview with Juan Martínez, November 23, 1986, Detroit; Paul S. Taylor interview with official, City Public Employment Office, July 30, 1928, Detroit, PTC.

41. Sugar-company representatives in turn accused the labor agents of unscrupulous recruiting techniques. Paid 0.50 to $1.50 for each recruit, the agents reportedly took advantage of Mexicans who could not read the work contracts even when written in Spanish. Mexican and Mexican American *enganchadores* (labor contractors) in the Texas border towns shared guilt for these abuses. By the mid-twenties the majority of Mexicans coming north to work on sugar-beet farms were families who relied less and less on the predatory labor agencies and *enganchadores,* who were known to hoodwink the workers. Paul S. Taylor interview with Juan Tovar, July 30, 1928, Detroit, PTC; Paul S. Taylor interview with Dr. Morris, August 2, 1928, Detroit, PTC; Montgomery, *Fall of the House of Labor,* 79; Valdés, "Betabeleros," 558–559.

42. Valdés, "Betabeleros," 560–561.

43. Sepulveda, "Research Note," 333; author interview with Mariano Alvarez, July 14, 1986, Detroit; George T. Edson, "Mexicans at Lorain, Ohio," 1926 PTC, 10; George T. Edson, "Mexicans in Detroit, Michigan," 1926, PTC, 19.

44. Morawska, *For Bread with Butter,* 116–117.

45. Montgomery, *Fall of the House of Labor,* 83; Humphrey, "Employment Patterns," 917, 922; Humphrey, "Mexican Repatriation from Michigan: Public Assistance in Historical Perspective," *Social Service Review* 15 (September 1941), 506, 510, 513; Baba and Abonyi, *Mexicans of Detroit,* 43–44.

46. Author interview with Juan Martínez, November 23, 1986, Detroit; Schwartz, *Seasonal Farm Labor*, 113; Taylor, *Chicago and the Calumet Region*, 98; Humphrey, "Employment Patterns of Mexicans in Detroit," 913, 916, 917. A family working under a labor contract in sugar beets on twenty-five acres at $23 per acre could earn $575 per season. However, a study commissioned by the National Child Labor Committee reported that $743 was the average income for these families from all sources combined. Linna E. Brisette, *Mexicans in the United States: A Report of a Brief Survey* (Washington, D.C.: National Catholic Welfare Conference, 1928), 13.

47. Shelton Stromquist, *A Generation of Boomers: The Pattern of Railroad Labor Conflict in Nineteenth-Century America* (Urbana: University of Illinois Press, 1987), 193–194.

48. Montgomery, *Fall of the House of Labor*, 62–63, 81; author interview with Juan Martínez, November 23, 1986, Detroit.

49. R. B. Mathews, immigration inspector, El Paso, Tex., to Inspector in Charge, Immigration Service, El Paso, Tex., July 26, 1918, USINS, 54261/ 202-C, Box 243; author interview with Juan Martínez, November 23, 1986, Detroit.

50. Quoted in Vernon Monroe McCoombs, *From over the Border: A Study of the Mexican in the United States* (New York: Council of Women and Home Missions, 1925), 23–24.

51. Author interview with Juan Martínez, November 23, 1986, Detroit.

52. Reisler, *By the Sweat of Their Brow,* 27–32.

53. One "Notice to Mexican Railroad Workmen" from the Rock Island Lines read as follows: "If any of you in your part of the country have a friend or a relative wishing to come to this country to work for a while, . . . you can advise them by letter that . . . they can come with all assurances that they will . . . secure work at good wages and free return transportation on the Rock Island Lines. . . . The most convenient place to cross from Mexico into the United States is through El Paso. . . . At that point is where we have our representative who will . . . arrange to ship you to places on our lines where there is work." General Manager, Chicago, Rock Island and Pacific Railway, to Anthony Caminetti, commissioner general of immigration, July 19, 1918, USINS, 54261/ 202-E, Box 243.

54. Año Nuevo-Kerr, "Chicano Experience in Chicago," 24; Reisler, *By the Sweat of Their Brow,* 99–100, 104; Sepulveda, "Origins of the Urban Colonias in the Midwest," 102; George T. Edson, "Mexicans in Chicago, Illinois," 1926, PTC, 2; Sanford M. Jacoby, *Employing Bureaucracy: Managers, Unions, and the Transformation of Work in American Industry, 1900–1945* (New York: Columbia University Press, 1985), 169–171.

55. Taylor, *Chicago and the Calumet Region,* 28, 33–34.

56. George T. Edson, "Mexicans in the Pittsburgh, Pennsylvania, District," 1925, PTC, 1; unsigned letter to U.S. Commissioner of Immigration, Philadelphia Immigration Station, Gloucester, N.J., February 24, 1921, USINS, 54261/ 202-J, Box 243; interview with David Limón, August 5, 1975, Minn. HS.

57. Edson, "Mexicans in Detroit, Michigan," 23–24; William Robinett,

commissioner of conciliation, Detroit, to H. L. Kerwin, director of conciliation, Department of Labor, Washington, D.C., June 24, 1925, USMCS, 165/223, Box 13.

58. Immigration Inspector, El Paso, Tex., to Inspector in Charge, Immigration Service, Cleveland, Ohio, January 21, 1919, USINS, 54261/202-G, Box 243; George T. Edson, "Mexicans in the Toledo, Ohio, Area", 1926, PTC, 1; George K. Apple, immigration inspector, Toledo, Ohio, to Inspector in Charge, Immigration Service, Cleveland, Ohio, May 16, 1919, USINS, 54261/202-G, Box 243; Montgomery, *Fall of the House of Labor,* 78; McWilliams, *North from Mexico,* 168–169.

59. Matt S. Meier and Feliciano Rivera, *The Chicanos: A History of Mexican Americans* (New York: Hill and Wang, 1972), 138.

60. Connell and Burton, "Survey of Labor Conditions"; Edson, "Northern Sugar Beet Mexicans," 24.

61. Jones, *Conditions surrounding Mexicans,* 106; Edson, "Mexicans in Our Northcentral States," 43; Montgomery, *Fall of the House of Labor,* 75; Susan L. Palmer, "Building Ethnic Communities in a Small City: Romanians and Mexicans in Aurora, Illinois, 1900–1940" (Ph.D. diss., Northern Illinois University, 1986), 133–134. In Aurora, Ill., over 100 Mexicans employed by the Burlington Northern lived with their relatives in a twenty-freight-car camp they shared with Romanian and Irish co-workers and their kin. While fathers, older brothers, and uncles worked sorting parts in the scrap yard and cutting and treating railroad ties, the children played together in the camp on their bicycles, scooters, and coaster wagons among a menagerie of dogs and cats. George T. Edson, "Mexicans in Aurora, Illinois," 1926, PTC, 4.

62. George T. Edson, "Mexicans in Fort Madison, Iowa," 1927, PTC, 3–4.

63. Author interview with Juan Martínez, November 23, 1986, Detroit; J. Blaine Gwin, secretary, Associated Charities, El Paso, Tex., to Assistant Supervisor of Immigration Harris, El Paso, Tex., June 21, 1918, USINS, 54261/202, Box 240, NA.

64. Hugh R. Osburn, King City, Calif., to Secretary of Labor, Washington, D.C., March 21, 1919, USINS, 54261/202G, Box 243; Montgomery, *Fall of the House of Labor,* 66, 81–83.

65. Rosales, "Mexicanos in Indiana Harbor during the 1920s," 88; Arthur F. Corwin and Lawrence A. Cardoso, "Vamos al Norte: Causes of Mass Mexican Migration to the United States," in Arthur F. Corwin, ed., *Immigrants—and Immigrants: Perspectives on Mexican Labor Migration to the United States* (Westport, Conn.: Greenwood Press, 1978), 50.

66. Record-card data on previous factory employment of Mexican Ford autoworkers and the field studies of Taylor and Edson substantiate this claim. The former factory workers who came to work in Detroit's auto plants arrived through a circuitous route that took them first to steel mills like South Works in Chicago and Indiana Steel in Gary, and then to Michigan, to Chevrolet Motors, the Gray Iron Foundry in Saginaw, Buick Motors in Flint, and the Wilson Foundry in Pontiac. From the Chicago-Gary area Mexicans traveled to Milwaukee, to work in leather factories. Mexican steelworkers in western Pennsylvania were first drawn to this region through work on the Pennsylvania Railroad

around mill towns like Homestead. Rouge Area Hourly Workers Employment Jackets, 1918–1947, Accession AR-84-58-1050, Ford Motor Company Industrial Archives and Record Center, Redford, Mich.; Taylor, *Chicago and the Calumet Region,* 77; George T. Edson, "Mexicans in the Pittsburgh, Pennsylvania, District," 11.

67. Richard Whipp, "'A Time to Every Purpose': An Essay on Time and Work," in Patrick Joyce, ed., *The Historical Meanings of Work* (New York: Cambridge University Press, 1987), 211. From their friends and relatives job applicants gained information about what to say at the factory employment office; whether safety goggles, masks, and leather gloves (essential for foundry work) were provided; whether outside work was required during the winter months; and whether the company utilized arbitrary swing shifts, speed-ups, and involuntary overtime.

68. David Brody, *Steelworkers in America: The Nonunion Era* (Cambridge: Harvard University Press, 1960), 267; Montgomery, *Fall of the House of Labor,* 238; Montejano, *Anglos and Mexicans in the Making of Texas,* 164, 174.

69. Their mills resembled the one described in the novel *Citizens:* "Those structures were stoves, heating up gas that went into the big blast furnace, to make heat, fire hotter than hell, to burn the iron out of the red earth. . . . They saw the stream of molten iron rushing out of the bottom of [the] huge furnace, into a great ladle like an inverted bell. . . . Sparks and lumps of fire jumped from the stream of liquid iron. . . . This liquid would make iron, . . . pig iron, but if it was cooked again in a different kind of furnace, in . . . open-hearth furnaces, . . . then iron became steel." Meyer Levin, *Citizens: A Novel* (New York: Viking Press, 1940), 98–99.

70. David Brody, *Labor in Crisis: The Steel Strike of 1919* (Urbana: University of Illinois Press, 1987), 162–163; Año Nuevo-Kerr, "Chicano Experience in Chicago," 24.

71. Ill will against Mexican strikebreakers became widespread in Pueblo, Colorado, the site of the Colorado Fuel and Iron Company steel mill. Most of the Mexicans were transient railroad workers and coal miners who had come to Pueblo in search of work. In 1920 tensions erupted, resulting in the lynching of two Mexicans on a hill outside the city. Philip S. Foner, *Organized Labor & the Black Worker, 1619–1981,* 2d ed. (New York: International Publishers, 1981), 144.

72. Edson, "Mexicans in Fort Madison, Iowa," 2–3.

73. Rosales and Simon, "Chicano Steelworkers and Unionism," 267–268; Edson, "Mexicans in Fort Madison, Iowa," 2–3; Edson, "Mexicans in the Pittsburgh, Pennsylvania, District," 19.

74. Brody, *Steelworkers in America,* 276–277; George T. Edson, "Mexicans in Bethlehem, Pennsylvania," 1926, PTC, 1; George Rivera, Jr., and Juventino Mejía, "Mas Aya del Ancho Río: Mexicanos in Western New York," *Aztlán* 7 (Spring 1976), 500–501; Rosales and Simon, "Chicano Steel Workers and Unionism," 268.

75. Edson, "Mexicans in the Pittsburgh, Pennsylvania, District," 2–3; Dennis C. Dickerson, *Out of the Crucible: Black Steel Workers in Western Pennsylvania, 1875–1980* (Albany: State University of New York Press, 1986), 96;

Brody, *Labor in Crisis,* 157–163; Robert J. Peters, director, Pennsylvania Bureau of Employment, Harrisburg, to R. H. Lansburgh, secretary of labor and industry, Harrisburg, May 18, 1925, USMCS, 165/223, Box 13. Edson reported that in Etna, Pa., 200 Mexicans worked at the Spang Chalfant Company, an iron-pipe manufacturer. The Mexicans constituted over 10 percent of Spang Chalfant's workforce of 1,600, alternating every other week between a ten-hour and twelve-hour night shift. Edson, "Mexicans in the Pittsburgh, Pennsylvania, District," 7.

76. Edson, "Mexicans at Lorain, Ohio," 7–8.

77. Gamio, *Mexican Immigration to the United States,* 143–144.

78. Montgomery, *Fall of the House of Labor,* 83.

79. A similar observation was made by a Mexican foundry worker in Detroit about the Mexican Ford autoworkers who showed up at the Saturday night dances downtown. The men were so handsomely dressed in suits that one forgot for a moment that they were machine operators and coremakers from the Ford River Rouge plant. Author interview with Pedro Escobar, November 20, 1986, Detroit.

80. Edson, "Mexicans at Lorain, Ohio," 21–22.

81. McWilliams, *North from Mexico,* 184.

82. George T. Edson, "Mexicans in Gary, Indiana," 1926, PTC, 1; Commissioner of Conciliation, Chicago, to H. L. Kerwin, director of conciliation, Department of Labor, Washington, D.C., April 29, 1925, USMCS, 165/223, Box 13. At the Gary-Indiana Steel Plant Mexicans were outnumbered only by Poles; Mexicans formed the second largest ethnic group and nearly 8 percent of the workforce. Another 1,100 Mexicans in Gary worked in plants of the American Sheet and Tin Plate Company and for the Gary Tube Company, both subsidiaries of U.S. Steel. Mohl and Betten, *Steel City,* 92.

83. Sepulveda, "Research Note," 327–328, 332; George T. Edson, "Mexicans in Indiana Harbor, Indiana," 1926, PTC, 7; Rosales, "Mexicans in Indiana Harbor during the 1920s," 89; Brody, *Steelworkers in America,* 265; Rosales and Simon, "Mexican Immigrant Experience in the Urban Midwest," 335; Taylor, *Chicago and the Calumet Region,* 25, 36.

84. Edson, "Mexicans in Indiana Harbor, Indiana," 15.

85. Edward Greer, *Big Steel: Black Politics and Corporate Power in Gary, Indiana* (New York: Monthly Review Press, 1979), 85; William Kornblum, *Blue Collar Community* (Chicago: University of Chicago Press, 1974), 42–43.

86. Jacoby, *Employing Bureaucracy,* 171–172; Montgomery, *Fall of the House of Labor,* 459–461; Morawska, *For Bread with Butter,* 115.

87. James R. Barrett, *Work and Community in the Jungle: Chicago's Packinghouse Workers, 1894–1922* (Urbana: University of Illinois Press, 1987), 50–51; Año Nuevo-Kerr, "Chicano Experience in Chicago," 25; Robert A. Slayton, *Back of the Yards: The Making of a Local Democracy* (Chicago: University of Chicago Press, 1986), 180; Mark Reisler, "The Mexican Immigrant in the Chicago Area during the 1920s," *Journal of the Illinois State Historical Society* 66 (Summer 1973), 149; author interview with Mariano Alvarez, July 14, 1986, Detroit; Taylor, *Chicago and the Calumet Region,* 94.

88. Barrett, *Work and Community in the Jungle,* 57.

89. Author interview with Mariano Alvarez, July 14, 1986, Detroit; Barrett, *Work and Community in the Jungle*, 69, 90–91.

90. Author interview with Guadalupe Morales, November 24, 1986, Detroit.

91. Zunz, *Changing Face of Inequality*, 286. In 1920, Detroit's twenty-nine automobile companies employed 135,000 workers, 40,000 of whom worked in the plants of the Ford Motor Company. Zunz, *Changing Face of Inequality*, 293.

92. Taylor, *Chicago and the Calumet Region*, 25; author interview with Pedro Escobar, November 20, 1986, Detroit; Dennis Nodín Valdés, "Perspiring Capitalists: Latinos and the Henry Ford Service School, 1918–1928" (Paper presented at the Seventy-fourth Annual Meeting of the Organization of American Historians, Detroit, April 3, 1981), 9.

93. Author interview with Ramón Huerta, November 19, 1986, Detroit.

94. Glen E. Carlson, "The Negro in the Industries of Detroit" (Ph.D. diss., University of Michigan, 1929), 46–47.

95. Author interview with Ramón Huerta, November 19, 1986, Detroit.

96. Henry Ford Service School, Foreign Student Research, Box 1319, June 10, 1920, EIA.

CHAPTER TWO

1. Mario T. García, *Desert Immigrants: The Mexicans of El Paso, 1880–1920* (New Haven, Conn.: Yale University Press, 1981), 235; Rodolfo Acuña, *Occupied America: A History of Chicanos*, 3d ed. (New York: Harper & Row, 1988), 169, 172, 181.

2. Montgomery, *Fall of the House of Labor*, 332; Ward, *Poverty, Ethnicity, and the American City*, 189; Taylor, *Chicago and the Calumet Region*, 277. Exposure of Mexicans to blacks in the Southwest and Mexico was minimal compared with exposure in the Midwest. Mexican and black cotton pickers and railroad workers toiled side by side in east Texas. Conceivably, some Mexicans had seen black soldiers under General John Pershing chasing Pancho Villa in northern Mexico after the Columbus, New Mexico, raid of 1916. In El Paso, Mexicans probably had contact with blacks brought in from east Texas and Louisiana during the 1913 smelter workers' strike. And east Texas Mexicans (along with foreign-born and black workers) were brought into the South, to Maryville, Louisiana, in November 1913 to break a local strike by lumbermen. Michael C. Meyer and William L. Sherman, *The Course of Mexican History*, 3d ed. (New York: Oxford University Press, 1987), 540–541; García, *Desert Immigrants*, 107–108; Foner, *Organized Labor & the Black Worker*, 118–119.

3. Valdés, "Perspiring Capitalists," 4; *Detroit News*, October 3, 1920; Baba and Abonyi, *Mexicans of Detroit*, 48; Valdés, *El Pueblo Mexicano en Detroit*, 16; Skendzal, *Detroit's Pioneer Mexicans*, 13–15; Edson, "Mexicans in Detroit, Michigan," 1.

4. Edson, "Mexicans in Detroit, Michigan," 4; Paul S. Taylor interview with Aureliano Aguilera, July 29, 1928, Detroit, PTC; Paul S. Taylor interview with

Mrs. Vollemear, International Institute, August 3, 1928, Detroit, PTC. Industry drew more and more Mexicans north, breaking their former migration to the farms in Texas. In Chicago a former scout for Laredo farmers told Taylor that he "used to get . . . cotton pickers in Laredo but now all they have in their heads is Chicago and Detroit. They won't stop in Texas." Taylor, *Chicago and the Calumet Region*, 34–35.

5. "Age-Grade and Nationality Survey," *Detroit Educational Bulletin* (Detroit Board of Education) 7 (January 1922); Baba and Abonyi, *Mexicans of Detroit*, 40; Taylor, *Chicago and the Calumet Region*, 98–99; Sepulveda, "Origins of the Urban Colonias in the Midwest," 103–104.

6. Data on the total number of Mexicans employed by the Ford Motor Company during this period are derived from the Rouge Area Hourly Workers Employment Record Jackets, 1918–1947. Gamio, *Mexican Immigration to the United States*, 160; Valdés, *El Pueblo Mexicano en Detroit*, 12; Taylor, *Chicago and the Calumet Region*, 266; Edson, "Mexicans in Detroit, Michigan," 2; Joyce Shaw Peterson, *American Automobile Workers, 1900–1933* (Albany: State University of New York Press, 1987), 1.

7. Paul S. Taylor interview with Aguilar, August 23, 1928, Detroit, PTC.

8. Paul S. Taylor interview with Juan Tovar, July 30, 1928, Detroit, PTC; Paul S. Taylor interview with Mexican at Howard Street Employment Agency, July 18, 1928, Detroit, PTC; Edson, "Mexicans in Detroit, Michigan," 15.

9. Peterson, *American Automobile Workers*, xii; Thomas J. Ticknor, "Motor City: The Impact of the Automobile Industry upon Detroit, 1900–1975" (Ph.D. diss., University of Michigan, 1978), 161; Melvin G. Holli, "The Impact of Automobile Manufacturing upon Detroit," *Detroit in Perspective* 2 (Spring 1976), 181–184; Stephen Meyer III, *The Five Dollar Day: Labor Management and Social Control in the Ford Motor Company, 1908–1921* (Albany: State University of New York Press, 1981), 78; Zunz, *Changing Face of Inequality*, 401.

10. Zunz, *Changing Face of Inequality*, 286; Gordon W. Davidson, "Industrial Detroit after World War I, 1919–1921" (Master's thesis, Wayne State University, 1953), 1; David Allan Levine, *Internal Combustion: The Races in Detroit, 1915–1926* (Westport, Conn.: Greenwood Press, 1976), 12.

11. Zunz, *Changing Face of Inequality*, 287; Ticknor, "Motor City," 161.

12. Detroit was the fifth largest industrial center in the United States. Ticknor, "Motor City," 107; Lois MacDonald, "Labor and Automobiles," in Lois MacDonald, ed., *Labor Problems and the American Scene* (New York: Harper and Brothers, 1938), 63; Zunz, *Changing Face of Inequality*, 293.

13. Peterson, *American Automobile Workers*, 14–16; Meyer, *The Five Dollar Day*, 26, 76–78; Davidson, "Industrial Detroit," 97–98, 165–166; Zunz, *Changing Face of Inequality*, 287.

14. Carlson, "The Negro in the Industries of Detroit," 40–42.

15. Levine, *Internal Combustion*, 44, 57–58; Rouge Area Hourly Workers Employment Record Jackets, Boxes 224, 296, 305, 437; Marks, *Farewell*, 34–44.

16. Carlson, "The Negro in the Industries of Detroit," 44; Peterson, *American Automobile Workers*, 24–28; Zunz, *Changing Face of Inequality*, 287–288.

17. Ticknor calculates the ratio of men to women in Detroit in 1920 as 120:100 for native white workers, 159:100 for foreign-born workers, and 144:100 for black workers. Ticknor, "Motor City," 181. Edson reported in 1927 that of the 20,900 Mexicans in the Detroit-Pontiac area, 11,843 (56.6 percent) were adult males, and the majority of females were between the ages of eighteen and thirty. Edson, "Mexicans in Our Northcentral States," 168. The annual reports of the U.S. Commissioner General of Immigration for the 1920s show that 70 percent of the Mexicans entering the country ranged in age from fifteen to fifty-four. Less than 7 percent were forty-five or older. The Mexicans traveling to Detroit matched these age characteristics. Cited in Cardoso, *Mexican Emigration*, 82.

18. Allan Nevins and Frank Ernest Hill, *Ford Expansion and Challenge 1915–1933* (New York: Scribner's, 1957), 534; Zunz, *Changing Face of Inequality*, 289–290. See Harvey Swados, *On the Line* (Boston: Little, Brown, 1957), 98–116, for a brilliant example of this wearing down of autoworkers. Historian Joyce Peterson states that one probable reason for the absence of older men in the car factories was that companies preferred to hire younger workers rather than take a risk with men past forty-five. Management believed the older men were less productive and more prone to injury. This arbitrary policy was enforced at the Detroit car plants throughout the twenties. Men eager for work in the factories dodged this requirement by lying about their age on job applications. Peterson, *American Automobile Workers*, 132–133.

19. MacDonald, "Labor and Automobiles," 159–160; Ticknor, "Motor City," 207; Chen-Nan Li, "A Summer in the Ford Works," *Personnel Journal* 6 (June 1928), 21.

20. Gordon, Edwards, and Reich, *Segmented Work, Divided Workers*, 100–101, 119; Meyer, *The Five Dollar Day*, 60; Harry Braverman, *Labor and Monopoly Capital: The Degradation of Work in the Twentieth Century* (New York: Monthly Review Press, 1974), 386; Andrew J. Steiger, "Autos and Jobs," *Nation* 126 (May 2, 1928), 506; Myron W. Watkins, "The Labor Situation in Detroit," *Journal of Political Economy* 28 (1920), 851.

21. Montgomery, *Fall of the House of Labor*, 371.

22. Peterson, *American Automobile Workers*, 108–116; Christopher H. Johnson, *Maurice Sugar: Law, Labor, and the Left in Detroit 1912–1950* (Detroit: Wayne State University Press, 1988), 91, 109.

23. Ticknor, "Motor City," 210; Johnson, *Maurice Sugar*, 51.

24. Zunz, *Changing Face of Inequality*, 319–320; Peterson, *American Automobile Workers*, 24.

25. David S. Weber, "Anglo Views of Mexican Immigrants: Popular Perceptions and Neighborhood Realities in Chicago, 1920–1940" (Ph.D. diss., Ohio State University, 1982), 119–121; Taylor, *Chicago and the Calumet Region*, 185.

26. Mohl and Betten, *Steel City*, 92; Acuña, *Occupied America*, 169; Rosales and Simon, "Mexican Immigrant Experience in the Urban Midwest," 336; Lance Trusty, *The Calumet Region: An Historical Resource Guide* (Hammond, Ind.: Calumet Regional Studies Institute, Purdue University, 1980), 221; Sepulveda, "Research Note," 329–330. Former residents described the Inland Steel

barracks as "too much like a prison; . . . we eat in a big place, all together, and sleep together. We never leave the walls of the factory." Quoted in Taylor, *Chicago and the Calumet Region*, 183.

27. Ticknor, "Motor City," 59, 79, 191; Zunz, *Changing Face of Inequality*, 342–343, 349; Davidson, "Industrial Detroit," 20–21.

28. Zunz, *Changing Face of Inequality*, 348–349.

29. Edson, "Mexicans in Detroit, Michigan," 1; Valdés, *El Pueblo Mexicano en Detroit*, 16; Zunz, *Changing Face of Inequality*, 348–349; Baba and Abonyi, *Mexicans of Detroit*, 51; Skendzal, *Detroit's Pioneer Mexicans*, 7.

30. Peterson, *American Automobile Workers*, 83; Paul S. Taylor interview with M. Alcosar, June 22, 1928, Detroit, PTC; Paul S. Taylor interview with Mexican in restaurant, June 21, 1928, Detroit, PTC. In 1921, an autoworker was able to save $2 a week. National Industrial Conference Board, *The Cost of Living among Wage Earners in Detroit, Michigan, September 1921* (New York, 1921), 17.

31. Davidson, "Industrial Detroit," 92–93; Peterson, *American Automobile Workers*, 75.

32. National Industrial Conference Board, *Cost of Living among Wage Earners in Detroit*, 3, 6–7; Ticknor, "Motor City," 190–191; Davidson, "Industrial Detroit," 95, 101; Zunz, *Changing Face of Inequality*, 291–292; Peterson, *American Automobile Workers*, 75, 88.

33. National Industrial Conference Board, *Cost of Living among Wage Earners in Detroit*, 7–8, 15; Peterson, *American Automobile Workers*, 74–75.

34. Rouge Area Hourly Workers Employment Record Jackets, Boxes 225, 305, 306, 307, 454, 491, 660, 1177, 1247, 1690, 1941, 2045.

35. Corwin and Cardoso, "Vamos al Norte," 50; Brisette, *Mexicans in the United States*, 20; Sepulveda, "Origins of the Urban Colonias in the Midwest," 102; Laird, "Argentine, Kansas," 26–55; Taylor, *Chicago and the Calumet Region*, 181.

36. Valdés, *El Pueblo Mexicano en Detroit*, 7, 16; Gamio, *Mexican Immigration to the United States*, 122; Paul S. Taylor interview with Mrs. Kel, Gershom Center, July 17, 1928, Detroit, PTC. For instance, prior to being hired by Ford Motors in the spring of 1920, autoworker Ernesto Mosquez had worked for the Pere Marquette Railroad, which supplied him and his family with housing in a boxcar. The autoworker listed the rail yards as his address when he applied for work at the Ford Highland Park plant. Rouge Area Hourly Workers Employment Record Jackets, Box 1480.

37. Jones, *Conditions surrounding Mexicans*, 55–64. This lamentable situation prompted one contemporary observer to liken the Mexican inhabitants of the boxcar camps to "rabbits in the cellar." Benjamin Goldberg, "Tuberculosis and the Mexican," *City of Chicago Municipal Tuberculosis Bulletin* 9 (March–April 1929), 22.

38. Author interview with Juan Martínez, November 15, 1986, Detroit.

39. An individual in Fort Madison further noted that track laborers injured on the job occasionally entered into common-law marriages with the women who moved into their bunk cars to take care of them. Another observer in Fort

Madison stated that the men and women "left their children with the grandparents in Mexico, came here and had more children, yet never sent for the others." Edson, "Mexicans in Fort Madison, Iowa," 4–6. Society of St. Vincent de Paul, Annual Report, 1920, St. Mary's Catholic Church, Detroit (hereafter cited as SMCC); Sepulveda, "Origins of the Urban Colonias in the Midwest," 105; Taylor, *Chicago and the Calumet Region*, 182; Laird, "Argentine, Kansas," 40.

40. Rouge Area Hourly Workers Employment Jackets, Box 1881.

41. The best example of this practice is found in Ernesto Galarza's autobiography *Barrio Boy* (South Bend, Ind.: University of Notre Dame Press, 1971). The late Chicano scholar supplies a detailed account of the step migration of his family from their mountain village of Jalcocotán, Nayarit, Mexico, to Sacramento, California.

42. Rouge Area Hourly Workers Employment Record Jackets, Boxes 521, 1629.

43. Ward, *Poverty, Ethnicity, and the American City*, 215; Leslie Woodcock Tentler, *Seasons of Grace: A History of the Catholic Archdiocese of Detroit* (Detroit: Wayne State University Press, 1990), 298.

44. Zunz, *Changing Face of Inequality*, 107, 324. In the Ford Highland Park plant, government agents investigated workers who made antipatriotic comments, and a few Mexicans came under surveillance. Those on the Ford profit-sharing plan were especially scrutinized. Meyer, *The Five Dollar Day*, 178–179; Rouge Area Hourly Workers Employment Record Jackets, Box 1691.

45. Ward, *Poverty, Ethnicity, and the American City*, 184–186; *Detroit News*, March 27, 1920; Skendzal, *Detroit's Pioneer Mexicans*, 25; Tentler, *Seasons of Grace*, 309.

46. Ward, *Poverty, Ethnicity, and the American City*, 215; *Michigan Catholic*, April 25, 1920; Baba and Abonyi, *Mexicans of Detroit*, 52; Skendzal, *Detroit's Pioneer Mexicans*, 20.

47. Society of St. Vincent de Paul, Minutes of the General Meeting, February 24, and March 9, 1920, SMCC; *Detroit News*, September 5, 1920; *Michigan Catholic*, May 6, 1920; Skendzal, *Detroit's Pioneer Mexicans*, 26; Tentler, *Seasons of Grace*, 228.

48. *Michigan Catholic*, May 15, 1920; Meyer and Sherman, *Course of Mexican History*, 548–549.

49. Garcia, *Desert Immigrants*, 214.

50. Ibid., 214, 218.

51. Montgomery, *Fall of the House of Labor*, 237; García, *Desert Immigrants*, 217–222; Sarah Deutsch, *No Separate Refuge: Culture, Class, and Gender on an Anglo-Hispanic Frontier in the American Southwest, 1880–1940* (New York: Oxford University Press, 1987), 104–106; George J. Sánchez, "*Go After the Women*": *Americanization and the Mexican Immigrant Woman 1915–1929*, Working Paper Series 6 (Stanford, Calif.: Stanford Center for Chicano Research, 1985); *Milwaukee Journal*, May 15, 1920; Mohl and Betten, *Steel City*, 114–115. A judge asked one Gary Mexican apprehended without legal papers whether he "was ready to fight for the United States." The Mexican opted to join the U.S. Navy and was assigned duty as a cook on a supply ship

during the German submarine blockade. When asked by Edson about naturalization, this Mexican answered: "What's the difference? It's a little matter and won't hurt any Mexican." Edson, "Mexicans in Gary, Indiana," 7.

52. *Detroit News,* March 27, 1920; García, *Desert Immigrants,* 218; Peterson, *American Automobile Workers,* 16–23; *Michigan Catholic,* July 21, 1921.

53. Quoted in *Detroit News,* March 27, 1920. Father Alanis's hopeful remarks were echoed by contemporary observers like *Detroit News* columnist James L. Devlin. In a series of articles he confidently reported on the progress of the Mexicans, highlighting for Detroiters the background of the newest arrivals: "They immigrated northward, guided by the star of Detroit's prosperity. . . . The exiles found in the soul of the great, dynamic city the warmth they craved for, and have hastened to conform themselves to the new environment. The unity of purpose among the Mexicans reveals . . . the infinite possibilities that are in the Mexicans for rapid Americanization." *Detroit News,* October 3, 1920.

54. Acuña, *Occupied America,* 171; Deutsch, *No Separate Refuge,* 117. A Texas Mexican LULAC member told Paul S. Taylor: "The world war taught us a lesson. We had thought we were Mexicans. The war opened our eyes. We have American ways and think like Americans." Paul S. Taylor, *An American-Mexican Frontier: Nueces County, Texas* (Chapel Hill: University of North Carolina Press, 1934), 245.

55. *Detroit News,* October 3, 1920.

56. Padilla was president of the St. Vincent de Paul Mexican Auxiliary from 1923 to 1930. Paul S. Taylor interview with Reyes Padilla, July 24, 1928, Detroit, PTC. During the Great Depression Muñoz edited the newspaper *La Chispa (The Spark)* and led the assault against Diego Rivera and La Liga de Obreros y Campesinos (The League of Mexican Workers and Peasants), one of the organizations the leftist Mexican muralist helped found. Skendzal, *Detroit's Pioneer Mexicans,* 48–49.

57. Valdés, *El Pueblo Mexicano en Detroit,* 18.

58. Rouge Area Hourly Workers Employment Record Jackets, Box 1314. That this ex-student had changed his name from Daniel to Dennis is another example of the Americanization Mexicans underwent in the Henry Ford Service School.

59. Ibid.

60. Zunz, *Changing Face of Inequality,* 309.

61. Quoted in Valdés, "Perspiring Capitalists," 3.

62. García, *Desert Immigrants,* 231.

63. Zunz, *Changing Face of Inequality,* 402; Montgomery, *Fall of the House of Labor,* 81.

64. Deutsch, *No Separate Refuge,* 38–39; Ward, *Poverty, Ethnicity, and the American City,* 182.

65. Skendzal, *Detroit's Pioneer Mexicans,* 55; *Detroit News,* December 11, 1920. Nonetheless, Detroit's Americanization campaign reached even to the Mexicans' celebrations of their national holidays. The *Michigan Catholic* (September 23, 1920) reported that at the 1920 Mexican independence celebration

"the Stars and Stripes held equal prominence with the flag of the Republic of the South."

66. A European immigrant worker said, "Festivities are shortened to one day. Who can afford to be merry for three days! The factory closes its doors to you if you are late 15 minutes. But what about being absent for two or three days?" Quoted in Thomas J. Woofter, Jr., *Races and Ethnic Groups in American Life* (New York: McGraw-Hill, 1933), 142. Mexican Ford autoworkers hired during World War I probably recalled that the company had discharged 900 immigrant workers for missing work to celebrate the Eastern Orthodox Christmas. This discharge occurred shortly after Ford Motors announced its $5 day and profit-sharing plan and simultaneously implemented stringent eligibility requirements for participation. Montgomery, *Fall of the House of Labor,* 236.

67. *Detroit News,* September 5, 1920.

68. Quoted in Taylor, *Chicago and the Calumet Region,* 261.

69. Reisler, *By the Sweat of Their Brow,* 49–53.

70. Ibid.; Martínez, *Mexican Emigration to the United States,* 52–53, Taylor, *Chicago and the Calumet Region,* 118.

71. Barrett, *Work and Community in the Jungle,* 256–261.

72. Mexican Consul Francisco Pereda, Chicago, to Mayor William Hale Thompson, Chicago, April 25, 1920, USINS, 54261/202, Box 243. The men under contract to the meat-packing houses in Wichita and Kansas City, Kansas, and in East St. Louis, Illinois, reached near-starvation. The companies donated meat to the jobless and famished Mexicans. About 1,700 without work and sleeping outdoors were being fed in the Kansas City area. The union president complained that the presence of this jobless workforce posed a threat to the welfare of his union men because the immigrants would willingly work for less than the set wages. John F. Hart, president, Amalgamated Meat Cutters and Workmen of North America, Washington, D.C., to Anthony Caminetti, commissioner general of immigration, Washington, D.C., April 13, 1921, USINS, 54261/202, Box 243.

73. Sepulveda, "Research Note," 332; Taylor, *Chicago and the Calumet Region,* 36; Reisler, *By the Sweat of Their Brow,* 50–51; Pereda to Thompson. The Mexican consul in New York City, however, was able to obtain help for the Mexicans in the vicinity who wanted to return to Mexico. On February 21, 1921, 110 Mexicans left New York City for Mexico aboard the *S.S. Antonio López.* Assistant Commissioner of Immigration, Ellis Island, New York Harbor, to Anthony Caminetti, commissioner general of immigration, Washington, D.C., February 24, 1921, USINS, 54261/202, Box 243.

74. Davidson, "Industrial Detroit," 123–127; Zunz, *Changing Face of Inequality,* 324.

75. Martin E. Sullivan, "On the Dole: The Relief Issue in Detroit, 1920–1939" (Ph.D. diss., University of Notre Dame, 1974), 32; Zunz, *Changing Face of Inequality,* 324. That area unemployment swiftly became a problem is revealed in the manpower reports submitted by the city's seventy-nine top corporations to the Detroit Employers' Association. The reports showed that in

March 1920 employment had reached a peak of 208,000. The workforce remained above 180,000 until September, then declined in November to 135,000 workers. Of these, 107,000 averaged a thirty-four-hour workweek. The lowest level of employment occurred in January 1921, when 25,339 workers were reported on the job—160,000 fewer than in the same period the preceding year. Almost one year passed before the number of workers employed in Detroit doubled to 52,156. A gradual recovery of the auto industry took place in January and February of 1922, and record production levels were attained in the spring of that year. Davidson, "Industrial Detroit," 127, 132–133; Peterson, *American Automobile Workers*, 118.

76. Davidson, "Industrial Detroit," 133; Ticknor, "Motor City," 209; Peterson, *American Automobile Workers*, 119; Sullivan, "On the Dole," 37.

77. Sullivan, "On the Dole," 33–34.

78. Only a small number of Mexican cases were reported however. District Director of Immigration, Detroit, to Anthony Caminetti, commissioner general of immigration, Washington, D.C., February 24, 1921, USINS, 54261/202, Box 243.

79. Approximately 458 (80.6 percent) of the 568 Mexicans hired by Ford Motors between 1918 and 1920 lost their jobs. These job terminations occurred on September 1, 1920, and appeared as "indefinite layoff" on the autoworkers' termination slips. Rouge Area Hourly Workers Employment Record Jackets, 1920.

80. Ten days after the mass layoffs at the Ford Highland Park plant in September 1920, autoworker Daniel López quit his foundry job and left for Texas, where he spent the fall and winter with relatives. López previously worked at Continental Motors and therefore was familiar with the seasonal fluctuations of auto work. He quit his job knowing that the auto companies would begin the series of layoffs as winter approached. Rouge Area Hourly Workers Employment Record Jackets, Box 1177. Dodge autoworker Salvador Villa lost his job in 1920. He left Detroit and traveled to southwestern West Virginia to look for work in the coal mines. In the summer of 1921, the United Mine Workers launched its organizing drive in this region, and Villa left the mines, probably in part to avoid the ensuing labor strife but even more to return to Detroit in anticipation of the seasonal hiring period. He stayed unemployed for several months, though he fortunately received aid from Detroit's DPW until finding work. Paul S. Taylor interview with Mr. Faris, Detroit Probation Department, July 26, 1928, Detroit, PTC; Melvyn Dubofsky and Warren Van Tine, *John L. Lewis: A Biography* (Urbana: University of Illinois Press, 1986), 59–60.

81. Society of St. Vincent de Paul, minutes of the General Meeting, January 24 and March 9, 1920, February 13, and July 24, 1921, SMCC; Paul S. Taylor interview with Mr. Fitzgerald, Society of St. Vincent de Paul, July 18, 1928, Detroit, PTC. The Society of St. Vincent de Paul filed reports on Mexicans it aided in order to properly regulate the distribution of provisions. The following was typical of the immigrants' hardships and illustrates the fate that awaited Mexicans most dependent on government aid. In late January 1921, Ford autoworker Rafael Espinosa died at Detroit's Receiving Hospital from a prolonged illness that a year earlier incapacitated the twenty-six-year-old foundry man and

forced him to quit his job at the Highland Park Plant. The day after Rafael's death, Bureau of Immigration agents arrested his widow and then deported her to Mexico. Mrs. Espinosa had been on assistance since her husband first became ill. She became conveniently expendable as the DPW pursued sharp reductions in its relief caseload. Society of St. Vincent de Paul, Annual Reports, 1920, 1921, SMCC. Ford autoworker Reyes Padilla joined the Mexican Auxiliary and devoted much time and energy to dispensing food and clothing to indigent Mexicans. During the Great Depression Padilla again would be a familiar and welcome sight in the Mexican colony as he made the rounds in his truck delivering bags of day-old bread, discarded produce, and clothing to the needy. Paul S. Taylor interview with Reyes Padilla, July 24, 1928, Detroit, PTC.

82. *Detroit News,* February 15 and 17, 1921.

83. Reisler, *By the Sweat of Their Brow,* 49–50; Immigration Service, Department of Labor, Detroit, to Anthony Caminetti, commissioner general of immigration, Washington, D.C., December 23, 1920, USINS, 54261/202, Box 243; Immigration Service, Department of Labor, Detroit, to District Commissioner of Immigration, Montreal, February 21 and 22, 1921, USINS, 54261/ 202, Box 243.

84. Martínez, *Mexican Emigration to the United States,* 74; Manuel C. Tellez, Mexican Embassy, Washington, D.C., to Mr. Quinn, commissioner of immigration, Saginaw, Michigan, January 31, 1921, USINS, 54261/202-I, Box 243; Reisler, *By the Sweat of Their Brow,* 53–55. The Mexican Honorific Commissions were established in 1921 at the first convention of Mexican general consuls held in San Antonio. Their main function was to provide indigent compatriots with assistance during the economic crisis, though the increasing Mexican population had been another reason behind their formation. Arthur F. Corwin, "Mexican Policy and Ambivalence toward Labor Emigration to the United States," in Arthur F. Corwin, ed., *Immigrants—and Immigrants: Perspectives on Mexican Labor Migration to the United States* (Westport, Conn.: Greenwood Press, 1978), 189.

85. By 1930, the Department of Labor was detaining 30,000 undocumented immigrants a year. Montgomery, *Fall of the House of Labor,* 460–461.

86. Arthur F. Corwin, "A Story of Ad Hoc Exemptions: American Immigration Policy toward Mexico," in Arthur F. Corwin, ed., *Immigrants—and Immigrants: Perspectives on Mexican Labor Migration to the United States* (Westport, Conn.: Greenwood Press, 1978), 141. A total of 21,400 Mexicans were deported by the Immigration Bureau in 1921. Martínez, *Mexican Emigration to the United States,* 53–55. The government deportation drives undertaken in January of the previous year, which targeted radicals, had been a dress rehearsal for these removals. Agents at that time rounded up 3,000 foreign aliens suspected of subversive activities. Robert K. Murray, *Red Scare: A Study in National Hysteria, 1919–1920* (New York: McGraw-Hill, 1964), 210–222.

87. Paul S. Taylor interview with Mr. Fitzgerald, Society of St. Vincent de Paul, July 18, 1928, Detroit, PTC; Society of St. Vincent de Paul, Minutes of the General Meeting, January 21, 1921, SMCC; Skendzal, *Detroit's Pioneer Mexicans,* 11–12, 27.

88. *Detroit News,* February 15, 1921; Martínez, *Mexican Emigration to the*

United States, 75–76; Reisler, *By the Sweat of Their Brow,* 55. The influx of sugar-beet workers may have inflated the latter figure of 2,500. Only fifty-seven Spanish surnames appeared in the 1921 *R. L. Polk's Detroit City Directory,* and just two Mexicans were hired at the Ford Highland Park plant in that year.

CHAPTER THREE

1. Restriction quotas on European immigration were a contributing factor in this migration as were an unstable Mexican economy and the social unrest produced by the de la Huerta (1923) and Cristero Revolutions (1927), which drove tens of thousands of immigrants across the American border. Despite attempts to control Mexican immigration, it continued unabated and created the labor force now essential to large-scale agriculture in the United States. George O. Coalson, *The Development of the Migratory Farm Labor System in Texas: 1900–1954* (San Francisco: R&E Research Associates, 1977), 12–13; Laird, "Argentine, Kansas," 66; Montgomery, "Thinking about American Workers in the 1920s," 10–11; Ward, *Poverty, Ethnicity, and the American City,* 199. Official estimates show that 249,248 Mexicans entered the United States between 1920 and 1924, and 238,527 arrived between 1925 and 1929; Mexicans contributed 15.6 percent of total immigration to the United States. Leo Grebler, *Mexican Immigration to the United States: The Record and Its Implications,* Mexican American Study Project Advance Report 2 (Los Angeles: Division of Research, Graduate School of Business, University of California, 1965), 8, 23.

2. Edson, "Mexicans in Our Northcentral States," 5; Daniel T. Simon, "Mexican Repatriation in East Chicago, Indiana," *Journal of Ethnic Studies* 2 (Summer 1974), 11; Reisler, *By the Sweat of Their Brow,* 267.

3. Montgomery, *Fall of the House of Labor,* 458. The heavy concentration of Mexicans in northern manufacturing during the twenties occurred in tandem with the decentralization of urban employment, eventually resulting in excessive joblessness. Racial and class dynamics further limited opportunities for succeeding generations of Mexican migrants, who were confined to deteriorating working-class neighborhoods. Ward, *Poverty, Ethnicity, and the American City,* 214–217.

4. Quoted in Mohl and Betten, *Steel City,* 92.

5. Mario Barrera, *Race and Class in the Southwest: A Theory of Racial Inequality* (South Bend, Ind.: University of Notre Dame Press, 1979), 222–223; Edson, "Mexicans in Detroit, Michigan," 22; Montgomery, *Fall of the House of Labor,* 81–82.

6. David Gartman, *Auto Slavery: The Labor Process in the American Automobile Industry, 1897–1950* (New Brunswick, N.J.: Rutgers University Press, 1986), 248–249; Gamio, *Mexican Immigration to the United States,* 55, 156; Mexican in Chicago quoted in Taylor, *Chicago and the Calumet Region,* 271; midwestern Mexican worker quoted in Taylor, *Spanish-Mexican Peasant Community,* 51.

7. Goldner, "The Mexican in the Northern Urban Area," 34; interview with Alfonso Galván, July 30, 1975, Minn. HS, 5–6; interview with Alfonso de

León, Sr., July 8, 1975, Minn. HS, 8; interview with George Galván, July 16, 1975, Minn. HS, 7–9.

8. Interview with Manuel Contreras, July 16, 1976, Minn. HS, 19, 22; interview with David Limón, August 5, 1975, Minn. HS, 4, 7, 9; Lorraine Esterly Pierce, "Mexican Americans on St. Paul's Lower West Side," *Journal of Mexican American History* 4 (1974), 2–3.

9. *Milwaukee Journal,* February 3, 1974; George T. Edson, "Mexicans in Milwaukee, Wisconsin," 1926, PTC, 1.

10. *Milwaukee Journal,* February 3, 1974.

11. Joe William Trotter, Jr., *Black Milwaukee: The Making of an Industrial Proletariat, 1915–45* (Urbana: University of Illinois Press, 1985), 53. By 1926 only 20 percent of the Mexicans hired as strikebreakers remained. Edson, "Mexicans in Milwaukee, Wisconsin," 5.

12. Edson, "Mexicans in Milwaukee, Wisconsin," 1, 4–5; Trotter, *Black Milwaukee,* 58–59.

13. Trotter, *Black Milwaukee,* 46.

14. Edson, "Mexicans in Chicago, Illinois," 1.

15. Brody, *Steelworkers in America,* 270; Edson, "Mexicans in Chicago, Illinois," 1–2. Edson mistakenly cited 16,000 Mexicans living in Chicago in 1927. The total number was 17,011.

16. Edson, "Mexicans in Chicago, Illinois," 2; Taylor, *Chicago and the Calumet Region,* 36–38; Barrera, *Race and Class in the Southwest,* 223.

17. Grossman, *Land of Hope,* 198; Taylor, *Chicago and the Calumet Region,* 32; Edson, "Mexicans in Chicago, Illinois," 2–3.

18. Brody, *Steelworkers in America,* 273–274; Taylor, *Chicago and the Calumet Region,* 157; Paul S. Taylor, "Mexicans at the Inland Steel Company," 1930, PTC; Edson, "Mexicans in Indiana Harbor, Indiana," 1.

19. Taylor, *Chicago and the Calumet Region,* 36.

20. Greer, *Big Steel,* 87; Edson, "Mexicans in Gary, Indiana," 1.

21. Martínez, *Mexican Emigration to the United States,* 69–70; *Detroit News,* November 10, 1932; Peterson, *American Automobile Workers,* 46.

22. Mike Davis, *Prisoners of the American Dream: Politics and Economy in the History of the U.S. Working Class* (New York: Verso Books, 1986), 42–43. Of the nation's autoworkers 13 percent worked in Ohio, 7 percent in Indiana, 6.7 percent in New York, 5 percent in Wisconsin, and 4.3 percent in Pennsylvania. The remainder worked in Michigan. Seventy-three percent of the 214,775 men employed by the auto industry in Michigan worked in the Detroit area, and over half (57 percent) were either foreign-born or black. This decrease in foreign-born workers was from 36 percent in 1920 to 30 percent in 1930. Sidney Fine, *The Automobile under the Blue Eagle* (Ann Arbor: University of Michigan Press, 1963), 4, 12. Peterson, *American Automobile Workers,* 14–20; Robert H. Zieger, *American Workers, American Unions, 1920–1985* (Baltimore: Johns Hopkins University Press, 1986), 4.

23. Coalson, *Development of the Migratory Farm Labor System in Texas,* 2–6.

24. Ramon Huerta, quoted in Edson, "Mexicans in Detroit, Michigan," 5;

U.S. Department of Commerce, *Mexican Immigration* (Washington, D.C.: Government Printing Office, 1930), 23; author interview with Ramón Huerta, November 19, 1986, Detroit. The company's appeal was repeatedly confirmed, as shown in the remarks of a Mexican Ford autoworker employed at the Rouge plant in 1928: "I think it is the best place to work. . . . It is quite a prestige to wear one of the [Ford] badges. Mexicans do not mind the steady fast pace which they have to keep up all the time. No loafing on the job there. They like Ford for two reasons. The first is that the wages are better than any place else. The second is that the work is steadier at Ford than elsewhere." This four-year employee added that Mexicans liked the automaker because even though they worked hard for eight hours and returned home tired, the men believed they had more job security than their compatriots did. Paul S. Taylor interview with Juan Tovar, July 30, 1928, Detroit, PTC.

25. Steve Babson, *Working Detroit: The Making of a Union Town* (New York: Adama Books, 1984), 48; author interview with Lauro Tienda, November 20, 1986, Detroit; Humphrey, "Employment Patterns of Mexicans in Detroit," 918–919; Edson, "Mexicans in Detroit, Michigan," 24; Carlson, "The Negro in the Industries of Detroit," 122; Paul S. Taylor interview with Mexican on Jones Street, September 14, 1928, Detroit, PTC. Mexicans were likely exposed to the black work habits that fashioned common labor, like the rhythmic work songs that set the mood and pace of the construction gangs. Grossman, *Land of Hope,* 192.

26. Edson, "Mexicans in Detroit, Michigan," 21; George T. Edson, "Mexicans in Pontiac, Michigan," 1926, PTC, 1–2. Approximately 400 Mexicans held jobs at the General Motors Central Foundry in Saginaw. Working conditions were hard and hazardous, but Mexicans persevered as long as possible before quitting. The $4.50-a-day wages kept them on the job. Paul S. Taylor interview with Mexican at an employment agency, September 4, 1928, Detroit, PTC.

27. H. F. Moorhouse, "The 'Work Ethic' and 'Leisure' Activity: The Hot Rod in Post-War America," in Patrick Joyce, ed., *The Historical Meanings of Work* (New York: Cambridge University Press, 1987), 241–242; author interview with Pedro Escobar, November 20, 1986, Detroit.

28. Testimony of María S. Montano, Visiting Housekeeper Association, Detroit, n.d. PTC.

29. Author interview with Ramón Huerta, November 19, 1986, Detroit.

30. Ibid.; author interview with Lauro Tienda, November 20, 1986, Detroit.

31. Edson, "Mexicans in Detroit, Michigan," 21–22. Briggs employed a sizable number of blacks; in 1937, 1,300 blacks worked for Briggs, constituting one-tenth of its workforce. At the Briggs Mack Avenue plant, blacks made up three-fourths of the workforce and with few exceptions were concentrated in the poorest jobs. August Meier and Elliott Rudwick, *Black Detroit and the Rise of the U.A.W.* (New York: Oxford University Press, 1979), 6–8.

32. Ford Motor Company's reputation was responsible for certain Mexicans' identifying Detroit as *la gran matris* (the grand matrix). Author interview with Ramón Huerta, November 19, 1986, Detroit.

33. Carlson, "The Negro in the Industries of Detroit," 121–122.

34. Robert W. Dunn, *Labor and Automobiles* (New York: International Publishers, 1929), 67; George T. Edson, "Mexicans in Flint, Michigan," 1926, PTC, 2.

35. Edson, "Mexicans in Detroit, Michigan," 21.

36. Edson, "Mexicans in Flint, Michigan," 1; Edson, "Mexicans in Detroit, Michigan," 6.

37. Carlson, "The Negro in the Industries of Detroit," 134; Robert N. McLean, "A Dyke against Mexicans," *New Republic* 59 (August 14, 1929), 335; Jones, *Conditions surrounding Mexicans*, 65–66. In 1928, Buick's employment manager was questioned about the company's Mexican employees. He remarked: "Two of them are among the finest valve grinders we have. They went in as laborers but are now earning big money." Quoted in Edson, "Mexicans in Flint, Michigan," 1–3.

38. Edson, "Mexicans in Pontiac, Michigan," 1–2; Gartman, *Auto Slavery,* 157–158.

39. David Rosner and Gerald Markowitz, eds., *Dying for Work: Worker Safety and Health in Twentieth-Century America* (Bloomington: Indiana University Press, 1989), 59; Dunn, *Labor and Automobiles*, 138–139.

40. Author interview with Lauro Tienda, November 20, 1986, Detroit.

41. Rouge Area Hourly Workers Employment Record Jackets, Box 1247; Edson, "Mexicans in Pontiac, Michigan," 2; Edson, "Mexicans in Detroit, Michigan," 21–22.

42. Peterson, *American Automobile Workers*, 36–38; Charles Reitell, "Machinery and Its Effect upon the Workers in the Automobile Industry," *Annals of the American Academy of Political and Social Science* 116 (November 1924), 40; Aronowitz, *False Promises*, 156; Meyer, *The Five Dollar Day*, 37.

43. Peterson, *American Automobile Workers*, 37; Meyer, *The Five Dollar Day*, 52.

44. Reitell, "Machinery and Its Effect upon the Workers," 43; Zieger, *American Workers, American Unions*, 6–7. In the summer of 1928, Yale engineering student Chen-Nan Li noted that nearly all the jobs at the Ford River Rouge plant consisted of a few operations that could be learned in five or ten minutes. One or two demonstrations by the shop foreman or by a worker were all the training needed by a newly hired autoworker to start his job. After a worker "automatized" the few operations to increase his work speed, he was considered a qualified "productive man." Li, "A Summer in the Ford Works," 23.

45. Peterson, *American Automobile Workers*, 37. Assembly workers (10 to 15 percent), skilled workers (5 to 10 percent), inspectors and testers (5 percent), helpers (15 percent), and laborers (10 to 15 percent) made up the remainder of the workforce. Already by 1917, 32 percent of Ford autoworkers held jobs as machine hands, and assemblers made up the next biggest job group (10 percent). Peterson, *American Automobile Workers*, 37.

46. Linda Downs, "The Rouge in 1932: 'The Detroit Industry' Frescoes by Diego Rivera," in Detroit Institute of Arts, *The Rouge: The Image of Industry*

in the Art of Charles Sheeler and Diego Rivera (Detroit: Detroit Institute of Arts, 1978), 7. A workforce of 5,000 men was required just to keep the gigantic Ford Rouge plant clean. Nevins and Hill, *Ford,* 292–293.

47. Paul S. Taylor interview with Aureliano Aguilera, August 23, 1928, Detroit, PTC; author interview with Guadalupe Morales, November 24, 1986, Detroit.

48. Peterson, *American Automobile Workers,* 27–28; Joyce Shaw Peterson, "Black Automobile Workers in Detroit, 1910–1930," *Journal of Negro History* 64 (Summer 1979), 181.

49. Plant managers quoted in Taylor, *Chicago and the Calumet Region,* 109, 244; employment manager quoted in Neil Betten and Raymond A. Mohl, "From Discrimination to Repatriation: Mexican Life in Gary, Indiana, during the Great Depression," *Pacific Historical Review* 42 (August 1973), 381. Historian Albert Camarillo noted that Chicanos in California knew of the subtle distinctions based on skin color that affected their treatment by Anglos: "If you were a huero [light-skinned] you could associate with any Gringo; . . . the color of your skin is what mattered. . . . If you were a little prieto [dark-skinned] you were an outcast." Albert Camarillo, *Chicanos in a Changing Society: From Mexican Pueblos to American Barrios in Santa Barbara and Southern California, 1848–1930* (Cambridge: Harvard University Press, 1979), 192.

50. In the Ford plants, shop foremen lacked outright power to discharge men, though they could lay off men for ten-day periods. The Ford Employment Office had the last say in discharges, but because autoworkers were regarded merely as "a badge number and very little else," a foreman did have considerable power. Gartman, *Auto Slavery,* 185; Humphrey, "Employment Patterns of Mexicans in Detroit," 915; Meyer, *The Five Dollar Day,* 84; Li, "A Summer in the Ford Works," 21, 26; Carlson, "The Negro in the Industries of Detroit," 234. The remark of a Mexican Flint autoworker was typical of this submission to Anglos: "My American foreman was a good man, he treated all nationalities good." Quoted in Taylor, *Spanish-Mexican Peasant Community,* 50.

51. Mariano Alvarez got along well with the foreman in his shop at the Ford Rouge plant, while Ford autoworker Guadalupe Morales faced a constant barrage of derogatory remarks about his nationality. On occasion the prejudiced foreman grabbed Morales by his shirt and shoved him about to emphasize the racial epithets. Frustrated by the demeaning treatment but aware that the unrestricted power of the foremen contributed to the repressive working conditions inside the Ford plant, this Mexican collared his foreman and threatened to hit him if he did not stop the haranguing. Author interview with Mariano Alvarez, July 14, 1986, Detroit; author interview with Guadalupe Morales, November 24, 1986, Detroit.

52. Gartman, *Auto Slavery,* 246, 248–249; Babson, *Working Detroit,* 50; author interview with Guadalupe Morales, November 24, 1986, Detroit.

53. Edson, "Mexicans in Detroit, Michigan," 14–15; Paul S. Taylor interview with former railroad worker, August 25, 1928, Detroit, PTC; Paul S. Taylor interview with Mexican at Howard Street Employment Agency, September 14, 1928, PTC.

54. Rouge Area Hourly Workers Employment Record Jackets, Boxes 19,

13, 799, 753. Elsewhere in the industrial North similar racial tensions between workers surfaced. For instance, in Indiana Harbor an area near the Inland Steel plant was known as "the bucket of blood" because of the host of savage fights between Mexican, immigrant, and black steelworkers. Against the shrieking and clattering of passing trains and the pall of dark smoke from the mill, Inland Steel's workers settled workplace disputes with fists, knives, and guns. Edson, "Mexicans in Indiana Harbor, Indiana," 1. This aspect of workers' lives has been neglected by labor historians in their examination of worker relations.

55. Gartman, *Auto Slavery*, 148.

56. MacDonald, "Labor and Automobiles," 161; Fine, *Automobile under the Blue Eagle*, 13–14; Dunn, *Labor and Automobiles*, 78; Peterson, *American Automobile Workers*, 46–50. Author interview with Ramón Huerta, November 19, 1986, Detroit.

57. Nevins and Hill, *Ford*, 519–520; Keith Sward, *The Legend of Henry Ford* (New York: Holt, Rinehart & Winston, 1948), 202–203, 218; Edmund Wilson, *The American Jitters* (1932; reprint, Freeport, N.Y.: Books for Libraries Press, 1968), 73; Gartman, *Auto Slavery*, 120–121.

58. Sward, *Legend of Henry Ford*, 216–217, 219; Dunn, *Labor and Automobiles*, 88; author interview with Victoria Rivas, November 11, 1986, Detroit.

59. Rouge Area Hourly Workers Employment Record Jackets, Box 304; Nevins and Hill, *Ford*, 515.

60. Rouge Area Hourly Workers Employment Record Jackets, Boxes 1719, 1159, 1484, 754.

61. Dickerson, *Out of the Crucible*, 79–82; Grossman, *Land of Hope*, 264; Rouge Area Hourly Workers Employment Record Jackets, Boxes 223, 229, 437, 799.

62. Rouge Area Hourly Workers Employment Record Jackets, Boxes 436, 847.

63. Nevins and Hill, *Ford*, 514–515; Rouge Area Hourly Workers Employment Record Jackets, Box 648; author interview with Victoria Rivas, November 11, 1986, Detroit.

64. Nevins and Hill, *Ford*, 514–515; Rouge Area Hourly Workers Employment Record Jackets, Boxes 645, 1734.

65. Gartman, *Auto Slavery*, 159–161.

66. Zieger, *American Workers, American Unions*, 6–7.

67. Ibid., 7; Coalson, *Development of the Migratory Farm Labor System in Texas*, 42; Montejano, *Anglos and Mexicans in the Making of Texas*, 217–218.

68. Quoted in Taylor, *Chicago and the Calumet Region*, 257, 260.

69. George T. Edson, "Mexicans in Milwaukee, Wisconsin," 1926, PTC, 4; Rosales, "Mexicanos in Indiana Harbor during the 1920s," 88–89, 94.

70. Holli, "Impact of Automobile Manufacturing upon Detroit," 185–186; Fine, *Automobile under the Blue Eagle*, 4–6, 15; Watkins, "Labor Situation in Detroit," 844–846, 851; Meyer, *The Five Dollar Day*, 81; Steiger, "Autos and Jobs," 506; Ticknor, "Motor City," 205–206. One-time Chrysler autoworker Ramón Huerta remembered how the new model year affected employment at

his plant. At the end of the production year the younger men were the first ones laid off, and when production resumed, the older workers were the first called back. Because uncertainty about production rates existed during model change-overs, auto companies circumvented worker contention about line speeds by bringing in the older, seasoned workers to set up the line. Instead of hiring additional workers plant inspectors and engineers verified that the lines were ready for production. Once everything was in place, the assembly lines started, and the workers were called in. They were expected to be ready to start any time. Author interview with Ramón Huerta, November 19, 1986, Detroit; Gartman, *Auto Slavery,* 157, 844–846.

71. Paul S. Taylor interview with Mexican, June 20, 1928, Detroit, PTC.

72. Peterson, *American Automobile Workers,* 54; Paul S. Taylor interview with Mexican carpenter, August 3, 1928, Detroit, PTC. Between 1923 and 1928 average monthly employment in the auto industry was 83.3 percent of annual employment according to a Bureau of Labor Statistics report. Cited in Fine, *Automobile under the Blue Eagle,* 4–6.

73. Peterson, *American Automobile Workers,* 54. For example, irregular employment caused Ford machine hand José Olmos to quit in August 1923 and return to his old job at Detroit's St. Regis Hotel. The hotel work paid less but was steady, which was essential in order for him to continue sending $50 per month to his family in Mexico. Rouge Area Hourly Workers Employment Record Jackets, Box 1472.

74. Edson, "Mexicans in Gary, Indiana," 12; Edson, "Mexicans in Fort Madison, Iowa," 12.

75. Nevins and Hill, *Ford,* 526; Taylor, *Chicago and the Calumet Region,* 102; Paul S. Taylor interview with Juan Tovar, July 30, 1928, Detroit, PTC; Rouge Area Hourly Workers Employment Record Jackets, Boxes 1177, 1190, 1371, 1881. One Mexican stated that he did not want to buy a Ford badge because men "who purchased passes into Ford's are being discharged; . . . the employees' list is being gone over carefully." Paul S. Taylor interview with Mexican at Howard Street Employment Agency, August 6, 1928, Detroit, PTC; Paul S. Taylor interview with E. López, July 23, 1928, Detroit, PTC.

76. Paul S. Taylor, "Mexicans in Detroit, Michigan."

77. Paul S. Taylor interview with Mexican carpenter, July 10, 1928, Detroit, PTC.

78. The Detroit Urban League and the Reverends R. L. Bradby of the Second Baptist Church and Everard W. Daniels of St. Matthews Episcopal Church wrote letters of recommendation to the Ford Motor Company on behalf of blacks applying for work. This process allowed Ford Motors to screen its black applicants in advance of hiring. The company was thus able to select from a pool of Detroit's "best" black workers. Levine, *Internal Combustion,* 97–98.

79. Paul S. Taylor interview with Juan Tovar, July 30, 1928, Detroit, PTC. In November 1925 Francisco Fuentes claimed on his application for work with Ford that he was a trained machinist. After one month, the Mexican was fired because he continually failed to execute his work as required. An exasperated shop foreman reported that the worker could not read his micrometer. Rouge Area Hourly Workers Employment Record Jackets, Box 636.

80. Approximately 60,000 Ford autoworkers were laid off or placed on two- or three-day work schedules. Over 11 percent of all Mexican Ford layoffs occurred at this time, with a mere nine men being hired in 1926 and 1927. The employment fluctuations in Detroit were twice the national average. Sward, *Legend of Henry Ford,* 199, 201; Ticknor, "Motor City," 209. Forty-five percent of Detroit's relief load was attributed to the Ford shutdown, and 28 percent (1,118) of the city's welfare cases were black families. Sullivan, "On the Dole," 36; Carlson, "The Negro in the Industries of Detroit," 99.

81. Meyer and Sherman, *Course of Mexican History,* 587–588. The predicament these newcomers faced was described in the *Michigan Catholic:* "Many of these people were brought here by lurid tales of employment managers during the boom days of several years ago. They were employed as laborers in the foundries and other shops and in the beet fields. Now in the present economic depression these people are fighting a losing game." *Michigan Catholic,* November 10, 1927. Author interview with Lauro Tienda, November 20, 1986, Detroit; Paul S. Taylor interview with Father Castillo, Our Lady of Guadalupe Church, August 30, 1928, Detroit, PTC; Paul S. Taylor interview with DPW officials, August 1928, Detroit, PTC.

82. Paul S. Taylor interview with Mr. Brock, Michigan Department of Labor, July 16, 1928, Detroit, PTC; Paul S. Taylor interview with Charles Benjamin, July 24, 1928, Detroit, PTC; Taylor, *Chicago and the Calumet Region,* 266; George T. Edson, "Mexicans in Waukegan, Illinois," 1926, PTC, 4. The wife and son of a track laborer who was killed in an accident while with the Trinity and Brazos Valley Railroad outside Houston received $12.60 compensation. Mexican Consul Ignacio Batiza, Detroit, to Mexican Consulate Office, Mexico City, July 1930, File IV-69-42, pp. 14, 16; October 1930, File IV-69-46, p. 26. Secretaria de Relaciones Exteriores, Archivo Nacional, Mexico City. (Hereafter cited as SRE.)

83. Rouge Area Hourly Workers Employment Record Jackets, Boxes 1485, 2138, 1359, 225, 968.

84. If the Detroit Mexican consul had not intervened to help them, Mexicans injured in work-related accidents would have lost the appropriate compensation. Paul S. Taylor interview with Reyes Padilla, July 24, 1928, Detroit, PTC; Paul S. Taylor interview with Charles Benjamin, July 24, 1928, Detroit, PTC.

85. Rouge Area Hourly Workers Employment Record Jackets, Box 1379.

86. Rouge Area Hourly Workers Employment Record Jackets, Boxes 968, 1457, 1987, 1914, 1376, 955; Peterson, *American Automobile Workers,* 63–67.

87. Paul S. Taylor interview with Mr. Johnson, Probation Department, Municipal Court, July 25, 1928, Detroit, PTC.

88. Edson, "Mexicans in Detroit, Michigan," 19.

CHAPTER FOUR

1. Martínez, *Mexican Emigration to the United States,* 69–72; Francisco A. Rosales, "The Regional Origins of Mexicano Immigrants to Chicago during the 1920s," *Aztlán* 7 (Summer 1976), 191; Sepulveda, "Research Note," 332; author interview with Lauro Tienda, November 20, 1986, Detroit. In 1926, ap-

proximately 10 percent of the 8,000 Mexican women in the Midwest lived in the Detroit-Pontiac area. Edson, "Mexicans in Our Northcentral States," 7.

2. Ronald Edsforth, *Class Conflict and Cultural Consensus: The Making of a Mass Consumer Society in Flint, Michigan* (New Brunswick, N.J.: Rutgers University Press, 1987), 16–17, 33–34.

3. Baba and Abonyi, *Mexicans of Detroit*, 56–57; Valdés, *El Pueblo Mexicano en Detroit*, 16–17.

4. *Detroit Saturday Night*, October 16, 1926; Eric H. Monkkonen, *America Becomes Urban: The Development of U.S. Cities and Towns, 1780–1980* (Berkeley: University of California Press, 1988), 194–197; Edson, "Mexicans in Our Northcentral States," 9. Information from the Ford employment record cards indicates that changes of residence generally coincided with wage readjustments.

5. Edson, "Mexicans in Detroit, Michigan," 19; Baba and Abonyi, *Mexicans of Detroit*, 56–57.

6. City lots purchased in the Chicago-Gary region usually had houses and cost between $3,000 and $10,000. Real estate purchases by Mexicans were limited to fifteen in the South Chicago and Brighton Park area, ten to fifteen in Indiana Harbor (including a hotel), and fifteen in Gary. Mexicans buying homes in this region usually rented out rooms to pay the mortgage. Raymond E. Nelson, "The Mexicans in South Chicago," 1928, PTC, 9–10; Taylor, *Chicago and the Calumet Region*, 165–166. Several dozen Mexican railroad workers in Fort Madison, Iowa, pooled their savings to buy property, paying $2,100 for twenty-one small lots. Despite the hostility of neighbors, the Mexicans eventually built their homes. Edson, "Mexicans in Fort Madison, Iowa," 6–7.

7. Paul S. Taylor interview with Javier Tovar, July 30, 1928, Detroit, PTC. A Spanish-speaking realtor remarked that he had little success with Mexican clients; they usually did not earn enough money, had irregular employment, or faced layoffs, which made them ineligible to purchase houses. Paul S. Taylor interview with López Real Estate agent, August 29, 1928, Detroit, PTC; Paul S. Taylor interview with Reyes Padilla, July 24, 1928, Detroit, PTC.

8. Nelson, "Mexicans in South Chicago," 14–15; Goldberg, "Tuberculosis and the Mexican," 22–23; Rosales and Simon, "Mexican Immigrant Experience in the Urban Midwest," 341; Sepulveda, "Research Note," 330; Simon, "Mexican Repatriation in East Chicago," 12–13; Brisette, *Mexicans in the United States*, 19–20; Edson, "Mexicans in Gary, Indiana," 2; Betten and Mohl, "From Discrimination to Repatriation," 372–374. A plan to move Mexicans in Gary west of Harrison Street, between 23rd and 25th Avenues, as a way to alleviate the problem of poor and congested living conditions was disapproved by the workers. *Gary Post-Tribune*, October 20, 1926.

9. Rosales, "Mexicanos in Indiana Harbor during the 1920s," 88; Edson, "Mexicans in Indiana Harbor, Indiana," 1–2; Sepulveda, "Research Note," 330, 334; Edson, "Mexicans in Detroit, Michigan," 1, 16.

10. Valdés, *El Pueblo Mexicano en Detroit*, 17; Skendzal, *Detroit's Pioneer Mexicans*, 16; Edson, "Mexicans in Detroit, Michigan," 7; Edson, "Mexicans in Our Northcentral States," 37; Gamio, *Mexican Immigration to the United States*, 21; Rosales, "Regional Origins," 196–197. One Detroit Mexican family that operated a *casa de asistencia* had a boarder who had been with them for

three years and had followed them as they traveled across the country. The number of Mexican families wanting boarders managed to meet demand. Paul S. Taylor interview with Mrs. Kel, Gershom Center, July 17, 1928, Detroit, PTC. In Chicago, two large industrial concerns established a boardinghouse as a way of stabilizing their new Mexican labor force. Taylor, *Chicago and the Calumet Region*, 184.

11. J. W. Nixon, "How Ford's Lowest-Paid Workers Live," *Social Service Review* 5 (March 1931), 44; Steiger, "Autos and Jobs," 506; Paul S. Taylor interview with Javier Tovar, July 30, 1928, Detroit, PTC.

12. Edson, "Mexicans in Our Northcentral States," 44–45; social worker quoted in Taylor, *Chicago and the Calumet Region*, 187–188.

13. Goldberg, "Tuberculosis and the Mexican," 24–25; Taylor, *Chicago and the Calumet Region*, 187–188. Tuberculosis was rumored to be caused by the cold air from Lake Michigan. In 1925, thirty-two cases of tuberculosis were reported, and seven proved fatal. Betten and Mohl,"From Discrimination to Repatriation," 373–374. Prior to 1927, Gary's hospital received many Mexican patients from East Chicago, which was without an infirmary. Edson, "Mexicans in Gary, Indiana," 4.

14. Valdés, *El Pueblo Mexicano en Detroit*, 17; Edson, "Mexicans in Detroit, Michigan," 5; Peterson, *American Automobile Workers*, 84–85; Mexican Consul Ignacio Batiza, Detroit, to Mexican Consulate Office, Mexico City, June 26, 1928, File IV-69-40, p. 1, SRE. Many Mexicans died at the Eloise Infirmary, Detroit's "poorhouse," and the ensuing poverty and homelessness forced the surviving family members to leave the city. In 1926, the family of one deceased Mexican autoworker went to Arkansas and obtained work picking cotton, but the widow and her children were cheated out of their earnings. The family next traveled to Memphis but failed to find work and were denied charity because of a one-year residency requirement. With no alternatives, the desperate widow decided to return to Detroit, where she resolved to support her family by washing clothes. Paul S. Taylor interview with DPW case worker, August 1928, Detroit, PTC.

15. Taylor, *Chicago and the Calumet Region*, 235–240; Palmer, "Building Ethnic Communities," 168; Grossman, *Land of Hope*, 175.

16. Edson, "Mexicans in Gary, Indiana," 8–10, 13–14; Gamio, *Mexican Immigration to the United States*, 120; Taylor, *Chicago and the Calumet Region*, 235, 240; *Milwaukee Journal*, February 3, 1927; Barrett, *Work and Community in the Jungle*, 176.

17. Paul S. Taylor interview with E. López, July 28, 1928, Detroit, PTC.

18. Nelson, "Mexicans in South Chicago," 14; Palmer, "Building Ethnic Communities," 171–172; Taylor, *Chicago and the Calumet Region*, 279–280.

19. Edson, "Mexicans in Waukegan, Illinois," 4; Edson, "Mexicans in Aurora, Illinois," 4; Rosales and Simon, "Mexican Immigrant Experience in the Urban Midwest," 343–344; Lizabeth Cohen, "Encountering Mass Culture at the Grass Roots: The Experience of Chicago Workers in the 1920s," *American Quarterly* 41 (March 1989), 16; Taylor, *Chicago and the Calumet Region*, 231–232; Simon, "Mexican Repatriation in East Chicago," 13; Mohl and Betten, *Steel City*, 95–96.

20. Babson, *Working Detroit*, 44; Peterson, *American Automobile Workers*, 90; Mary Frances Berry and John W. Blassingame, *Long Memory: The Black Experience in America* (New York: Oxford University Press, 1982), 235.

21. Baba and Abonyi, *Mexicans of Detroit*, 55–56; Valdés, *El Pueblo Mexicano en Detroit*, 20–21; Paul S. Taylor interview with Javier Tovar, July 30, 1928, Detroit, PTC; Edson, "Mexicans in Our Northcentral States," 32–33; *Detroit News*, August 1, 1926.

22. George T. Edson, "Mexicans at Davenport, Iowa, and Moline, Illinois," 1927, PTC, 13; Taylor, *Chicago and the Calumet Region*, 252–254.

23. Palmer, "Building Ethnic Communities," 169; Taylor, *Chicago and the Calumet Region*, 245–246, 255; Paul S. Taylor, *Mexican Labor in the United States: Bethlehem, Pennsylvania* (Berkeley: University of California Press, 1931), 21 (hereafter cited as *Bethlehem, Pennsylvania*); John Cervantes, *My Moline: A Young Illegal Immigrant Dreams* (Canoga Park, Calif.: Canyon, 1986), 55; Paul S. Taylor interview with Mrs. Vollemeare, interpreter, International Institute, August 3, 1928, Detroit, PTC; Rosales, "Mexicanos in Indiana Harbor during the 1920s," 94.

24. Taylor, *Chicago and the Calumet Region*, 255–256; Montgomery, *Fall of the House of Labor*, 110; Taylor, *Spanish-Mexican Peasant Community*, 53, 55; Taylor, *Bethlehem, Pennsylvania*, 23.

25. *Detroit News*, September 5, 1920; author interview with Lauro Tienda, November 20, 1986, Detroit; Leslie Woodcock Tentler, *Wage-Earning Women: Industrial Work and Family Life in the United States, 1900–1930* (New York: Oxford University Press, 1979), 14–15. For example, one Mexican woman in Moline, Illinois, prepared lunch for all the section hands on the Milwaukee Railroad and for those on the Burlington line. Cervantes, *My Moline*, 44–45.

26. Tentler, *Wage-Earning Women*, 117; Palmer, "Building Ethnic Communities," 134–137; *R. L. Polk's Detroit City Directory*, 1928; *R. L. Polk's Detroit City Directory*, 1926–1929; Edson, "Mexicans in Detroit, Michigan," 23; Paul S. Taylor interview with Mrs. Gonzáles, n.d., Detroit, PTC.

27. Edson, "Mexicans in Our Northcentral States," 18; Edson, "Mexicans in Gary, Indiana," 4; Morawska, *For Bread with Butter*, 127. Both the Alamo Hotel and the Cass Hotel were managed by Mexican women and served a large Mexican clientele. *R. L. Polk's Detroit City Directory*, 1918–1929.

28. Paul S. Taylor interview with the director, Visiting Housekeeper's Association, July 20, 1928, Detroit, PTC; Brisette, *Mexicans in the United States*, 10–12. By 1930, 25 percent of the Southwest's Mexican and Mexican American women were low-wage industrial workers, a percentage comparable to that of East Coast foreign-born women engaged in blue-collar employment. Vicki L. Ruiz, *Cannery Women, Cannery Lives: Mexican Women, Unionization, and the California Food Processing Industry, 1930–1950* (Albuquerque: University of New Mexico Press, 1987), 14.

29. Alice Kessler-Harris, *Out to Work: A History of Wage-Earning Women in the United States* (New York: Oxford University Press, 1982), 236. According to a 1926 report, women constituted 59, 259 (or 61.6 percent) of the 96,141 workers in domestic and personal services in Michigan. Clara Menger, *Women Workers of Michigan: Numbers and Occupations of Women Workers in the*

State of Michigan and in the Fourteen Largest Cities of the State, Vocational Education Bulletin 222 (Lansing, Mich.: State Board of Control for Vocational Education, April 1926), 12–13. A small number of single, middle-class Mexican and Mexican American women in Detroit obtained clerical and sales jobs because they knew English and had formal educations and citizenship. However, within these categories, it is likely that these women held the low-wage and unattractive jobs, which offered little opportunity for advancement. Paul S. Taylor, "Mexican Women in Los Angeles Industry in 1928," *Aztlán* 11 (Spring 1980), 116–125; Tentler, *Wage-Earning Women,* 96.

30. Tentler, *Wage-Earning Women,* 22, 35.

31. Author interview with Manuela Alvarez, July 14, 1986, Detroit; Melissa Hield, "'Union-Minded': Women in the Texas ILGWU, 1933–50," *Frontiers* 4 (1979), 61.

32. Tentler, *Wage-Earning Women,* 30–33; Lois Rankin, "Detroit Nationality Groups," *Michigan History Magazine* 23 (Spring 1939), 151–152.

33. Author interview with Olga Huerta, November 19, 1986, Detroit; Taylor, "Mexicans in Detroit, Michigan"; Sánchez, *"Go After the Women,"* 13.

34. Ruiz, *Cannery Women, Cannery Lives,* 13; Paul S. Taylor interview with Miss Baker, International Institute, July 20, 1928, Detroit, PTC. A handful of Mexican women in Detroit during the 1920s were schoolteachers, like the two sisters mentioned previously who had followed their husbands to Detroit from El Paso, and students in local high schools. *R. L. Polk's Detroit City Directory,* 1918–1929.

35. Palmer, "Building Ethnic Communities," 143–144; Tentler, *Wage-Earning Women,* 35–36.

36. Rosalinda M. González, "Chicanas and Mexican Immigrant Families, 1920–1940: Women's Subordination and Family Exploitation," in Lois Scharf and Joan M. Jensen, eds., *Decades of Discontent: The Women's Movement, 1920–1940* (Westport, Conn.: Greenwood Press, 1983), 4; Palmer, "Building Ethnic Communities," 143–144; Ruth Milkman, *Gender at Work: The Dynamics of Job Segregation by Sex during World War II* (Urbana: University of Illinois Press, 1987), 112–116.

37. Tentler, *Wage-Earning Women,* 141–142.

38. Quoted in Taylor, *Chicago and the Calumet Region,* 267.

39. Paul S. Taylor interview with autoworker Martínez, July 5, 1928, Detroit, PTC.

40. Tentler, *Wage-Earning Women,* 73–74; Paul S. Taylor interview with Aureliano Aguilera, August 23, 1928, Detroit, PTC; Paul S. Taylor interview with autoworker Martínez, July 5, 1928, Detroit, PTC; Ruiz, *Cannery Women, Cannery Lives,* 18–19.

41. Paul S. Taylor interview with autoworker Martínez, July 5, 1928, Detroit, PTC. Working women in the Midwest proved competent and self-reliant as they adapted to the male-dominated urban environment. In unruly, working-class Indiana Harbor, a Mexican woman earned her living by operating a combination barbershop and beauty parlor out of a pool hall. She was not offended by the colorful language of the steelworkers who came in to shoot pool. On the contrary, the woman freely used the same profanities as the men and shared in

their bawdy jokes as she gave haircuts and shaves to her customers. Edson, "Mexicans in Indiana Harbor, Indiana," 11.

42. Tentler, *Wage-Earning Women,* 61–64; García, *Desert Immigrants,* 201; Cervantes, *My Moline,* 47; author interview with Olga Huerta, November 19, 1986, Detroit.

43. Edson,"Mexicans in Chicago, Illinois," 18.

44. Morawska, *For Bread with Butter,* 258–259; Palmer, "Building Ethnic Communities," 144; Taylor, *Chicago and the Calumet Region,* 169, 279; Steven A. Riess, *City Games: The Evolution of American Urban Society and the Rise of Sports* (Urbana: University of Illinois Press, 1989), 74–75; Skendzal, *Detroit's Pioneer Mexicans,* 18; Rosales and Simon, "Mexican Immigrant Experience in the Urban Midwest," 343.

45. Taylor, *Chicago and the Calumet Region,* 167, 169; Murillo, "Detroit Mexican 'Colonia,'" 38–41.

46. Ibid., 170. The Mexican proprietor of a restaurant in Chicago commented on the mainly Mexican patronage of his establishment: "Most of our customers are Mexicans who come here to eat their . . . home dishes. . . . We have many who come in regularly for all their meals." Taylor, *Chicago and the Calumet Region,* 167, 169. Mexican restaurants in Detroit opened in low-rent districts, but the food typically cost more than in American restaurants. Consequently, Detroit's Mexican restaurants had a limited compatriot clientele. Edson, "Mexicans in Detroit, Michigan," 20; Paul S. Taylor interview with E. López, August 2, 1928, Detroit, PTC. Yet there were probably men who willingly paid the higher price for the food and the ambience because eating there served as a brief respite from the mayhem of the factories and reminded them of their homeland. Edson described a typical Mexican restaurant in Indiana Harbor: "The odor of burning garlic, the tin pan music of a mechanical piano, colors and decorations on the wall, the Spanish language on every tongue and señoritas waiting on tables furnish a setting where the frequenters may eat . . . in an atmosphere as Mexican as in their native pueblos." Edson, "Mexicans in Indiana Harbor, Indiana," 17.

47. Edson, "Mexicans in Indiana Harbor, Indiana," 11–12; clerks quoted in Simon, "East Chicago Repatriation," 12; Trusty, *Calumet Region,* 221–222; Edson, "Mexicans in Our Northcentral States," 101–102. In 1924, a Mexican restaurant on East Congress Street was open for business on a part-time basis during the owner's off-time as a painter. A Mexican barbershop that did business on Michigan Avenue in 1918 closed briefly in 1924 when one of the barbers left to work in a local auto factory. It later reopened when the remaining Mexican barber established a partnership with an Armenian. *R. L. Polk's Detroit City Directory,* 1918, 1924.

48. Taylor, *Chicago and the Calumet Region,* 170–171.

49. Edson, "Mexicans in Detroit, Michigan," 22.

50. *R. L. Polk's Detroit City Directory,* 1918–1924, 1926–1929; Riess, *City Games,* 73.

51. Gamio, *Mexican Immigration to the United States,* 79; Skendzal, *Detroit's Pioneer Mexicans,* 16, 19. In 1926, Mexicans in East Chicago had made a similar appeal to their compatriots to invest in a moviehouse that would show

Spanish-language films. Rosales and Simon, "Mexican Immigrant Experience in the Urban Midwest," 343.

52. Paul S. Taylor interview with Mexican at Abbott Street Pool Room, August 30, 1928, Detroit, PTC; Cohen, "Encountering Mass Culture at the Grass Roots," 10–11; author interview with Olga Huerta, November 19, 1986, Detroit.

53. Gamio, *Mexican Immigration to the United States,* 118; quote from Betten and Mohl, "From Discrimination to Repatriation," 376; Nelson, "Mexicans in South Chicago," 12, 26.

54. Gamio, *Mexican Immigration to the United States,* 115–117; Morawska, *For Bread with Butter,* 261–262; Taylor, *Spanish-Mexican Peasant Community,* 36–37; Cardoso, *Mexican Emigration,* 72; Skendzal, *Detroit's Pioneer Mexicans,* 14–15; Rosales, "Regional Origins," 195–196; Sepulveda, "Research Note," 329; Nelson, "Mexicans in South Chicago," 26; Palmer, "Building Ethnic Communities," 148; David Montgomery, "Nationalism, American Patriotism, and Class Consciousness among Immigrant Workers in the United States in the Epoch of World War I," in Dirk Hoerder, ed., *"Struggle a Hard Battle": Essays on Working-Class Immigrants* (DeKalb: Northern Illinois University Press, 1986), 330–331.

55. Gamio, *Mexican Immigration to the United States,* 115–117.

56. Deutsch, *No Separate Refuge,* 50–51; Ruiz, *Cannery Women, Cannery Lives,* 6; Palmer, "Building Ethnic Communities," 147; author interview with Manuela Alvarez, July 14, 1986, Detroit.

57. Edson, "Mexicans at Lorain, Ohio," 4.

58. Gamio, *Mexican Immigration to the United States,* 119; Mohl and Betten, *Steel City,* 96–97; Edson, "Mexicans in Indiana Harbor, Indiana," 5; Rosales, "Regional Origins," 196; Palmer, "Building Ethnic Communities," 145–146; Nelson, "Mexicans in South Chicago," 119.

59. *Detroit News,* March 27, 1920; *Michigan Catholic,* July 21, 1921; Paul S. Taylor interview with Father Heenan, Holy Trinity Catholic Church, August 28, 1928, Detroit, PTC.

60. Father Juan P. Alanis to Bishop Gallagher, Archdiocese of Detroit, July 25, 1923, Archives of the Archdiocese of Detroit. Small groups also met at Providence Hospital's chapel and for rosary recitals at Mexican homes. Skendzal, *Detroit's Pioneer Mexicans,* 29–30.

61. *Michigan Catholic,* May 13, 1920, and July 21, 1927; Valdés, *El Pueblo Mexicano en Detroit,* 20. The societies were Sociedad San José (St. Joseph's Society), El Circulo Mutualista Mexicano (Mexican Mutual Aid Circle), La Cruz Azul Mexicana (Mexican Blue Cross), and Sociedad Anáhuac (Anáhuac Society).

62. Paul S. Taylor interview with Father Luis Castillo, Our Lady of Guadalupe Church, August 30, 1928, Detroit, PTC; Father Alanis quoted in Skendzal, *Detroit's Pioneer Mexicans,* 28–29. A photograph of the newly constructed church with several members and religious guests appeared on the first page of the November 1, 1923, issue of the *Michigan Catholic.*

63. Valdés, *El Pueblo Mexicano en Detroit,* 20; *Michigan Catholic,* December 2, 1926, and November 10, 1927.

64. Valdés, *El Pueblo Mexicano en Detroit,* 20; Paul S. Taylor interview with Father Luis Castillo, Our Lady of Guadalupe Church, August 30, 1928, Detroit, PTC; Tentler, *Seasons of Grace,* 306, 316. The sardonic remarks of a Mexican Indian autoworker in response to a question by Paul S. Taylor about the Cristero Revolution revealed that maltreatment and exploitation by the Church along class lines had not been forgotten: "The government did not shut the churches. The priests did that themselves. What the government did was to keep money from being sent to Rome. The rich are to blame. They took the properties and the money that has been taken away from the Church for themselves." Mexicans of Indian origin were mindful of how in their home country Catholic priests ostentatiously exhibited their class and caste differences, treating their flocks as racially inferior. Patronizing references to Mexicans as "my Indians" by priests were not uncommon and were even uttered by priests in the North. Paul S. Taylor interview with Mexican Indian autoworker, n.d., Detroit, PTC. In Chicago, a non-Catholic Mexican told Taylor that if Mexicans were able to vote in the presidential election of 1928, they would vote for Herbert Hoover rather than Al Smith, who was Catholic. Chicago Mexicans believed that if Smith were elected, he would continue the Cristero Revolution in their homeland. Taylor, *Chicago and the Calumet Region,* 209. The parish priest of South Chicago's Mexican Catholic church stated that his worshippers were "made up of the lowest and most ignorant Indian stock." Quoted in Nelson, "Mexicans in South Chicago," 11.

65. Author interview with Pedro Escobar, November 20, 1986, Detroit; Taylor, *Chicago and the Calumet Region,* 210; Edson, "Mexicans at Lorain, Ohio," 4; Taylor, *Spanish-Mexican Peasant Community,* 58; Roy Rosenzweig, *Eight Hours for What We Will: Workers & Leisure in an Industrial City, 1870–1920* (Cambridge: Cambridge University Press, 1983), 204, 213.

66. Deutsch, *No Separate Refuge,* 63; García, *Desert Immigrants,* 219–222; Camarillo, *Chicanos in a Changing Society,* 195–196; Riess, *City Games,* 157.

67. Protestant missionary quoted in R. Douglas Brackenridge and Francisco O. García-Treto, *Iglesia Presbiteriana: A History of Presbyterians and Mexican Americans in the Southwest,* 2d ed. (San Antonio, Tex.: Trinity University Press, 1987), 128.

68. Martha Caroline Mitchell Remy, "Protestant Churches and Mexican-Americans in South Texas" (Ph.D. diss., University of Texas, Austin, 1970), 169; Nelson, "Mexicans in South Chicago," 25.

69. Cervantes, *My Moline,* 25–26.

70. *Gary Post-Tribune,* October 6, 1926; Taylor, *Chicago and the Calumet Region,* 212–213; Nelson, "Mexicans in South Chicago," 26. East Chicago's Spanish-speaking Protestant movement was led by a Mexican pastor from Mexico City, the center of that country's largest non-Catholic population. Rosales, "Regional Origins," 196.

71. Skendzal, *Detroit's Pioneer Mexicans,* 43–44; *Detroit News,* August 1, 1926; Paul S. Taylor interview with Mexican member of Baptist Church, August 7, 1928, Detroit, PTC.

72. Paul S. Taylor interview with Father Heenan, Holy Trinity Church, August 28, 1928, Detroit, PTC; Taylor, *Chicago and the Calumet Region,* 210.

73. Gamio, *Mexican Immigration to the United States,* 135–136; Arthur F. Corwin, "Mexican Policy and Ambivalence toward Labor Emigration to the United States," 189; Martínez, *Mexican Emigration to the United States,* 74, 78; García, *Desert Immigrants,* 223.

74. Morawska, *For Bread with Butter,* 229; author interview with José Allende, November 22, 1986, Detroit; author interview with Pedro Escobar, November 20, 1986, Detroit.

75. Montgomery, "Nationalism, American Patriotism, and Class Consciousness," 332–333.

76. Edson, "Mexicans in Gary, Indiana," 5; Taylor, *Chicago and the Calumet Region,* 131–133; Rosales, "Regional Origins," 191. The Mexican newspaper *El Nacional* of Chicago noted that the majority of the local clubs in Chicago had lasted from one to six years. *El Nacional,* March 3, 1934.

77. Rosales, "Mexicanos in Indiana Harbor during the 1920s," 92; Mohl and Betten, *Steel City,* 94.

78. Rosales, "Mexicanos in Indiana Harbor during the 1920s," 92; Riess, *City Games,* 105–106.

79. Nicolas Kanellos, "Fifty Years of Theater in the Latino Communities of Northwest Indiana," *Aztlán* 7 (Summer 1976), 255–256; Spencer Leitman, "Exile and Union in Indiana Harbor: Los Obreros Católicos 'San José' and El Amigo del Hogar, 1925–1930," *Revista Chicano Riqueña* 2 (Winter 1974), 52; Edson, "Mexicans in Indiana Harbor, Indiana," 6; Rosales and Simon, "Mexican Immigrant Experience in the Urban Midwest," 339–340; Rosales, "Mexicanos in Indiana Harbor during the 1920s," 91.

80. Edson, "Mexicans at Lorain, Ohio," 19–21; *Detroit Saturday Night,* October 16, 1926; *Detroit News,* August 1, 1926; Skendzal, *Detroit's Pioneer Mexicans,* 59; Edson, "Mexicans in Detroit, Michigan," 3; Paul S. Taylor interview with Javier Tovar, July 30, 1928, Detroit, PTC. In Detroit, in addition to the Mexican Honorary Commission, the Mexican Blue Cross, and the Sociedad de San Jose, there were other organizations: Chapultepec, Chihuahenses Unidos, Club Recreativo Azteca, Circulo Mutualista Mexicano, Circulo Anáhuac, Obreros Libres, Circulo Progresista Tlaltenanguense, Damas Catolicas, and Padres de Familias.

81. Skendzal, *Detroit's Pioneer Mexicans,* 55; *Detroit News,* December 11, 1920; Baba and Abonyi, *Mexicans of Detroit,* 54–55; *Detroit News,* September 16, 1926; Morawska, *For Bread with Butter,* 245–246; Mexican Consul Ignacio Batiza, Detroit, to Mexican Consulate Office, Mexico City, 1931, File IV-657-63, unpaged, SRE.

82. Edson, "Mexicans in Detroit, Michigan," 23; Morawska, *For Bread with Butter,* 246.

83. Paul S. Taylor, "Sociedad 'Anáhuac,'" n.d., PTC; Valdés, *El Pueblo Mexicano en Detroit,* 18; Edson, "Mexicans in Our Northcentral States," 112.

84. Paul S. Taylor, "Sociedad 'Anáhuac'"; Paul S. Taylor, "Circulo Mutu-

alista Mexicano," July 3, 1928, PTC; Paul S. Taylor interview with Javier Tovar, July 30, 1928, Detroit, PTC.

85. Paul S. Taylor, "Circulo Mutualista Mexicano"; Skendzal, *Detroit's Pioneer Mexicans,* 58–59; Edson, "Mexicans in Our Northcentral States," 113; Edson, "Mexicans in Detroit, Michigan," 3; Baba and Abonyi, *Mexicans of Detroit,* 52–53.

86. Taylor, *Chicago and the Calumet Region,* 136–137; Valdés, *El Pueblo Mexicano en Detroit,* 21; Paul S. Taylor interview with Javier Tovar, July 30, 1928, Detroit, PTC; Paul S. Taylor interview with Reyes Padilla, July 24, 1928, Detroit, PTC.

87. Quoted in Taylor, *Chicago and the Calumet Region,* 136–137.

88. Palmer, "Building Ethnic Communities," 142.

89. Cervantes, *My Moline,* 113; Palmer, "Building Ethnic Communities," 149.

90. Morawska, *For Bread with Butter,* 263–264.

91. Green, *Grass-Roots Socialism,* 329; Frank Nills Hanson, "Texas Justice, 99 Years," *International Socialist Review* 16 (February 1916), 476–478; Edson, "Mexicans in Gary, Indiana," 13; superintendent quoted in Gamio, *Mexican Immigration to the United States,* 119.

92. Rosales and Simon, "Chicano Steel Workers and Unionism," 269; Deutsch, *No Separate Refuge,* 173; labor agent quoted in Taylor, *Chicago and the Calumet Region,* 121.

93. *México,* February 6, 1929; steelworker quoted in Edson, "Mexicans in Indiana Harbor, Indiana," 14. Many Mexicans knew about American intervention in Nicaragua and expressed pride that President Calles had condemned this aggression. Meyer and Sherman, *Course of Mexican History,* 583–587.

94. Vasconcelos criticized the progressive American labor movement because of what the Mexican intellectual deemed its isolationist stance in excluding non-naturalized immigrant workers. John Skirius, "Vasconcelos and México de Afuera (1928)," *Aztlán* 7 (Fall 1976), 487.

95. Skendzal, *Detroit's Pioneer Mexicans,* 60; Paul S. Taylor, "Sociedad Obreros Libres," July 3, 1928, PTC. Another Mexican-worker organization in Detroit was El Circulo Progresista Tlaltenanguense (Tlaltenango Progressionist Circle), formed in the mid-1920s by autoworkers from the village of Tlaltenango, Michoacán. Its primary objective was to construct a school in the members' home village. Edson, "Mexicans in Our Northcentral States," 93, 112.

96. Montgomery, *Fall of the House of Labor,* 463–464; Reisler, *By the Sweat of Their Brow,* 34–35, 169; Gamio, *Mexican Immigration to the United States,* 135; Paul S. Taylor, interview with Mexicans at Howard Street Employment Agency, July 14, 1928, Detroit, PTC.

97. Cardoso, *Mexican Emigration,* 92–93; Morawska, *For Bread with Butter,* 233–235; Cohen, "Encountering Mass Culture at the Grass Roots," 8. Carey McWilliams noted that Mexicans indeed had an appreciation for consumer goods: "High on the list of items which 2,104 immigrants brought back to Mexico from the United States . . . were . . . bathtubs; wooden and metal toilets; refrigerators; metal kitchen utensils; washing machines; metal stoves;

sewing machines; and automobiles (thirty-seven percent returned with cars)." McWilliams, *North from Mexico*, 214.

98. García, *Desert Immigrants*, 200; Paul S. Taylor interview with Mrs. Vollemeare, interpreter, International Institute, August 3, 1928, Detroit, PTC.

99. Taylor, *Chicago and the Calumet Region*, 189–190; *Milwaukee Journal* August 14, 1927; author interview with Olga Huerta, November 19, 1986, Detroit.

100. Taylor, *Chicago and the Calumet Region*, 163–164; Gamio, *Mexican Immigration to the United States*, 70; Edson, "Mexicans in Gary, Indiana," 3; Cohen, "Encountering Mass Culture at the Grass Roots," 8; Stewart Ewen, *Captains of Consciousness: Advertising and the Social Roots of the Consumer Culture* (New York: McGraw-Hill, 1976), 30. According to one contemporary observer, installment buying by some Mexican Detroiters occasionally led them to contract debts that they could not repay and resulted in a number of families being forced to seek public aid. Paul S. Taylor interview with Mrs. Kel, Gershom Center, n.d., Detroit, PTC. Another stated: "The installment plan companies do a good deal of wrong to the Mexicans. As soon as the Mexicans get a little bit ahead they begin to make payments on a victrola or a player piano and when there is a period of depression they lose everything." Paul S. Taylor interview with Mrs. Vollemeare, interpreter, International Institute, August 3, 1928, Detroit, PTC.

101. Gamio, *Mexican Immigration to the United States*, 68–69; McWilliams, *North from Mexico*, 214; Edson, "Mexicans in Detroit, Michigan," 4, 8–9; Edson, "Mexicans in Our Northcentral States," 20.

102. Edson, "Mexicans in Our Northcentral States," 20.

103. Taylor, *Bethlehem, Pennsylvania*, 20; executive quoted in Edson, "Mexicans in Bethlehem, Pennsylvania," 2; Paul S. Taylor interview with Mexican Ford autoworker Huerta, August 18, 1928, Detroit, PTC. One Detroit autoworker who died left his mother in Michoacán, Mexico, a $1,000 Woodmen of the World insurance policy as well as a $1,250 Aetna Life Insurance policy. Mexican Consul Ignacio Batiza, Detroit, to Mexican Consulate Office, Mexico City, October 1930, File IV-69-46, p. 26, SRE.

104. Taylor, *Chicago and the Calumet Region*, 161–163; Edson, "Mexicans in Our Northcentral States," 21.

105. Edson, "Mexicans at Lorain, Ohio," 5; Edson, "Mexicans in Gary, Indiana," 5; Edson, "Mexicans in Milwaukee, Wisconsin," 4; Edson, "Mexicans in Detroit, Michigan," 3; Edson, "Mexicans in Our Northcentral States," 92–93; Paul S. Taylor interview with Mrs. Vollemeare, interpreter, International Institute, August 3, 1928, Detroit, PTC.

106. Edson, "Mexicans in Detroit, Michigan," p. 32.

107. Morawska, *For Bread with Butter*, 240.

108. Palmer, "Building Ethnic Communities," 187. Visits to the Mexican colonies in nearby Gary and South Chicago were popular pastimes. The trams and buses connecting these cities along Lake Michigan's shoreline facilitated interaction among the immigrants. Rosales and Simon, "Mexican Immigrant Experience in the Urban Midwest," 337.

109. Cervantes, *My Moline*, 28; Edson, "Mexicans at Lorain, Ohio," 13; Edson, "Mexicans in Indiana Harbor, Indiana," 11.

110. Rosenzweig, *Eight Hours for What We Will*, 191; Edson, "Mexicans in Chicago, Illinois," 12.

111. Riess, *City Games*, 110–112; interview with George Galvin, July 16, 1975, Minn. HS, 7–18.

112. Li, "A Summer in the Ford Works," 30–31.

113. Paul S. Taylor interview with Mexican autoworker Martínez, August 6, 1928, Detroit, PTC; author interview with José Allende, November 22, 1986, Detroit.

114. Ralph Janis, "The Brave New World That Failed: Patterns of Social Structure in Detroit, 1880–1940" (Ph.D. diss., University of Michigan, 1972), 77; Valdés, *El Pueblo Mexicano en Detroit*, 20; Edson, "Mexicans in Detroit, Michigan," 9; Paul S. Taylor interview with Mexican autoworker Martínez, July 11, 1928, Detroit, PTC; Paul S. Taylor interview with Mexican autoworker Huerta, n.d., Detroit, PTC. Major Spanish-language newspapers were available to Detroit's Mexicans: *La Prensa* (San Antonio); *El Diario* (New York City); *La Opinión* (Los Angeles); *El Norte* (Monterrey); *El Informador* (Guadalajara); and *Universal, Excelsior,* and *Novedades* (Mexico City). Edson, "Mexicans in Detroit, Michigan," 20; Skendzal, *Detroit's Pioneer Mexicans*, 50.

115. Gamio, *Mexican Immigration to the United States*, 136–137; Taylor, *Chicago and the Calumet Region*, 170. Acuña, *Occupied America*, 175; Simon, "Mexican Repatriation in East Chicago," 12. The newspaper titles suggested a working-class readership; for example, Mexican workers in Davenport, Iowa, read *El Trabajo (The Work)*; steelworkers in East Chicago read *El Amigo del Hogar (Friend of the Hearth)* and *Humo (Smoke)*.

116. Mario T. García, "Chistes and Caricaturas in the Mexican American Press, Los Angeles, 1926–1927," *Studies in Latin American Popular Culture* 1 (1982), 86.

117. Rosenzweig, *Eight Hours for What We Will*, 220–221; Paul S. Taylor interview with Mexican autoworker Martínez, July 11, 1928, Detroit, PTC.

118. Paul S. Taylor interview with Mexican in a restaurant, June 21, 1928, Detroit, PTC; Paul S. Taylor interview with Mexican autoworker Huerta, n.d., Detroit, PTC; author interview with Olga Huerta, November 19, 1986, Detroit; Nelson, "Mexicans in South Chicago," 30.

119. Manuel Peña, *The Texas-Mexican Conjunto: History of a Working-Class Music* (Austin: University of Texas Press, 1985), 39–40; Batiza to Mexican Consulate Office, 1931; Taylor, *Bethlehem, Pennsylvania*, vii; Nelson, "Mexicans in South Chicago," 28; Cohen, "Encountering Mass Culture at the Grass Roots," 8–9. The film *Ballad of an Unsung Hero* (1983) portrays the importance of Spanish-language radio programming for Mexicans in Los Angeles during these early years.

120. Sidney Fine, *Frank Murphy: The Detroit Years* (Ann Arbor: University of Michigan Press, 1975), 102; Ticknor, "Motor City," 48. One dance hall was a redecorated apartment located over an auto-accessories store owned by a Mexican; it was managed by his nineteen-year-old daughter. The father had helped his daughter get the hall started and fully supported this venture. Paul S.

Taylor interview with Mrs. Hutzel, Detroit Police Department Women's Head-quarters, July 11, 1928, Detroit, PTC; author interview with Guadalupe Morales, November 24, 1986, Detroit.

121. Cohen, "Encountering Mass Culture at the Grass Roots," 16–27.

122. Taylor, *Bethlehem, Pennsylvania,* 19. The Mexicans Taylor interviewed in Arandas, Jalisco, who had been in the North brought suits, hats, and oxfords out of trunks to show the American scholar. They also had photographs of themselves dressed in American clothing. Taylor, *Spanish-Mexican Peasant Community,* 57.

123. Edson, "Mexicans in Chicago, Illinois," 7–8.

124. *Milwaukee Journal,* August 14, 1927.

125. García, *Desert Immigrants,* 200; González, "Chicanas and Mexican Immigrant Families," 74; Paul S. Taylor interview with Mexican, July 7, 1928, Detroit, PTC; Paul S. Taylor interview with Mexican worker, September 5, 1928, Detroit, PTC; Paul S. Taylor interview with Mexican in restaurant "Texas," June 21, 1928, Detroit, PTC; quote from Paul S. Taylor interview with Aureliano Aguilera, August 23, 1928, Detroit, PTC; Paul S. Taylor interview with Father Castillo, Our Lady of Guadalupe Church, August 30, 1928, Detroit, PTC. "Women no longer stood for what they meekly accepted in Mexico," remarked a social worker from the International Institute in Detroit. "If their husband beats them they go to the police." Paul S. Taylor interview with Mrs. Larsen, International Institute, June 25, 1928, Detroit, PTC.

126. Watkins, "Labor Situation in Detroit," 840–841; Edson, "Mexicans in Detroit, Michigan," 8.

127. The following exchange was probably typical of the haggling that took place: "'I can get a paper suitcase like that for $2,' said one to a Jewish merchant. 'Paper'? said the Jew. 'This one isn't paper, it's fiber. Fiber.'" Edson, "Mexicans in the Pittsburgh, Pennsylvania, District," 28.

CHAPTER FIVE

1. The purchasing power of these midwestern Mexican workers had also been reduced by the inflation that marked the decade of the 1920s, as a large part of their earnings went to pay for food, housing, and heating bills. Alexander Keyssar, *Out of Work: The First Century of Unemployment in Massachusetts* (Cambridge: Cambridge University Press, 1986), 149; David Brody, *Workers in Industrial America: Essays on the Twentieth Century Struggle* (New York: Oxford University Press, 1980), 64–65.

2. Deutsch, *No Separate Refuge,* 174.

3. Albert Bawaski, Gary, Ind., to U.S. Bureau of Immigration, Washington, D.C., September 5, 1930, USINS, 55639/616.

4. H. B. Robertson, Mansfield, Ohio, to U.S. Commissioner General of Immigration Harry E. Hull, Washington, D.C., April 2, 1930, USINS, 55639/616. In a letter addressed to President Franklin Roosevelt but rerouted to Immigration Commissioner Harry E. Hull, an irate resident of Traverse City, Mich., remarked that "if there were two million less Mexicans in our country the same number of Americans would have jobs." He probably had in mind the high

number of Mexicans in the state who worked in sugar beets. Arthur A. Caulkett, Traverse City, Mich., to U.S. Commissioner General of Immigration Harry E. Hull, Washington, D.C., April 22, 1930, USINS, 55639/616.

5. Reisler, *By the Sweat of Their Brow,* 228–229.

6. Rosales and Simon, "Chicano Steel Workers and Unionism," 269; Humphrey, "Employment Patterns of Mexicans in Detroit," 914; Humphrey, "Mexican Repatriation from Michigan," 498; Mexican Consulate Office, Mexico City, to Mexican Consul Ignacio Batiza, Detroit, June 11, 1930, File IV-76-3, SRE. The Bureau of Immigration refused to grant visas to Mexican workers and justified this policy by stating that Mexicans "could become public charges." Reisler, *By the Sweat of Their Brow,* 231.

7. Mexican Consul Ignacio Batiza, Detroit, to Mexican Embassy, Washington, D.C., March 7, 1930, File IV-76-3, SRE.

8. Betten and Mohl, "From Discrimination to Repatriation," 380–381. The lack of work in the steel mills of Indiana Harbor, Ind., forced an estimated 3,000 Mexicans to leave for Mexico between 1929 and 1933. Rosales, "Mexicanos in Indiana Harbor during the 1920s," 95.

9. Fine, *Frank Murphy,* 246–247; Ticknor, "Motor City," 212. Because some auto companies retained on their payrolls workers who were buying automobiles, men would attempt to keep their jobs by having auto dealers report that they were buying cars. Fine, *Frank Murphy,* 201–202; Peterson, *American Automobile Workers,* 130–131; author interview with Lauro Tienda, November 20, 1986, Detroit.

10. Samuel M. Levin, "The Ford Unemployment Policy," *American Labor Legislation Review* 22 (March 1932), 101–102; Peterson, *American Automobile Workers,* 131; author interview with Mariano Alvarez, July 14, 1986, Detroit; Ticknor, "Motor City," 212; Brody, *Workers in Industrial America,* 67–68. Undoubtedly, the most publicized and controversial relief measure undertaken by the Ford Motor Company during the depression was its extensive renovation of the black community of Inkster. Ford set up a commissary, paid the back bills of Inkster families, refurbished houses, and provided residents with clothing. Black autoworkers from this community more than paid for this act of Ford benevolence through outrageous deductions from their pay. Inkster's males were given work at Ford at $4 a day, but $3 a day was deducted for the renovation of Inkster. In 1933, after Ford had abandoned the Inkster renovation project, some black autoworkers from this community were still being paid $1 a day. Peterson, *American Automobile Workers,* 137. See Meier and Rudwick, *Black Detroit and the Rise of the U.A.W.,* 15.

11. Levin, "Ford Unemployment Policy," 105; Roger Keeran, *The Communist Party and the Auto Workers' Unions* (New York: International Publishers, 1980), 71–74; author interview with Guadalupe Morales, November 24, 1986, Detroit.

12. Peterson, *American Automobile Workers,* 136–137.

13. Levin, "Ford Unemployment Policy," 107–108; Fine, *Frank Murphy,* 309–310; Richard D. Lunt, *The High Ministry of Government: The Political Career of Frank Murphy* (Detroit: Wayne State University Press, 1965), 35.

14. Author interview with Pedro Escobar, November 20, 1986, Detroit.

15. Peterson, *American Automobile Workers*, 135. Following the example of other states, the Los Angeles Police Department established a "bum blockade," albeit unconstitutional, of 150 city police officers at entry points along the California border to selectively expel undesirable migrants. In 1935, the governor of Colorado declared martial law along the state's southern border and called out the National Guard to patrol the boundary with New Mexico in order to keep Mexicans from migrating into the state. Irving Bernstein, *A Caring Society: The New Deal, the Worker, and the Great Depression* (New York: Pantheon, 1985), 282; Deutsch, *No Separate Refuge*, 165–166.

16. Press release, March 7, 1932, Governor Wilbur M. Brucker Papers, Box 13, Michigan Historical Collection, Ann Arbor.

17. Peterson, *American Automobile Workers*, 135; Fine, *Frank Murphy*, 202–204; Helen Hall, "When Detroit's out of Gear," *Survey* 64 (April 1, 1930), 9–10.

18. Lunt, *High Ministry of Government*, 36. The personal concern that Mayor Frank Murphy had for the unemployed was shown in his efforts to furnish them with clothing and shoes and, as winter approached, in his request that the homes of the unemployed remain supplied with gas and light. Lunt, *High Ministry of Government*, 30–31.

19. Ibid., 31–34.

20. Author interview with Lauro Tienda, November 20, 1986, Detroit; author interview with Victoria Rivas, November 19, 1986, Detroit.

21. Lunt, *High Ministry of Government*, 37, 49; Fine, *Frank Murphy*, 305–306.

22. Lunt, *High Ministry of Government*, 49. The DPW also made eligibility for assistance more stringent. It cut off support to single adults, adult families of two or more members, childless couples and those with fewer than three children, families with incomes, families that could be supported by relatives, families residing in Detroit fewer than three years, families with bank accounts, families that engaged in illegal activities, and legally resident families refusing transportation to other communities that would provide them with relief. Fine, *Frank Murphy*, 325–327.

23. Lunt, *High Ministry of Government*, 52–53; Fine, *Frank Murphy*, 339.

24. Mexican Consul Ignacio Batiza, Detroit, "Report on the Mexican Honorary Commissions," April 30, 1931, File IV-338-35, SRE; Tentler, *Seasons of Grace*, 313–316.

25. Lunt, *High Ministry of Government*, 50–52.

26. George C. Kiser and Mary Woody Kiser, "Introduction," in George C. Kiser and Mary Woody Kiser, eds., *Mexican Workers in the United States: Historical and Political Perspectives* (Albuquerque: University of New Mexico Press, 1979), 33; Valdés, *El Pueblo Mexicano en Detroit*, 29–30.

27. Detroit District Director of Immigration John L. Zubrick, Detroit, to U.S. Commissioner General of Immigration Harry E. Hull, Washington, D.C., October 20, 1932, USINS, 55784/585; *El Nacional*, May 14 and May 28, 1932; Murillo, "Detroit Mexican 'Colonia,'" 140; George C. Kiser and David Silverman, "Mexican Repatriation during the Great Depression," in George C. Kiser and Mary Woody Kiser, eds., *Mexican Workers in the United States: His-*

torical and Political Perspectives (Albuquerque: University of New Mexico Press, 1979), 59; Valdés, *El Pueblo Mexicano en Detroit,* 34; Humphrey, "Mexican Repatriation from Michigan," 498.

28. Humphrey, "Mexican Repatriation from Michigan," 501; Abraham Hoffman, *Unwanted Mexicans in the Great Depression: Repatriation Pressures, 1929–1939* (Tucson: University of Arizona Press, 1974), 120; Murillo, "Detroit Mexican 'Colonia,'" 160.

29. Mexican Consul Ignacio Batiza, Detroit, to C. Delegado, minister of migration, Nuevo Leon, Tamaulipas, December 11, 1932, File IV-335-5, SRE.

30. Hoffman, *Unwanted Mexicans,* 121; Humphrey, "Mexican Repatriation from Michigan," 501; *Detroit News,* October 10, 1931.

31. Ignacio Batiza, "Mexican Consul Agrees to Repatriation of Detroit Mexicans," in George C. Kiser and Mary Woody Kiser, eds., *Mexican Workers in the United States: Historical and Political Perspectives* (Albuquerque: University of New Mexico Press, 1979), 44; Kiser and Silverman, "Mexican Repatriation," 59.

32. Downs, "The Rouge in 1932," 47–48. The information about Guillermo Kahlo's ties to the Ford Motor Company is from the author's telephone conversation in the winter of 1984 with Linda Downs of the Detroit Institute of Arts. From March 19 to March 27, 1933, the *Detroit Times* ran a series of articles that covered the controversy created by Rivera's murals at the Detroit Institute of Art.

33. Downs, "The Rouge in 1932," 48–49.

34. Ibid., 51; Keeran, *Communist Party and the Auto Workers' Unions,* 71–74.

35. Author interview with Guadalupe Morales, November 24, 1986, Detroit.

36. Author interview with Pedro Escobar, November 20, 1986, Detroit; author interview with José Allende, November 22, 1986, Detroit.

37. Valdés, *El Pueblo Mexicano en Detroit,* 40; Skendzal, *Detroit's Pioneer Mexicans,* 10.

38. Simón Muñoz et al. to Bishop Michael J. Gallagher, Archdiocese of Detroit, October 18, 1932, Our Lady of Guadalupe Church file, Archives of the Archdiocese of Detroit; Skendzal, *Detroit's Pioneer Mexicans,* 48–49.

39. Michigan Governor Wilbur M. Brucker, Lansing, to Detroit District Director of Immigration John L. Zubrick, Detroit, October 21, 1932, USINS, 55784/585; Valdés, *El Pueblo Mexicano en Detroit,* 31–32.

40. Zubrick to Hull; Murillo, "Detroit Mexican 'Colonia,'" 141–146; Skendzal, *Detroit's Pioneer Mexicans,* 63; Valdés, *El Pueblo Mexicano en Detroit,* 32, 40; Humphrey, "Mexican Repatriation from Michigan," 501–502; Baba and Abonyi, *Mexicans of Detroit,* 58.

41. Batiza, "Mexican Consul Agrees to Repatriation," 44–45.

42. "It is believed that this is the first concerted movement of this type that has been organized in the United States. . . . If this movement proves to be a success, there is no doubt that it will be taken up by adjoining states and possibly may also result in the same system being used to remove indigent Europeans who are not deportable." Zubrick to Hull.

43. Ibid.; Kiser and Silverman, "Mexican Repatriation," 59; Valdés, *El Pueblo Mexicano en Detroit*, 34; Humphrey, "Mexican Repatriation from Michigan," 498. Detroit District Director Zubrick was given authorization to cooperate with Michigan officials in charge of the repatriation program by the U.S. Immigration Department in Washington. The Immigration Department informed Zubrick that the district directors of immigration in El Paso and San Antonio, Texas, were going to be notified in advance of the movement of Mexicans from Michigan. Acting U.S. Commissioner General of Immigration Edward J. Shaughnessy, Washington, D.C., to Detroit District Director of Immigration John L. Zubrick, Detroit, October 27, 1932, USINS, 55784/585.

44. Mexican repatriation from Detroit was being financed by funds acquired from the Reconstruction Finance Corporation, and for this reason city officials attempted to reduce costs even more by requesting a 25 percent fare reduction from the Central Passenger Association. This request was later denied. Murillo, "Detroit Mexican 'Colonia,'" 147–148.

45. Humphrey, "Mexican Repatriation from Michigan," 497; Valdés, *El Pueblo Mexicano en Detroit*, 32–33; Baba and Abonyi, *Mexicans of Detroit*, 58; Murillo, "Detroit Mexican 'Colonia,'" 150; *Detroit News*, November 16, 1932; author interview with Juan Martínez, November 23, 1986, Detroit; *Detroit Evening Times*, November 16, 1932.

46. Industrial Relations–Sociological Department, Ford Motor Company Milk Fund, Case Study 5369, Accession 237, Box 19, 1932, EIA. After receiving District Director Zubrick's report that the first trainload of repatriates was on its way to Mexico, U.S. Commissioner General of Immigration Hull wired back to express the bureau's pleasure "that so many citizens of Mexico and their children, who are entirely or partly destitute, have been started to their home country." U.S. Commissioner General of Immigration Harry E. Hull, Washington, D.C., to Detroit District Director of Immigration John L. Zubrick, Detroit, November 18, 1932, USINS, 55784/585.

47. Immigrant Inspector Harry Yeager, Laredo, Texas, to Detroit District Director of Immigration John L. Zubrick, Detroit, November 21, 1932, USINS, 55784/585.

48. Ibid.

49. Kiser and Silverman, "Mexican Repatriation," 61–62; Immigrant Inspector R. W. Gangwere, Laredo, Texas, to Detroit District Director of Immigration John L. Zubrick, Detroit, November 29, 1932, USINS, 55784/585.

50. Batiza to Delegado, November 28, 1932, File IV-335-5, SRE; Zubrick to Hull, December 22, 1932, and November 16 and 23, 1932, USINS, 55784/585.

51. Batiza to Delegado, November 28, 1932, File IV-335-5, SRE.

52. Ibid.

53. Delegado to Batiza, December 10, 1932, File IV-335-5, SRE.

54. Quoted in Betten and Mohl, "From Discrimination to Repatriation," 386–387.

55. Kiser and Silverman, "Mexican Repatriation," 62–63; Valdés, *El Pueblo Mexicano en Detroit*, 33; Humphrey, "Mexican Repatriation from Michigan," 503.

56. Detroit District Director of Immigration John L. Zubrick, Detroit, to Inspector in Charge, U.S. Immigration Service, Laredo, Texas, November 23, 1932, USINS, 55784/585; Detroit District Director of Immigration John L. Zubrick, Detroit, to Mexican Consul Ignacio Batiza, Detroit, November 23, 1932, USINS, 55784/585. The poor conditions in Ciudad Juárez, the repatriation depot for Mexicans from Gary, Ind., were appalling. In 1931, the *New York Times* reported that in Ciudad Juárez pneumonia and exposure had caused the deaths of twenty-six Mexicans, and that 2,000 repatriates were sheltered in a large, open corral. Lack of food was also a problem. The Mexicans who returned to Gary likewise described their difficulties and the scarcity of work in Mexico. Betten and Mohl, "From Discrimination to Repatriation," 386.

57. Valdés, *El Pueblo Mexicano en Detroit*, 34; Humphrey, "Mexican Repatriation from Michigan," 504–505, 510–511; Baba and Abonyi, *Mexicans of Detroit*, 59; Reisler, *By the Sweat of Their Brow*, 232.

58. Valdés, *El Pueblo Mexicano en Detroit*, 34. Rivera wrote, "I . . . tried to convince them . . . that a return to Mexico would not solve their problems; that having established roots in the United States, they must act with other Americans to achieve a betterment of their economic position." Quoted in Baba and Abonyi, *Mexicans of Detroit*, 59.

59. Zubrick to Hull, December 5, 1932, USINS, 55784/585. For an account of Rivera's disastrous speech at New York City's John Reed Club, see Albert Halper, "Comrade Rivera Gets the Business," in Albert Halper, *Good-bye Union Square: A Writer's Memoir of the Thirties* (Chicago: Quadrangle Books, 1976), 89–97.

60. Pierce, "Mexican Americans on St. Paul's Lower West Side," 3; Simon, "East Chicago Repatriation," 17; Gary resident quoted in Betten and Mohl, "From Discrimination to Repatriation," 384–385.

61. Quoted in Sepulveda, "The Origins of the Urban Colonias in the Midwest," 107.

62. Keyssar, *Out of Work*, 153; Murillo, "Detroit Mexican 'Colonia,'" 163–164; Fine, *Frank Murphy*, 306–307; Valdés, *El Pueblo Mexicano en Detroit*, 34–37; author interview with Ramón Huerta, November 19, 1986, Detroit; author interview with Victoria Rivas, November 19, 1986, Detroit; Humphrey, "Mexican Repatriation from Michigan," 505, 509.

63. C. M. Greene, director of public welfare, Dearborn, Mich., to Mexican Consul Ignacio Batiza, Detroit, July 26, 1932, File IV-314-42, SRE.

64. Mexican Consul Ignacio Batiza, Detroit, to mayor of Dearborn, Dearborn, Mich., May 19, 1932, File IV-314-42, SRE.

65. Irving Bernstein, *The Lean Years: A History of the American Worker, 1920–1933* (Boston: Houghton Mifflin, 1960), 297–298; *El Nacional*, August 13, 1932; Betten and Mohl, "From Discrimination to Repatriation," 385.

66. Humphrey, "Mexican Repatriation from Michigan," 505; Hoffman, *Unwanted Mexicans*, 121–122; Lunt, *High Ministry of Government*, 74; Valdés, *El Pueblo Mexicano en Detroit*, 37–38. Pedro Escobar remembered the day a policeman came to his house with news that a public cafeteria had opened on nearby Jefferson Avenue. The laid-off foundry worker was told that from then on he and his family could receive three meals a day at the cafeteria. But

Escobar's dignity prevented him from going. "I did not go near it. I was ashamed." Author interview with Pedro Escobar, November 20, 1986, Detroit.

67. Author interview with Victoria Rivas, November 19, 1986, Detroit; author interview with Josefina Aldama, August 7, 1986, Detroit. In East Chicago, several hundred Mexican families were fed by the Mt. Carmel Mission from food donated by local supermarkets. Sometimes the food made available to Mexicans consisted of a steady diet of pumpernickel bread and canned clam chowder. Rosales and Simon, "Mexican Immigrant Experience in the Urban Midwest," 344–345.

68. Valdés, *El Pueblo Mexicano en Detroit*, 39–40; Skendzal, *Detroit's Pioneer Mexicans*, 12, 18; Murillo, "Detroit Mexican 'Colonia,'" 159; Humphrey, "Mexican Repatriation from Michigan," 502–503; Batiza to Delegado, December 12, 1932, File IV-335-5, SRE.

69. Rosales and Simon, "Mexican Immigrant Experience in the Urban Midwest," 348; Simon, "Mexican Repatriation in East Chicago," 13–14; Betten and Mohl, "From Discrimination to Repatriation," 383; *Milwaukee Journal*, October 8, 1932; Goldner, "The Mexican in the Northern Urban Area," 36–37; *La Defensa*, January 18, 1936.

70. Keyssar, *Out of Work*, 146; author interview with Ramón Huerta, November 19, 1986, Detroit; Keyssar, *Out of Work*, 159; author interview with Mariano Alvarez, July 14, 1986, Detroit; author interview with Josefina Aldama, August 7, 1986, Detroit. Lauro Tienda learned about track work from his mother, who in turn got the information from the two Mexican track laborers she cooked for as a means of supporting the family. Author interview with Lauro Tienda, November 20, 1986, Detroit.

71. Humphrey, "Employment Patterns of Mexicans in Detroit," 919–920. Although most Mexican workers in Detroit in the early 1930s certainly suffered because they remained unemployed for long periods, others fared relatively well. For example, laid-off Ford autoworker Francisco Azcarate had recently applied for work at Hudson Motors and was anticipating being called back to work when investigators from the Ford Sociological Department visited him at his St. Clair Shores home on December 28, 1932. Asked by the investigators what he would do if he did not get a job with Hudson Motors, Azcarate simply answered that he "would struggle along somehow." This autoworker adamantly refused assistance because he believed that other men needed welfare more than he did. He did, however, accept the offer of a Christmas basket of food. Industrial Relations–Sociological Department, Ford Motor Company Milk Fund, Case Study 376, Box 19, 1932, EIA.

72. Keyssar, *Out of Work*, 157. A worker with exceptional planning and investing abilities, thirty-five-year-old Joaquín Sepulveda refused help from Ford Sociological Department investigators who visited him in Dearborn on December 8, 1932. Joaquín had been employed at the Ford Rouge foundry since 1926 but had not worked in six months. He supported his wife and their four children on withdrawals from his savings, his Ford Investment Plan, and bonds. The Ford Sociological Department investigators reported that the resourceful Mexican autoworker repaid all the assistance the Dearborn Welfare Department gave him, $30.73. They noted that Sepulveda had $50 cash on hand, $523

in a Ford Investment Plan, and forty shares of Class A Hearst Consolidated valued at $1,000 purchased in the previous year. In addition, the Ford investigators reported that Sepulveda owned three Prudential insurance policies taken out in each of the last three years, $2,346 equity in his four-room home, and the family's 1930 Ford sedan. Industrial Relations–Sociological Department, Ford Motor Company Milk Fund, Case Study 4306, Box 19, 1932, EIA.

73. Ford autoworker Placido Hernández had been in the United States since 1918 and arrived in Detroit in the spring of 1928 from Indiana Harbor. He was hired as a molder at the Ford Rouge foundry, the same job he held when he was laid off in early June 1931. Hernández lived with his three young children in a house the widower was purchasing on Detroit's west side. Dwindling resources caused him to miss payments on his furniture and his mortgage payments. He was having problems feeding and clothing his children. Hernández lost his home when the mortgage company foreclosed, and the DPW shortly thereafter took custody of his children and placed them in a Detroit foster home. Rendered jobless and homeless, Hernández continued to search for work to regain custody of his children. Rouge Area Hourly Workers Employment Record Jackets, 1932, Box 838.

74. Author interview with Victoria Rivas, November 19, 1986, Detroit.

75. Rouge Area Hourly Workers Employment Record Jackets, Box 1258.

76. Ibid.

77. Ibid.

78. Keyssar, *Out of Work,* 157–158, 164.

79. Industrial Relations–Sociological Department, Ford Motor Company Milk Fund, Case Study 3093, Box 19, 1932, EIA.

80. Ibid.

81. Ibid., Case Study 3821, 1932.

82. Ibid.

83. Ibid., Case Study 191, 1932.

84. Ibid., Case Study 2902, 1932, and Miller School Case Study, 1932.

85. Keyssar, *Out of Work,* 169.

86. Industrial Relations–Sociological Department, Case Study 13, Box 19, 1932, EIA.

87. Batiza to Delegado, May 16, and July 11, 1933, File IV-335-5, SRE.

88. When one Mexican client was asked by his case worker whether he would like to return to Mexico he answered that "he would be glad to return . . . if he had money" but quickly added that he was ashamed to return without having prospered. Quoted in Humphrey, "Mexican Repatriation from Michigan," 506, 510, 513.

89. Kiser and Kiser, "Introduction," 34; Batiza to Delegado, December 12, 1932, File IV-335-5, SRE.

90. *El Nacional,* May 7, 1932, and February 17, 1934; Simon, "Mexican Repatriation in East Chicago," 18; Laurence Leslie Waters, "Transient Mexican Agricultural Labor," *Southwestern Social Science Quarterly* 22 (June 1941), 49; Pierce, "Mexican Americans on St. Paul's Lower West Side," 2–3.

91. Author interview with Ramón Huerta, November 19, 1986, Detroit.

92. Author interview with Lauro Tienda, November 20, 1986, Detroit.

93. Author interview with Pedro Escobar, November 20, 1986, Detroit.

94. Author interview with Victoria Rivas, November 19, 1986, Detroit; author interview with Pedro Escobar, November 20, 1986, Detroit.

95. Author interview with Guadalupe Morales, November 24, 1986, Detroit.

96. Ibid.; Batiza to Delegado, February 16, and March 14, 1932, File IV-335-5, SRE; Peterson, *American Automobile Workers,* 139–148.

97. Humphrey, "Mexican Repatriation from Michigan," 498; Valdés, *El Pueblo Mexicano en Detroit,* 29–30; Kiser and Kiser, "Introduction," 33.

98. Simon, "Mexican Repatriation in East Chicago," 18–19.

99. Keyssar, *Out of Work,* 172–173.

100. Mexican workers formed Centro de Cultura de Detroit (Detroit Culture Center) specifically to counter the discriminatory propaganda. Centro de Cultura de Detroit, Detroit, to Mexican Government, Mexico City, February 1, 1932, File IV-338-34, SRE; Batiza to Delegado, December 12, 1932, File IV-335-5, SRE. George H. Malatt, Chicago, to Secretary of Labor Frances Perkins, Washington, D.C., July 9, 1933, USINS, 55639/6616-A.

101. *El Nacional,* April 29, 1933; *La Defensa,* December 14, 1936; Rosales and Simon, "Mexican Immigrant Experience in the Urban Midwest," 351–352; interview with George Galvin, July 16, 1975, pp. 19–21, Minn. HS. East Chicago Mexican steelworkers made up three-fourths of the picket lines during the 1937 "little steel strike" and constituted 15 percent of the demonstrators during the "Memorial Day massacre." Rosales and Simon, "Chicano Steel Workers and Unionism," 271–272. One Flint Chicana recalled that her father, who had been a striking General Motors autoworker at the time, told her about the sit-down like a man recounting war stories. Jane Bushong Haney, "Migration, Settlement Pattern, and Social Organization: A Midwest Mexican-American Case Study" (Ph.D. diss., Michigan State University, 1978), 269–270.

CONCLUSION

1. Morawska, *For Bread with Butter,* 44.

2. Montgomery, "Thinking about American Workers in the 1920s," 21. Like the values and attitudes of the Mexicans, homes always showed a blend of two cultures, one American and the other Mexican. Those of Lorain's Mexican steelworkers were typical: "American radios . . . are covered with zarapes [sic] and bits of Indian pottery. Stone metates grind out corn which is cooked on gas and even electric ovens. American phonographs play South American tangos and Mexican marches." McWilliams, *North from Mexico,* 222.

3. Edson, "Mexicans in Detroit, Michigan," 13–14.

4. Louis Peden, Galveston, Tex., to Secretary of Labor, Washington, D.C., January 5, 1921, USMCS, 165/223A, Box 13.

5. Montgomery, *Fall of the House of Labor,* 461–462; author interview with Ramón Huerta, November 19, 1986, Detroit.

6. Trotter, *Black Milwaukee,* 277; Rosales, "Regional Origins," 195; author interview with Ramón Huerta, November 19, 1986, Detroit.

7. Cervantes, *My Moline,* 41.

8. Peterson, *American Automobile Workers,* 38.

9. Ibid., 40. African American labor historian Joe Trotter has noted a similar effect on the job performance of southern West Virginia black coal miners. Joe William Trotter, Jr., *Coal, Class, and Color: Blacks in Southern West Virginia, 1915–32* (Urbana: University of Illinois Press, 1990), 108.

10. Montgomery, *Fall of the House of Labor,* 462–463; Montgomery, "Thinking about American Workers in the 1920s," 19–21.

11. Author interview with Ramón Huerta, November 19, 1986, Detroit.

12. Peterson, *American Automobile Workers,* 156.

13. David Montejano, *Anglos and Mexicans in the Making of Texas,* 265–269.

14. William Serrin, "The Myth of the 'New Work': A Great American Job Machine?" *Nation* 249 (September 18, 1989), 272. One of the longest strikes of the 1980s was waged by Chicano and Chicana Phelps-Dodge copper miners in Arizona. In northwest Ohio, the Farm Labor Organizing Committee engaged in a seven-year boycott of the Campbell Soup Company. Through a powerful labor-community coalition of Chicanos, blacks, and Asian Americans, UAW Local 645 in Van Nuys, Calif., successfully contested the power of General Motors to close the local plant. In 1987, Chicana and Mexican women frozen-food workers in Watsonville, Calif., won an eighteen-month strike for fair wages and benefits. Chicano labor activists are leading drives to organize undocumented Mexican workers in low-wage, nonunionized sweatshops, underground operations, and service industries, where working conditions resemble those in the Third World. Zaragosa Vargas, "Report, Fifth Annual National Association of Chicano Studies Conference," *International Labor and Working Class History* 33 (Spring 1988), 102–103, 105. The devastating effects of deindustrialization in the Chicago area are discussed by David Bensman and Roberta Lynch, *Rusted Dreams: Hard Times in a Steel Community* (Berkeley: University of California Press, 1987), 101–102. For a description of the fate of Michigan's Latinos, see Richard A. Navarro, "Structural Changes in the Midwest Economy and the Hispanic Labor Force: Trends, Future Prospects, and Needs" (unpublished paper, 1989, Michigan State University, East Lansing), 8–9. For an analysis of the potential impact of the North American Free Trade Agreement on the United States, see Kim Moody and Mary McGinn, *Unions and Free Trade: Solidarity vs. Competition* (Detroit: Labor Notes, 1992), ch. 5.

Bibliography

PRIMARY SOURCES

Connell, Charles T., and R. W. Burton, "Survey of Labor Conditions on the Mexican Border and Contiguous Territory as Related to Unskilled Labor." 1922. Report for the secretary of labor. U.S. Mediation and Conciliation Service, RG 280, Subject Case Files 165, 223 B, Box 13, NA.

Edson, George T. "Mexicans at Lorain, Ohio," 1926. Paul S. Taylor Collection, Bancroft Library, University of California, Berkeley.

———. "Mexicans in Aurora, Illinois," 1926. Paul S. Taylor Collection, Bancroft Library, University of California, Berkeley.

———. "Mexicans in Bethlehem, Pennsylvania," 1926. Paul S. Taylor Collection, Bancroft Library, University of California, Berkeley.

———. "Mexicans in Chicago, Illinois," 1927. Paul S. Taylor Collection, Bancroft Library, University of California, Berkeley.

———. "Mexicans in Detroit, Michigan," 1926. Paul S. Taylor Collection, Bancroft Library, University of California, Berkeley.

———. "Mexicans in Flint, Michigan," 1926. Paul S. Taylor Collection, Bancroft Library, University of California, Berkeley.

———. "Mexicans in Fort Madison, Iowa," 1927. Paul S. Taylor Collection, Bancroft Library, University of California, Berkeley.

———. "Mexicans in Gary, Indiana," 1926. Paul S. Taylor Collection, Bancroft Library, University of California, Berkeley.

———. "Mexicans in Indiana Harbor, Indiana," 1926. Paul S. Taylor Collection, Bancroft Library, University of California, Berkeley.

———. "Mexicans in Milwaukee, Wisconsin," 1926. Paul S. Taylor Collection, Bancroft Library, University of California, Berkeley.

———. "Mexicans in Our Northcentral States," 1927. Paul S. Taylor Collection, Bancroft Library, University of California, Berkeley.

———. "Mexicans in Pontiac, Michigan," 1926. Paul S. Taylor Collection, Bancroft Library, University of California, Berkeley.

———. "Mexicans in the Pittsburgh, Pennsylvania, District," 1926. Paul S. Taylor Collection, Bancroft Library, University of California, Berkeley.

———. "Northern Sugar Beet Mexicans," 1927. Paul S. Taylor Collection, Bancroft Library, University of California, Berkeley.

———. "Mexicans in the Toledo, Ohio, Area," 1926. Paul S. Taylor Collection, Bancroft Library, University of California, Berkeley.

———. "Mexicans in Waukegan, Illinois," 1926. Paul S. Taylor Collection, Bancroft Library, University of California, Berkeley.

Henry Ford Service School. Foreign Student Research. Accession ARG-15. Edison Industrial Archives, Edison Institute, Ford Motor Company, Dearborn, Mich.

Industrial Relations-Sociological Department. Ford Motor Company Milk Fund. Accession 237. Edison Industrial Archives, Edison Institute, Ford Motor Company, Dearborn, Mich.

Minnesota Historical Society, Archives and Manuscripts Division. Oral Histories Collection. St. Paul.

Nelson, Raymond E. "The Mexicans in South Chicago," 1928. Paul S. Taylor Collection. Bancroft Library, University of California, Berkeley.

R. L. Polk's Detroit City Directory. Detroit: R. L. Polk Company, 1918–1929.

Rouge Area Hourly Workers Employment Record Jackets, 1918–1947. Accession AR-84-58-1050. Ford Motor Company Industrial Archives and Record Center. Redford, Mich.

Secretaria de Relaciones Exteriores. Archivo Nacional, Mexico City.

Society of St. Vincent de Paul. Annual Reports, 1920, 1921. St. Mary's Catholic Church, Detroit.

———. Minutes of the General Meetings, 1920, 1921. St. Mary's Catholic Church, Detroit.

Taylor, Paul S. "Circulo Mutualista Mexicano." July 3, 1928. Paul S. Taylor Collection, Bancroft Library, University of California, Berkeley.

———. "Mexicans in Detroit, Michigan." 1928. Paul S. Taylor Collection, Bancroft Library, University of California, Berkeley.

———. "Sociedad 'Anáhuac." N.d. Paul S. Taylor Collection, Bancroft Library, University of California, Berkeley.

U.S. Immigration and Naturalization Service. Record Group 85. National Archives, Washington, D.C.

U.S. Mediation and Conciliation Service. Case Files, Record Group 280. Washington National Records Center, Suitland, Md.

NEWSPAPERS

Detroit Evening Times
Detroit Free Press
Detroit News
Detroit Saturday Night

Detroit Times
El Nacional, 1932–1934
Gary Post-Tribune
La Defensa, 1935–1936
Mexico, 1928–1929
Michigan Catholic
Milwaukee Journal

SECONDARY SOURCES

Acuña, Rodolfo. *Occupied America: A History of Chicanos.* 3d ed. New York: Harper & Row, 1988.

Año Nuevo-Kerr, Louise. "The Chicano Experience in Chicago: 1920–1970." Ph.D. diss., University of Illinois at Chicago Circle, 1976.

Aronowitz, Stanley. *False Promises: The Shaping of American Working Class Consciousness.* New York: McGraw-Hill, 1973.

Baba, Marietta Lynn, and Malvina Houk Abonyi. *Mexicans of Detroit.* Detroit: Wayne State University Press, 1979.

Babson, Steve. *Working Detroit: The Making of a Union Town.* New York: Adama Books, 1984.

Barrera, Mario. *Race and Class in the Southwest: A Theory of Racial Inequality.* South Bend, Ind.: University of Notre Dame Press, 1979.

Barrett, James R. *Work and Community in the Jungle: Chicago's Packinghouse Workers, 1894–1922.* Urbana: University of Illinois Press, 1987.

Batiza, Ignacio. "Mexican Consul Agrees to Repatriation of Detroit's Mexicans." In *Mexican Workers in the United States: Historical and Political Perspectives,* edited by George C. Kiser and Mary Wood Kiser. Albuquerque: University of New Mexico Press, 1979.

Betten, Neil, and Raymond A. Mohl. "From Discrimination to Repatriation: Mexican Life in Gary, Indiana, during the Great Depression." *Pacific Historical Review* 42 (August 1973): 370–388.

Brisette, Linna E. *Mexicans in the United States: A Report of a Brief Survey.* Washington, D.C.: National Catholic Welfare Conference, 1928.

Brody, David. *Labor in Crisis: The Steel Strike of 1919.* Urbana: University of Illinois Press, 1987.

———. *Steelworkers in America: The Nonunion Era.* Cambridge: Harvard University Press, 1960.

———. *Workers in Industrial America: Essays on the Twentieth Century Struggle.* New York: Oxford University Press, 1980.

Camarillo, Albert. *Chicanos in a Changing Society: From Mexican Pueblos to American Barrios in Santa Barbara and Southern California, 1848–1930.* Cambridge: Harvard University Press, 1979.

Cardoso, Lawrence A. *Mexican Emigration to the United States, 1897–1931: Socio-Economic Patterns.* Tucson: University of Arizona Press, 1980.

Carlson, Glen E. "The Negro in the Industries of Detroit." Ph.D. diss., University of Michigan, 1929.

Cervantes, John. *My Moline: A Young Illegal Immigrant Dreams.* Canoga Park, Calif.: Canyon, 1986.

Coalson, George O. *The Development of the Migratory Farm Labor System in Texas: 1900–1954.* San Francisco: R&E Research Associates, 1977.

Cohen, Lizabeth. "Encountering Mass Culture at the Grass Roots: The Experience of Chicago Workers in the 1920s." *American Quarterly* 41 (March 1989):6–33.

Corwin, Arthur F. "Mexican Policy and Ambivalence toward Labor Emigration to the United States." In *Immigrants—and Immigrants: Perspectives on Mexican Labor Migration to the United States,* edited by Arthur F. Corwin. Westport, Conn.: Greenwood Press, 1978.

Corwin, Arthur F., and Lawrence A. Cardoso, "Vamos al Norte: Causes of Mass Mexican Migration to the United States." *In Immigrants—and Immigrants: Perspectives on Mexican Labor Migration to the United States,* edited by Arthur F. Corwin. Westport, Conn.: Greenwood Press, 1978.

Corwin, Arthur F., and Walter F. Fogel, "Shadow Labor Force: Mexican Workers in the American Economy." In *Immigrants—and Immigrants: Perspectives on Mexican Labor Migration to the United States,* edited by Arthur F. Corwin. Westport, Conn.: Greenwood Press, 1978.

Davidson, Gordon W. "Industrial Detroit after World War I, 1919–1921." Master's thesis, Wayne University, 1953.

Deutsch, Sarah. *No Separate Refuge: Culture, Class, and Gender on an Anglo-Hispanic Frontier in the American Southwest, 1880–1940.* New York: Oxford University Press, 1987.

Dickerson, Dennis C. *Out of the Crucible: Black Steel Workers in Western Pennsylvania, 1875–1980.* Albany: State University of New York Press, 1986.

Downs, Linda. "The Rouge in 1932: 'The Detroit Industry' Frescoes by Diego Rivera." In Detroit Institute of Arts, *The Rouge: The Image of Industry in the Art of Charles Sheeler and Diego Rivera.* Detroit: Detroit Institute of Arts, 1978.

Dunn, Robert W. *Labor and Automobiles.* New York: International Publishers, 1929.

Fine, Sidney. *The Automobile under the Blue Eagle.* Ann Arbor: University of Michigan Press, 1963.

———. *Frank Murphy: The Detroit Years.* Ann Arbor: University of Michigan Press, 1975.

Foner, Philip S. *Organized Labor & the Black Worker, 1619–1981.* 2d ed. New York: International Publishers, 1981.

Gamio, Manuel. *Mexican Immigration to the United States: A Study of Human Migration and Adjustment.* Chicago: University of Chicago Press, 1930.

García, Mario T. *Desert Immigrants: [The Mexicans of El Paso, 1880–1920.]* New Haven, Conn.: Yale University Press, 1981.

García, Richard A. "Class, Consciousness, and Ideology—The Mexican Community of San Antonio, Texas: 1930–1940." *Aztlán* 9 (Spring 1979):23–69.

Gartman, William David. *Auto Slavery: The Labor Process in the American Automobile Industry, 1897–1950.* New Brunswick, N.J.: Rutgers University Press, 1986.

Goldberg, Benjamin. "Tuberculosis and the Mexican." *City of Chicago Municipal Tuberculosis Bulletin* 9 (March–April 1929):3–36.

Goldner, Norman S. "The Mexican in the Northern Urban Area: A Comparison of Two Generations." Ph.D. diss., University of Minnesota, 1959.

Gonzáles, Kathleen May. *The Mexican Family in San Antonio, Texas.* San Francisco: R&E Research Associates, 1971.

González, Rosalinda M. "Chicanas and Mexican Immigrant Families 1920–1940: Women's Subordination and Family Exploitation." In *Decades of Discontent: The Women's Movement, 1920–1940,* edited by Lois Scharf and Joan M. Jensen. Westport, Conn.: Greenwood Press, 1983.

Gordon, David M., Richard C. Edwards, and Michael Reich. *Segmented Work, Divided Workers: The Historical Transformation of Labor in the United States.* Cambridge: Cambridge University Press, 1982.

Green, James R. *Grass-Roots Socialism: Radical Movements in the Southwest, 1895–1943.* Baton Rouge: Louisiana State University Press, 1978.

Grossman, James R. *Land of Hope: Chicago, Black Southerners, and the Great Migration.* Chicago: University of Chicago Press, 1989.

Hoffman, Abraham. *Unwanted Mexicans in the Great Depression: Repatriation Pressures, 1929–1939.* Tucson: University of Arizona Press, 1974.

Holli, Melvin G. "The Impact of Automobile Manufacturing upon Detroit." *Detroit in Perspective* 2 (Spring 1976):176–188.

Hufford, Charles H. *The Social and Economic Effects of Mexican Migration into Texas.* San Francisco: R&E Research Associates, 1971.

Humphrey, Norman D. "Employment Patterns of Mexicans in Detroit." *Monthly Labor Review* 61 (November 1945):913–923.

———. "Mexican Repatriation from Michigan: Public Assistance in Historical Perspective." *Social Service Review* 15 (September 1941):497–513.

Jacoby, Sanford M. *Employing Bureaucracy: Managers, Unions, and the Transformation of Work in American Industry, 1900–1945.* New York: Columbia University Press, 1985.

Johnson, Christopher H. *Maurice Sugar: Law, Labor, and the Left in Detroit 1912–1950.* Detroit: Wayne State University Press, 1988.

Jones, Anita E. *Conditions surrounding Mexicans in Chicago.* 1928. Reprint. San Francisco: R&E Research Associates, 1971.

Keeran, Roger. *The Communist Party and the Auto Workers' Unions.* New York: International Publishers, 1980.

Keyssar, Alexander. *Out of Work: The First Century of Unemployment in Massachusetts.* Cambridge: Cambridge University Press, 1986.

Kiser, George C., and Mary Woody Kiser. "Introduction." In *Mexican Workers in the United States: Historical and Political Perspectives,* edited by George C. Kiser and Mary Woody Kiser. Albuquerque: University of New Mexico Press, 1979.

Kiser, George C., and David Silverman. "Mexican Repatriation during the Great Depression." In *Mexican Workers in the United States: Historical and Political Perspectives,* edited by George C. Kiser and Mary Woody Kiser. Albuquerque: University of New Mexico Press, 1979.

Laird, Judith Finchar. "Argentine, Kansas: The Evolution of a Mexican American Community, 1905–1940." Ph.D. diss., University of Kansas, 1975.

Levin, Samuel M. "The Ford Unemployment Policy." *American Labor Legislation Review* 22 (March 1932):101–108.

Levine, David Allan. *Internal Combustion: The Races in Detroit, 1915–1926.* Westport, Conn.: Greenwood Press, 1976.

Li, Chen-Nan. "A Summer in the Ford Works." *Personnel Journal* 6 (June 1928):18–32.

Lunt, Richard D. *The High Ministry of Government: The Political Career of Frank Murphy.* Detroit: Wayne State University Press, 1965.

MacDonald, Lois. "Labor and Automobiles." In *Labor Problems and the American Scene,* edited by Lois MacDonald. New York: Harper and Brothers, 1938.

McWilliams, Carey. *Ill Fares the Land: Migrants and Migratory Labor in the United States.* 1941. Reprint. New York: Barnes & Noble, 1967.

———. *North from Mexico: The Spanish-Speaking People of the United States.* 1949. Reprint. Westport, Conn.: Greenwood Press, 1968.

Marks, Carole. *Farewell—We're Good and Gone: The Great Black Migration.* Bloomington: Indiana University Press, 1989.

Martínez, John R. *Mexican Emigration to the United States, 1910–1930.* San Francisco: R&E Research Associates, 1972.

Meier, August, and Elliot Rudwick. *Black Detroit and the Rise of the U.A.W.* New York: Oxford University Press, 1979.

Meyer, Michael C., and William L. Sherman. *The Course of Mexican History.* 3d ed. New York: Oxford University Press, 1987.

Meyer, Stephen, III. *The Five Dollar Day: Labor Management and Social Control in the Ford Motor Company, 1908–1921.* Albany: State University of New York Press, 1981.

Mohl, Raymond A., and Neil Betten. *Steel City: Urban Patterns in Gary, Indiana, 1906–1950.* New York: Holmes & Meier, 1986.

Montejano, David. *Anglos and Mexicans in the Making of Texas, 1836–1986.* Austin: University of Texas Press, 1987.

Montgomery, David. *The Fall of the House of Labor: The Workplace, the State, and American Labor Activism, 1865–1925.* Cambridge: Cambridge University Press, 1987.

———. "Nationalism, American Patriotism, and Class Consciousness among Immigrant Workers in the United States in the Epoch of World War I." In *"Struggle a Hard Battle": Essays on Working-Class Immigrants,* edited by Dirk Hoerder. DeKalb: Northern Illinois University Press, 1986.

———. "Thinking about American Workers in the 1920s." *International Labor and Working-Class History* 32 (Fall 1987):4–24.

Morawska, Ewa. *For Bread with Butter: The Life-Worlds of East Central Europeans in Johnstown, Pennsylvania, 1890–1940.* Cambridge: Cambridge University Press, 1985.

Murillo, Christopher Louis. "The Detroit Mexican 'Colonia' from 1920 to 1932: Implications for Social and Educational Policy." Ph.D. diss., Michigan State University, 1981.

National Industrial Conference Board. *The Cost of Living among Wage Earners in Detroit, Michigan, September 1921.* New York, 1921.

Nevins, Allan, and Frank Ernest Hill. *Ford: Expansion and Challenge 1915– 1933.* New York: Scribner's, 1957.

Palmer, Susan L. "Building Ethnic Communities in a Small City: Romanians and Mexicans in Aurora, Illinois, 1900–1940." Ph.D. diss., Northern Illinois University, 1986.

Peterson, Joyce Shaw. *American Automobile Workers, 1900–1933.* Albany: State University of New York Press, 1987.

Pierce, Lorraine Esterly. "Mexican Americans on St. Paul's Lower West Side." *Journal of Mexican American History* 4 (1974):1–18.

Reisler, Mark. *By the Sweat of Their Brow: Mexican Immigrant Labor in the United States, 1900–1940.* Westport, Conn.: Greenwood Press, 1976.

Reitell, Charles. "Machinery and Its Effect upon the Workers in the Automotive Industry." *Annals of the American Academy of Political and Social Science* 116 (November 1924):37–43.

Riess, Steven A. *City Games: The Evolution of American Urban Society and the Rise of Sports.* Urbana: University of Illinois Press, 1989.

Rosales, Francisco A. "Mexicanos in Indiana Harbor during the 1920s: From Prosperity to Depression." *Revista Chicano Riqueña* 4 (1976):88–98.

———. "The Regional Origins of Mexicano Immigrants to Chicago during the 1920s." *Aztlán* 7 (Summer 1976):187–201.

Rosales, Francisco A., and Daniel T. Simon. "Chicano Steel Workers and Unionism in the Midwest, 1919–1945." *Aztlán* 6 (1975):267–275.

———. "Mexican Immigrant Experience in the Urban Midwest: East Chicago, Indiana, 1919–1945." *Indiana Magazine of History* 77 (December 1981): 333–357.

Ruiz, Vicki L. *Cannery Women, Cannery Lives: Mexican Women, Unionization, and the California Food Processing Industry, 1930–1950.* Albuquerque: University of New Mexico Press, 1987.

Sánchez, George J. *"Go After the Women": Americanization and the Mexican Immigrant Woman 1915–1929.* Working Paper Series 6. Stanford, Calif.: Stanford Center for Chicano Research, 1985.

Schwartz, Harry. *Seasonal Farm Labor in the United States: With Special Reference to Hired Farm Workers in Fruit and Vegetable and Sugar Beet Production.* New York: Columbia University Press, 1945.

Sepulveda, Ciro H. "The Origins of the Urban Colonias in the Midwest, 1910– 1930." *Revista Chicano Riqueña* 4 (1976):99–109.

———. "Research Note: Una Colonia de Obreros: East Chicago, Indiana." *Aztlán* 7 (Summer 1976):237–336.

Simon, Daniel T. "Mexican Repatriation in East Chicago, Indiana." *Journal of Ethnic Studies* 2 (Summer 1974):11–23.

Skendzal, Edward Adam. *Detroit's Pioneer Mexicans: A Historical Study of the Mexican Colony in Detroit.* Grand Rapids, Mich.: Little Shield Press, 1980.

Steiger, Andrew J. "Autos and Jobs." *Nation* 126 (May 2, 1928):505–506.

Sullivan, Martin E. "On the Dole: The Relief Issue in Detroit, 1920–1939." Ph.D. diss., University of Notre Dame, 1974.

Sward, Keith. *The Legend of Henry Ford.* New York: Holt, Rinehart & Winston, 1948.

Taylor, Paul S. *Mexican Labor in the United States: Bethlehem, Pennsylvania.* Berkeley: University of California Press, 1931.

———. *Mexican Labor in the United States: Chicago and the Calumet Region.* Berkeley: University of California Press, 1932.

Tentler, Leslie Woodcock. *Seasons of Grace: A History of the Catholic Archdiocese of Detroit.* Detroit: Wayne State University Press, 1990.

———. *Wage-Earning Women: Industrial Work and Family Life in the United States, 1900–1930.* New York: Oxford University Press, 1979.

Ticknor, Thomas J. "Motor City: The Impact of the Automobile Industry upon Detroit, 1900–1975." Ph.D. diss., University of Michigan, 1978.

Trotter, Joe William, Jr. *Black Milwaukee: The Making of an Industrial Proletariat, 1915–45.* Urbana: University of Illinois Press, 1985.

Trusty, Lance. *The Calumet Region: An Historical Resource Guide.* Hammond, Ind.: Calumet Regional Studies Institute, Purdue University, 1980.

Valdés, Dennis Nodín. "Betabeleros: The Formation of an Agricultural Proletariat in the Midwest, 1877–1930." *Labor History* 30 (Fall 1989):536–562.

———. *El Pueblo Mexicano en Detroit y Michigan: A Social History.* Detroit: Wayne State University Press, 1982.

———. "Perspiring Capitalists: Latinos and the Henry Ford Service School, 1918–1928." Paper delivered at 74th Annual Meeting of the Organization of American Historians, Detroit, April 3, 1981.

Ward, David. *Poverty, Ethnicity, and the American City, 1840–1925: Changing Conceptions of the Slum and Ghetto.* Cambridge: Cambridge University Press, 1989.

Watkins, Myron W. "The Labor Situation in Detroit." *Journal of Political Economy* 28 (1920):840–852.

Zieger, Robert H. *American Workers, American Unions, 1920–1985.* Baltimore: Johns Hopkins University Press, 1986.

Zunz, Olivier. *The Changing Face of Inequality: Urbanization, Industrial Development, and Immigrants in Detroit, 1880–1920.* Chicago: University of Chicago Press, 1982.

Index

Abbott, Edith: *The Tenements of Chicago 1908–1935,* 8
Alanis, Juan P., 71–74, 83, 145
Amalgamated Association of Iron, Steel, and Tin Workers, 199
American culture: impact on immigrant Mexican culture, 9–12, 204
American Federation of Labor (AFL), 157–58, 207
Americanization programs: Catholic Church promotes, 73–74, 85; and Mexican auto workers, 70–74, 84, 87, 133, 204, 228n53; and Mexican children, 73; and proficiency in English, 73
Amigo del Hogar, El (newspaper), 31, 48, 151
Assimilation. *See* Americanization programs
Associated Industries of Detroit, 63
Automobile industry: anti-union tactics, 62–63; artificial job hierarchies, 106–7, 111, 122–23; black workers in, 51–52, 102; collapses in Great Depression, 169, 172–73; collusion with employment agencies, 119; economic decline, 11, 171–72; effects of mass production, 106–9, 125; employment methods, 50–51; European immigrants in, 57, 60, 62; hazardous working conditions, 104–5, 114–15, 121–23, 179; hierarchy of status among companies, 101, 104, 125;

high wage levels, 94, 103–4; job-sharing during Great Depression, 172; labor stratification, 50–52, 59, 204; labor turnover problem, 51, 129, 206; loss of jobs in Great Depression, 169, 172–73; Mexican promotion opportunities, 51, 102–3, 106; Mexicans prefer, 5–7, 50; and naturalization requirements, 101, 105–6, 120, 122, 227n51; recruitment methods, 63, 225n18; restricts hiring to U.S. citizens, 176; role in Detroit's economy, 5–6, 51, 59, 81; seasonal layoffs and retooling, 58, 61–62, 95, 117–18, 120, 123, 125, 128, 203, 237n70; as secondary industrial employment, 50, 96, 122; technical innovations, 6; working conditions, 52, 106–7; work-related stress, 52, 61, 112–15, 123
Automobile ownership: and worker status, 159
Auto-parts industry: hazardous working conditions, 100–101; subcontracts from Ford Motor Company, 172
Auto Workers Union, 62

Batiza, Ignacio: aids Mexican factory workers, 175–76, 188–89; cooperates in Mexican repatriation, 176–77, 180–81, 183; encourages Mexican immigrants to remain in Detroit, 185–86

269

Compositor: Graphic Composition, Inc.
Text: 10/13 Sabon
Display: Sabon
Printer and Binder: Braun-Brumfield, Inc.